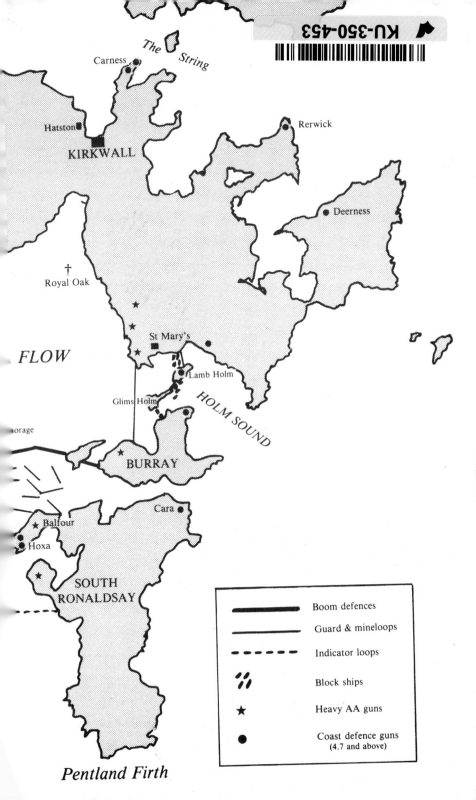

Carness

The String

Hatston

KIRKWALL

Rerwick

Deerness

† Royal Oak

FLOW

St Mary's

Lamb Holm

Glims Holm

HOLM SOUND

orage

BURRAY

Cara

Balfour

Hoxa

SOUTH RONALDSAY

Pentland Firth

▬▬▬▬	Boom defences
————	Guard & mineloops
– – – –	Indicator loops
⁄⁄⁄	Block ships
★	Heavy AA guns
●	Coast defence guns (4.7 and above)

ASPECTS OF ORKNEY 3

THIS GREAT HARBOUR
SCAPA FLOW

This series has been developed in order to provide detailed and thorough texts on a range of aspects of the life, history and environment of the Orkney Islands. Each book is designed to make specialist knowledge available to the general reader.

Editor — Howie Firth
Consultant Editor — William P. L. Thomson

1. Kelp-making in Orkney   William P. L. Thomson

2. The Birds of Orkney   Chris Booth, Mildred Cuthbert and Peter Reynolds

3. This Great Harbour — Scapa Flow   W. S. Hewison

4. The People of Orkney   (ed.) R. J. Berry*

*Publication in 1986

Subjects to be covered in forthcoming volumes will include the history of aviation in Orkney, old Orkney industries, and old Orkney songs. Up-to-date details are available from the publishers.

Series design — Bryce Wilson

King George V and Admiral Sir David Beatty, Commander-in-Chief of the Grand Fleet, on the quarter-deck of the flagship HMS *Queen Elizabeth* during the King's visit to Scapa Flow in 1917.

ASPECTS OF ORKNEY 3

THIS GREAT HARBOUR
SCAPA FLOW

W. S. HEWISON

1985
THE ORKNEY PRESS

Published by The Orkney Press Ltd., 72 Victoria Street, Stromness, Orkney

© Text: W. S. Hewison, 1985

ISBN 0 907618 11 1

Printed by the Kirkwall Press, "The Orcadian" Office, Victoria Street, Kirkwall, Orkney
Bound by James Gowans Ltd., Glasgow

The publishers wish to thank Orkney Islands Council for financial assistance towards the publication of this volume.

To Nancy

without whose forbearance, encouragement and active assistance this book would never have been written.

Contents

Photographs

Maps
by Nancy Hewison

Foreword

by

Rear Admiral J. C. K. Slater LVO
Assistant Chief of the Defence Staff

'The British Battle Fleet is like the queen on the chessboard; it may remain at the base but it still dominates the game.' Admiral of the Fleet Lord Chatfield must surely have had the great Fleet anchorage in Scapa Flow uppermost in his mind when he wrote those words. The life span of the Flow as a naval base has been relatively short but extremely full. Twice this century Scapa has played a key role in the struggle for supremacy at sea.

The defences of a naval base are seldom given high priority in peacetime and Scapa Flow was no exception. The Grand Fleet found its principal base dangerously vulnerable in 1914. Twenty-five years later, Scapa Flow again became the Home Fleet's main base, a vital anchorage ill-defended against both submarine and air attack. While the deficiencies were being made good, we cannot but be inspired by the determined struggle to protect the harbour and its ships against the onslaught of the Luftwaffe. Bill Hewison paints a vivid picture from his own and others' personal experience.

Orkney was not only home for the ships but it was also home for the thousands of men and women who have served both afloat and ashore there over the years. Some will remember the months and years spent in the North with long spells at sea, often in terrible weather and with infrequent clashes with the enemy. Others will recollect the day and night tactical manoeuvres, screening the battlefleet, and others the torpedo, gunnery and anti-submarine exercises and, of course, the interminable harbour drills. All will have carried away striking impressions of this dramatic, wild and land-locked anchorage and memories of the friendliness and kindness of the Orkney people.

Although the Royal Navy has now left Scapa Flow, the famous anchorage remains and its strategic importance is undiminished. Modern naval warfare, with its computer technology

i

and advanced weapons and sensors together with its integrated afloat support, bears little resemblance to that of forty years ago. However today, in Scapa, it is oil that must be protected and ships must still have shelter; so the Flow is as important as ever.

Who knows what tomorrow will hold? One thing is certain: we are an island people and we will continue to depend on the sea for our survival. Our maritime expertise and experience give us a unique role in the North Atlantic Alliance. At a geographical key point of that Alliance lies Scapa Flow.

The Royal Navy values highly its tradition and Scapa Flow is part of that tradition. As a naval officer of the new generation and particularly proud of my Orcadian connections, I am delighted to be associated with this book. Bill Hewison has written an authoritative and comprehensive story of a unique harbour. It will bring back many memories to those who have lived or been based there. People worldwide know of Scapa Flow; this book will give them a fascinating insight into its remarkable history.

Ministry of Defence
London
November 1985

Jock Slater

Prologue

NO ASPECT of Orkney is so familiar in the public mind, at home or abroad, as Scapa Flow. For close on a century-and-a-half hundreds of thousands of British, Commonwealth, American and now NATO Servicemen and women have enjoyed, or endured, its hospitality and shelter not only from stress of weather, wind and tide but from the even greater ferocity of man-made attack.

Orcadians themselves, of course, know it well with so many of them living on or near its shores. Many of them, indeed, played an active part in its defence, for in two world wars — three if you count the Napoleonic conflict — this land-locked sheet of sheltered water embraced by Orkney's South Isles has been the strategic base for the Royal Navy when it confronted hostile European, and even on one occasion, trans-Atlantic powers. And on all three occasions it has been quite unprepared for that role when war actually broke out, its main defences being completed each time only when the main danger had passed; an indictment of Britain's national strategic planning, no doubt, but the Flow itself has a proud record of achievement.

Many historic events have taken place on its waters, and not all of them warlike. It has, for instance, many 'firsts' to its credit — the first aeroplane to make a successful landing on an aircraft carrier under way, for example; the first enemy bomber to be shot down by anti-aircraft guns in Britain in World War II, and the first enemy bomb to explode on British soil in that same war and almost at the same time. Unhappily, too, there was the first civilian to be killed in Britain by enemy bombing in the Second War. Between the wars it saw the greatest salvage operation of all time in the raising of the German Fleet scuttled there in 1919 — in itself a unprecedented instance of naval self-immolation.

Through the centuries it has seen the kings and heroes and villains too, come and go across its waters; great fleets have sailed from it to do battle, and even more sinister and dangerous fleets have attacked it from the air. But in the long periods of peace between these warlike irruptions it has provided shelter for fishing fleets and a livelihood for those who lived round its shores, and it has even been a launching-pad for early attempts to fly the Atlantic.

It is, however, mainly as a naval base that it is remembered outside Orkney; but how much is known generally about its selection to play this important part in British affairs? How it evolved and how, when the wars were 'all over', its guard was dropped?

When it was first suggested that I might write a book about Scapa Flow my reply was what I suspect would be that of most Orcadians of my generation — 'Write a book about Scapa Flow? But everybody knows all about Scapa Flow already.'

But do they? The more I thought about it the less I found I knew — and I had served on its defences at the beginning of World War II, and members of my family had been on these same defences in the First War, often in the self-same batteries. Conversations with some of my contemporaries and even more with members of generations too young to know anything directly about the war convinced me that there were many gaps in our knowledge of what had actually happened in our own great harbour — even among those of us who were there at the time. It seemed there was, indeed, a place for a history of Scapa Flow not only to remind the wartime generation of what they had experienced but to let their children, grandchildren and great-grandchildren know what their forbears had been doing in the wars, along with the many thousands from outside the islands who came to defend the Scapa Base and the ships which sought safety and protection in it.

Quite a few books have been written about isolated events in or near the Flow such as the sinking of the *Royal Oak* or the loss of the *Hampshire* off Birsay, but these have not provided an overall connected picture of the vital part it has played in our naval history. Then again individuals, myself among them, remember various incidents or happenings on the defences, but again they are largely unconnected and we are getting thinner on the ground, while there are very few indeed now who remember Scapa between 1914 and 1918. And with the passage of time human memory becomes less and less reliable, as I know from personal experience. It is not only Henry V's soldiers before Agincourt who remember the battle 'with advantages' — we all do it, but it does not make things easier when trying to discover what really happened. It is interesting that estimates in Intelligence Reports and War Diaries of units round the Flow during the spring air-raids of 1940 even can vary as much as

iv

from 14 attacking aircraft to 35 for one raid; similarly, newspaper reports at one point in the first year of the war suggested that there had already been over a hundred air-raid warnings in Orkney, whereas the total for the whole war was officially put at 65 by the Civil Defence authorities in 1945.

I have tried to use documented evidence from as near the time of an actual event as possible, and even so to try and find corroborative evidence to support it. For this I have found the reports of the two local newspapers to be of inestimable value, especially for the pre-1914 run-up-to-war period and again for the inter-war years, supplemented, of course, by the naval, military and official documents now available in the Public Record Office at Kew which were unknown to the newspapers of the time. The Admiralty and War Office records for the actual war years themselves are, of course, all-important, the newspapers being subject to war-time censorship.

A glance at the 'Notes and References' section of this book will show that I have leaned heavily on the files of 'The Orcadian' for much of my local information, and for this I must thank the proprietor and the Editor, Mr James Miller, for the freedom of the newspaper's fileroom at all times. From my years on the editorial staff of 'The Orcadian' I was, of course, already familiar with these files which is why they are so frequently quoted, but this is not to decry those of 'The Orkney Herald' now in the County Library, which are equally valuable and as a rule provide the same basic information as that in 'The Orcadian' for the same relevant dates. Orkney is indeed fortunate to have two such valuable sources of material for anyone researching the period from 1854 onwards.

And it is also fortunate in the excellent County Library under its Chief Librarian, Mr David Tinch, who has given me much help and suggested new sources I might follow, but inevitably the main burden of my frequent importunities has fallen on the willing shoulders of the Deputy Chief Librarian, Mr Bobby Leslie, who has been unfailingly encouraging and helpful towards my persistent requests, and what is even better, he has usually come up with the answers. I am most grateful to them both and also to the Archivist, Miss Alison Fraser, for her help in providing me with material such as the Minute Books of the local authorities, and plans of the Lyness base complex, while Mr Bryce Wilson, the County Museums Officer, kindly provided me with photographs from the Stromness Museum and from the Tankerness House Museum collection, as well as casting a professional eye over their selection and layout.

Members of the Royal family have been frequent visitors to

Scapa and the Fleet in war and peace, one of them indeed, King George VI, serving in it as a naval officer in World War I. His father, George V, too, both as a naval officer and as Monarch was familiar with Orkney waters and, in fact, the title of this book comes from a suggestion he made after the First War that there should be a national memorial to those who gave their lives either in, or sailing from 'this great harbour, Scapa Flow'. Throughout his life he kept a day-to-day diary now preserved in the Royal Archives at Windsor Castle and I wish to express thanks to Her Majesty The Queen for her gracious permission to quote extracts from it concerning his visits to Orkney.

In the early months of the war I had the privilege of serving in the same unit as Eric Linklater and no one could capture in words the 'feel' of Orkney at war better than he, so I am very indebted to Mrs Marjorie Linklater for permission to quote from his volume of essays, 'The Art of Adventure'. I must also thank Mr James MacDonald for his help in letting me study the maps and other material in his excellent Orkney Wireless Museum in St Margaret's Hope.

I have also received great help from the Naval Historical Library and the Naval Historical Branch of the Ministry of Defence and I would like in particular to thank Mr A. J. Francis and Mr R. M. Coppock for their assistance.

Most of the prime source material for this book is in the Public Record Office at Kew and I am extremely grateful to the staff there also for the help and courtesy I received during my frequent visits, and this is also true of the Imperial War Museum in London, especially in the photographic prints department where Mr Michael Willis and Mr James Lucas were particularly helpful.

In this respect I am also very indebted to my cousin, Miss Brenda Smith, for her unstinting hospitality which meant that I was able to spend much longer periods of research in these two establishments than would otherwise have been possible. I was also fortunate in being able to write much of the first draft of the book in the Spanish home of my friends Brian and Judith Reason — it is much easier to write about the 'cold, grey waters of Scapa Flow' when the warm winter sun is glinting on the blue Mediterranean just down the road.

And then there are the countless people who during conversations have supplied me with material, or at least have pointed me in the right direction to find it for myself. Prominent among these, of course, have been former members of 226 HAA Battery which might almost be called 'Kirkwall's Own', the Orkney Heavy Regiment RA and my own Orkney (Fortress)

The British Fleet used Scapa Flow in the years before World War I.

Tragedy — as Commander Dunning's Sopwith Pup goes over the side of HMS *Furious* in the Flow in 1916. He had made the first-ever successful landing on a carrier at sea only the day before — on this second occasion he lost his life.

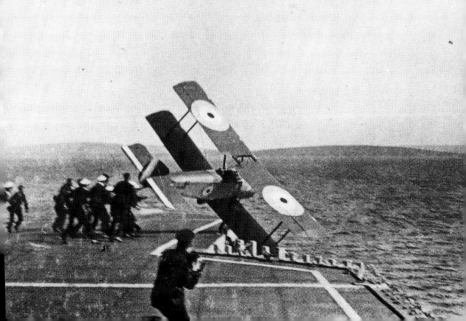

Taking in the harvest alongside one of the Martello Towers built to protect Longhope in the Napoleonic Wars.

Burray had a thriving fishing industry until the eastern channels to the Flow were closed by blockships and then barriers.

Company RE; but conversations with members of the Services from outside Orkney have also been very useful, as have those with people outside the Forces altogether but who have spent their lives within sight of the Flow and who in the course of a chat have 'minded on'. To them I am deeply grateful, for this is really the story of Scapa Flow as seen from the Orcadian point of view, although I hope it will also be of interest outside the islands.

On the technical side I would like to thank my former colleagues on the printing staff of The Kirkwall Press for their help, advice and expertise, in particular the Foreman, Stewart Davidson, and his Deputy Bryan Leslie. It is not often that a writer knows who actually sets up his work, but in this case, through my time on the editorial staff of 'The Orcadian', I do know the two typesetters involved, having worked with them before, Angus Windwick and Drew Kennedy, and to them I can only say a big Thank You for initiating me into the mysteries of the electronic printing age — new since my day — and my thanks go too to the Head Machineman, Kenny Thomson, and Adrian Harray who carried out the printing.

I am also indebted to Mr John D. M. Robertson for reading the final proofs and discussing them with me but, of course, any errors appearing in the text are entirely my own responsibility.

Finally I must express gratitude to my publishers, The Orkney Press, epitomised in the person of Howie Firth whose idea it was originally to produce a book on Scapa Flow, and whose enthusiastic encouragement over the years has been a constant source of stimulation while still curbing most of my wilder excesses — his mailed fist has a very soft velvet glove over it.

W.S.H.
October 1985

Newark
Weyland Bay
Kirkwall
Orkney

Ojo del Sol
La Herradura
Prov. de Granada
Spain

vii

CHAPTER 1

In the Beginning

ISLANDS, we were told at school, are areas of land entirely surrounded by water. Conversely, an area of water entirely surrounded by land is a lake — or, if you live in Scotland, a loch. But what about the other phenomenon, an area of water almost entirely surrounded by islands? A natural harbour certainly — possibly a naval anchorage and base or, more specifically perhaps, Scapa Flow.

For that is what the Flow is, a large area of water, some 120 square miles of it, almost totally enclosed by a ring of islands, the South Isles of Orkney, and this whole mosaic of land and sea, poised strategically just off the north coast of Scotland, divides the long grey surges of the Atlantic Ocean from the equally inhospitable waters of the North Sea. It is this combination of geographical location and natural formation which has given Scapa Flow its unique character and its potential as a naval base; a potential it has held throughout the centuries, for whoever controls it commands the North Sea with easy access to either side of the British Isles and the wide oceans of the world beyond.

These advantages have been recognised by mariners certainly since the time of the Norsemen who not only used the Flow but named it, somewhere about the end of the eighth century or the beginning of the ninth. The 'Scapa' part of the name probably comes from the Old Norse word *skálpr,* meaning 'a sword scabbard' or in a more poetic sense 'a ship', to which was added *eið* meaning an isthmus. This word *skálpeið* is used in both the *Håkonarsaga* and the *Orkneyinga Saga* in connection with the landing and beaching of ships. Scapa Bay with its fine sandy beach is a perfect example of such a landing place, situated as it is on the south side of the one-and-a-half mile wide isthmus dividing the Orkney Mainland into East and West and on which Kirkwall, the island capital, occupies the north shore. So much for the 'Scapa' part — the 'l' and the 'r' being dropped through time and the 'eið' gradually becoming just 'a'.

The 'Flow' part of the name is also Old Norse originally,

being derived in all probability from *floi,* or possibly flóð or *fljot,* meaning 'plenty of water' or 'fjord', and here again with the passage of time, the 'i', 'd' or 't' would be dropped, leaving 'flow' or 'flo' — which, with the English influence of the Navy in two world wars became pronounced to rhyme with 'mow', but which the older Orcadians always rhymed with 'how' or 'now', and they often used the pronunciation 'Scappy' to rhyme with 'happy' rather than Scapa. So we have the complete name Scapa Flow, derived from the Old Norse word *Skálpeiðflói* meaning the 'fjord or loch of the ship isthmus'.[1] Incidentally, the modern Norwegian word *flo* means 'flood' or 'flood tide', presumably being derived from the same source.

Oddly enough although the name 'Over Scapa' appears in Blaeu's maps of the 17th century for the farm near Scapa Bay, the word 'Flow' itself does not appear until 1750, in Murdo Mackenzie's chart of the South Isles of Orkney.[2] Perhaps even more strangely, although the maps of Blaeu, Moll, And. Johnston, Isaak Tirion, Bennet and others have no reference to Scapa Flow as such, some of them do name the very small skerry more or less in the middle of the Flow, the Barrel of Butter, and give it its correct position — perhaps they were intrigued by its unusual name. In a written text as opposed to a map or chart, the full name seems to have its first reference in George Low's 'Tour thro' Orkney & Schetland' dated 1774 where, in the section on South Ronaldsay referring to what he calls 'the How of Hoxa', he writes 'here one of a Danish king's sons was buried who was slain in a battle at sea in Scapa flow or bay' — and he spells it with a small 'f'. Legend has it that Earl Thorfinn Skullsplitter, son of the celebrated Torf Einar, was buried in this very prominent mound.

By the beginning of the 19th century there are further references to Scapa 'Flow', notably in Sir Walter Scott's 'Diary' of his voyage round the north of Scotland with the Lighthouse Commissioners in 1814 where he writes 'a deep bay called Scapa Flow indents it' — a capital 'F' this time.[3]

A couple of years earlier in 1812 it had been put firmly on the naval map, or rather, chart, by Graeme Spence, Maritime Surveyor to the Admiralty, in his 'Proposals for Establishing a Temporary Rendezvous for Line of Battle Ships in a National Roadstead called Scapa Flow found by the South Isles of Orkney'.[4]

But obviously from its Old Norse origins the name had been in common use among seafarers for many centuries before this, and usually seafarers with war on their minds who wanted an anchorage sheltered not only from the stress of weather common in these latitudes but also from their enemies — a place in which to hide securely behind natural defences of tide and rock but from which they could sally forth easily to do battle or to raid as necessity or inclination demanded.

It is doubtful, however, if many of the sailors or soldiers obliged to stay either in its shelter or round its shores in the two world wars would entirely agree with the Reverend Mr Liddell, Minister of the Parish of Orphir, the coastline of which forms the northern shore of the Flow, when he writes in the 'Old Statistical Account' published between 1795 and 1798, 'Scapa Flow — The sea opposite to this coast is the most beautiful piece of water, being a small Mediterranean.'[5] Beautiful it certainly can be in certain conditions, but it lacks the warm climate and the lush vegetation of the southern sea, to put it mildly. Those servicemen expressed their rather different opinion of the place with considerable vigour if not quite the same eighteenth century elegance in such compositions as the 'Scapa Hymn of Hate'[6] during World War I and more forcibly still, but with less finesse, in 'Bloody Orkney' in the Second World War.[7]

It was also sometimes described rather differently from the school-day version as — 'miles and miles of damn-all surrounded by miles and miles of more damn-all'. And quite often the expletives were more forceful than that. But a 'small Mediterranean'? No — hardly that. Still, the rest of Liddell's 'Account' stands nearly as true today as when he wrote close on two centuries ago, for he goes on —

> It is surrounded with twelve different islands, through which are several outlets to the Pentland Firth, and German and Atlantic Oceans. This, particularly in time of war, is the great thoroughfare for ships coming north about. It abounds in safe roadsteads and fine harbours; such as Holm Sound, Floxa [sic]Sound, St Margaret's Houp, Pan Houp and Long Houp, in the Island of Walls; where there is good anchorage and a sufficient depth of water for the largest ship in the British Navy.[8]

Prophetic words indeed, although his later comment that the 'principal entrance to Scalpa Flow is through Holm Sound on the East' no longer holds good nor has done since its blocking by sunken merchant ships in World War I as a defence against submarine attack, and more permanently in World War II by the Churchill Barriers for the same reason.

The 'twelve different islands' with which Liddell says the Flow is surrounded must still be there, even in a slightly different form, but it is not clear which ones he included in his round dozen. On the north and east side, going clockwise, there are the Orkney Mainland, Lamb Holm, Glims Holm, Burray and South Ronaldsay; then on the south there are Flotta, Switha, South Walls and Hoy; and finally, in the Hoymouth opening, Graemsay — and that makes nine, or ten if you treat South Walls and Hoy as two separate islands, ignoring the narrow isthmus at Brims. So where are Mr Liddell's two, or even three other islands? It may be that he includes Swona — near the southern entrance — and Cava and Fara, which are both actually inside the Flow, for he does mention that 'it is remarked of the island of Cava, and some other small islands, that neither rat nor mouse will live there'.[9] But he can hardly have included in his twelve the Barrel of Butter, that low, flat skerry with its cairn making it look like a primitive submarine, though he does refer to it as being 'formerly known as Carlin Skerry . . . a seal hunting ground for which the farmer paid a barrel of oil a year. But shipping scared the seals away and the proprietor changed the rental to one of one barrel of butter a year.'[10]

So by the end of the eighteenth century certainly, there were enough ships using the Flow to drive away the seals from this skerry, although they are still to be found not so far away, notably in South Ronaldsay.

It is difficult to delineate Scapa Flow in strict measurements — it all depends on what one includes in it. From Scapa Bay in the north to where the Hoxa Boom used to be in wartime, stretching from Hoxa Head in South Ronaldsay to near Stanger Head in Flotta, the distance is some twelve miles, and it is a little more than that from Cairston Roads, outside Stromness in the west, say, to the Churchill Barriers on the east between Holm, Lamb Holm, Glims Holm, Burray and South Ronaldsay — an area of between 120 and 160 square miles according to what reference points one takes.

There were originally nine major entrances to the Flow proper. On the east there was Kirk Sound, Skerry Sound, Weddel Sound and Water Sound — all subject to strong tides of anything up to ten knots. To the south there was Hoxa Sound between South Ronaldsay and Flotta, the main entrance for the larger naval craft, battleships, carriers, cruisers and so on; Switha Sound between Flotta and Switha, used mainly by the smaller ships such as destroyers, and sometimes nicknamed the 'tradesmen's entrance'; and Cantick Sound between Switha and Cantick Head. Finally, there was Burra Sound (between Hoy and Graemsay) and Hoy Sound (between Hoy and Stromness), both with very strong tides, on the west. The four eastern sounds are

Orkney

Dennis Head

North Ronaldsay

Noup Head

Papa Westray

✝ Pierowall

Westray

Start Point

Sanday

+ Air Stations WWI

✈ Airfields WWII

® Main Radar Stations

⊙ Lighthouses

Eday

Stronsay

Brough of Birsay

Rousay

Egilsay

Wyre

Birsay

Marwick Head

Gairsay

Auskerry

✈ Twatt
✈ Skeabrae

Mainland

Harray Loch

Shapinsay

The String

Helliar Holm

Finstown

Stromness

✝ Stenness

Hatston ✈

KIRKWALL

✈ Grimsetter

Deerness

Hoy Sound

⊙ Hoy Low

Graemsay ⊙ Hoy High

+ +

® Netherbutton

Copinsay

St Mary's

Bring Deeps

⊙ Houton

Scapa Flow

Lamb Holm

Glims Holm

Roseness

Norway

Faroe

Cava

Holm Sound

Shetland

Rysa

Hunda

Burray

Orkney

Cromarty

Hoy

Fara

Lyness

Flotta

St M'gts Hope

Jutland

L'hope

® S. Walls

Switha

Cantick Head

South Ronaldsay

Rosyth

Dogger Bank

Torness

Pentland Firth

Burwick

Stroma

Pentland Skerries

Dunnet Head

Duncansby Head

Scotland

now all completely blocked by the massive causeways constructed in World War II, it having been discovered too late that the ten-knot swirling tides and the blockships sunk across them in World War I were not sufficient deterrent to a resolute submariner such as Günther Prien, who successfully forced them in his *U 47* on the night of 13/14 October 1939, to torpedo and sink the anchored battleship *Royal Oak* with the loss of over 800 lives. So now there are only five entrances to the Flow and one of them, at least, Burra Sound, still has wartime obstructions in it.

The contours of the land round this great expanse of water are, for the most part, low and gently rounded, rising to just over 1,500 feet with Orkney's highest hills in Hoy to the west and south-west — fortunately the direction from which the worst of Orkney's gales of 100 mph and more usually come. And so even the biggest ships, including the vast supertankers of the oil-boom era as well as the earlier battleships and aircraft carriers, can ride out these violent storms tucked into the shelter of the Hoy land — although passengers in smaller craft such as the wartime drifters might be forgiven for describing it as only 'comparative shelter' if they were caught out in the middle by a sudden gale whipping the tops off the waves in a driving mist of spindrift obscuring the land only a mile or two away.

The bottom of the Flow is pretty regular. As Dr A. C. O'Dell writes in *The Highlands and Islands of Scotland,* 'Its flat floor, the result of infilling with sediment or from the decay of dead ice, is very prominent on the charts.' Nowhere is it deeper than 62 metres, just over 30 fathoms, and most of it is less than that, averaging perhaps 35 metres or some 20 fathoms, but it was still more than enough to swallow up the great ships of the Kaiser's High Seas Fleet which scuttled itself in these waters on Midsummer Day, 1919, as well as to cover several of our own ships which lie on its 'flat floor'. The deepest point is actually in the Bring Deeps on the west, but just outside its main entrance in Hoxa Sound the depth is 35 fathoms or 64 metres.[11]

But what does this place really look like? — this great seawater lake with its enclosing necklace of islands which, in fine weather, seem to float in their own bubble of clear air below the wide arch of a pale blue summer sky but which in winter gales are merely darker shadows in an all-pervading greyness, conditions which inspired the doggerel 'Bloody Orkney' or the 'Scapa Hymn of Hate', but which in the first example can bring an awareness of the serene beauty of natural things and places still unspoiled, an awareness heightened and intensified in time of war by the ever-present fear that such beauty cannot last much longer.

One man who knew it in all its moods was the Orkney author Eric Linklater. As a young man he had sailed his boat on its waters and had walked its shores; much of the action of his first novel, *Whitemaa's Saga,* takes place either on, or around, the Flow, and in World War II as Company Commander of the Orkney (Fortress) Company of the Royal Engineers he played his part in its defence. Who better to paint the Flow's portrait in words? In his essay, 'The First Attack' in *The Art of Adventure,* he writes:

On calm days the islands floated on a deep-blue sea in a charm of shadowed cliffs and reddish moors, the harvest was ripe, and the fields were bearded with bright gold or gay in a lovely green. The forehead of the hills rose in smooth lines against a lucent sky, and rippled lakes provoked a passion for mere water. In such weather one could live by the eye alone, and beautify oneself with the delighted torture of love-at-seventeen. To suppose that war might invade that landscape, or snatch one from it, seemed quite outrageous; yet it was, beyond doubting, the threat of war that opened one's eyes, as if to a new thing, to the beauty of the islands and their sea.

That was Orkney and Scapa in the valedictory sunshine of those last few doom-fraught summer days of 1939 as the world slid helpless over the brink to war. They could not last for ever and the storms were bound to come. Eric Linklater caught this other side of the picture, too, in another essay from the same volume 'The Atlantic Garrisons':

To stand in a south-easterly gale on the weather-worn headlands of Hoxa and Stanger, at the Fleet's entrance to Scapa Flow, was to endure such a hurly-burly, so rude and ponderous a buffeting, that one could hardly deny a sense of outrage, a suspicion that the wind's violence was a personal enmity. In the crested tumult of the sea there were colours of wildly derisive beauty above the monstrous procession of the waves, and the spectator, battered by the gale, and resentful, was humbled by the immensity of the pageant that careered before it. The sky was pitiless, and the young soldiers in their shabby khaki were dwarfed and lonely in the vast confusion of the storm.

Those are the two faces of Scapa Flow and there are countless shades of expression in between.

CHAPTER 2

A Viking Lair

THE NORSEMEN may have named it, somewhere about 800 AD, but they were not the first people to know and use it.

Orkney has been lived in for at least five thousand years and it is inconceivable that, in the four millenia or so before the first Viking keel crunched into the sands of Scapa Bay, some other earlier people had not lived along its shores or on its islands. There is ample archaeological evidence, in fact, that they did.

The broch-builders of more recent, although still remote times, around 100 or 200 AD or so, also knew Scapa Flow. Indeed it may well have been a centre of political power at times for what are sometimes called the proto-Picts — the loose amalgam of peoples and tribes from which the still mysterious Picts themselves evolved. Writing in the chapter on 'Brochs and Broch Builders' in *The Northern Isles*, J. R. C. Hamilton suggests that these unique circular stone towers may have originated and been developed in the Scapa Flow area, where the type of stone used in them is readily available, the design and technique of building them then spreading out from this centre to the rest of Orkney, Shetland, Caithness and the Western Isles as the need for defensive structures demanded.[1] One such broch was, in fact, situated at Lingro on the banks to the west of Scapa Bay and just above it, until it was destroyed in the late 1970s during agricultural development.

Were these brochs built as a defence against the Romans perhaps? The Romans certainly sailed round the north of Scotland and must have seen Orkney. It is unlikely that with their efficiency and thoroughness, not to mention their inquiring minds, they did not at least sail into the Flow if only to assess its military value. But there is no hard and fast evidence that they did so nor that they landed on Orkney soil. Any Roman artefacts found during excavations in the islands, and they are few, can be traced to the trading activities of the people already living there.

It is with the coming of the Norsemen that hard evidence of the use of Scapa Flow begins to be found, notably from their sagas and, as one might expect, particularly in the *Orkneyinga*

Saga — the story of the Norse Earls of Orkney and their henchmen as told by the skalds and sagamen between the ninth and twelfth centuries, handed down orally and subsequently given the permanence of writing in Iceland in the twelfth and thirteenth centuries. And much of this story, or rather stories, has been backed up by subsequent archaeological and place-name study which still goes on with parallel study of whatever documentary sources may provide.

The Norsemen showed their appreciation of the anchorage and the need to keep a watchful eye on its approaches by building castles at Paplay overlooking Holm Sound on the east and at Cairston in the west from which Hoy Sound could be kept under observation. In addition the Norse Earls had a favourite residence at the Bu, further inside the Flow on the Orphir shore.

One of the earliest, and most dramatic, events in the recorded history of the Flow occurred in 995 AD when King Olaf Tryggvason on his way back to claim the Norwegian throne, having been himself converted to Christianity while in the West, arrived in the Pentland Firth burning with evangelising zeal. He surprised Earl Sigurd II of Orkney in the enclosed bay of Osmundwall, now Kirk Hope in South Walls at the southern entrance to the Flow, where he carried out not so much a shotgun wedding as a battle-axe conversion.

Sigurd, along with his followers, was given the choice of forsaking the old pantheon of Norse gods and embracing the Christian faith — or to be killed on the spot along with his son and henchmen. Pragmatically he chose to live, but how sincerely he accepted the new faith is open to doubt. To make sure that he remained Christian, at least outwardly, Olaf took Sigurd's son back to Norway as hostage. After the boy's death there, Sigurd certainly seems to have reverted to the old gods, for he was allied with pagan vikings when he was killed in 1014 at the battle of Clontarf outside Dublin, bearing the magic raven-shaped banner made by his mother Edna which brought death to anyone who bore it into battle but victory to those who followed it. And so Orkney became Christian, at least nominally, although the Faith had been, in fact, established long before the advent of the Vikings, by the Celtic monks and missionaries, the remains of whose holy places can still be seen on such places as the Broughs of Birsay and Deerness.

There are frequent references to Scapa in the *Orkneyinga Saga*, often associated with Sweyn Asleifsson, called by Eric Linklater 'The Ultimate Viking' in his book about him by that title. It is an apt name, for Sweyn was a swashbuckling, piratical character living some 200 years too late, for the real Viking age had passed by the time he was at his full potential in the mid-twelfth century.

We hear of him at 'Knarston at Scapa' — not far from Scapa Bay — at Yule, 1135. His father had just been murdered in his house at Duncansby in Caithness while Sweyn was fishing in the Pentland Firth. To escape a similar fate he was on his way to the Earl's Bu in Orphir, also on the shores of the Flow, where Earl Paul was holding a great Yule feast. It proved to be a doom-laden festival, for during it Sweyn killed his namesake, the sinister Sweyn Breastrope, and had to make his escape across the dark hills to the North Isles, staying with Bishop William in Egilsay before sailing to the safety of Tiree.[2]

In the Spring of 1136, the year before Earl Rognvald began his great project of building St Magnus Cathedral to the memory of his uncle, the martyred St Magnus, Sweyn was engaged in darker deeds — the capture of Earl Paul from Westness in Rousay after which he carried him south through Scapa Flow where his ship was seen from Gaitnip on the east side as it bore the captive earl to mutilation and death in Scotland.[3] But Sweyn was back again later in the year when 'nine armed men were seen coming from Scapa to the Thing'. Sweyn was one of the nine for 'Sweyn had sailed in a ship from the south to Scapa and left the ship behind him there'.[4] He had arrived to make his peace with the all-powerful Earl Rognvald, sole ruler of Orkney now that Earl Paul was no more. Earl Rognvald was holding a 'Thing' (a Court or Parliament) in Kirkwall.

From 1154 Sweyn is frequently connected with Scapa Flow as when in that year he sailed from Scotland with a cargo ship and a cutter to Orkney: 'And when they came to [Scapa] they captured a ship from Fogl Ljotolf's son.'[5]

From later that year comes the first saga record of an event which was to become familiar in the Flow right down to our own times, a fleet assembling and preparing for battle, when 'the Earls then moved their ships to Scapa' and Sweyn, having made a feint rounding of Cape Wrath before doubling back through the Pentland Firth, arrived at Walls, possibly Osmundwall again, or Longhope where 'they learned that the Earls lay off Scapa with fourteen ships below [Knarston]'.[6] Knarston, situated on the west side of Scapa Bay, probably derives its name from another Old Norse word connected with the berthing and beaching of ships, Knarrarstoðum, meaning 'ships' place', the ships in this case being merchant vessels or cargo ships — knarr.

The Earls that Sweyn 'learned' of were Rognvald and his co-holder of the Earldom, Harald. Sweyn, with his own nominee for the Earldom, Erlend — for once again it was in the nature of a three-cornered contest for the islands — decided to attack that same night and did so with devastating effect. Rognvald and Harald were routed and had to escape across the Flow and the Pentland Firth to Scotland in small rowing boats while many of their followers died in the surprise attack. One man, indeed, was so scared that he bolted for Kirkwall and sanctuary in the Cathedral with his shield still strapped to his back, but so great was his haste that he forgot to slacken it off and he got jammed in the doorway.

So this battle of Knarston gave Sweyn and Erlend control of Orkney — in the meantime — and also added their opponents' fleet of fourteen ships to their own seven.

Scapa is mentioned again in 1155 when 'Thorbjorn sailed secretly out to the Orkneys in a cutter with thirty men and landed at Scapa'.[7] From there he walked to Kirkwall and again Sweyn Asleifsson was involved — this time on the side of Earl Rognvald.

So far the number of ships or galleys mentioned as being in the Flow at any one time has been comparatively small, fourteen for Rognvald and Harald, or twenty-one if they are added to Sweyn's seven after Knarston.

It is more than a century later before we hear of a really big war fleet in these waters, that of King Håkon Håkonsson of Norway when he came west-over-sea in an attempt to shore up his crumbling empire in Scotland and the Western Isles. Sailing from Bergen late in the summer of 1263, he called at Shetland then consolidated his force off Shapinsay's Elwick Bay in Orkney, just north of Kirkwall, before sailing east-about the islands to concentrate in Rognvaldsvoe, now St Margaret's Hope, in South Ronaldsay. It was late in the year now for a war cruise to Scotland even though his fleet numbered some 120 large well-found ships, including his own magnificent oak-built, 37-bench flagship, *Kristsuðin, the Christship* — certainly the greatest naval force ever seen in Scapa Flow up till then, possibly the largest assembly of fighting ships anywhere at that time.

But the omens were not good. Just before he sailed out through Hoxa Sound into the Pentland Firth there was an eclipse of the sun, presaging the eclipse of Norse power in the west. Apprehensive, but undeterred by this portent, Håkon pushed on round Cape Wrath to meet with disaster at the Battle of Largs in the Clyde when his punitive intentions were frustrated as much by bad weather as by the Scots. It was one of those indecisive victories which both sides claim but neither side wins, rather like another great naval battle fought out of Scapa Flow in our own century, Jutland in 1916. The fact remains, however, that from that time on, Norse power in the west waned and only Orkney and Shetland continued as Scandinavian possessions off Scotland. The sun of the Viking dawn which had risen over the fjords in the east four centuries before was setting fast in the sea lochs of the west, and even the Norse hold on the Northern Isles had only two more centuries to run.

Håkon, with the remnants of his shattered fleet, struggled north again through the stormy seas of that late autumn to reach the haven offered by Scapa Flow, probably lying first in Switha Sound or Longhope before returning whence he had set out, Rognvaldsvoe. Some of his ships sailed straight on back to Norway but he took his own great ship, along with some others, across the Flow to Houton and its sheltered bay, where they were hauled for the winter. Others were beached at Scapa Bay.

From Houton he went to Kirkwall, to die, for he was a broken man — 'After that he fared into Scapa-neck . . .' as Dasent's translation of the Håkon Saga has it.[8] He took up residence with Bishop Henry in the Bishop's Palace there, where his life ended at Yuletide while he had the Scriptures read to him. He was buried temporarily in St Magnus Cathedral, which was then just a century old. In the Spring of 1264 he made his last Voar cruise from Scapa, where his body was carried and taken on board his ship brought round from Houton — bound for Bergen where he was to lie with his fathers. 'And all the bodyguard went out with it [the body] across Scapa-neck and the body was carried out in a boat to the ship.'[9]

And so ended, in effect, the Norse era in the story of Scapa Flow, although the islands which form its perimeter along with the rest of Orkney remained Scandinavian possessions until 1468, when they became part of a still unredeemed pledge for the dowry of Margaret, daughter of King Christian I of Denmark, who was to marry James III of Scotland, Norway then being ruled by Denmark.

There have been suggestions that another Princess Margaret, the Maid of Norway, died in Scapa Flow, giving her name to St Margaret's Hope in South Ronaldsay. There is no truth in this story whatsoever. She was the seven-year-old granddaughter of Alexander III of Scotland and legal heiress to the Scottish throne. She was being brought back to Scotland from Norway, where she was born, by Sir Patrick Spens of ballad fame in 1290 to marry Edward, Prince of Wales, son of Edward I of England — a marriage which would have united the Scottish and English crowns three centuries before it actually did happen. She fell ill on the way across the North Sea and died, possibly off Orkney or in its shelter. At all events she was not the eponymous Margaret of St Margaret's Hope as she was never canonised. It may even be that she was drowned off Aberdeen or Aberlour as the ballad has it.

St Margaret's Hope, in fact, derives its name from a chapel dedicated to yet another Margaret, the beautiful, learned and pious Hungarian-born wife of Malcolm III Canmore, King of Scotland, who was canonised by Pope Innocent IV in 1251, nearly two centuries after her death in Edinburgh Castle.

CHAPTER 3

The Scots Take Over

IT IS perhaps appropriate that as the Norse chapter of Scapa's story closes in true Nordic fashion with a lost battle and the departure of a dead king, the new Scottish era should open with a successful battle from Orkney's point of view and the visit of a very live king, James V, in 1540, when Orkney had been under Scottish rule for seventy-two years — at least nominally.

Oddly enough, he too had been having trouble with his chieftains of the Western Isles and West of Scotland, just as Håkon Håkonsson had in a different context. James's voyage, too, was in the nature of a punitive expedition to bring them to heel.

He was accompanied by Cardinal Beaton and had a fleet of sixteen ships, including his own flagship, the *Salamander* (Captain John Ker) and a complement of three or four thousand men. Sailing from the Forth in an atmosphere of considerable secrecy to conceal the purpose of the expedition, they cruised up the east coast of Scotland by way of Aberdeen, the Moray Firth, Sutherland, Caithness and Orkney, through the Pentland Firth to the Western Isles, where they sorted things out with the chieftains, and so on to the south again. In Orkney they were entertained by Bishop Robert Maxwell, and it is virtually certain that they lay in Scapa Flow in order to land and visit Kirkwall across the 'ships' isthmus' of the former owners of the islands.

In order to make a voyage like this in the days when charts and even navigational instruments were rare, a skilled pilot was an essential member of the expedition and James V had one such in Alexander Lindsay, who had prepared his *Rutter of the Scottish Seas,* probably specially for this important state cruise.[1]

A 'Rutter' was a sixteenth century set of sailing instructions used by a pilot in coastal navigation and it preceded charts and instruments. The word is of the same French origin as 'route'.

Lindsay's 'Rutter' in the Balfour Collection in the National Library of Scotland covers the whole coast of Scotland, starting even south of the Border, from the Humber, round to the Solway Firth by way of the Pentland Firth and the Western Isles.

Headlands, harbours, tides and dangerous rocks are listed and described along with advice on how they should be negotiated. If James V's fleet followed this Rutter, which it probably did, it would have had very explicit information about the dangers of the Pentland Firth, how to avoid them and how to enter the Flow between South Ronaldsay and Swona, for Lindsay obviously knew all about these treacherous waters just as our latter-day sailors did, and still do, although he did not have their scientific aids to help him.

In his section on 'Hauins, sounds and dangers from Dungisbe [Duncansby] Head to the Mulle of Cantyre both on the Mayneland and throw the Iles', he writes:

In the middes of Pethland Fyrth betuixt Dungisbe and Orknay there is a great daunger causit be nepe tydis whiche is called the Boir. To avoid the daunger ye sal mak your cours from Dungisbe northwest till you come north to est from Stroma. At the north end of Stroma is a greater daunger called the Swelle whiche is the meeting of iiij or v contrary tydes with great circulationne of watter causing a deip hurlepoole in the middes, dangerous for all shippis both great and small.[2]

And these waters remain dangerous today even to greater ships than Lindsay could have possibly imagined, both men-o'-war and merchant ships, for quite apart from passing two of the main entrances to Scapa Flow the Pentland Firth is a passage in the great ocean highway from the northern ports of Europe to the Atlantic and the New World.

The Rutter continues:

Betuixt Swinna [Swona] and Ronaldsa are great dangerous poplynis of watter called the Hoppers.
On the southwest syd of Ronaldsa is a dangerous tyde called the Crelis.
A halff a myle from the May Head lyeth dangerous rockis called the Men of May.

In the Flow itself Lindsay advises:

Iff ye will lye in Orknay cast anker south or southwest from Kirkwall in the sound and ye sall find x or xij fadomes. Betuixt Ronaldsa and Glowmis Home is a good rode for all windis called St Margaretis Howip.[3]

His first instruction for anchoring would seem to put him

somewhere in Scapa Bay or just along the Orphir shore where ships still anchor today, and it would have provided James V and Cardinal Beaton with a comparatively short journey on foot or on horseback to meet Bishop Maxwell in Kirkwall.

The Rutter is right again in recommending St Margaret's Hope as a 'good rode for all winds', but a bit out in placing it 'betuixt Ronaldsa and Glowmis Home [Glims Holm]' — Lindsay apparently means Burray which comes between Glims Holm and South Ronaldsay.

After this incursion into the Flow the Rutter goes on to give directions for sailing from Scrabster in Caithness, to the west and ultimately south through the Western Isles.

And so another great fleet led by a king's flagship headed out into the Pentland Firth between the Heads of Hoxa and Stanger. Many more, both kings and fleets, were to follow but not for quite a long time.

The last battle to be fought on Orkney soil had taken place in 1529, eleven years before James V visited the islands. It was at Summerdale on the borders of Orphir and Stenness and about three miles from the shores of Scapa Flow where the invading force under the Earl of Caithness must have landed — either in Waulkmill Bay or possibly Houton as the most likely bridge-heads, but it could have been anywhere between these two points. How many vessels with their armed invaders crossed the Flow that fateful day of 7 June 1529 is not known, but the invasion fleet must have been of considerable size. What is certain is that not so many went back across the Flow after the battle, as it is variously estimated that between three hundred and five hundred men, including the Earl himself, were slain or killed 'fleeand to their botis'. It was claimed by some that there was Divine intervention on the side of the Orcadians with the reported appearance of St Magnus fighting for them — others hinted that witchcraft had played a part. At all events the Orkneymen were the undoubted victors.

The battle arose out of a family feud among the Sinclairs both in Orkney and Caithness which boiled over into open rebellion in the islands when Lord William Sinclair, whose father, Henry, Lord Sinclair, was killed at Flodden, was appointed Justice Depute of Orkney with residence in Kirkwall Castle. He made himself generally obnoxious to the Orkney folk and in 1528 they rose, headed by James Sinclair of Brecks and his brother Edward, both illegitimate sons of Sir William Sinclair of Warsetter by the same mother. They seized the Castle and sent Lord William packing, killing a number of his supporters. He appealed to James V for help to put down the uprising and in 1529 a royal command to the Orkney rebels instructed them to hand over the castle and submit themselves to judgement. Not surprisingly, the command was ignored and with royal authority Lord William and his kinsman the Sinclair Earl of Caithness raised an army, in Caithness, and embarked to bring the Orkney insurgents to heel. The Battle of Summerdale was the result.

The Flow now faded into one of its periods of historical obscurity as far as the written records are concerned, though it obviously continued to be used by shipping of all kinds.

Sir Martin Frobisher with his three ships, *Gabriel, Michael* and *Aid* probably anchored in it in 1576, when they took on water before sailing again in search of the elusive but ever-beckoning North-West Passage round Arctic Canada to the Pacific. The Hudson's Bay ships were to do the same annually three centuries later when bound in the same direction.

Dionyse Settle, one of Frobisher's company, wrote of landing in Orkney and of the fear of Orcadians about English fishermen who were raiding the islands on their way to and from the Iceland fishing grounds.[4] These fishermen also doubtless knew the Flow well.

There is no evidence that any ships of the Spanish Armada entered Scapa Flow, although in that disastrous and stormy autumn of 1588 they would doubtless have welcomed its shelter as they wallowed wounded through the North Sea gales to escape the English men-o'-war snapping at their heels. They must have seen the islands as they limped into the Atlantic and made for Spain, leaving many of their galleons on our rock-bound shores — one certain wreck was *El Gran Griffon* on Fair Isle; whether Orkney claimed any victims itself is uncertain but some survivors did make Westray, where a group of families was known as the Dons until quite recently. Another, but unsubstantiated story is that a Spanish ship perished along with the crew at Yesnaby, quite close to the Castle.

In 1650 the Marquis of Montrose embarked his army of pressed Orkneymen and others at Holm on the east side of the Flow, before the debacle of the Battle of Carbisdale and his subsequent betrayal and humiliating death on the Grassmarket gallows in Edinburgh for supporting the wrong cause, that of the Stewarts.

On a more cheerful note there was a famous cup said to be kept at Scapa. It was apparently of gargantuan proportions, and visiting celebrities were expected to do it appropriate justice. It is recorded that when Bishop Mackenzie visited his diocese in 1677 and landed at Scapa, he knocked it back in one draught and then, anticipating Oliver Twist by several centuries, asked for more.[5]

Another visitor at the end of the seventeenth century must have been Captain Greenville Collins RN, for Orkney featured in three of the charts in his 'atlas', officially entitled 'Great Britain's Coasting Pilot being a New and Exact Survey of the Sea-Coast of England and Scotland with the Scilly Islands and Orkney and Shetland'. Collins was Hydrographer to Charles II and was a Younger Brother of Trinity House. His recommended harbours are Deer Sound in the east and Cairston near Stromness on the west side of the Flow — a word he does not actually use, although the name 'Scapa' appears in the bay of that name and he also indicates the 'Barrill' — the Barrel of Butter.

It would seem that Collins, like all the early map and chart makers, regarded Scapa Flow not as a harbour itself but as an inland sea which had good harbours in it. His charts, one of which is dedicated to Prince George of Denmark, First Lord of the Admiralty at the time, are claimed to be the first of their kind produced in Britain, the previous ones having originated for the most part in Holland.

The eighteenth century saw sporadic activity in these waters, some of it highly illegal such as the sacking of the Stewart Depute's Hall of Clestrain on the Orphir shore by Gow's pirate crew in January 1725. Gow, a Stromness man, would have known the Flow well in his youth before he embarked on his career of piracy which ended in Calf Sound, Eday when his stolen ship, the *Revenge,* grounded and he began the long trail to Execution Dock in London, and death.[6]

Orkney did not feature particularly prominently in the Jacobite risings of 1715 and 1745, although it had its share of the action. In 1746 a Jacobite force landed in South Walls and made its way across the Flow to Scapa Bay. The Government ship *Sheerness* was lying in Stromness at the time, but the two sides did not meet.[7]

Earlier that year, a mysterious Spanish brig with three Caithness Jacobites on board hovered to the eastward of Orkney before being piloted in to the Flow through Weddel Sound to Pan Hope in Flotta. She lay there for a week while her three passengers were entertained by, and presumably discussed plans with, Sir James Stewart at the Bu of Burray, who shared their views on the restoration of the Stewarts.

A little later HMS *Shark* came up through the Flow to take that same Burray laird prisoner, putting an end to his anti-Hanoverian activities. He was taken to London where he died, probably of typhus, in Southwark jail, having been arraigned on a charge of high treason only the previous day.

Towards the end of the century Orkney, in common with the rest of Britain's east coast, was plagued by French privateers. The 'Edinburgh Magazine' of 1782, for instance, quotes an example of their depredations. The privateer in question — she is not named — landed a party in South Ronaldsay where they robbed a 'lady and gentleman' of two watches, which would be, as the magazine points out, a large proportion of the watches on the island at that time. The ship then crossed to Longhope, where a sloop was captured and sunk after the privateers had taken its rigging. At night nine of them were landed and they raided the premises of Messrs Smeck, possibly Bremen merchants. Next day they landed again and took 'a great deal of wearing apparel and blankets' as well as 'some sheep, swine and oxen' which they shot, although they also took a milking cow back to their ship alive. They 'stripped one of the people of his cloathes' before leaving the district in pursuit of a brig which they took.

'The Edinburgh Magazine' also records a murder on Cava in the middle of the Flow in 1774. Hugh Inksetter and William Mallich apparently lived on the island and on this occasion had landed there from a boat with a party of other islanders. The two men fell out for some reason and started to fight, but were parted by the others. Some time later, however, Inksetter started the fight again further up the island and tried to strangle Mallich with his own neckerchief; Mallich pulled a knife to cut his neck free, as he claimed, but instead 'ran it into Inksetter's belly from which he died in great pain'. Thirty-six hours later, Mallich escaped by boat to Hoy and then crossed the Pentland Firth, never to be heard of again.[8]

'Scalpa Flow', however, had its peaceful activities during the eighteenth century, too, as the Reverend Mr Liddell points out in the 'Old Statistical Account' and these probably were of much more interest to the Orkney people themselves than the comings and goings of pirates, Royalists and mysterious ships.

'It abounds with many other kinds of fish such as scate, flounders, haddock, mackerel and, occasionally, herring,' he writes. This was apart from the dogfish which provided an important source of income from their oil as well as being a major item of food. When smoked they were said to resemble kippers.

'The common kinds of shellfish are also to be found here,' continued Liddell, 'such as lobster, partans, spouts, and cockles; there are likewise a few seals, and otters, whose skins are valuable. Sometimes, too, the small whales called the bottlenosed, make their appearance on this coast and when embayed, are surrounded with boats and forced on shore.

C

'There are no fewer than fifteen smacks employed through-out the season, in fishing and carrying lobsters to the London market; all of which rendezvous in one or other of the harbours of Scalpa Flow.'

Big skate are still caught in the Flow, mainly by sea anglers nowadays, and schools of whales are not unknown though no longer hunted and slaughtered, as happened in the 18th, 19th and early 20th centuries, for their oil.

Now in the latter half of the 20th century when Scapa is coping with a different kind of oil, whales are an embarrassment rather than an asset when they become 'embayed' and stranded with the resulting difficulty of getting rid of the unwanted carcases.

Another important source of wealth based on the Flow to a large extent in the 19th and early 20th centuries, was the herring fishing. It was, of course, seasonal but it provided a livelihood for many people round the herring stations of St Mary's, Holm, Burray, St Margaret's Hope and Stromness serving the fleets of smacks from all over the east of Scotland and even further afield, on their annual visitations as they followed the shoals south from Shetland along the east coast to Yarmouth and Lowestoft. This was followed by the processing and salting for export, largely to Germany, Russia and the Baltic countries. The first war and the advent of the steam drifter killed this trade and its kindred crafts, while the wartime blocking of the eastern entrances to the Flow by sunken ships also rendered the fishing harbours useless.

So quite apart from its value as an anchorage throughout history, the Flow was obviously a fairly prolific source of food and livelihood for the people who lived round its shores. Grimmer harvests were to be reaped in the future.

CHAPTER 4

Shape of things to come

EARLY in the nineteenth century Scapa Flow began to assume the role that was to be its destiny for the next century and a half — at least in times of war.

France held most of the Continent in thrall. Britain, as was to happen again in the twentieth century, stood alone against this tyranny, her international trading brought almost to a standstill. The Napoleonic Wars raged on land and sea. To make matters worse, the United States of America, Britain's lost trans-Atlantic colonies, declared war on what had been the mother-country, in 1812, and instead of a friendly ally across the ocean as in later world conflicts there were American privateers raiding shipping off our northern and western coasts. Sir Walter Scott was troubled by the proximity of these raiders and actually sighted one of them when he made his voyage round the north of Scotland, Orkney and Shetland in the summer of 1814.

On the east side, French privateers were active and indeed had made the passage of merchant ships through the English Channel and Straits of Dover dangerous if not actually impracticable. As a result, more and more merchant ships from the west of England and the Clyde used the Pentland Firth route when Baltic-bound, so having to run the gauntlet of the American threat to their peaceful passage. As this threat increased, so the rudiments of the convoy system were introduced. And the rendezvous and collecting point for these merchantmen was Scapa Flow, or at least Longhope, where at times there were as many as a hundred sail waiting for a warship escort. If, however, a naval escort was not immediately available, then these hundred or so, mainly defenceless, vessels had to wait, lying completely unprotected in a narrow land-locked bay, admittedly sheltered from storm and tempest but very vulnerable to enemy attack. For the first time the authorities realised that if Scapa Flow was to be used strategically as a base in time of war, it needed more than just its natural defences of tide-rips, rocks and stress of weather. Guns were needed.

In the year following the American declaration of war, work

started on an eight-gun battery and two Martello towers sited to guard the entrance to Longhope Bay. The two towers, similar to those built against the Napoleonic threat of invasion along the south coast of England, were, and still are, 33 feet high, the circular walls being nine feet thick on the seaward side where there was the greater danger of damage from bombardment by attacking warships, and six feet thick on the landward side. It has been claimed, with some justification, that they contain some of the finest masonry ever executed in Orkney. They were each to have a 24-pounder cannon on the top and the estimated cost of each tower was £5,264 16s 2½d.[1] Sited at Hacksness and Crockness, they were a familiar site to the many servicemen who passed them in the two later world wars, just as they are today to the oilmen and visitors on more peaceful missions.

The battery is not so well known, being naturally less conspicuous. It was sited to the east of Hacksness and its eight 24-pounders covered the approaches to the anchorage. Its estimated cost was £1,162 16s 4½d, which along with the Martello towers make the total cost of Scapa's defences in 1812 or '13 just under £12,000 all told — quite a difference from the £2 million or so spent on the Churchill Causeways alone in the 1940s. The towers and battery were completed in 1815, the same year that the state of war between Britain and America ended, and so they were never tested by enemy action and their guns were never fired in anger. No use was found for them in the later wars either, although one tower at least, did have a radar scanner mounted on it in World War II. It is one of the ironies of history that guns sited not far from this original battery, some of them made in America but manned by the British Royal Marine Artillerymen, were protecting the United States Navy's Sixth Battle Squadron when it joined the British Grand Fleet in the Flow in 1917.

As was to happen again in 1914 and 1939, Scapa's defences were not merely inadequate but virtually non-existent at the time of greatest need — the beginning of hostilities. The Longhope battery and the Martello towers were only completed after the need for them had gone — indeed, after the Napoleonic Wars were over.

Perhaps this unpreparedness arose from the official ignorance about Orkney in London, from which had emanated the query on several occasions — 'Where is Longhope?' The same lack of official knowledge about Scapa generally was also too often apparent in later times when the need for adequate defence of the anchorage was being discussed in Whitehall.

All the same, these meagre defences were kept under some

sort of precautionary review from time to time, for the Longhope Battery and the towers were up-graded in 1866 when the threat of Fenian trouble in Ireland and the possibility of Britain becoming embroiled in further wars with France or Russia underlined the need for a secure base in home waters for the British Fleet, the most powerful weapon in our armoury at that time.

The towers were given new gun mountings and the battery's armament was changed from the eight 24-pounders to four 64-pounders — a reduction in the number of guns but a big increase in the weight of shot. The 64-pounders were, moreover, the same type of guns as those being used by the Orkney Volunteer Force which was being recruited at that time against these same French and Russian threats.

The Navy, however, had been advised much earlier to have a good long look at the possibilities of Scapa Flow as, at least, a rendezvous base for its ships. This was in 1812 at the height of the Napoleonic Wars and at the same time as the Longhope battery and towers were begun. The advice came from Graeme Spence, who had been Maritime Surveyor to the Admiralty, and it was printed on a chart of the South Isles of Orkney based on the Mackenzie survey and charts of 1750, and rather cumbrously entitled 'Proposal for Establishing a Temporary Rendezvous for Line of Battle Ships in a National Roadstead called Scapa Flow formed by the South Isles of Orkney' — 'most humbly submitted to the consideration of the Rt. Honble the Lords Commissioners of Admiralty'.[2]

In it Spence points out that from earliest times the 'Northern Maritime Nations of Europe, such as the Danes, Swedes and Norwegians' had appreciated the value of Orkney and its numerous harbours as bases for their fleets intent on invasion of the British Isles. He goes on to give a rather inaccurate account of how Scotland, whose rulers also realised the islands' strategic value, managed to acquire possession of them. Having quoted the historical precedents for using Scapa Flow as a naval base, Spence then tells Their Lordships:—

... I shall be happy if in what I have to propose, I could dispel that Cloud of Neglect which has hung over this Thule of the Ancients for the last 500 years, in order to view the Orcades in their true Northern Light in which they must appear to be not only the most Northern Maritime Advanced-Post about Britain but one of the most important also when we are at War with the Northern Nations of Europe, provided we would Occupy it to the extent it seems capable of and which the Norwegians from the bad use they made of it against Britain and Ireland, seem so well to have understood.

After warning of the dangers, and possibility, of Orkney and Scapa Flow being occupied by a hostile power such as Napoleonic France with the resultant strategic consequences to Britain, Spence lists the advantages of using it as a naval base ourselves, for 'it is doubtless the finest natural Roadstead in Britain and Ireland except Spithead'. With its three main channels to the east, south and west — Holm Sound, Hoxa Sound and Hoy Sound — he points out that no ship would be windbound in it: 'from whatever Point the Wind blows, a vessel in Scapa Flow may make a fair wind of it out to free sea . . . a property which no other Roadstead I know of possesses, [and] without waiting for Tide on which account it may be called the Key to both Oceans.' He puts its area as 'upwards of 30 square miles', a greater area than any other British roadstead apart from Spithead. He thinks it would provide anchorage for sixty sail of the line, but as he suspects some foul ground he restricts this to half that number. And he marks the possible moorings on the chart — pretty well in the middle of the Flow. The depth of water all over he puts at ten to twenty fathoms. Another point in its favour as a naval anchorage, Spence says, is that 'the Stream of Tide is scarce sensible in Scapa Flow, so that if there is any wind, a vessel is sure to lie Wind-rode'.

Next he emphasises the Flow's strategic value, with the Navy being able to protect merchant ships going north-about Britain in time of war, to avoid the narrows of the English Channel with its risk of attack by hostile forces. Conversely, the Navy would be in a position to intercept an enemy country's trade through the same northern waters. This, of course, is exactly what did happen in the two World Wars.

He admits that critics of his 'Proposal' will quote the dangerous nature of the tides, rocks and skerries round Orkney, but he cites Mackenzie as writing sixty years earlier: 'by inspecting my Survey of Orkney, it will appear that there is as little, perhaps less, foundation to apprehend danger on the coast of Orkney than on any other part of Britain.'

Spence agrees that navigation of Orkney waters may be risky for strangers, but argues 'that the Native Pilots would think light of it and that it would be easy for them to Navigate any Ship, however large, into Scapa Flow, with a fair wind after matters were first put in proper train for so doing; such as laying a few Channel Buoys and Beacons upon some of the most dangerous shoals'. After all, he points out, warships were being piloted almost daily into more intricate channels than the Pentland Firth, Holm Sound, Hoxa Sound and Hoymouth. And of course, the Pentland Skerries had their warning light as early as 1812, followed by the establishment of Cantick Head light less than half a century later in 1850. Even so, Spence suggests that before his 'Proposal' is taken up, if it should be, it would be advisable to carry out a more detailed survey of the whole area.

Much of what Spence 'Proposed' was sound strategic and hydrographical common sense, not only in the days of sail but even in the steam and oil-driven era of warships, about which he could know nothing. But Government departments, perhaps especially the Admiralty of those days, grind slowly like the mills of God if not always so surely; and so, apart from the Longhope Battery, the Martello towers and, a little later, the formation of the Orkney Volunteer gunners with their 64-pounder muzzle-loading cannon, nothing much was done to make Scapa Flow a secure naval base for another hundred years or so — and then the threat came not from France but from Germany and the Kaiser's High Seas Fleet, nearly as powerful as our own. But much of Graeme Spence's 'Proposal' still held good and although the Admiralty had had over a century to absorb its advice and implement it, the Flow was still virtually defenceless when the Grand Fleet concentrated there at the end of July and beginning of August 1914.

CHAPTER 5

Lull Before The Storm

THE END of the Napoleonic Wars in 1815 saw comparative peace descend on Europe and indeed the world. As usual after a major conflict it was a fragile peace with sporadic outbreaks of minor wars. But it was peace — Pax Britannica, in fact, a peace maintained by the British Empire at its zenith, enforced by the Royal Navy showing the flag, and sometimes its teeth, all over the globe as it kept the Imperial trade routes open and safe from possible predators.

With these global commitments spreading the men-o'-war far and wide, there was no real need to maintain a naval base in the uncongenial climate of northern Britain. No threats were apparent from the smaller northern European nations, and with the United States of America no longer hostile the North Atlantic routes were reasonably secure. The Navy could forget Scapa Flow meantime — even as a 'rendezvous'. And it did.

The Flow could revert to its customary peace and quiet, disturbed only by winter tempests and summer squalls. Great Northern Divers and Long-tailed Ducks could spend their winters in the shelter of its shores before gathering in great yodelling rafts ready for the north-bound migration to their Arctic breeding grounds; gannets could dive like flashing darts into its waters when the sea outside was too stormy; tysties, black, white and vivid scarlet, could bob and curtsey in its lonely waves while, with the cormorants and eiders, they watched the aquatic antics of great schools of ca'ing whales or dolphins. Under the grey skies of autumn, Atlantic seals could haul themselves ashore on undisturbed rocky beaches to breed and perpetuate their kind, their only predators, like the whales, being man, and not too many of them. In winter the mountain hares of Hoy changed their coats to white until spring brought the golden eagles back to their eyries in those same hills looking out across the Flow. Summer saw the banks above the beaches sparkle with the freshness of June flowers, pink and carmine of campion, pale blue of squill echoing the northern sky, the tiny yellow jauntiness of tormentil and the rich regal purple of violets and orchis presaging the autumn glories of the heather-clad hills. It was all very peaceful.

But times change and even if History does not always repeat herself word for word, she has a disturbing habit of telling the same story time after time, changing only the accent, emphasis or language.

At the beginning of the nineteenth century the threat to Britain had been the domination of Europe by Napoleonic France, and the language of that threat was, of course, French, with occasional American overtones. By the end of the century the message was still the same: European, even world domination, but now the language was uncompromisingly German with an unmistakable Prussian accent. Germany had evolved from a conglomeration of petty states and principalities, usually at odds with each other, into a Prussian-dominated, arrogant and bellicose nationhood under Bismarck's direction.

It was a nation jealous of Britain's power and influence in the world, an attitude epitomised in its eventual ruler, Kaiser Wilhelm II. Inevitably his eyes turned to one of the main sources of British power — the Royal Navy. He must have at least its equal but preferably its superior. And so the lines were drawn for the naval arms race, and the drift towards war began to move ever more swiftly.

At the same time big technological changes were taking place. The Industrial Revolution was in full spate. At sea, sail had to give way to steam. Bigger and more powerful guns were made possible, and they needed bigger and more powerful ships to carry them. The outcome was HMS *Dreadnought,* launched in 1906 — the first all-big-gun fighting machine which helped Britain maintain her naval superiority. But soon, as always in an arms race, the other side began to catch up. The threat to Britain's command of the sea and to her mercantile and Imperial power in the world, increased.

How was this threat to be met? First of all, of course, the British fleet had to be built up with more modern ships and armaments to match or surpass those of Germany. Up until this time Britain had operated under a vague system known as the 'two-power plan', whch meant roughly that the British fleet must always be stronger than the second and third navies of the world, which really meant that it had to be stronger than those of France and Russia put together. Now all that changed. These two nations were no longer the major threat; they were, in fact, to become allies. It was the ambitious and jealous Germany which was the bogeyman.

In addition to building up her fleet, Britain also had to find bases from which these new ships could best deter Germany's ambitions. The traditional naval bases on the south coast of England, such as Portsmouth and Plymouth, were no longer adequate and, more importantly, they were not in the right place to meet the German threat, for they had grown up when France was the traditional enemy.

So new bases along the east coast looking out to the North Sea were planned and gradually, very gradually, came into being — Harwich, Felixstowe, the Humber, even Rosyth in the Firth of Forth, although the Admiralty began to feel that this was getting a bit too near the Arctic, and as for Invergordon in the Cromarty Firth — well, it was even further north and like the Forth had only one narrow entrance which could be fairly easily closed either by an enemy or by weather. Scapa Flow was almost beyond the pale, in spite of its natural advantages of several navigable entrances and the protection afforded by its tides, skerries and climate. Then again, it was not on the British mainland. It had no rail access for stores, nor could have, although an extension of the Highland Railway from Georgemas Junction in Caithness to Gills Bay near John o' Groats was actively considered for a time. This would have brought the railhead to within 20 miles of Scapa Flow, but even so at least half of that distance would be across the ferocious tideway of the Pentland Firth.

Nonetheless, the Flow still had its champions as a naval base; among them, at least if one can believe his later writings, was the man almost literally at the helm of Britain's drive for technological and numerical naval superiority — the ebullient Admiral of the Fleet, as he subsequently became, Sir John (Jacky) Fisher, later Lord Fisher of Kilverstone, First Sea Lord at the Admiralty from 1904 to 1910 and again later for a short period during the early part of the war.

He was a brilliant strategist, gunnery expert and administrator, very forceful and quite ruthless when it came to getting things done for his beloved Navy and nation. It was he who forced through the development of the *Dreadnought* class of battleships and more or less scrapped the older ships. He foresaw the advantages of using oil fuel instead of coal, and was said to have predicted accurately the date of the beginning of World War I. He was also the bluff, blunt seaman in many of his pronouncements and writings, where he was deliberately outrageous at times, especially in later life.

In one of his articles which appeared in 'The Times' in 1919, the year before his death at the age of 79, he wrote:

. . . once looking at a chart in my secluded room at the
Admiralty, in 1905, I saw a large landlocked sheet of water
unsurveyed and nameless. It was Scapa Flow. One hour after
this an Admiralty survey ship was en route there. Secretly she
went for none but myself and my most excellent friend the
Hydrographer knew. No one, however talented, except myself
could explain how, playing with a pair of compasses, I took
the German Fleet as the centre for one leg of the compasses
and swept the chart with the other leg to find a place for our
Fleet beyond the practicability of surprise by the Germans.
The Fleet was there in Scapa Flow before war broke out.

'Unsurveyed and nameless'? Sir John, it would seem, had
forgotten the 1812 'Proposal' by the earlier Admiralty hydrographer Graeme Spence for a 'Rendezvous base' in that
'nameless' sheet of water, which he very definitely and correctly
called Scapa Flow and described in detail using maps and charts
based on those of an even earlier surveyor, Murdo Mackenzie,
produced in 1750, half a century before. Perhaps Lord Fisher
was better at predicting the date of the outbreak of World War I
than remembering later the lead-up to it. Nonetheless, the British
fleet was certainly in Scapa Flow before those hostilities began.
    The weekly magazine, 'Passing Show', commenting on Lord
Fisher's claim to have 'discovered' Scapa Flow, wrote: 'We will
now sing hymn 364 — "Praise Jack from whom all Scapas
Flow". As a matter of fact I'd never heard of the damned place
until I spotted it on the map one day. But I was there five
minutes afterwards,' the magazine added in an imitation of
Fisher's own sometimes 'breezy' style.
    There does not seem to be any record of whether Lord
Fisher ever actually visited the Flow himself; most of his
seagoing experience was in warmer climes, but few naval officers
this century have avoided sailing in through Hoxa Sound
some time in their careers.
    Of course, Orkney was by no means unknown to the Navy
long before 1905, although the ships then tended to use Kirkwall
Bay rather than Scapa and continued to use it off and on right
up to the outbreak of war. In July 1898, for instance, a total of
fourteen vessels, eight of them battleships, dropped anchor in
Kirkwall Roads.[1] They were from the Channel Fleet, the main
home fleet of the time, and they were joined a little later by the
cruiser Crescent, commanded by the Duke of York, who later
became King George V. He was making a farewell cruise round
the coast of his future kingdom — his last, commanding a ship,
before he left the Navy owing to pressure of his growing Royal

duties. He had, in fact, resigned his regular commission in the Navy in 1892, and this cruise was a last goodbye to a life he loved.

During the Kirkwall visit, the future king — who wished to be known as the 'Captain of the *Crescent*', not as Duke of York — watched from the 17th century Mercat Cross on Broad Street as 3,800 bluejackets from the fleet set out on a route march under the command of his cousin, Flag Captain of the Fleet Prince Louis of Battenburg, leading them on horseback.

The previous day, a contingent of about a thousand Marines had landed for a route march which took in the main streets of the Burgh including Broad Street where the Admiral commanding the fleet, Sir H. C. Stephens, along with Battenburg, the Duke, and the Provost of Kirkwall, took the salute before the Duke went to lunch on board the *Magnificent* with General and Mrs Burroughs from Rousay.

The *Crescent* had come up by the west coast of Scotland and the weather did not treat her kindly — indeed, George V nearly always had bad weather when he visited Orkney. In his diary for Saturday, 16 July, 1898 he wrote:

We are still going 14 knots, rolling about 12 to 15 degrees, squally with showers and cold, we passed through the Orkneys by the North passage not through the Pentland Firth as we should have had an 8 knot current against us. We arrived at Kirkwall at 6.0 and found the Channel Squadron and moored on a bearing from the *Arrogant* ahead of the cruisers, it was blowing very hard and we were too close to the *Arrogant* so we weighed again and came in a second time, didn't finish mooring till 8.15, beastly bore and very cold on the bridge.

For Sunday, 17 July, he noted there were now eight battleships and six cruisers, with a total complement of 9073 officers and men, in the Bay. He decided to explore and later wrote:—

In the afternoon went on shore with the two Admirals and Sir Baldwin Walker, we visited the Cathedral and the ruins of the palace of the Earl of Orkney and then for a walk, it came on to rain so we returned to Kirkwall and had tea at the hotel, came on board again at 6.30 still raining and cold.

It was damp and cold next day too after having rained all

night, then '. . . it came on to blow hard and the glass fell, perfectly beastly weather', but he spent two-and-a-half hours in the afternoon calling on eight of the ships.

It was still 'Blowing, cold and beastly' in the diary for Wednesday 20 July when

> The Fleet weighed at 1.30 . . . Cruisers went out first, formed single line ahead to go through the Northern passage, as we were 12th ship astern of *Furious* we had a pretty lively time, as we were never straight or in station, owing to the tide rips and bad steering of the other cruisers.

Prince Louis of Battenburg had been in Orkney before, apparently in 1892 when he was Chief Secretary to the joint Naval and Military Committee for the Defence of the United Kingdom. He was said to have surveyed possible coast defence positions with other officers but, whatever their conclusions, nothing appeared on the ground until after the First World War had begun, by which time, of course, Battenburg was First Sea Lord.[2] The visit was probably part of what he called his '1000 Forts in 1000 hours' tour, during which he certainly visited Scotland.[3]

Nothing concrete had emerged from two previous surveys either, apart from a report by Col. Phillpots, Commanding Royal Engineers, in November 1852 regarding the condition of the Longhope Battery dating from the Napoleonic War.[4] Four years later in July 1856 there was another survey. 'The Orcadian' reported — 'The Government has at last, we are glad to understand, come to a definite resolution on erecting lines of defence along the northeastern coast of Scotland. On Saturday last, Col. Moodie of the Royal Engineers, along with two assistants, arrived here by steamer, and the object of their visit, we believe, is to select a site for the erection of a battery. We have not yet heard what spot has been fixed by them.' And they never did hear, nor did a battery appear unless it was the up-dating of the Longhope one some years later.

There were surveyors in Flotta again in 1876, and possibly on other islands as well.[5] The Flotta correspondent of 'The Orkney Herald' in 1912 recalls that these surveyors raised a number of mounds of earth and stones round the shores, besides chiselling marks in various cornerstones on a number of houses in the island. Some thirty years later, members of the crew of a survey vessel, HMS *Triton,* landed and also raised heaps of stones round the shores, and they whitewashed the cornerstones of some houses as well.

This period saw the beginning of a defence movement, local in enthusiasm if national in concept — the Volunteers, forebears of the Territorial Army. From this time on they manned what meagre coastal defences Orkney was given, right up to and into World War I, although by 1909 they had become, much against their will, Territorial Army soldiers; and during the war itself many were transferred, also against their will, to the Royal Marines, for in those days the Navy liked to control its own land defences. At the outbreak of World War II their descendants in the TA again manned the still meagre and inadequate defences, both coastal and anti-aircraft, round the Flow, often in batteries on the same sites as those occupied by their fathers a quarter of a century before.

The Volunteer movement, which had a tremendous impact on Orkney's social life, quite apart from its military aspect, started in 1860 when the first Company of the Orkney Royal Garrison Artillery (Volunteers), the ORGA(V), was formed in Kirkwall, although the Force was not given that official title until twenty years later by which time there were seven Companies or Batteries throughout the islands at Stronsay, Holm, Firth, Evie, Rousay, Stromness, Shapinsay, with a further two in Kirkwall. They trained on 64-pounder muzzle-loading cannon firing at floating targets moored offshore, like the one in Kirkwall Bay, with the guns sited at the old Cromwell's Fort, near where the Coastguard Station stands today. They held ceremonial parades on such occasions as Royal Birthdays, went to firing camps in the south, to Buddon or Kinghorn on the Forth, and became as proficient with their big guns as with their carbines and rifles. At the Kinghorn camp in June 1907, their last as Volunteers, the Orkney contingent mustered thirteen officers and two hundred other ranks.[6]

Much to their chagrin, the Volunteers were disbanded the following year on 1 April — All Fools Day, as 'The Orcadian' pointed out with feeling — and they were offered enrolment in the new Territorial Army being formed under the Haldane Act. The Orkney Volunteers were deeply suspicious of the new set-up, especially as at first it seemed that the local unit would be infantry and not artillery.[7] This idea was stoutly opposed by the Orcadians of all ranks, and there was also a feeling that all this might be just the thin end of a wedge leading to conscription. In any case they had always been gunners, and gunners they wished to remain. The powers-that-be gave way. An agreement between the Admiralty and the War Office allowed the Orkney men to retain their artillery status, and they were asked to form seven companies of Royal Garrison Artillery which represented a third of the RGA Force in the whole of Scotland.[8] And within less than four months, two 4.7-inch breech-loading quick-firing guns were landed at Kirkwall Pier from the ss *St Rognvald* and installed forthwith at Cromwell's Fort on the Munt for practice.[9]

Others followed for the West Mainland units. But in spite of these enticements of new and more modern equipment, not all the old Volunteers transferred to the new TA. At the beginning of 1908 there had been nine companies of the 1st ORGA(V), with 32 officers and 584 other ranks. In June of the following year, just fourteen months after the changeover, the ORGA(T) had a strength of only 19 officers and 353 other ranks, although the establishment was for 533 men in seven companies. It was also reported that the Orkney Force was short of seven subalterns for their 1909 annual firing camp, which that year was held at Weyland Farm near the Fort.[10]

Whether the Orkney RGA was intended for the defence of Scapa Flow is not clear; it must be presumed that it was, but certainly it had no fixed batteries to cover any of the entrances, and the Navy's attitude towards this potential northern base had, at best, been ambivalent.

But that attitude was to change. Early in 1907, an article in the 'Naval Annual' on 'Strategical Features of the North Sea' suggested that the Atlantic Fleet should make much more use of, and spend more time in, the vicinity of Orkney and Shetland. It also advocated the establishment and maintenance of a cruiser squadron in these waters, to keep a watchful eye on German activities and trade in the North Sea area. Scapa Flow as such was not specifically mentioned but '. . . possibly a good anchorage could be found somewhere in the vicinity of Wick'. Both Peterhead and Rosyth were considered to be too far south to serve this surveillance purpose.[11]

Not surprisingly, 'The Orcadian' was able to report a few days after the appearance of this suggestion that 'Rumours are rife that Kirkwall stands high in the estimation of Naval authorities as a suitable place for a naval base'. No confirmation for this rumour was found but it was maintained by the newspaper that 'Kirkwall is certainly under consideration in connection with some naval arrangements'. Guarded inquiries had been made from the south as to the town's facilities, it was claimed.[12]

And the survey vessel HMS *Triton* was certainly in the area, while later that year, in September 1907, the old 5760-ton cruiser *Furious*, later to be converted as one of the early aircraft carriers, was in Kirkwall Bay in connection with wireless telegraphy experiments.[13]

It had also been rumoured that the Fleet might visit Orkney soon after the autumn manoeuvres which were to take place in North of Scotland waters, and indeed twenty-one warships were seen in the Pentland Firth one day, before the fog came down. Seventeen of them crept through the haar to anchor off Scrabster, but the only report of the Navy being in Orkney was from some fishermen who saw a 'small warship' in Inganess Bay.[14] No ships of the Navy were seen in Scapa Flow that year. With 1908, however, naval interest in Orkney and Scapa Flow began to gather momentum. HMS *Triton* was again busily surveying Orkney waters for quite a time, based this time on Stromness.[15]

In July there were more naval manoeuvres around the islands, during which Wick was reported 'captured' in a mock battle, and eleven battleships had been sighted going east through the Pentland Firth earlier in the year.[16]

And the Navy **did** eventually arrive in Orkney, and in some force, with a depot ship and the Eastern Destroyer Flotilla dropping anchor in Scapa Bay on 26 July — 27 ships in all. It was understood they were to stay for a month, and local contractors were kept busy supplying them with the 1500 lbs of bread, 1500 lbs of beef and 3000 lbs of potatoes they needed every day. It was also understood that the ships would land 80 to 100 men who would live ashore under 'war conditions' — no tents.

The destroyers carried out gunnery practice in the Flow but all was not work and no play, for the officers at least, who were invited to be guests of Kirkwall Town Council at a ball in aid of the Balfour Hospital.[17]

And it may be that lying in Scapa Bay as they did, they found the new Wason's buoy on Scapa Skerry, just off the pier. a comforting guiding light when returning from such late-night entertainments as the hospital ball. The buoy had been placed in position in March that year, having been donated by the MP for the Orkney and Shetland landward constituency, Cathcart Wason. He had long advocated putting a warning beacon on this awkwardly-situated skerry in the middle of the bay, as part of the Flow's defences against shipwreck, but had found no support from the authorities concerned. So, he put up the money himself. The Northern Lighthouse Commissioners, however, graciously agreed to maintain it once it was in position.[18]

It was in 1909, however, that the navy really began to use Scapa Flow, and Orkney generally. From April onwards until well into October that year there were naval vessels in or around the islands, sometimes in large numbers, as, for instance, in

April when 82 warships, comprising 38 large ships and 44 destroyers manned by a total of over 20,000 men, sailed into the Flow through Hoxa Sound in four divisions, led by the great battleship *Dreadnought* herself wearing the flag of Admiral Sir William May.

'An Imposing Spectacle; Flotta Encircled by Warships', wrote that island's correspondent in 'The Orcadian', describing the Fleet's stately progress on its way to anchor in Scapa Bay on the north side of the Flow. The Atlantic Fleet was there, too, under command of Prince Louis of Battenburg, no stranger to Orkney. He was, of course, father of Earl Mountbatten, who also knew the Flow, serving in it during the first War like so many naval officers and again in World War II when he commanded a flotilla of destroyers led by his own famous *Kelly* which I once heard described by a navyman as 'the most efficient thing afloat'.

The Fleets caused intense interest among Orcadians, who flocked to Scapa's various shores to see this vast armada. Boat trips round the ships were organised from Kirkwall, Stromness and St Margaret's Hope, and the two burghs declared a public holiday so that people could take advantage of them.

The local supply contractors were almost run off their feet — R. Garden for bread, James Leith for beef and J. T. Harcus and J. & W. Tait for vegetables and other victuals. Some of the ships sailed again after only four days but the repair ship *Cyclops*, hospital ship *Maine* and the distilling ship *Aquaris* to supply fresh water, all arrived along with the Admiralty yacht *Surprise*. It looked as if the Navy had decided to use the Flow seriously, for they engaged in gunnery and exercised in it frequently until the end of May, the longest period they had ever spent there.[19]

Negotiations were also opened for the acquisition of ground on which to construct a golf course for officers in Burray, 'as a visit of the Fleet to Scapa Flow waters is now to be so frequent that the officers wish for a course of their own', wrote 'The Orcadian'. Up till now they had been playing on the Kirkwall course, and in gratitude for the use of this facility the Fleet Destroyer Flotilla presented the Orkney Golf Club with a silver challenge trophy still known and played for as the Flotilla Cup.

Provost Baikie and local dignitaries dined on board the flagship HMS *Dreadnought,* many bluejackets were ashore on liberty passes, or for various sporting fixtures, and there were dances both ashore and on the ships. Some of the destroyers came round to Kirkwall Bay and held gunnery practice in the Bay of Firth. It was certainly a stirring time for the islands. Still,

D

there was no word of any permanent defences being installed to protect the Flow — golf courses, perhaps, but batteries, no.[20]

The battleship *New Zealand* did land two detachments of bluejackets at Scapa Pier one day, complete with two 12-pounder guns with which they came at the double all the way to Grainshore and engaged a target moored in Kirkwall Bay with shrapnel — but no permanent gunsites were installed.

And in spite of the buoy so thoughtfully provided on Scapa Skerry by Mr Cathcart Wason MP, the destroyer *Itchen* managed to ground on it, though fortunately with little damage except to naval pride.[21] *Itchen* was not so lucky a little later when, apparently accident-prone, she ran aground on the Head of Work when returning to Kirkwall Bay after a night exercise, and had to be towed off by other naval craft, badly holed and making water forward. After a court-martial at Chatham in December, her commander was found 'not guilty of negligence' but 'guilty of suffering the vessel to be stranded by default', and severely reprimanded.

The Fleet sailed from Orkney in mid-May, leaving 'the town very quiet', according to 'The Orcadian'. But four weeks later they were back, eight battleships, seven cruisers and 27 destroyers, returning to Scapa with the depot ship of the Second Destroyer Flotilla, *Blake,* and the repair ship *Assistance.*[22]

Almost inevitably, all this naval activity produced a spy scare. The Flotta news in 'The Orcadian' reported a 'Mysterious Visitor' to the island in June when the Fleet was in the Flow. Described as a 'somewhat foreign-looking gent in a Norfolk jacket with binocular slung from his shoulder', he landed from a Caithness fishing yawl whose crew had rowed him across the Pentland Firth from Huna. He was, according to the Flotta correspondent, 'a not unnaval looking man', who went at once to the highest point of the island from which vantage point he scanned intently the lines of warships anchored in Scapa Bay.

He spoke, it was said, 'very London English' but with a foreign accent. He asked for something to eat and paid 'munificently' before going back across the Firth. The Caithness crew of his boat knew nothing about him, not even his name, but he had been staying in Caithness and had been out with them fishing on several occasions. Speculation was rife in Flotta as to his identity and the purpose of his visit.[23] The first of so many 'mysterious visitors' throughout the history of Scapa Flow as a naval base, even into World War II with its 'mysterious watchmaker' who never existed, this one vanished after crossing the Firth and was never heard of again.

Warships were back in Orkney in the end of August, 1909,

when seventeen destroyers and a couple of cruisers — or rather a cruiser, *Sapphire,* and a 'scout', *Skirmisher,* which were attached to the Second Destroyer Flotilla — arrived in Kirkwall Bay. They were later joined by the Nore Destroyer Flotilla, which stayed there or in the Flow, usually with Longhope as headquarters, until mid-October. A 'scout' was a light cruiser which acted as a flotilla leader.

There now seemed to be a possibility that Orkney would become at least a permanent destroyer base.

Towards the end of the year, there were speculations in the national press about the possibility, even probability, that Scapa Flow would become a much bigger permanent base than just one for destroyer flotillas. The 'Daily Record and Mail' thought the Admiralty was going to base the Fleet there to 'put a stopper in the North Sea Bottle'. This would contain the German naval threat but land defences would be needed, and one suggestion was for a heavy battery on Dunnet Head in Caithness.

'Lloyds News' stated that 'With the Home Fleet spending most of its time at Scapa Flow the North Sea will be effectively bottled'. Rosyth was too far south and would be a cul-de-sac unless a Forth-Clyde canal capable of taking capital ships, like the Kiel Canal on the other side of the North Sea, were constructed. 'The Daily Mail' on the subject of 'Orkney Naval Base' wrote about Kirkwall as getting a wireless station; Scapa Flow becoming a first class naval base; and Wick a secondary base with a wireless station.

'The Daily Telegraph' and the 'Naval and Military Record', however, both discounted these speculations. It would not become a first class naval base but would continue to be used as a 'rendezvous base' and for gunnery and torpedo practice as during the current year's manoeuvres. The only foundation for the rumours of a base at Scapa, these papers maintained, was the plan (which had indeed been discussed) for Scapa Pier to be extended for the convenience of the Fleet — nothing more. 'There is no intention to carry out extensive works, these being unnecessary,' stated the 'Naval and Military Record' quite emphatically, and, as it eventually turned out, wrongly.

CHAPTER 6

The Pace Quickens

THE NEXT year, 1910, saw increasing pressure on the Liberal Government which was in power, to make Scapa Flow a permanent naval base in order to counter the growing menace of Germany's rapidly expanding fleet. The pressure came mainly from the politicians — for there was a general election looming large early in the new year — and was closely tied to the great public debate going on about the need or otherwise, for increasing the Naval Estimates.

Sir Arthur Bignold, the sitting Unionist MP for the Northern Burghs constituency (which comprised Dingwall, Tain, Cromarty, Dornoch, Wick and Kirkwall but not their surrounding landward areas) set the tone in a speech in Kirkwall during January, when, in addition to demanding more ships for the Navy, he also wanted a dock at Scapa Flow, 'large enough to take a Dreadnought'. On the question of establishing a naval base in Orkney he said, to cheers from a packed hall: 'Any Government which longer delays the dock at Scapa will be false to the greatest of all public trusts.'

'Orcadian hearts of oak,' he went on, 'I feel that I can look forward across the waves of time and see the Kirkwall of the future, a hive of industry with the fleet at Scapa Flow and our city no longer dependent on agriculture and fishing alone, but her sons reaping the benefit of her position in the Empire where she stands ready to meet the enemies of Britain at the gate.'[1]

Of course, politicians do have these visionary spasms at election time, especially when their party is not in power, but there is no doubt that he was expressing the hopes of many, in the Orkney part of his constituency, at least. Some other parts of it, like Wick and Cromarty, who also hoped to benefit economically from the establishment of a naval base in their areas, were not so happy about his enthusiasm for Scapa Flow and, after ten years as their MP, he was defeated by his Radical opponent Robert Munro. But Cathcart Wason, Liberal MP for the landward part of the Orkney and Shetland constituency — which meant all of the two groups of islands except Kirkwall — was also in favour of a naval base for Scapa.

The national press, too, was still campaigning vigorously in favour of the idea, with the 'Aberdeen Free Press' referring to Scapa's use by the Navy during the previous year and strongly advocating the extension of the Highland Railway line to Gills Bay near John o' Groats where a harbour would have to be constructed but which would, it was claimed, provide a more sheltered passage to Scapa Pier. The writer must have had some experience of Pentland Firth crossings for he added that there was 'more potency for evil to a pint in that bit of water than any other stretch of water in the wide world'.[2] And many Servicemen and women who made the Pentland Firth passage in the two World Wars would say he was by no means exaggerating.

In face of this growing barrage of political, public and press demand for the establishment of a permanent naval base at Scapa Flow, what was the Admiralty's reaction?

Up until this point its traditional War Plan, if indeed it had a formal one, was the imposition of a 'close blockade' on enemy ports as soon as war was declared. This meant that the smaller warships were to be sent in close to the enemy ports to prevent their ships, either warships or merchantmen, from getting in or out. These smaller vessels would be supported by the bigger capital ships from their secure bases not far away on the English south coast. It was comparatively easy to maintain such a blockade against the French ports which were only twenty to sixty miles away across the Channel — and France, of course, had been the traditional enemy. After all, even as late as 1898, the Fashoda Incident in the Sudan had shown that war with France was by no means impossible.

But now, in the first decade of the twentieth century, everything was changed. France was no longer the potential enemy. Germany had assumed that role and it was not really feasible to suggest maintaining a 'close blockade' on her ports three or four times further away than those of France.

Yet in spite of this shift in the international balance, the old 'close blockade' policy and War Plan was maintained unchanged by the Admiralty, which probably accounts for its lukewarm attitude towards Scapa as a naval base.

There was, at the beginning of the century, no such thing as a Naval Staff. That function was carried out by the Board of Admiralty — Their Lordships, the professional Sea Lords and the political First Lord. It was a very closed shop, and a very conservative one, too.

Then things began to move. A War Plan was formulated in considerable secrecy by the newly-set-up Admiralty War Division — the beginnings of a Naval Staff comparable to the Army's

General Staff which was already functioning. The process was considerably speeded up with the eruption on the naval scene of Winston Churchill as the dynamic new First Lord at the end of 1911. Closely concerned with drawing up the War Plan was Captain (later Admiral) Sydney Fremantle as head of the War Division. He was later to be deeply involved with events in the Flow during June 1919 when the interned German High Seas Fleet scuttled itself.

With these new brooms sweeping clean the dusty corridors of power in Whitehall, the new policy of a 'distant blockade' of Germany was adopted, and was included in the new Admiralty War Orders of 1912. This meant that what was to be named the Grand Fleet with all its supporting vessels and auxiliaries was to be based on Scapa Flow to close off the North Sea, while the older battleships would be in bases further south to close the English Channel. 'By this means,' wrote Churchill in *The World Crisis 1911-1918,* 'the British Navy seized and kept the effective control of all the oceans of the world,' and, he added, 'If our naval strength were maintained we were safe and sure beyond the lot of any other European nation; if it failed, our doom was certain and final.'[3]

The implications of the new War Plan and the adoption of the 'distant blockade' system were tested in the big manoeuvres of 1912, when Flotta was defended by Marines, and in 1913 with a mock attack on the Humber.

In 1912 an experiment was tried of having an immense cordon of cruisers and destroyers, supported by the Battle Fleet, stretched from Norway to the north-east coast of England. It did not work. Instead the Admiralty fell back on the system which Churchill calls 'prowling squadrons and occasional drives'. 'In other words,' he wrote, 'it was recognised that we could not maintain any continuous control of the North Sea. The best we could do was sweep it in strength at irregular intervals and for the rest await the action of the enemy.'

The importance of Scapa Flow became even more apparent in these circumstances as a place from which to 'sweep' and then to 'wait'. It had obviously featured pretty prominently in Fremantle's Plan, for in his book *My Naval Career* he claims credit for the fact that not only the Grand Fleet, but all the auxiliaries, store ships, repair ships and hospital ships were there before war broke out; but even so, there were no land-based defences whatsoever. Lord Fisher, it may be recalled, also claimed credit for ensuring that the Grand Fleet was in the Flow before the war began.

Fremantle also chaired two Committees, one on 'Combined

Operations', and the other on 'Regulations Governing the entry to Defended Ports in Time of War', but he admits that the War Office had given these matters much more attention than the Admiralty mainly because it had formed a General Staff so much earlier. But these joint discussions formulated only the 'Regulations', not the means of enforcing them, especially in the case of Scapa Flow.

The sea-going Navy itself was obviously showing continued and growing interest in Scapa Flow. At the end of April 1910, ninety warships, including dreadnoughts, battle-cruisers, battle-ships and cruisers as well as forty destroyers and a number of auxiliary vessels preceded by nine colliers carrying 25,000 tons of coal, anchored off Scapa Pier while a flotilla of eight destroyers with two repair ships, two cruisers and a depot ship arrived in Kirkwall Bay. This Atlantic Fleet had as its Commander-in-Chief, Admiral Prince Louis of Battenburg. Coming into the Flow through Hoxa Sound the ships had taken two hours to steam past Flotta before they anchored off Scapa Pier, passing within a quarter-of-a-mile of Howequoy Head in Holm on their way in.

After they had been in harbour for a week the local contractors were beginning to feel the strain. They had begun slaughtering cattle the week before the Fleet arrived and had to bring in extra staff from Aberdeen to cope with the demand of up to six carcases per ship per day. The main beef contract during this year appears to have been with a Glasgow firm which had its own boats to supply the ships, but R. Garden still supplied the bread from Kirkwall bakehouses and J. & W. Tait and Harcus also supplied victuals and meat. George Leonard and George Leslie of Kirkwall showed considerable enterprise by putting up a store at Scapa Pier for the sale of newspapers and groceries, temporary branches of their existing shops in the town.

But the Fleet did not stay as long on this visit as had been anticipated, and indeed hoped for, and when they began to disperse after only four or five days some contractors found themselves in difficulties through being over-stocked; this did not apply to the people who kept poultry, for by this time the demands of the Navy men had resulted in what the local press described as 'an egg famine'. The efforts of the contractors, however, were praised by the Navy who complimented them on their service as they sailed away 'in boisterous weather and heavy rain' out through Hoxa Sound again, except for the *Cyclops* which went out through Hoy Sound. During their stay the telegraph cable between Kirkwall Post Office and the *Cyclops* at Scapa Pier was in operation for the first time, and sailors were also on duty in the Post Office itself to cope with very heavy mail. Officers had played golf at the Bu in Burray, and the possibility of building a jetty at the Point of Weddel in the island to facilitate such recreation was again mooted.[4]

The Admiralty also wanted a 140-foot extension to Scapa Pier, but the Orkney Harbour Commissioners did not agree with the plans.

On the other hand, it was strongly rumoured that Orkney might see less of the fleet in future, as the new First Sea Lord, Sir Arthur Wilson, was known to attach less importance to Scapa Flow as a training base than the previous First Sea Lord, Lord Fisher, had done, although he still considered it important as a 'war base'[5] — another example of the strangely ambivalent attitude of the Admiralty towards the Flow. This Whitehall attitude, which persisted in some quarters right up to the outbreak of war in 1914, and even occasionally after hostilities had begun, could perhaps best be summed up as: 'Yes, we know we should have a proper naval base at Scapa, but we don't really want to put one there.' The result was unpreparedness on an unprecedented scale. It was fortunate that the Germans with their highly professional military outlook just did not believe that their potential powerful enemy on the sea could conceivably have left the protection of its most strategically vital naval base to no more than the mere chance of rocks, tides and weather.

Nevertheless, in spite of the Admiralty's lukewarm attitude to the place, the Second Destroyer Flotilla of seventeen ships was back in the Flow in August, carrying out exercises and anchoring in Longhope '. . . and other convenient places', reported 'The Orcadian'; these included Stromness.[6] The ships stayed around until September exercising, and this increasing use of the area may well have speeded up the provision of more warning lights. Scapa Skerry had already got its Wason's Buoy and now as the nights grew longer the new Graemsay lighthouse was lit for the first time in August, to be followed by the beacon on Lother Skerry off Burwick in South Ronaldsay which so many ships had to round when making Hoxa Sound from the east.[7]

And during the year two more 4.7-inch guns had arrived for the Orkney RGA's Stromness and Birsay Batteries. The guns were hauled into position by teams of horses, and Stromness Town Council complained that their weight had damaged the Burgh's paved streets. The Burgh Surveyor put the cost of repairing the damage at £4 14s and informed the Ordnance Department of this. Whether the Council ever got the money is not recorded.[8]

As 1910 drew towards its close, Orkney was given a faint

indication of what lay ahead — a promise, and a threat. Two Germans did something which no man had ever done before. They arrived in Orkney by air. They came by balloon, and admittedly, by mistake, but they were the first human beings to reach the islands without using a boat or ship. It was the evening of 4 December.

The previous afternoon three men had gone aloft from a field near Munich in Bavaria, intending to be up for twenty-four hours, reaching Switzerland or perhaps even the south of France. But the weather took a hand. The wind veered to the south-east, piling up thick cloud. Soon darkness fell, and they had no idea of where they were. In the morning they heard the sound of the sea breaking — but where? And what sea? They came down to have a look but overdid it and hit the waves as they were throwing out ballast to regain height. This caused them to bounce back off the sea up into the cloud again where, having re-established their equilibrium, and looking round, Herren Distler and Joerdens found they were alone in the basket — the third member of the crew, Herr Metzger, had been thrown out when they bounced. He was never seen again.

They carried on before the gale all day, failing to attract the attention of the few ships they saw. Darkness fell again over the grey immensity of the ocean. Would they see the dawn? About 9 p.m. they did see a light, possibly Auskerry Lighthouse. Then more lights. Desperately they pulled the plug, came down fast and bounced on the sea again, probably in Inganess Bay just to the east of Kirkwall, before being dragged ashore by the now deflated balloon, fetching up on the edge of a quarry.

Making for the nearest house with lights, which happened to be Park Cottage in Berstane Road, the home then, as now, of the Leonard family, they asked where they were, and learned they were in Orkney some 1,500 miles and thirty harrowing hours from their starting-point, having averaged about 50 mph over the ground and sea — an indication of the strength of the gale.[9] And, inadvertently, they had shown that the sea was no longer the only road to the isles. It may have been only a small pointer to the future, but it was a significant one.

Almost another three years were to pass before the first heavier-than-air machines flew over Orkney and over Scapa Flow in particular. This happened when HMS *Hermes,* parent ship of the Naval Wing of the Royal Flying Corps, arrived in Scapa on 22 August 1913 carrying two hydroplanes, as seaplanes were then called. One was French-built with blue wings and the other, with white wings, was British, according to 'The Orcadian' report which went on to describe the intense interest among local people who watched their occasional flights with an avid interest contrasting strongly with the blasé attitude of the *Hermes* crew who just went on fishing for sillocks and cuithes over the side, paying no attention to these new technological wonders, typically a Serviceman's outlook — 'Seen it all before.' The aircraft, of course, took off and landed on the water, being hoisted over and in board from the parent ship.[10]

The day of the lighter-than-air craft, however, was by no means over — neither was the speculation about mysterious and sinister strangers spying out the land, and in the case of Orkney, perhaps the sea as well. The two phobias, if that is not too strong a word, coalesced to some extent in the 'spy airship' scares.

Earlier in 1913 an airship had been reported as flying south past Sanday in daylight, or at least, dusk, about 5 p.m. in February. The press in the south took up the story but were very doubtful as to its truth — it was inferred that it had arisen from the bucolic imagination of some island hicks who had not been able to tell the difference between a flock of starlings and an airship. The Sanday folk were justifiably indignant, and to some extent they got confirmation of their story when the skipper of a merchant ship in the North Sea also reported an airship off the Humber that same night. And it might be significant that only a few days later the Government issued regulations forbidding intrusion into British airspace by foreign aircraft.[11] How these regulations would have been enforced is a matter for conjecture, especially as two of the 'forbidden zones' were Kirkwall and Flotta and there was certainly no means of controlling intruders in the sky over Orkney at that time.

Was it a Zeppelin having a look at Orkney's potential naval anchorages? It **is** possible, and the German High Seas Fleet was, in fact, out in the North Sea about this time flexing its muscles in exercises.

A few weeks later, in April 1913, another airship was reported, this time from Stronsay. It was at night but its lights were plainly visible and the engine clearly heard as it hovered some 300 feet over the island. More than a dozen people saw it and had no doubts as to what it was. What it was doing was another matter, but the Stronsay folk were of the opinion that it might have been have been having a good look at Rothiesholm Bay which they thought would make an excellent anchorage for hostile ships wanting to control the entrance to Kirkwall Harbour through the String.[12]

The interest in air activity at this time is underlined by the fact that the Orkney writer, poet and farmer, John G. S. Flett of

Nistaben in Harray, was sufficiently inspired to write the lyric of a popular song entitled 'Out with Angeline in an Airship' which was published in the United States.[13]

But in 1911 the threat to Britain was still very much more likely to be seaborne than to come from the air. The other threat from **under** sea was still also a matter of speculation, so much so that no attempt had been made to block the channels into Scapa Flow through which a submarine might creep.

This year the naval activity in Orkney was on the Kirkwall side to start off with. Sixteen ships of the Second Destroyer Flotilla arrived in Kirkwall Bay early in May for a five-week visit. It was expected that they would exercise in the Flow and come round to the fleshpots of Kirkwall for the weekends but, in fact, they also carried out torpedo practice runs in the Bay of Firth as well, during which the *Lyra,* one of the latest class, ran ashore on Puldrite Skerry off the Rendall shore, but refloated on the rising tide without trouble.[14]

The Flotilla finally moved to Longhope before leaving Orkney, to be replaced by the First Destroyer Flotilla which coaled and oiled in Kirkwall Bay before going round to the Flow and Longhope. It was joined there by the battleship *Hibernia* which later moved across the Flow to anchor off the Orphir shore, where it was said that she was taking soundings for 'an oil tank', and possibly also for a torpedo range.[15] What sort of oil tank was envisaged, apparently in the sea, was not revealed, but this was the year when the Navy ordered its first experimental diesel engine. Oil was already being used to replace coal, of course, in some of the Navy's ships, no doubt a welcome change-over from the crews' point of view, obviating, as it did, the hated chore of 'coaling' which involved the entire ships' company at frequent intervals, covering everything and every-body with grit and grime.

In the next few years Churchill as First Lord committed the Navy entirely to the use of oil in place of coal — not without considerable criticism and trepidation, for it meant having to rely entirely on a fuel obtained only in the Persian Gulf which had to be transported to this country, whereas we had more than ample supplies of coal under our own soil. On the other hand, oil was much more efficient than coal for warships which as a result of its use could be built bigger, could carry heavier armament and were very much faster. But it was a big step to take, with dire consequences should anything go wrong.[16]

All through the spring and summer of 1911 there was a constant coming and going of naval vessels, mostly destroyers, commuting between the Flow and Kirkwall Bay and usually going in and out through Holm Sound rather than taking the long way round through Hoxa or Switha Sounds. The Flotta correspondent of 'The Orcadian' wrote that 'naval ships still cause interest in the island but not so much as they used to do when they were less common'. Familiarity not quite breeding contempt, it would seem.

There were, of course, many social and sporting occasions where the navymen and Orcadians mixed and made friends, and every now and again there would be a spectacular searchlight display.

The First Lord of the Admiralty, Reginald McKenna MP — Churchill did not take over until the end of the year — cruised into the Flow, accompanied by his wife, on board the Admiralty's 3470-ton, 18-knot yacht, *Enchantress* early in June; it was said his visit was in connection with the proposed extension to Scapa Pier which was still under consideration.[17] The Fourth Cruiser Squadron and Fifth Destroyer Flotilla called at Kirkwall where Provost Slater and Baillies Baikie and Garden went aboard the *Leviathan* 'to pay their respects' to Rear Admiral Bradford. There followed a big sports day with 900 boys from the ships taking part while 200 Marines exercised on Wideford Hill and *Leviathan's* band played in front of St Magnus Cathedral.

The ships then dispersed 'for various parts of Orkney', turning up in some odd places like the two destroyers which anchored in Burwick, South Ronaldsay — not one of the safer anchorages, one would have thought.[18] Signallers were landed on various headlands, with three on one of the Martello towers where they could communicate with the flotilla leader *Leander,* lying in Longhope.

And getting a view of all this naval activity that summer were at least two German cruise liners with full complements of several hundred passengers each. One of them, the ss *Kronprinzessin Cecilie* of the Hamburg-Amerika Line, came into Kirkwall one Sunday in August and was not at all popular with the Kirk.[19] These German cruise liners with their calls at Kirkwall were a feature of the time, with several visits each summer. There was one German cruise liner, the ss *Prinz Friedrich Wilhelm,* with 500 passengers on board, anchored in Kirkwall Bay only eight days before the declaration of war on 4 August, 1914.

Eighteen ships of the Third Destroyer Flotilla called at Kirkwall early in September intending to stay for two weeks to carry out boiler cleaning, but it soon became known in the town that they were at very short notice to sail. Shore leave was stopped and a telegraphist was landed to do all-night duty at the

Post Office, with signallers at the pier to relay any urgent messages. Some trouble was obviously brewing internationally, and indeed the flotilla sailed out through the String very abruptly and much earlier than had been expected.[20]

There was considerable international tension at this time caused by the Agadir incident when the Germans tried a bit of gunboat diplomacy by sending the *Panther* to the Moroccan port, claiming it was to protect their nationals from alleged French expansion. Britain was worried about all this happening so close to Gibraltar, fearing that the Germans might turn Agadir into a rival naval base. France and Germany started negotiations, which almost broke down in September, raising the international temperature and so causing the destroyers in Kirkwall Bay to go on short notice to raise steam — and eventually to sail hurriedly.

The cruisers, however, stayed in the Flow and by the end of the month what was described as 'the most powerful fleet ever to visit Orkney' was also there, a battle squadron of dreadnoughts with accompanying cruisers, a flotilla of twenty destroyers — and the Admiral's yacht, *Surprise*. They exercised in the Flow and carried out night firing right into October in bitterly cold weather with severe gales, during which the cruiser *Blonde*, parent ship of the First Flotilla, grounded on the Pentland Skerries, but although holed forward she got off unaided.[21]

During the exercise the destroyer *Saracen* and the battleship *Agincourt* lost a torpedo apiece off Hunda. Rewards of £10 — quite a lot of money in those days — were offered for their recovery. One was found a week or so later on Howequoy Head in Holm by Robert Bews from the village of St Mary's, and the other turned up near Graemeshall where it was salvaged by Charles Langskaill, both men getting their £10. The destroyer *Saracen* herself and another, the *Swift,* came up from Fortrose to collect the torpedoes.[22]

CHAPTER 7

Time Runs Out

IN 1912 it looked at long last as if some kind of land-based defences were going to be established at Scapa. The cruiser *Blonde* risked passing the Pentland Skerries where she had grounded the previous year, and anchored in the Flow, while two 'scouts' were reported to have arrived in Pan Hope about the same time, early April, to land men on Flotta. These men were said to have taken observations and 'waved flags'.[1] The 'Orkney Herald' thought they were also looking for the whitewash and chisel-marks made by the earlier surveyors in 1876 and 1900.[2] In addition to Flotta, sites appear to have been surveyed in Graemsay, Lamb Holm and in Holm, as possible defence points, while there was also talk of an air station — one of a chain which the Admiralty planned, stretching from Dover up the east coast now that the North Sea had become the focus of strategic interest. There was also a suggestion that what was then the vast sum of £30,000 might be spent on Stronsay harbour, but for what purpose was never made clear.[3]

The Flotta correspondent of 'The Orcadian' was surprised when he saw even more naval activity, with the arrival of nine destroyers of the First Flotilla, their support ship, *Blenheim,* and their leader, *Boadicea,* in Longhope. He had thought that movement of naval ships had been restricted owing to the miners' strike which was holding up fuel supplies. But then the Third Flotilla also arrived for exercise in the Flow, going round to Kirkwall at weekends. Sports, regattas, and other social functions were planned, and the King's Birthday was marked by the firing of a Royal Salute by all eighteen ships.

Ashore it was understood that the Admiralty had increased its proposed grant in aid of extending Scapa Pier from £1,000 to £9,000.

In Flotta, what 'The Orcadian' correspondent named as 'Fort Stanger' and 'Fort Warth' had been surveyed and 'pegs had been put in the ground' — but nothing more. Warth, of course, would cover Switha Sound and the entrance to Longhope while the Stanger Head position looked across Hoxa Sound, the main entrance to the Flow. But it was still only 'pegs in the ground' — not guns.

Following a big naval review off Spithead there were manoeuvres in the North Sea, and great excitement in Flotta on a Saturday in mid-July when a joint force of Royal Marine Artillery and Royal Marine Light Infantry landed at Kirk Bay on the south side of the island from the 2802-ton Elder Dempster steamer *Bakana*. Given the temporary title of 'The Scapa Flow Expeditionary Force', it was composed mainly of young Marines. The objective of the Force, commanded by Major G. W. Poole RMA, was the defence of the Flow during the current manoeuvres, with 4-inch guns on Stanger Head and 12-pounders at Neb, both of which became battery sites in 1914 and again in 1939. The total Force of four companies, two artillery and two infantry, numbered about 350 men who had embarked at Portsmouth from their Eastney Barracks in some secrecy. In addition to the CO, Major Poole, there was his adjutant, Capt. Rookes, and a Staff Surgeon RN as Medical Officer besides a full complement of officers, Warrant Officers and NCOs, not forgetting no fewer than eight buglers, four each for the artillery and the infantry. And according to the schedule of stores and equipment they might need, in addition to the more war-like items, such as guns and rifles, were 'four sets of handcuffs, pans frying for officers, and latrine paper as required'. It was felt, however, that as their stay on the island would be comparatively short, they would not need either a wet or a dry canteen although '. . . it is considered desirable that a supply of rum be sent'.

And they might well have needed it, for they arrived in fog with a stiff south-easterly bringing a 'lumpy' sea into the rather exposed bay. It was thought locally that the African civilian crew — the *Bakana* normally ran to West Africa — had brought the ship in much too close to rocks for comfort, much closer than a Flotta boat would have risked. Still, she made it and the Marines were soon getting guns of various calibres ashore in a steel 'horse-boat' and on pontoons. During this operation the ship's steel mast and derrick collapsed, but with a running repair and the rigging of a jury mast the unloading of gear (which, in addition to guns included stores, water carts, field kitchens and camouflage paint) continued under the direct charge, it was noted locally, of an officer wearing a monocle. Even so, they had to work for seventeen hours at a stretch to get everything ashore, some of them not even stopping to eat.

Although they did not occupy it, they reconnoitred Hoxa Head across the Sound, the site of another main coastal battery in both wars.[4]

While all this was going on, five submarines and two
cruisers were sighted — one of the submarines, *C 61,* going
ashore on the Pentland Skerries, but she got off again and went
round to Kirkwall.[5]

After a week ashore defending Flotta, the Marines re-
embarked from Kirk Bay along with all their guns and gear, and
the *Bakana,* whose Captain, like his black crew, never came
ashore, sailed, taking away '. . . a body of men of whom, during
their brief stay amongst us, we had formed a very good opinion
indeed', according to the correspondent of 'The Orcadian', who
added that they 'liked cockles and periwinkles and almost any
'buckie' they could find'.

It was claimed in an unsigned article in 'The Orcadian' of 6
September, 1923, referring to this practice landing, that the
Admiralty had a 'well-defined plan' for the defence of the base,
but Jellicoe in his book *The Grand Fleet* says only that '. . . it
had been discussed on more than one occasion after examination
on the ground by a committee of officers but no action was
taken due to economy measures'.

So — still no permanent defences for the Flow and time was
running out.

In fact, quite a lot had been going on behind the scenes in
the Admiralty and the War Office, both in the preparations for
the Flotta exercise and in the consequent study of what was to be
learned from it. But apart from the exercise itself, it was in the
main, an 'office operation' and its results remained in Whitehall
rather than being projected on to the ground itself.

As early as June 1912, the possibility of a permanent
garrison of 250 Royal Marines at Scapa to prevent a *coup de
main* was being considered by the Admiralty, but nothing was
done pending a decision about blocking the channels to the Flow
and also the findings from the Flotta exercise.

A high level conference of representatives from the
Admiralty and War Office later considered another defence plan
for the Flow with an estimated cost of nearly £1 million and
requiring sixteen 4-inch and four 6-inch guns. Nothing happened
about that either, although it was felt that the use of smaller
guns would lower the cost. This conference was told that the
blocking of the channels was not feasible.

It was considered that 100 of the 450 men of the Orkney
RGA could be called out to reinforce the suggested 250 Marines
during a precautionary period and that the fleet's own guns
could cover Hoxa and Switha Sounds.[6]

On the general situation, the Admiralty pointed out in a
Minute that in the event of war with Germany, Scapa Flow

offered the Grand Fleet, as it was to be called, the following advantages **not** to be found in any other war anchorage in the British Isles along the 'war front':—

(a) it would hold the entire Grand Fleet with all the auxiliaries
(b) its insular position would prevent the Fleet movements from being reported by spies
(c) the hydrographic conditions of the approaches rendered submarine attack practically impossible; the only danger was from torpedo attack by night through various channels, even by cruisers against which the Fleet could defend itself.[7]

The next idea, which had Churchill's approval as First Lord, was for a 'flying column' of 3,000 Marines which would be rushed to Scapa or elsewhere in the event of trouble, to take up temporary defence positions previously prepared. The force could also be used, it was suggested, for 'securing and occupying an advanced base for the fleet either in British, neutral or hostile territory, the use of a portion of it in manning the defences at Scapa Flow in an emergency, being kept in mind'.[8]

And in October 1912 the almost inevitable Committee on Defence of Scapa Flow was set up, with Lieut. Col. Mercer RMLI, as president, 'to formulate proposals for the efficient and expeditious method of establishing temporary defences at Scapa Flow whenever required and at the shortest possible notice'. It was to base its recommendations on the outcome of the Flotta exercise for the most part, so still no permanent defence of the Flow was anticipated and the 'emergency' was less than two years away.[9] But realisation of the strategic importance of Orkney and Shetland to either side, however, would not go away. And there were doubts in Whitehall as to what the people who lived in these islands thought about it all, with one report studied in the Admiralty and War Office stating that: 'In the Shetlands particularly the detached situation of the islanders has tended to weaken their sense of British nationality.'[10] Shades of island independence movements to come.

It was also thought significant that Germany had been keen to pay Shetland a great deal of attention with naval visits and so on. Churchill thought that the establishment of a local TA unit would be a great influence for good in this respect — a marked contrast to his moves later on to get the Army out of Orkney and for the Marines to take over the defence of Scapa in both wars.

By early 1913 the War Office, too, had come round to this

E

line of thought, suggesting in a letter to the Admiralty that in future the Navy should be solely responsible for the defence of both Orkney and Shetland. If this happened the Orkney RGA would have no artillery role, it was pointed out in the letter, and would not be in sufficient numbers to provide infantry protection and so, it continued, 'Under present circumstances there is no possibility of giving adequate military protection for these islands.' Nor could they be reinforced by the Army from the mainland and, the letter added, 'Moreover the actual efficiency of the two companies is considerably less than other TA units as the great majority of the men are unable to attend camp owing to the fact that the training season coincides with the season of herring fishing upon which their livelihood depends.' And so the situation was that '. . . if therefore an enemy attempts to seize the islands by a *coup de main* before mobilisation is ordered under the existing system of military defence, no guarantee could be given there would be any military force whatsoever available to deal with the landing'.[11]

Obviously these northern islands so far away from Whitehall were an awkward military commitment, and the War Office was making the best possible case from its own point of view for getting rid of it, so it formally asked the Admiralty to assume responsibility for all defence of Orkney and Shetland, well knowing, of course, that the Navy had its eye pretty firmly, if reluctantly, fixed on Scapa Flow as at least a 'war anchorage' if not a full scale naval base. If the Admiralty agreed to this hand-over, the War Office suggested, the Orkney Territorials should either be disbanded or converted into Naval Volunteers and they would be happy to facilitate such a move. The Orkney soldiers themselves were not, of course, consulted but rumours of their uncertain future did seem to have reached them, and the possibility that they might be absorbed into some naval volunteer force was not received with any great enthusiasm — but, of course, it did happen eventually and many of them became rather unwilling Royal Marines. Surprisingly, this argument as to whether the Army or the Navy should man the land-based defences of the Flow still rumbled on into the Second World War, by which time the Navy was not so keen on manning the land-based defences of its bases.

In 1913, however, the Navy most certainly preferred to man defences of its bases itself, and so the Admiralty was only too pleased to accept the War Office invitation to take them over at Scapa but felt that Shetland should remain under War Office control — after all, they did not have a naval base as far north as that just then. The Orkney gunners would be converted to

Naval Volunteers, as it was felt that there was not so much need for purely infantry defence in Orkney where the approaches to the Flow would be protected by guns. The scheme was for twenty-two 4.7-inch guns with permanent searchlights, all in concrete emplacements, to be installed in peacetime, and the implementation of the scheme was referred to the bigger Cromarty Committee from the *ad hoc* Scapa Flow Defence Committee which had been set up only a few months previously.[12]

Discussion continued as to the status of whatever force was to be entrusted with the 'forward defence' of the Flow and which could be used not only to deny the islands to an enemy, now openly acknowledged to be Germany, but also to strike at other strategic points across the North Sea if necessary.

In the meantime it seemed that the Orkney gunners would be retained to man these naval guns to be emplaced round the Flow, but the War Office was not entirely happy about this arrangement, saying that it would give every assistance in converting them to Naval Volunteers and that it felt that the whole matter should be referred back to the Committee of Imperial Defence for reconsideration.

The Chief of Naval Staff suggested that Scapa's status itself should be changed, and in a Minute he noted that the decision to erect forward defences there meant that it could no longer be classed as a 'Temporary Naval Base' but should now be termed a 'War Anchorage'.[13]

Two destroyer flotillas with four submarines used Kirkwall Bay that August and September of 1912, twenty-two ships in all, and the 'special vessel' HMS *Hearty* was in Deer Sound for six weeks, during which her crew put up a flagpole on top of Wideford Hill as well as others elsewhere in the islands.

There was a scare story in the national press at this time about a German gunboat said to be lying in Baltasound in Shetland. It proved to be just a routine visit by a German fishery cruiser which had taken place some time before and which had been blown up into an exaggerated story by the popular press — but it indicated the edginess of the international scene.[14]

Scapa Flow continued to be described in some newspapers as 'the new strategic base' and there was further speculation about a possible air station for Orkney, possibly on South Ronaldsay, but the only tangible signs on the ground were the holes made by those 'pegs' in Flotta. And it was later reported that 'there was no thought of putting land defences on Scapa Flow meantime although it could be an important coaling base'. It might also be useful for storing oil fuel for the Navy, said the national press.

But whatever kind of base the Admiralty in Whitehall had in mind, if it had any coherent thoughts on the matter at all, the sea-going navy certainly realised Scapa's value, amply demonstrated by the presence of four flotillas of destroyers totalling 56 ships anchored in line in Longhope, stretching from end to end and side to side of the bay where they were joined by the battleship *Neptune* wearing the flag of Admiral Callaghan, C-in-C Home Fleet, early in October. Bad weather, however, held up the projected exercises and the fleet sailed away on 12 October, leaving the Flow to its customary winter solitude.[15]

Quite early in 1913, the last complete year of peace and 'the old order', the 'Glasgow Herald' was writing about 'Naval Activities in the North Sea', but it seemed, in fact, to be underlining the lack of such activities on the British coast of that sea, apart from work going on at Rosyth. 'Next in importance to the scheme at Rosyth,' wrote the paper, 'are proposals to establish naval bases at Scapa Flow in the Orkneys and Lamlash in the Isle of Arran. No construction work has been carried on at either during the past year [1912] but preliminary operations are not likely to be delayed much longer.' A pious hope on the part of the 'Herald', one feels, rather than a statement of fact. It was expected that the erection of coal and oil stores would begin soon at both Lamlash and the Flow, probably in a few months time. The proposal, said the 'Herald', was that Scapa Flow would be made a 'jumping off place', a port of call for ships from Rosyth, where they could coal, take on ammunition and generally complete their arrangements immediately before going into action. A rather leisurely way to go to war, one would think, but then, a year before the horrors of 1914-18, war was still expected to be conducted along gentlemanly lines.

It was also anticipated that Scapa would have a naval air station, one of a chain of such establishments being planned for the east coast of Britain, and, indeed, Orkney did see its first heavier-than-air machines later that year when the *Hermes* called with her two hydroplanes. In February a party of Marine and Naval officers in a special service vessel visited Holm Sound, Water Sound, Hoxa Sound and Scapa Pier, the first three being vital areas in any scheme for defending the Flow against sea-borne attack.[16]

The Naval Estimates for 1913/14 were published in March amounting to £46,409,300, an unprecedented increase for those days of £1¼ million on the previous year — but of this vast amount the figure of £5,000 for what were called 'improval works' at Scapa Flow seems pretty meagre, to put it mildly, although a further £6,000 was also proposed for equally unspecified 'new works' there — 0.01% of the total estimate, or at best, perhaps 0.02%.[17]

By early May the ships were back in the Flow, 18 destroyers of the Second Flotilla and more were expected — as many as four flotillas, all part of the First Fleet, with four cruisers of the Third Squadron. They found little to encourage them climatically, for the weather was vile with south-easterly gales screaming across the islands for anything up to a week at a time. The destroyer *Hope,* going through Holm Sound with the rest of her flotilla, was damaged when the flood tide, which could reach over 8 knots there before it was blocked, met the gale, piling up tremendous seas. Her after-hatch was carried away and her First Lieutenant was washed overboard and drowned, another officer being injured so badly that he had to be admitted to Balfour Hospital when they reached Kirkwall.[18]

The Flotta folk had been doing good business with the ships by going out to them in their yoles when they were at anchor to sell fresh farm produce and fish, while traders in Longhope and Kirkwall also enjoyed a welcome boom in their business enterprises.

The four extra flotillas duly arrived off Longhope at the beginning of June, all 68 ships of them. As so often in June, it was foggy, so what with the earlier gales and now fog, the Navy was getting a foretaste of what it could expect in this northern fastness. They anchored without trouble, however, in a capital 'T' formation with each arm some two miles long — the top of the 'T' was north and south along the west shore of Flotta, and the other arm stretched up into Longhope Bay itself. Going out on exercises, as they frequently did, two flotillas would use Switha Sound, and the other two would go out through Holm Sound. They were watched by the Commander-in-Chief Home Fleet, Admiral Sir George A. Callaghan, from his flagship, the Super Dreadnought *Neptune* anchored off Longhope.

It was all part of the run-up to the annual summer manoeuvres in which, the Admiralty announced, 344 ships would take part that year, including 42 submarines and three hydroplanes. Also in preparation for these 'war games' and mock battles, the First Battle Squadron of HMS *Collingwood* and seven other battleships, along with the First Battle Cruiser Squadron of HMS *Lion* and two other battlecruisers, were in the Flow, all coaling. And before they left the Flow, members of the ships' companies attended a church parade in St Magnus Cathedral.

The actual manoeuvres did not touch Orkney this year but involved a successful landing in force in the Humber area under the command of Admiral Jellicoe. It was said to be so successful, in fact, that strenuous efforts were made to keep the details secret in case it gave the German High Command ideas.

But although the action did not touch Orkney directly, the Navy kept its ships, mainly cruisers and destroyers, to-ing and fro-ing in and out of Scapa right up until October, and the survey ship *Endeavour* spent a lot of time in the islands, seeming to concentrate on the Deer Sound area.

And there was one very important and significant visitation to the Flow, when the Admiralty yacht *Enchantress* dropped anchor off Scapa Pier in the first week of October. On board were Asquith, the Prime Minister, Churchill, First Lord of the Admiralty, Seely, Secretary of State for War, and Montague, Under-Secretary of State for India, along with Mrs Churchill, Lady Gwendoline Churchill and Churchill's private secretary. Apart from seeing Scapa Flow for themselves the party landed and visited Kirkwall including St Magnus Cathedral, where they climbed the tower before walking back to Scapa Pier to re-embark and sail to Invergordon.[19] While there they attended a very high-powered naval conference on the yacht where, in addition to their own party, the First Sea Lord, Battenburg, the Second Sea Lord, Jellicoe, the C-in-C Home Fleet, Callaghan, and nine other Flag Officers were also present. Churchill, however, still found time to make a couple of flights round the area in one of the hydroplanes from the *Furious*.

The outcome of this conference was contained in a 'Secret Memorandum on the necessity of defending Scapa Flow against attack by torpedo craft', issued by the Admiralty on 23 October, three weeks after the meeting, in which it was stated:—

> The strategic value of this great natural harbour [Scapa Flow] was strongly emphasised at a conference on board the *Enchantress* at Cromarty on 3 October at which the Board of Admiralty met all the Flag Officers commanding units of the Home Fleet to discuss the results of recent manoeuvres and the general strategic situation in the North Sea. All these officers adverted to the great value of Scapa Flow as a war anchorage and fuelling base, and after careful discussion, expressed a preference for that port over the alternative bases in the neighbourhood on the mainland.[20]

There would thus seem to be no doubt as to which base the sea-going navy wanted, but at the Admiralty itself Cromarty was apparently the chosen harbour, for on 21 November a memo from the First Lord, Churchill, to the First Sea Lord,

Battenburg, stated that the Committee of Imperial Defence had been 'persuaded with difficulty to authorise the fortification of Cromarty after the whole question [Scapa Flow versus Invergordon] had been thrashed out', and this fortification of Cromarty was in full swing, as 'having to choose between the two we deliberately chose Cromarty as the vital place to be fortified'. Churchill's minute went on:—

> The Admiralty has been so frequently charged with changeableness in its views that the greatest care must be taken to avoid any justification for such an accusation as a long, and in my opinion, unjust disparagement of Cromarty would have the worst effects on the Admiralty credit before the Committee of Imperial Defence. It ought to be possible to make the case for some light armament for Scapa Flow without reflecting on Admiralty policy in regard to Cromarty.[21]

So it would seem that the Admirals' advocacy for Scapa as their base, voiced at the *Enchantress* conference, had fallen on deaf ears — and the erecting of defences at Cromarty, already in hand, was to go ahead while Scapa was to be fobbed off with 'light armament' which, when war did come, proved to be so light that it was non-existent.

At the end of the year, in spite of the worsening international situation, the future of the Orkney Territorials in the RGA and their role in the defence of Scapa was still in doubt. The Admiralty wanted to take over defence of the Flow, as suggested by the War Office, but this had been a bone of contention locally ever since the change-over from the old Volunteer movement to the Territorial Army set-up. Disbandment had been considered several times but in face of the Orkney soldiers' forceful expression of their desire to man what defences there were as Army gunners, Whitehall had always backed down; but the possibility of a change-over obviously still existed and was favoured by the Admiralty who wanted, in fact, to take control of the coast defence of all naval ports away from the Army. It was a situation hardly conducive to the formulation of a firm policy over the defence arrangements ashore.[22]

In the meantime the Admiralty was in its own element when it placed an order for seven 30-foot sailing cutters with brass and copper fittings, sails and so on with Stanger's Yard in Stromness; and another Orkney firm, S. Baikie & Son, secured the contract for building the look-out station at Brough Ness in South Ronaldsay which was, however, now to be a visual signal station and not a radio station as had at first been thought. It was completed just before war broke out.[23]

Strangely enough, the first half of 1914 brought no naval ships to the Flow, which must have looked as empty and deserted as in early times. But it was not going to be like that for long. The Flotta correspondent of 'The Orcadian' made the point on 6 June in the island's news column — ' . . . one small cruiser so far' — but continued, 'We are just wondering if she is not the harbinger of other ships to follow.' How right he was, for only two months later his column says plaintively: 'We have had sights and doings not only round but in the island, such as would give us a great deal to write about . . .' But it was not to be. Britain had declared war on Germany and strict censorship, which grew ever tighter, forbade the telling of those 'sights and doings', which, of course, included the arrival of the renamed 'Grand Fleet' in what was to be its main wartime home, Scapa Flow.

CHAPTER 8

Zero Hour

IT IS an odd fact that as the remorseless seconds ticked towards midnight on 4 August 1914, zero hour, when Britain's ultimatum to Germany would run out and 'let slip the dogs of war', there were virtually no fighting ships in the nation's most vital strategic base — Scapa Flow. But they were not far away.

The Fleet had been in the Flow for several days previously as the European crisis deepened and the threat of war slid towards being reality. The 'always ready' First Fleet with its four squadrons of Britain's most powerful battleships, some two dozen of them, accompanied by supporting cruisers and destroyers, had slipped quietly through Hoxa Sound out of the North Sea mist on 1 August. On 4 August, renamed the Grand Fleet, under its new Commander-in-Chief, Admiral Sir John Jellicoe, in his flagship HMS *Iron Duke,* the ships had been ordered to sea again at 8.30 in the morning by the Admiralty.[1]

With them went the light cruisers *Southampton, Birmingham, Boadicea* and *Blonde* along with the Fourth Destroyer Flotilla, to be joined by other ships from Rosyth and the First Battlecruiser Squadron under Admiral Sir David Beatty, which was already at sea with its attendant cruisers and destroyers, off Fair Isle searching for potential enemy ships, including possibly the cruise liner *Kronprinzessin Cecilie,* a frequent visitor to Orkney in pre-war days, which was later reported to have passed through the Stronsay Firth within 24 hours of the declaration of war.[2] This British show of naval strength was formidable and there were still two other fleets further south — the Second, assembling at Portland, and the Third, in home ports awaiting the return of its Reserve crews.

The fleet's arrival in Scapa Flow had been largely hidden by a summer sea fog and, as far as the general public knew, and the Germans too, it had just disappeared from its English south coast bases into the concealing greyness of the North Sea, bound, no one knew where. Orcadians, of course, knew very well where it was but it remained generally a well-kept secret.

The comparative dearth of naval ships in the Flow earlier in the year and referred to by the Flotta correspondent of 'The Orcadian', was now to some extent explained, though not publicly. The Navy had been in the habit of holding annual manoeuvres during the summer, often in recent years, involving Orkney and the Flow. In 1914, however, this routine was changed. Winston Churchill, First Lord of the Admiralty, and Prince Louis of Battenburg, First Sea Lord, decided instead to hold a test mobilisation of the fleet reservists to be followed by a Royal Review off Spithead. The First Fleet, being on an 'always ready' status, needed no reservists — it could go into action at any time. The Second Fleet of two battle squadrons, also with attendant smaller craft, needed only to collect personnel re-training at various naval schools, or on other duties ashore, and it too could be ready for action almost as soon as the First. The Third Fleet was the one which the test mobilisation would most affect. It consisted of two battle squadrons of the Navy's oldest ships manned by care and maintenance crews only, needing the naval reservists to be called out before it could put to sea.

The test mobilisation, which Churchill in his book *The World Crisis 1911-1918,* says had no connection with the deteriorating European situation, began on 15 July when 20,000 reservists were called out. The ships were coaled, always a tedious, unpleasant chore, and made ready for sea. The test was an entire success, with the ships raising steam and sailing from their home ports to join the First and Second Fleets for the Review to be held off Spithead on 17 and 18 July.

As Churchill wrote, 'It constituted incomparably the greatest assemblage of naval power ever witnessed in the history of the world.'[3] Some indication of the size of this great armada can be gained from the fact that when it put to sea for exercises on the following day, 19 July, with bands playing, flags flying, ships' companies lining the rails and aircraft circling overhead, it took six hours to pass the saluting base on the Royal Yacht, even steaming at 15 knots. As Churchill wrote in *World Crisis* — 'They were going on a longer voyage than any of us could know.' It was a voyage from which many would not return.

The test mobilisation over, the Second and Third Fleets dispersed to their home ports where the Reservists paid off. The First Fleet, although at full readiness, was also due to disperse for various exercises and cruises.

The international situation deteriorated rapidly following the assassination of Archduke Franz Ferdinand of Austria at Sarajevo in Serbia on 28 June, and the resulting impossible ultimatum from Austria. Battenburg, on his own initiative, ordered the First Fleet **not** to disperse but to remain at Portland, an order almost immediately approved and endorsed by Churchill. A communiqué was issued informing the world of the British action, in the hope that it would steady and calm the European ferment.

The majority of the British Cabinet was determined that Britain should not be drawn into a conflict unless herself attacked. Churchill, for his part, wanted to ensure that the diplomatic situation did not get ahead of the naval one and that the Grand Fleet should be in its War Station, Scapa Flow, before Germany could know whether or not Britain would be a belligerent. He also felt that the Fleet should be in position before even the Cabinet itself had decided this.

On 29 July the 'Warning Telegram' was sent out bringing in a 'Precautionary Period' — naval harbours were closed, bridges guarded, coast-watchers posted and so on. And that same morning the First Fleet under its Second-in-Command — the C-in-C, Admiral Sir George Callaghan, having been called to the Admiralty for consultations — received orders to weigh. The Fleet was to time its sailing from Portland so that it would pass through the Straits of Dover in darkness and without lights.

Describing the departure Churchill wrote of:

> . . . squadron by squadron, scores of gigantic castles of steel wending their way across the misty, shining sea, like giants bowed in anxious thought. We may picture them again as darkness fell, eighteen miles of warships running at high speed and in absolute blackness through the narrow Straits, bearing with them into the broad waters of the North Sea the safeguard of considerable affairs.[4]

A future King of Britain, Prince Albert, then a midshipman in the dreadnought *Collingwood,* later to be King George VI, described the sailing more prosaically: 'We left Portland and steered west then east, starting war routine at 1 p.m. After dinner we went to night defence stations, all ready for a destroyer attack, and passed the Straits of Dover at midnight.'[5]

Their destination was secret, only flag officers and captains had been told — 'Shape course for Scapa Flow.' Not even the Cabinet was told till later; only the Prime Minister and the First Lord knew.

The German ambassador in London did not like it at all when he found out that the Fleet had sailed but he was curtly informed by the Foreign Office: 'The movements of the Fleet are free of all offensive character'; and it was further added that the ships were not going near German waters.

On Thursday, 30 July, the flagship, *Iron Duke,* reported to the Admiralty that they were well out in the middle of the North Sea and there was a general sigh of relief in Whitehall.

As the German Official Naval History has pointed out, 'the strategic concentration of the Fleet had actually been accomplished with its transfer to Scottish ports'. Churchill agreed when he wrote — 'We were now in a position, whatever happened, to control events, and it was not easy to see how this advantage could be taken from us.' There was no longer the danger of a surprise torpedo attack on the Fleet in harbour coinciding with a declaration of war or even preceding it.

He went on:

> If war should come no one would know where to look for the British Fleet. Somewhere in that enormous waste of waters to the north of our islands, cruising now this way, now that, shrouded in storms and mists, dwelt this mighty organisation . . . The king's ships were at sea.

Indeed they were but although it was not apparent at this time the threat of surprise torpedo attack had by no means disappeared, not even from the supposed security of Scapa Flow itself.[6]

But, from the last day of July until the morning of that final day of peace, this great fleet lay at anchor off Scapa Pier on the north side of the Flow, stretched out in meticulous lines from Holm to Orphir.

It was probably on 29 July, the day the fleet sailed from Portland, that Orcadians, like so many of their countrymen, first realised that war was not just a possibility but, in fact, a probability. On that day the Territorials were called out and small parties drawn from the Orkney Royal Garrison Artillery made their way to war stations — usually guard duty in an infantry role on telegraph cable terminals where these vital links in the communications chain came ashore.[7]

These guards were usually parties of ten men but the one in Rackwick in Hoy was of twice that number, under an officer, for this was the all-important telegraphic link across the Pentland Firth to the Admiralty in London. Radio was still not a reliable form of communication, quite apart from the security problems which it posed.

Coastguards were also sent to take up watch-keeping duties at the new signal station on Brough Ness in South Ronaldsay past which the fleet would sail so many times in the next four-and-a-half years.

The first warships of the Navy to arrive in the Flow were destroyers of the Fourth Flotilla, which had been on patrol duties in the Irish Sea on account of the Irish troubles arising from the Home Rule crisis which had occupied the political minds of Britain almost to the exclusion of the greater danger developing in Europe. They were oil-burners and refuelled from a tanker already in the Flow. Next day, 31 July, they moved from the middle of the Flow, where they had first anchored, to form a long line along the Orphir shore so that the Grand Fleet when it arrived later that day could come straight into Scapa Bay.[8]

Colliers and tankers had been arriving for some days and that night there were over a hundred ships in the Flow altogether. The Grand Fleet itself numbered 96 ships — with the 1st, 2nd, 3rd and 4th Battle Squadrons of 21 dreadnoughts, 8 pre-dreadnoughts, and 4 battlecruisers; attached were 8 armoured cruisers of 2nd and 3rd Cruiser Squadrons and 4 light cruisers of 1st Light Cruiser Squadron, along with 9 other cruisers and 42 destroyers.[9] On arrival the ships were being cleared for action. Ships' boats were put ashore and hauled up on the beaches in their hundreds looking like 'schools of stranded whales'. Wooden fittings and anything else likely to burn were wrenched out in feverish haste and either taken ashore or, more often, just dumped over the side. The shores were strewn with mahogany and teak fittings, while boats piled high with chests of drawers, furniture and even an occasional wardroom piano, put off to be anchored here and there round the Flow. Dozens of steam pinnaces gleaming with polished brass and bell-shaped funnels, even a private motor launch found moorings in sheltered bays; while an officer's motor car was also landed, it was said.[10]

Captain Swanson, Master of the mail boat St Ola, said later — 'The Flow was full of warships and they launched many boats and beached them in Scapa Bay. Many of them were full of wardrobes, pianos and luxurious fittings which had been stripped to prepare the warships for action. We ran through them many a time.' It was 'panic stations' with a vengeance and there were rich pickings for local 'beachcombers'.

Lean and hungry-looking destroyers patrolled the entrances scrutinising all merchant ships in the prevailing fog — even the St Ola on her regular run. Capt. Swanson said he was hailed by one of them outside Hoxa. The Navy offered to escort him in, but it soon became obvious that the destroyer's Commanding Officer was less sure of the way than the much more experienced Master of the Ola. They parted company in the murk and Capt. Swanson, finding that he was unable to hear any of the foghorns or the man he had under contract at Hoxa to 'blow' for him in thick weather, anchored for the night, not wishing to run the gauntlet of a Flow full of invisible warships.[11]

The rest of the Orkney Territorials were called out on 2 August, when parties of 25 men were detailed for Stanger Head on Flotta and Hoxa Head in South Ronaldsay where naval ratings from the ships had been preparing emergency gun positions. They were later reinforced by ten Marines at each site with a further addition of Royal Marine pensioners, recalled to the Colours, joining them six weeks later.[12] Nor surprisingly there was some friction between the local soldiers and the naval-controlled newcomers, especially as the Marines were thought to have better accommodation and equipment than that provided by the Army. Still, the Orkney gunners did fire in some degree of anger in the first day or so of the war when a trawler entered an unspecified 'prohibited area', probably Hoy Sound, and had to be stopped by a 'bring-to' round of gunfire until such time as a destroyer could come up and take over the examination.

On the opening day of the war, too, 5 August, the first German prisoners were landed at Scapa Pier, thirteen unlucky members of the crew of a fishing-boat caught at sea by the declaration of war. They were taken under guard by the Orkney Territorials to Naval headquarters before being sent south.[13]

Admiral Sir John Jellicoe had arrived in Scapa Flow on 2 August from Wick aboard the cruiser Boadicea, having been delayed by the fog which had concealed the arrival of the Fleet two days earlier.[14] He had sealed orders from the Admiralty instructing him to take over as Commander-in-Chief from the 62-year-old Admiral Sir George Callaghan, now approaching retiring age, who had been in command for three years. Churchill and Battenburg had agreed that Jellicoe should take over in the event of war, especially as Callaghan was not in good health, and they felt that he might not be physically able to stand up to the strain of supreme war command. But he was a fine naval commander, very much liked and trusted by the Fleet. Again, it was risky to change such an important command at this juncture when the Fleet might well have to fight a major battle at any time. That same night Jellicoe was instructed to break the seals on his orders and act on them at once, Churchill and Battenburg now being of the opinion that war was inevitable. Jellicoe and Callaghan both protested to the Admiralty, protests which were echoed by practically all the flag officers who had served under Callaghan, but to no avail. The First Lord and the First Sea Lord were adamant. It was a grave decision to take but they were sure it was the right one; it was no time to consider the feelings of individuals.

Jellicoe took over, hoisting his flag on *Iron Duke,* on the evening of 3 August while Callaghan, with a heavy heart, was piped over the side for the last time. Almost at once Jellicoe received instructions to take the Grand Fleet to sea at 8.30 the next morning which he did to the sound of cheering from ships and shore. By the time he returned at six o'clock in the evening of 7 August, Britain had been at war for two days — it was to last for more than another 1,500 days during many of which the Fleet would lie in Scapa Flow. But on this, its first actual wartime visit, the Fleet did not stay long — only 12½ hours in fact.[15]

Jellicoe was very worried about the lack of defences at Scapa — there were virtually none apart from those provided by the Fleet itself. 'The greatest anxiety constantly confronting me,' he wrote in *The Grand Fleet 1914-1916,* 'was the defenceless nature of the base at Scapa, which was open to submarine and destroyer attacks.'[16]

His predecessor, Callaghan, had also had these worries but all he could do was to land some 12-pounder guns from the Fleet and mount them at the entrances to the anchorage. There were, however, no searchlights available so the guns were of little value at night and were of too small a calibre in any case to be really effective against a determined attack. Jellicoe makes the point that when, a year or two previously, the Admiralty had decided that Scapa Flow would be the main Fleet base, the question of providing shore-based defences had been discussed on 'more than one occasion' after an on-the-spot examination by a committee of officers, but that nothing had been done owing to lack of funds.[17] The main defence against submarine attack, he wrote, indeed the only defence, 'lay in the navigational difficulties attendant upon entry into the harbour . . . due to strong and varying currents'. But he added that the Germans were well acquainted with Orkney, indeed there had been German cruise liners in and out of the islands for many years before the war, not to mention fishing-boats, and they were well able to judge the difficulties as well as our own navy, '. . . and seeing that we used it as a main Fleet Base, they could deduce the fact, if they did not know it already, that the difficulties of entry were not insuperable'.[18] In fact, a German destroyer was said to have been in the Flow only a 'short while' before the outbreak of war, which is quite possible for, after all, quite a number of British warships were in Kiel on a courtesy visit at the actual time of the assassination of Archduke Franz Ferdinand in Sarajevo which triggered off the war.

In its wisdom, and basing its assessment on the performance

of its own submarines, the British Admiralty also believed that Scapa was beyond the effective range of U-boats from Germany. The Germans, however, found in the first week of war that they could get as far as Scapa but did not attempt then to penetrate it because they gave the British, wrongly as it happened, the credit of defending their main naval base as strongly as they had protected their own.

As an emergency measure, cruisers and destroyers had been stationed at the main entrances to assist the '12-pounders ashore and when the Fleet was in the Flow patrols were maintained to the eastward of the Pentland Firth. It was not felt in the Fleet generally, however, that these measures gave much security, even against destroyer attack on a dark night and none at all against submarines. The only answer to that threat was the siting of obstructions under water as well as on the surface. Only with these in position would the Fleet feel really secure.[19] Much work had been done on the design of such measures but at the outbreak of war the fact remained that no satisfactory anti-submarine obstruction had been devised.

Experienced British submariners generally were of the opinion that while the minor entrances to the Flow, such as Hoy Sound or the Holm Sound channels on the east, would certainly present great difficulties for entry by a submarine, Hoxa Sound was quite practicable for a determined U-boat commander.[20]

It is not surprising that Jellicoe was worried. To make matters worse there were re-fuelling difficulties and delays on that first wartime return of the Fleet, caused by a shortage of colliers to bring the coal from Cardiff.

So, at 6.30 that evening the Grand Fleet put to sea again where it felt safer.[21] They went west-about Orkney through the Pentland Firth and into the North Sea by way of the Fair Isle channel. It was soon evident that fears of submarine attack were by no means groundless when, somewhere east of Orkney the next day, the cruiser *Birmingham* claimed to have rammed and sunk the *U 15* — the first U-boat 'kill' of the war.[22]

CHAPTER 9

Settling In

SCAPA FLOW base installations at this point — the outbreak of war — were, to say the least, very thin on the ground, or on the water for that matter. There were just the two sea-going repair ships, *Cyclops* and *Assistance,* anchored close in-shore off Scapa Pier.

The first official indication that the Flow had indeed achieved, at least nominally, the status of a naval port came on 2 August in a notice posted and signed by Captain Coke RN, as King's Harbour Master, which warned that navigational lights in the area might be ordered to be extinguished. There were, however, few concrete signs of this new status ashore as yet. In view of Captain Coke's notice about the possible extinguishing of navigational lights it is interesting that nothing further seems to have been done in this direction until 1 October, when regulations to put out coastal lights actually came into force for Orkney waters and were extended to cover all the north of Scotland ten days later. At the same time east coast ports were closed to neutral fishing vessels for the first time.[1]

The *Cyclops* was connected to a shore telegraph cable through Kirkwall Post Office. This had been installed during Fleet exercises a year or two earlier and she now became a floating post office herself as well as the base for what few auxiliary vessels there were in the anchorage, mainly requisitioned drifters. Shortly after the declaration of war, Rear Admiral Francis S. Miller was appointed to her as Senior Naval Officer (SNO) of the Base and he found facilities on board cramped in the extreme, with the Staff in many instances having to sleep on the deck.[2]

By September the Base installations were beginning to build up. The *Imperieuse,* formerly the *Fisgard I,* arrived from Portsmouth to become Headquarters of the SNO and mail office for the Base, so relieving some of the pressure on the *Cyclops.* She was in addition HQ for the Fleet Coaling Officer, Naval Stores Officer, Victualling Officer, Naval Ordnance Officer, Cashier and Base Censor, and for a time she also accommodated dockyard working parties sent north to maintain and to carry out modifications to the ships of the fleet.[3]

There should have been another Base HQ ship, the *Fisgard II* which sailed from Portsmouth in company with the *Fisgard I* or *Imperieuse,* but unfortunately she capsized and sank off Portland Bill; and another ship intended to house the dockyard personnel, the *Caribbean,* did not make it either, when she foundered off Cape Wrath in heavy weather the following year with the loss of fifteen of her crew. It was not until March 1916 that conditions for the large numbers of these dockyard workers began to improve, with the arrival of HMS *Victorious* which at times housed as many as 500 civilian tradesmen. Some of these men, of course, stayed on the warships themselves in order to complete their work aboard on the engines, boilers, and other machinery, besides fitting such complicated instrumentation as the Director Fire Control for the guns which made such a vast improvement in naval gunnery. On occasion these civilians found themselves at sea if the ship they were working on was suddenly ordered out on patrol or on a sweep.[4]

One of the lessons of the Battle of Jutland, learned the hard way, was that the deck armour of the British ships was inadequate to withstand the plunging shells of long-range gunnery. Additional armour had to be fitted, and much of this work was carried out by the dockyard teams while the ships were moored in the Flow ready for action.

An important appointment made early on was that of Vice-Admiral Sir Stanley Colville to be Vice-Admiral Commanding Orkney and Shetland (ACOS) and he became virtually 'Governor' of the area with an ever-growing control over matters not only military or naval, but to a considerable extent, civil as well.[5] It was a control which grew tighter as the war progressed, becoming very irksome to Orcadians who found the mounting restrictions, especially on their movements, beginning to smack of martial law. He was in charge of all the Base defences, such as they were, and he was responsible for their strengthening by the installation of nets, booms, and other underwater obstructions to deter both submarine and surface attack on the anchorage. The actual blocking of the channels by nets, booms and blockships was under the direct supervision of Captain Stanley Dean RN.[6]

So things were beginning to move in the defence of Scapa, and nothing moved faster or more often than the Grand Fleet itself as the ships' companies became more and more aware of their insecurity while at anchor there, and their Commander-in-Chief was perhaps the most anxious of anyone, for it was truly

said of him by Churchill that 'he was the only man on either side
who could lose the war in an afternoon'.

The anxiety boiled over on 1 September in what came to be
known as 'The First Battle of Scapa Flow'.[7] It was about six
o'clock in the evening. The Dreadnought Fleet of battleships,
Sixth Cruiser Squadron, and First Light Cruiser Squadron with
the Fourth Destroyer Flotilla were all anchored off Scapa Pier
engaged in cleaning boilers, taking on stores and ammunition,
and other harbour chores. The Second Destroyer Flotilla was
similarly engaged in Longhope. They were all at two hours
notice to steam, however, and those vessels equipped with them
had their anti-torpedo nets out.

All was apparently quiet and peaceful on this dull, rather
misty, evening with rain showers trailing their grey skirts across
the sombre scene, when suddenly the *Falmouth,* one of the light
cruisers, opened up with her six-inch guns on what she reported
as a U-boat periscope. What is more, she claimed a probable hit.
Shortly afterwards the battleship *Vanguard* fired on an object
which was also reported as a periscope and an E Class destroyer,
on patrol between Hoxa and the fleet, had a go as well, while at
6.30 the *Drake* signalled that she too, had sighted the submarine.
The cat was well and truly among the pigeons.

With all this excitement the Fleet was ordered to raise steam
'with all despatch and to prepare for torpedo attack'. The Light
Cruiser Squadron and the Second Destroyer Flotilla weighed
anchor and carried out a search.

It was now 8.30 p.m. and getting dark. Small craft were
ordered to cruise up and down the lines of bigger ships to
confuse the enemy and searchlights were used for the same
purpose, as well as to locate any possible target, and just to
make doubly sure, the colliers and store ships were ordered
alongside those battleships with no anti-torpedo nets to take the
brunt of any attack. No doubt the crews of these, mainly
merchant, ships did not think much of this role, but it was vital
to preserve the capital ships to fight another day.

The Fleet itself was ordered to sea as soon as the ships had
raised steam, a difficult operation in the dark enclosed waters
with the additional hazard of thick weather but by 11 p.m. they
had all cleared, not only the Flow, but the Pentland Firth as
well, breathing more easily as they rose to the surge of the open
sea. Just to speed their already hasty departure came news from
the repair ship *Assistance* that she had sighted a submarine just
as she was clearing Hoxa Sound.

Cyclops, with her vital telegraph link to the south, was by
this time the only ship left in the Flow, apart from some

destroyers left behind to search for and sink any intruder. They found nothing.

It was the first of many such scares, some of which ended up with heavy gunfire and occasional shells landing on farms in the surrounding islands. In one such action, it was reported, a shell pitched very close to a postman on his rounds, so near, in fact, that both he and his horse were covered with earth. His comments have not been recorded but it was also reported that a dead whale came ashore a few days later. Jellicoe himself wrote of this first 'battle':—

No trace of a submarine was discovered, and subsequent investigation showed that the alarm *may* have been false, the evidence not being conclusive either way. The incident, however, made it clear that protection against submarine attack was an absolute necessity, as the Fleet could not remain at a base that was so open to this form of attack as Scapa Flow.[8]

Jellicoe maintained that the only possible action during any such alarm was to take the Fleet to sea as quickly as possible, even with the difficulties and dangers attendant upon such a hurried operation at night or in thick or stormy weather. With this feeling that its main base was not a safe place, it is not surprising that in the first three months of the war the Grand Fleet steamed a total of 15,000 miles in the open sea.[9] This all created a feeling of unease among the crews, quite apart from the fact that such routine work as boiler cleaning, refitting machinery and repairs could not be carried out and the almost constant steaming of the Fleet in the first few weeks of war had shown that such maintenance was vital to the ships' continued efficiency.

This feeling of insecurity which pervaded the Fleet is exemplified in Jellicoe's remark to Admiral Sir Percy Scott, the gunnery expert, who developed the gunnery director system for the Navy. When he visited Scapa Flow he is quoted as saying — 'A Hun submarine could have come in and sunk them any night. I slept on board the *Iron Duke*. My last remark to Lord Jellicoe was — "Shall we be here in the morning?" His reply was — "I wonder." '

A story was told in a BBC radio programme between the wars of a party of French naval officers who visited Scapa Flow in 1915 aboard a British destroyer. As they came up with the Orkney land through the Pentland Firth before entering the Flow, and again as they approached the boom, they expressed

their amazement at the excellence of the defence's camouflage —
the strong points were entirely invisible, they remarked. 'That's
not surprising,' replied a British officer. 'There are none.' It may
be an apocryphal story but it illustrates the position early in the
war.

Writing to Churchill, the First Lord, on 30 September,
Jellicoe said —

> I long for a submarine defence at Scapa. It would give such a
> feeling of confidence. I cannot sleep half so well inside as
> when outside, mainly because I feel we are risking such a mass
> of vulnerable ships in a place where, if a submarine did get in,
> she practically has the British Fleet at her mercy up to the
> number of torpedoes.[10]

The feeling of insecurity increased and the ships spent more
and more time at sea. At the Admiralty Churchill was well aware
of this jittery atmosphere which pervaded the Fleet and he too
was worried. In *World Crisis 1911-1918* he wrote — 'Everything
depended upon the Fleet and during these same months of
October and November the Fleet was disquieted about the very
foundations of its being . . . The Grand Fleet was uneasy. She
could find no resting place except at sea . . . The idea had got
around — the German submarines were coming after them in the
harbours.' After reiterating that Scapa was supposed to be
protected by its currents from submarine attack Churchill went
on: '. . . but no one, we believed, could take a submarine
submerged through the intricate and swirling channels. Now, all
of a sudden the Grand Fleet began to see submarines in Scapa
Flow.'

Although even as late as December 1914 Germany had only
35 U-boats, the first having been launched in 1906, there was
considerable justification for the Fleet's disquiet. On 22 September
three 12,000-ton British cruisers, *Aboukir, Crecy* and *Hogue,*
were torpedoed one after another and sunk by a single
submarine, the *U 9,* commanded by Kapitän Leutnant Weddigen
in the Broad Fourteens, Dogger Bank area of the North Sea,
with the loss of 1,400 men. Less than a month later *U 9* was 20
miles off Orkney when Weddigen tried to repeat his Dogger
Bank exploit by attacking five destroyers. He was unsuccessful
this time, but he helped to scare the Grand Fleet out of the Flow
and down to Northern Ireland.

This climax was reached on 16 and 17 October with
considerable U-boat activity being reported round Orkney, and
one was said to have been seen by look-outs on a Switha shore

battery. Reports that there was a submarine actually inside the Flow increased the tension — it was described as the equivalent of reporting 'a cobra in a drawing room'. What became known as 'The Second Battle of Scapa Flow' was soon in full swing.[11]

There was the usual panic and all the Grand Fleet left during the night, while it was reported by ACOS that there was still a U-boat inside the Flow next morning. It was alleged to have fired a torpedo inside the anchorage but this was subsequently found to have been one let off accidently by one of our own destroyers. Still, as Churchill wrote — 'Guns were fired, destroyers thrashed the waters, and the whole gigantic Armada put to sea in haste and dudgeon.' He went on — 'Of course there never was a submarine in Scapa Flow. None during the whole war achieved the terrors of the passage.'

Jellicoe was not quite so dogmatic, saying that the presence or otherwise of a U-boat in the Flow had never been determined with certainty, but it would seem that he doubted the validity of most of the reported sightings as far as the 17 October scare was concerned, although he cautiously added:— 'Many of the officers concerned in the search were convinced at the time that there actually was a submarine inside, and that they had seen her. Indeed a good many rounds were fired during the day at objects which were thought at the time to be a periscope.'

Sometimes it is suggested that seals may have caused the confusion, or could it possibly have been an inquisitive skarfie poking up its long neck and being glimpsed briefly in bad light?

There was no doubt at all, however, about the presence of an enemy submarine in Hoxa Sound on the morning of 23 November. *U 18*, commanded by Kapitän Leutnant Heinrich von Hennig, was one of several U-boats in Orkney waters at this time — at least three were reported in the Copinsay/Pentland Firth area and one was actually identified the following day as the *U 16*, and yet another was pursued but escaped off Fair Isle travelling at an estimated 18 knots, proof of their capabilities on the surface.[12]

Passing eastward of the islands on the night of 22/23 November, von Hennig saw searchlights in the general direction of Kirkwall and the Flow, confirming his suspicion that the Grand Fleet was in Scapa. He decided to try an attack in the anchorage itself.

The Pentland Skerries light was lit — as it happened this was to assist the Fleet departing from the Flow but von Hennig was not to know this. He used the light to cruise on the surface as far as the Skerries where he dived, his batteries now fully charged. Soon after, helped rather than obstructed by the tide,

he was off Swona and by 11 a.m. *U 18* was in Hoxa Sound.
From here he could see into the Flow through his periscope and
to his great disappointment saw that the Grand Fleet had gone;
all that remained in the anchorage were a few destroyers and
patrol boats, targets which he had previously ignored in the hope
of much bigger game. He saw a net boom between Hunda in
Burray and Roan Head in Flotta and though he guessed,
probably correctly, that he could have dived under it, he decided
that discretion was the better part of valour with no worthwhile
targets for him, and so at 11.20 a.m. he began the tricky
operation of getting himself out to the open sea again.

He saw two destroyers coming out through the boom and
thought that with nothing better on offer he might have a go at
them. But when he raised his periscope again to aim and fire his
torpedoes he found that the boot was on the other foot. He had
been spotted by the examination steamer *Tokio* on the way in
and now the whole patrol was looking for him.

He stayed submerged but had to come to periscope depth
from time to time in order to navigate his way out through the
tormented currents and rocky bottom of the Sound. For a time
he was lucky but he did it once too often, and a mile-and-a-
quarter off Hoxa Head he was rammed good and proper by
Minesweeper No. 96, which in peacetime was the Aberdeen
trawler *Dorothy Gray,* still commanded by her normal skipper,
Alex Youngson. *U 18* was thrown on her beam ends, her reserve
steering-gear put out of action and her periscope bent over at
right angles. Owing to the sharp-edged rocks on the bottom he
could not lie there and wait, so von Hennig was faced with the
almost impossible task of trying to get a blind and nearly
unmanageable submarine to the comparative safety of deep
water, with the patrol in full cry after him. He then hit a rock
about 160 feet below the surface. There was a loud crack and the
hull seemed to bend before he shot to the surface only to be
rammed for a second time by another minesweeper, the
Kaphreda. It was really just a nasty scrape on her upper deck,
and it was the hard cutting rocks of the Pentland Skerries which
administered the real *coup de grace.*

It was all over. The forepart of the submarine was in an
awful mess; some of the welding gave way and the propeller
crunched itself to a grating halt on the boulders of the seabed.
Von Hennig, to save the lives of his crew, blew the tanks and
surfaced. There were no ships anywhere near, so he hoisted a
white flag to attract attention. It was seen at the Brough Ness
Signal Station and duly reported. Two destroyers, *Garry* and
Erne, came up at full speed whereupon von Hennig gave the

order to scuttle; the seacocks were opened and *U 18* went down as the *Garry* came alongside. The crew had been on deck and took to the water as their vessel sank — three officers and 23 ratings were saved and taken prisoner. Only one man was drowned.

The lookout at Brough Ness was an Orkney Territorial, Robert Wilson, an employee of the Post Office who later became a Kirkwall Town Councillor. At a naval reunion dinner after the war he said that when he reported the *U 18* to naval HQ he was asked if he could tell the difference between a U-boat and a whale, to which he replied — 'Well, if it's a whale it's got 25 men standing on its back.'

Two more U-boats tried to force the Hoxa boom next day but the tides were too strong for *U 22* which had a defective engine; *U 16,* however, got far enough through to have a good look into the Flow but seeing no sign of the Grand Fleet retired without being spotted.

U 18 thus became the first, but by no means the last German warship to commit suicide in Orkney waters. Details as to just how she had been sunk were kept absolutely secret so that the enemy might be led to believe that her destruction was due to mines and nets which were, in fact, not in position there until some time later. The secrecy seems to have had the desired effect for there were few, if any, further direct attempts by U-boats to get into the Flow until near the end of the war, by which time of course, the defences were more than adequate to deal with that incursion. By the end of November 1914 considerable progress had been made on the defences. Two old battleships, *Hannibal* and *Magnificent,* had been anchored in positions to cover the Hoy and Hoxa entrances respectively as floating coastal batteries, as early as 10 August, while work went ahead to mount the 6-inch and 4-inch guns, some of them American, in the shore batteries at Hoxa, Stanger, Neb, Stromness and Holm. They were eventually manned under dual control by both the Orkney Territorials and the Royal Marine Reservists recalled to the Colours and commanded by Lieutenant Colonel N. A. Harris RMA.

The shore batteries were still apparently not complete by the spring of 1915 when the two old battleships were relieved and replaced by the equally old cruisers, *Crescent* and *Royal Arthur.*

In his book, *The Grand Fleet* written in 1919, Jellicoe, referring to the gun defences of Scapa, says that they were 'manned by Royal Marine personnel who had to endure considerable hardships in the early days'. When the book was published after the war this statement brought sharp criticism in the correspondence columns of 'The Orcadian' where several letters pointed out that the hardships were over by the time the Marines arrived.[13] Early hardships **were** endured but by the Orkney gunners who had to use cold, draughty shelters and who were billeted in old barns and so on. The writer of one letter said that Jellicoe had insulted the Orkney soldiers. When the Marines did arrive they found hutted accommodation waiting for them.

The editor of 'The Orcadian', who would have been James Mackintosh at this time, agreed in a footnote to the letter, saying that the Marines always enjoyed preferential treatment, probably due to the dual control by the War office and the Admiralty over the ORGA. There had been many grievances and he thought the Navy could well have provided the Orkney gunners with the same sort of stores as were provided for batteries going overseas. In one instance it had taken the Admiralty four years to provide even a stove for an army hut — something that would not have happened to a Marine unit.

An anonymous Marine replied, and while grudgingly admitting some delay over stores, pointed out that the Navy had mounted the guns and anyway 'old barns' would have been better than the leaky bell tents that some of the Marines had to put up with.

The Orkney gunner correspondent came back at him — the Navy might indeed have mounted the guns but it was the Orkney soldiers who had had to dig them in. What was more, the first time they were fired they almost jumped out of the ground, so badly were they mounted, and the Orkney men had to re-mount them all over again. This jumping of badly mounted guns had resulted in a number of the Orkney gun layers getting black eyes while sighting through telescopic sights, added the letter. There was obviously considerable ill-feeling between the Orkney gunners and the Navy about the manning of these coast defence batteries, although quite a few of the Marine officers were Orcadians who had transferred from the Army to the Navy.

Marines also had a grievance which surfaced after the war. In a letter to 'The Times' of London, one of them complained that service on the Scapa Flow defences did not qualify for the 1914-18 Medal or even the Victory Medal. They had done all they could, he wrote, to get away from Orkney for service elsewhere but to no avail, adding, 'It was not home service, it was banishment from home', so why should they be penalised?

It was the end of August, 1914, before the Admiralty at last approved the defences for the Flow and St Margaret's Hope became a subsidiary base, with as many as 2000 men engaged there at times on this work. The first anti-submarine obstructions were little more than buoys moored across the channels with herring nets strung between them and, even though they may have deceived some U-boat commanders such as von Hennig into thinking the entrances were adequately blocked, the weather and tides played havoc with them.

Work began on the more efficient steel nets, and blockships were sunk across the eastern channels during November. This operation was only partly successful. They were merchant ships, brought up to the Flow light and with no cement ballast. In the first place it was difficult to sink them in just the right spot with tides of up to eight or nine knots as in Holm Sound posing particular problems. It had to be done during the very brief intervals of slack water. Then, once they were in position, there was the danger of Orkney's very severe winter gales shifting them or even breaking them up.[14]

Nonetheless they were eventually positioned and became part of Orkney scenery right up until the more efficient Churchill Barriers were built in the Second World War. They were particularly conspicuous in Holm Sound where the graceful, if rusty, lines of ss *Thames* with her three masts, two funnels and clipper bow with its bowsprit, gave the impression that she was still afloat and sailing into Lamb Holm. She had, incidentally, at one time been commanded by Jellicoe's father.

Astern of her stretching towards the Holm shore were the *Minieh*, *Aorangi* and *Numidian*. Altogether, nineteen blockships were sunk in defence of Scapa in the first war, the cthers being *Teeswood*, *Elton*, *Rheinfeld*, *Almeria* and *Argyle* in Skerry Sound between Lamb Holm and Glims Holm; *Gartshore*, *Lapland* and *Reginald* in Weddel Sound between Glims Holm and Burray; and *Clio*, *Lorne* and *Pontos* in Water Sound between Burray and South Ronaldsay. On the other side of the Flow in Burra Sound, between Hoy and Graemsay, another five were sunk, *Budrie*, *Urmstone Grange*, *Ronda*, *Gobernador Bories* and *Rotherfield*. This left the three main entrances of Hoxa, Switha and Hoy Sounds to be closed by nets, buoys, booms and minefields, with 'gates' to permit the entry and exit of ships about their lawful occasions.

Many of these blockships were sunk more or less 'as they stood' by blowing their bottoms out so that they sank quickly to cheat the tides. With much of their furnishings and equipment still on board, they provided rich pickings for years to come. There must have been a number of houses round the Flow which owed quite a few of their furnishings and amenities to these ships. Quite a lot of the furnishings of the messes at the Holm Battery at Breckan came from the *Thames,* where it was quite possible to walk the decks and go below by the fine staircases at low water. And when peace came they were still able to yield valuable scrap for those with the courage and skill to go and get it.

The winter of 1914/15 brought bad weather with frequent and violent storms holding up defence works or, even worse, destroying them just after they had been completed. Even so, the Grand Fleet still used Scapa Flow occasionally although, in view of the U-boat scares, it had retired first to Loch Ewe on the west coast of Scotland, and later, after a submarine alarm there as well, to Lough Swilly in Northern Ireland and to Loch-na-Keal in Mull.[15] These harbours, of course, were manifestly too far away to keep 'the stopper firmly in the North Sea bottle' and Jellicoe was anxious to get back to Scapa as soon as it was safe.

Vice-Admiral Beatty, commanding the battlecruisers, did not scare easily but he too was obviously worried when he wrote to Churchill at the Admiralty saying that the menace of mines and U-boats was getting bigger every day.

'We are gradually being pushed out of the North Sea and off our particular perch,' he wrote, continuing '. . . we have no base where we can with *any* degree of safety, lie for replenishing, coaling and refitting, after two-and-a-half months of war. This spells trouble . . . The remedy is to fix upon a base and make it impervious to submarine attack.' He added: 'I think you know me well enough to know that I do not shout without cause. The Fleet's tail is still well over the back. We hate running away from our base and the effect is appreciable. We are not enjoying ourselves. But morale is high and confidence is higher.'

Beatty would probably have preferred Rosyth to Scapa, but the arguments were the same for either base.

News that something was at last moving came on 24 October when Battenburg telegraphed Jellicoe: 'The defences for Scapa will leave Dockyards 24 October.' It must have been one of the last signals he made to the C-in-C before he resigned as First Sea Lord at the end of the month in face of a virulent press and public smear campaign regarding his Teutonic ancestry — his father had been the Grand Duke of Hesse and his mother was Princess Alice, a daughter of Queen Victoria. He was a loyal British subject and he had spent his life following a brilliant career in the British Navy, but the stigma of a Germanic background played on by the press brought him down. He was succeeded by Lord 'Jacky' Fisher, now over seventy, who later claimed to have 'discovered' Scapa Flow in 1905.

The defence material mentioned in the signal may well have been on its way from the Dockyards, but there was still a long way to go before it was in position and the Fleet safe behind it — still, action was being taken and at the highest level.

On 2 November Churchill issued a list of decisions which had been taken by the Admiralty. These included the sending of 48 armed trawlers and three yachts with guns and radio to be placed at the disposal of the C-in-C Grand Fleet and they were to be at Scapa by 5 November; rafts and barges were to be fitted with anti-submarine nets and also sent to Scapa; 12 extra destroyers would join the Grand Fleet immediately; 12 armed merchant cruisers were to strengthen the Northern Patrol and were to be at Scapa within a week; the North of Scotland and the islands were to be a 'Prohibited Area' while parts of the adjacent North Sea were to be closed to all shipping other than that allowed by the Navy. Censorship of postal and telegraph offices was to be imposed within the Prohibited Area and lookouts would be posted at vantage points throughout.

Heavy booms for the anchorages were to be supplied without delay and lines of contact mines, electrically operated, were to be sent to Scapa Flow within ten days. Another light cruiser squadron was to be formed for the North Sea patrol work and eight light-draught vessels were to be converted for minesweeping and dispatched to the Grand Fleet as soon as possible. It was a typical Churchillian 'Action this day' edict.

All these items had been requested by Jellicoe, and obviously Churchill and the Admiralty had got the message very loud and clear. As the First Lord had stressed in a personal and private message to Jellicoe some time earlier: 'Every effort will be made to secure you rest and safety at Scapa . . . I wish to make absolute sanctuary for you there'.[16] He was as good as his word.

Owing to the exposed nature of Scapa Bay and its pier and with the storms of winter not far off, the Base was moved across to Longhope in October and its Headquarters established in and around the Longhope Hotel. It was to remain there for the rest of the war, the final move to Lyness taking place only in 1919. The Fleet moved too, its anchorage now being to the north of Flotta for the big ships and in Longhope itself and along the Hoy shore for the auxiliaries and smaller craft.[17]

The number of auxiliaries increased rapidly. On 1 September 1914 there were still virtually none apart from a few requisitioned drifters, but by the summer of 1915 they numbered four yachts, 85 trawlers and 27 drifters, and, as the base became safer with the Fleet spending more time in port, these numbers continued to grow.

Among the auxiliaries, besides the two repair ships *Cyclops* and *Assistance* which arrived at the outbreak of war, and the *Imperieuse*, which followed soon after, also as a depot ship, there was the Royal Fleet Auxiliary *Ruthenia,* which for a time had been disguised as a dummy battleship but which now relieved the *Imperieuse* by becoming storeship and HQ for the Victualling and Naval Stores Officer, while the Coaling Officer for the fleet took up quarters in the RFA *Perthshire* moored in Pegal Bay. The torpedo depot ship *Sokoto,* and the repair ship *Zaria,* which looked after the small craft, both lay in Longhope. The importance of these auxiliaries is reflected in the fact that RFA *Perthshire* and her attendant vessels handled four million tons of coal for the Fleet during the war; the *Imperieuse* sent off 42 million letters and parcels from lonely sailors and delivered 85 million letters to the various ships. Seafaring is hungry work and needed 320 tons of meat, 800 tons of potatoes, 6,000 bags of flour each weighing 140 lbs, 1,500 bags of sugar each of 120 lbs and 80,000 loaves of bread every month to satisfy these sharpened appetites.[18] The Victualling Officer was a very important man.

The Fleet did still use the Flow from time to time in those early days but always in some trepidation. On arrival the various ships prepared make-shift anti-U-boat measures by rapidly placing sections of rope-net detectors attached to buoys across Hoxa, Switha and Hoy Sounds, with armed trawlers detailed to watch each section. Jellicoe was disappointed at the slow progress of the permanent steel wire obstructions, although the increase in the number of trawlers relieved some of his hard-pressed destroyers from having to patrol the entrances.

There was a particularly bad three-day gale from 11 to 13 November when the Fleet, or most of it, was in the harbour. All defence work stopped and the ships lay with steam up for safety. They stayed in harbour for a few more days after the gale and for the first time during the war carried out gunnery and torpedo practice inside the Flow itself. Guns of up to six-inch calibre were used for both day and night firing, the start of a routine which proved very beneficial to the standard of proficiency in these branches of the service and which was continued from then on whenever the Fleet was in Scapa Flow.[19]

At this time the Grand Fleet numbered 26 battleships, four battlecruisers, eleven cruisers, five light cruisers, 30 destroyers, two armed merchant cruisers and five minesweeping gunboats.

Just a fortnight later, at the beginning of December 1914, they were caught by an even worse gale when, in spite of all ships having two anchors down, several dragged their moorings and all communication between ships was suspended, even by drifter. Several men were washed overboard and drowned. Even during this storm there was a U-boat alarm when one was sighted and engaged by patrols in Holm Sound, where she had presumably been sheltering. Torpedoes were also, it was said, 'exchanged'. She escaped to seaward, however, without damage.[20]

The gales continued and two cruisers were badly damaged in the Pentland Firth, the *Boadicea,* in which Jellicoe had arrived at Scapa to take over command of the Grand Fleet, lost her bridge and several of her crew, and the *Blanche* was also in trouble.[21]

Just before Christmas a report of a U-boat being in the Flow was shown 'not to be well-founded' but there was considerable concern a few days later when it was discovered that the Hoxa boom had been pierced. A search was made and small craft exploded charges on the seabed, a form of attack instituted in areas where U-boats had been reported and a forerunner of the depth-charges which took such a heavy toll of submarines later in the war.

Two days after Christmas the Grand Fleet returned to Scapa and had a very bad time of it, an exceptionally severe south-easterly gale making the entry through the narrow sounds not only difficult, but dangerous. With the wind dead astern fuel smoke obscured everything ahead and two battleships, *Monarch* and *Conqueror,* were rendered unseaworthy when they collided while trying to avoid a trawler in the darkness.[22] The Fourth Battle Squadron, led by the *Iron Duke,* decided to stand off until daylight and kept on westward through the Pentland Firth. The winter dawn came late and reluctantly in this murky weather, and turning the ships through 180 degrees in order to return to harbour proved extremely hazardous in the furious gale still blowing. As well as the two battleships which had been in collision, three destroyers had to go into dock for repairs to damage caused by the huge seas.

As far as weather was concerned, the new year started off no better than the old. It came in with a gale on New Year's Day which was followed by more from 16 to 19 January. Just to add a little variety there was a fog in February and two destroyers went aground in the North Isles — the *Goldfinch* ran ashore near Start Point in Sanday and became a total loss but the *Sparrowhawk* managed to refloat herself.[23] U-boats continued to be active all round the coast but none penetrated the growing defences, although one was reported in Hoy Sound but not found after a search by patrol craft. And to facilitate reporting of U-boats in the Pentland Firth area Swona was connected to Base by telephone.

Following the shelling of English east coast ports by German warships in early 1915 and what some critics thought was a lack of initiative by the British in the Battle of Dogger Bank on 24 January, the Navy was not in very good odour in the country. It was felt that our ships should at least have headed off these raids and preferably have sunk more German ships. There was a feeling that Scapa was too remote for the Grand Fleet to be able to intercept such forays. Both Churchill and Fisher were in favour of bringing the Fleet to the Forth where Beatty's battle-cruisers were already based, or even as far south as the Humber. Jellicoe did not agree. Scapa was his chosen base and all he wanted was to get his fleet there as soon as it was secure. The Forth, he pointed out, could be easily closed by mines or bad weather — much more easily than the Flow. Moreover, the Fleet could get to sea much more quickly from the Flow than from the Forth, quite apart from the advantages Scapa held for training and exercises. He had his way and Scapa remained the main fleet base.

But the Orkney climate showed no gratitude for his faith in the Flow and the early part of April brought a week of fierce gales with fog and snow later — a typical Orkney spring, in fact, which must have done much to inspire such literary efforts as the 'Scapa Hymn of Hate' from ratings cooped up in the anchored ships, for the Fleet was now in Scapa much more often, especially after May when the second line of submarine obstructions advanced considerably towards completion. This second line was designed to prevent the entry of hostile destroyers as well as such submarines as might succeed in piercing the first line of booms and nets.

On the west side of the Flow the first anti-submarine defences were double lines of drifters moored to nets, one line stretching from Houton to Cava and the other from the Orphir shore to Hoy. These were later reinforced by 'barriers of steel' from Clestrain to Graemsay. This barrier, composed of steel girders or hurdles assembled at Ness near Stromness, was started in 1915 and completed the following year. After the war there was considerable trouble in removing it, the icebreakers *Sviator, Solatoga* and *Alexandra* being brought up in late 1919 and early 1920 to crush the barrier sufficiently to allow ships to pass over it. The girders were cleared later and shipped south for scrap.[23]

To increase the security of the Flow still further, minefields were now laid in 1915 — the 'Observation' minefield off Hoy Sound being completed by June. As a result, the Grand Fleet spent much longer periods at Scapa carrying out extensive gunnery and torpedo training as well as coaling, victualling, maintenance and all the other routine harbour activities.

The first phase of converting this great stretch of grey water between its sheltering belt of islands into an armed camp and fortress was over. The Grand Fleet at last began to feel safe in its harbour, for was it not the great Nelson himself who had been quoted as saying '. . . any sailor who attacks a fort is a fool'. The British hoped that the German Navy knew that dictum and had taken it to heart.

CHAPTER 10

Welcome Visitors

WITH THE WAR now nearing the end of its first year, and the Grand Fleet safer in its northern fastness under the hazy blue skies and softer winds of summer, a little of the grim tension of the earlier winter days relaxed, even if the vigilance did not. It was now reluctantly admitted that the war would last a long time; the deadlock on the Western Front and in Gallipoli made that clear. The hopeful sentiment of August 1914 that 'it'll all be over by Christmas' had taken a severe knock long since. The probability now had to be accepted that these great ships, their companies totalling many thousands of men wrenched from their homes, families and familiar amenities of life, would be in this bleak and often hostile environment of Scapa Flow for many more months, perhaps even years, to come. It has been said by someone who must have known all about it that 'war is long periods of extreme boredom interspersed by moments of intense fright'. That was very true for the Navy at Scapa Flow in World War I.

The 'fright' part of it could be controlled by training and discipline, but what about the boredom of being cooped up in the confined mess-decks of a warship swinging round and round her moorings with little to relieve the monotony except the occasional patrol or North Sea sweep? As early as February 1915 Jellicoe had expressed concern at the lack of recreational facilities at Scapa and had instituted a system of sending ships down to Invergordon periodically, where, although it was still isolated, there was more opportunity for recreation ashore, it having been a naval base rather longer than Scapa Flow.

Football pitches were established at Longhope and on Flotta and the long-projected naval golf course did actually come into being, not at the Bu Sands of Burray as had been envisaged in peacetime but on Flotta near Roan Head.[1] Jellicoe himself used to play here when time permitted and so did Beatty, and in any case, the course was in sight of the flagships should an emergency blow up and the Fleet have to put to sea. King George V told the then Provost of Stromness J. G. Marwick at a

Holyrood Garden Party in the thirties that he had played golf there too with Jellicoe during one of his visits.

A later addition to the auxiliary fleet, and a welcome one, was the ss *Borodino* which had an arrangement with the Army & Navy Stores then in Lower Regent Street, London for supplies. Prices, as a rule, were lower than in London and the ship had an annual turnover of £50,000, a big sum in those days.

On one particular day there were as many as 2,700 officers and men on board at one time or another from the various ships of the Fleet anchored nearby. A frequent customer was Prince Albert, serving in the battleship *Collingwood* 'and known just as Mr Johnstone — later still, of course, he was better known as King George VI. Whether he was one of the buyers of the thousand pots of honey sold on one single day is not recorded but it is unlikely that he shared the American sailors' taste for raw kippers and jam together when their ships joined the Grand Fleet in 1917.

The *Borodino* had other facilities as well, including a small theatre, billiard tables, a laundry, barber's shop and so on. A frozen-meat ship, ss *Gourko,* later became a theatre ship in the Flow with full stage facilities and the auditorium just above the refrigeration deck, so there was plenty of excuse for any of the perfomers who got cold feet when their turn came to face the footlights.[2]

Gardening also became a popular pastime with some of the sailors, providing the opportunity of getting ashore to work their plots as well as supplying the galley with welcome fresh vegetables. Hens, too, were kept and there was said to be at least one instance of a pig being fattened to grace the mess tables in due course.

For most of the war up till now the whereabouts of the Grand Fleet had been shrouded in a good deal of mystery as far as the general public was concerned. And it was hoped the Germans would also be mystified as to where the ships actually were — but this was rather much to hope for, as the frequent U-boat probes round Orkney demonstrated only too well. These probes had, of course, kept the Fleet on the move. But now in midsummer 1915 it could pause to draw breath, and indeed breathe more freely behind its reasonably secure defences in Scapa Flow.

Visitors, official and welcome, rather than those who came in U-boats, began to travel north to see this massive display of Britain's naval might and the men who were the most important part of it.

One of the first to come was the Archbishop of York, Dr

Cosmo Lang, who later became Archbishop of Canterbury, and it was, as far as is known, the first time an Archbishop of the Anglican Church had ever set foot in Orkney. He arrived on 26 June and held a Fleet Confirmation Service in the Flagship, *Iron Duke,* as well as conducting great open-air services in Flotta and Longhope, attended by many thousands of sailors. He also visited quite a few individual ships during his short stay, in addition to dedicating the Anglican part of the Naval Cemetery at Lyness.[3]

That same summer of 1915 saw another ecclesiastical visit to the Fleet in the Flow, this time by the Moderator of the General Assembly of the Church of Scotland, the Very Reverend Dr. Wallace Williamson. He was accompanied by the Reverend Norman Maclean, Minister of St Cuthbert's in Edinburgh, and together they went out to the Fleet in a drifter, the significance of whose name would not have escaped their notice. She was the *Jenny Geddes* named after the celebrated, or should it be notorious, Edinburgh lady of strong Presbyterian convictions who one Sunday in the 17th Century threw her stool at the head of Dean Hanna in St Giles Cathedral when he tried to introduce the English form of prayer in the service, with the objuration — 'Dost thou say the mass at my lug?' Dr Williamson also performed a Dedication Service at Lyness Cemetery and later preached in St Magnus Cathedral in Kirkwall.

Commenting on the visit in 'The Orcadian' and emphasising the growing efficiency of radio, Norman Maclean had no doubt as to the importance of Scapa Flow when he wrote:

And through the air from all the seas there came ceaseless messages to a room where the brain of the Fleet controls it all. It is that telegraph of the air which has transposed the centre of the world's mightiest empire. That centre is no longer London — it is now in the circuit of lonely isles, desolate and rockbound. Did the nerve-centre here fail — the Empire would pass as the baseless fabric of a dream.[4]

Shortly after this, on 7 July, the Grand Fleet had its first royal visitor in Scapa, King George V, himself a former naval officer who had intended to make the Navy his career until the death of his older brother made him next in the line of succession to the Throne, forcing him to leave the sea in order to concentrate on affairs of state. He had previously been in Orkney in 1898 when commanding the cruiser *Crescent,* which now, in World War I, was guard ship covering Hoy Sound until the shore batteries became operational.

This time he was met at Thurso by his son Prince Albert
and Admiral Colville, ACOS, a former shipmate, and they
crossed to Scapa in the destroyer *Oak,* the Commander-in-
Chief's despatch boat, with an escort from the Second Flotilla.
At Hoxa they were met by the C-in-C, Admiral Jellicoe, who
came on board while they steamed round the 11 miles of booms
and their attendant trawlers.[5] 'I then inspected the fleet by
steaming between the lines,' the King wrote in his diary that
night, 'Each ship cheered as we passed, splendid sight, but it was
cold and overcast with NE breeze which was a pity.'

After visiting the hospital ship *Drina* where Prince Albert
was soon to go for observation, 'as he has not been quite the
thing', the King landed at Longhope where he was greeted by
Colville and his staff. He inspected the officers and men of
destroyers, trawlers, store ships and dockyardmen who were
drawn up 'on the road to his [Colville's] house and they cheered
at the end. I am staying with Colville, his house is quite
comfortable, it was a small inn. Bertie [Prince Albert] is staying
here too,' wrote the King in his diary. Colville's 'house' was, in
fact, the Longhope Hotel.

Next day, Thursday 8 July, he went out to the *Iron Duke*
where he was received by Jellicoe and 'all his Admirals'. He
went on to the *Emperor of India* (Adm. Duff), *Benbow* (Adm.
Sturdee), *St Vincent* (Adm. Evan Thomas), *Marlborough* (Adm.
Cecil Burney) where he lunched, *Collingwood* (Captain Ley,
Prince Albert's ship), *Defence* (Adm. Sir R. Arbuthnot),
Shannon (Adm. Calthorpe) and *Agincourt* (Captain Nicholson)
where he had tea. In his diary he wrote, 'Onboard each flagship
all the officers and men, not only of the flagships, but of their
respective divisions marched past me on the quarter deck.
Everything was beautifully arranged, I must have seen close on
20,000 men. I also walked round some of the ships when there
was time. Got back to Longhope at 6.30, a distinctly long but
interesting day. The spirit of the fleet is splendid. Dined onboard
Iron Duke with Commander in Chief at 8.30. 26 at dinner
including 11 Admirals.'

Friday 9 July started off with something unusual for the
Longhope Hotel — an investiture. The King's diary records:
'Gave Cecil [Adm. Colville] the GCVO [Grand Cross of the
Victorian Order] after breakfast.' They then left Longhope in the
Oak and visited Stanger Head Battery in Flotta, landing in the
geo below the guns which was still known as King's Hard in
World War II.

He had seen his old command, the *Crescent,* and then, on
Flotta, inspected officers and men of the light cruisers, attached

cruisers, minesweepers, sloops and destroyers of the Second and Fourth Flotillas, 4,550 of whom were on parade. After lunch on board the *King George V* there was a march-past of her officers and men along with those of *Ajax* and *Centurion* which, he wrote in his diary, 'was beautifully arranged with massed bands playing'. On to *Orion, Monarch* and *Conqueror* where 'unfortunately it came on to rain and blow rather hard, but it did not damp their spirits'. Finally he boarded the *Queen Elizabeth* which had been in action in the Dardanelles, being hit 17 times but with no casualties; then the *Benbow* again for tea before saying farewell to Jellicoe and the Vice-Admirals. He left Scapa in the *Oak,* again accompanied by Bertie and Colville, sailing through the Fleet which manned ship and cheered as they passed and he wrote: 'It was a great success in every way, I saw over 35,000 men in two days and the spirit of both officers and men is splendid. We had an escort of destroyers . . .'[6]

A month later his eldest son, Edward, Prince of Wales, later to be briefly Edward VIII before his abdication, spent a week in the Flow staying with Admiral Colville at Longhope and visiting many of the ships lying at anchor.[7] He, too, of course, had trained as a naval officer.

Prince Albert, his younger brother who became George VI, did not enjoy good health while serving in the *Collingwood* at Scapa. Shortly after arriving in the Flow at the beginning of the war he was transferred to the hospital ship *Rohilla* lying at Wick, with suspected appendicitis. Intelligence reports indicated that the German fleet might be putting to sea at this time, so *Rohilla* with Prince Albert on board still under observation was sent to Scapa with a destroyer escort, to take patients from the sick bays of the fighting ships in the event of their going into battle. She then sailed to Aberdeen on Jellicoe's orders so that Prince Abert could undergo the necessary operation in a hospital ashore. In the meantime *Collingwood* was engaged in the Battle of Heligoland Bight which the Prince thus missed, to his great disappointment.

When his father, George V, visited Scapa in July 1915 Albert was back aboard *Collingwood* and, indeed, went across to Thurso to meet his father. Shortly afterwards he was taken to the hospital ship *Drina,* which was lying in Longhope; he did not return to seagoing service in his old ship, *Collingwood,* for nearly a year, rejoining her on 5 May 1916 less than a month before she went into action at Jutland.[8]

Rather less exalted but still important were the visitors on 2 September described by Jellicoe in his book as 'five French gentlemen of eminence and a representative of the United States

Press'. The French party included journalists as well as politicians. After visiting several ships, including the flagship, they watched as the Fleet put to sea on one of its sweeps — a very impressive sight, as recorded by the American war correspondent, Frederick Palmer. This was the first time the Grand Fleet had been visited by anyone not directly concerned with it, a first step in what we now call Public Relations.[9]

Some other Americans, not quite so welcome, also visited, or rather, called in at Orkney later in the year on board the specially chartered 'Peace ship', Oscar II. Heading the party was the famous millionaire motor-car manufacturer of Model T fame, Henry Ford himself, who had conceived this self-imposed 'Peace Mission' to warring Europe — the United States, of course, was still neutral at this time. The Oscar II was passed through Kirkwall contraband control like any other neutral vessel but none of the party was allowed to land. Their departure from the United States had been extensively covered by the Press but by the time they reached Oslo, their first main neutral port of call, all the 'peace delegates' had fallen out among themselves and were at one another's throats in a most unpeaceful manner. It was generally looked on as a ship-load of pro-German stop-the-war-at-any-price cranks. Nothing more was heard of them.[10]

But all was not peace and quietness by any means in this second northern summer of the war. The U-boat menace outside the Flow was ever-present. Just before the King's visit, for instance, no fewer than sixteen fishing-boats were sunk by gunfire from a U-boat off Shetland. The conventions of war at sea, however, were strictly observed by the German Commander and all the crews were allowed to take to the boats before he opened fire. There were no casualties.[11]

Just before this the 2000-ton ss Iona had been sunk by U-boat gunfire off Orkney, along with two trawlers. There were no fatalities but the crew, including a Burray man, James Petrie, Chief Officer of the Iona, were twenty hours in their open boats before being landed at Kirkwall. Three more trawlers were sunk in the area two days later, while the 'North' boat, St Clair, tried unsuccessfully to ram a U-boat off Fair Isle.[12] And at the end of July an American and a Russian ship as well as several trawlers were sunk off the west coast of Orkney. Again there appear to have been no casualties and the Russians were landed at Birsay.

There were no casualties either on 10 July when the Kirkwall-registered schooner Sunbeam, owned by the Finstown merchant W. B. Firth and skippered by Captain W. Moodie, also of Finstown, was sunk by a submarine off Wick.[13] Besides the skipper the crew were William Laird, Burray, Robert Walls,

Finstown and James Seatter, Westray. All of them reached land safely, having been given five minutes to clear the schooner in their lifeboat before the submarine opened fire, and they certainly 'lived to fight another day' and to have their revenge.

The *Sunbeam,* on a normal trading trip on this occasion, was about to be taken over by the Admiralty for what was rather vaguely described as 'special service'. All four of the ship's company had volunteered to go with her to the Navy. But that was not to be — not in the *Sunbeam.* The Navy did, however, give Captain Moodie and his crew another ship 'for operations in the North Sea'. It was about this time in 1915 that the idea of 'Q' ships was born and tried out, in and from Scapa Flow.[14] This scheme was to produce an innocent-looking merchant ship carrying concealed equipment that was anything but innocent — guns. These usually rather dilapidated vessels went to sea, often alone, hoping to lure a U-boat to the surface. Then with the crew exhibiting every sign of panic as they took to the boats the U-boat would close to point-blank range, only to find that it was point-blank range too for the gun crew left concealed on board the 'doomed' merchantman. But they had to be quick and accurate in getting the first round off before the submarine, for unless the German was holed within a minute she could dive for safety and escape or even torpedo the 'Q' ship.

Five of these 'Q' ships, colliers or store ships for the most part, were operating from Scapa by the end of the year, having been developed, disguised and fitted out by Captain Farrington of the repair ship *Cyclops.* Manned by volunteers from the Fleet there was never any shortage of crews for this arduous and dangerous work in the stormy waters round Orkney, Shetland, the Western Isles, or on the routes to neutral Norway or the White Sea used regularly by normal merchantmen, the appearance of the 'Q' ships being adapted accordingly to look like one of the regular ships. The five Scapa 'Q' ships were the *Prince Charles, Vala, Duncombe, Penhurst* and *Glen Isla* and they had to steam many weary sea miles often in heavy weather with only the occasional chance of engaging a U-boat.

But the first successful 'Q' ship 'kill' did fall to one of these Scapa-based vessels, the *Prince Charles* under the naval command of Lieutenant W. P. Mark-Wardlow RN, a member of Admiral Colville's ACOS staff at Longhope.[15] Cruising west of Orkney on 28 July 1915 they sighted a neutral Danish ship, the *Louise,* hove-to near North Rona with a U-boat on the surface close by.

Observing this more inviting quarry, the submarine left the *Louise* and made for the *Prince Charles,* opening fire at 5,000 yards. The 'Q' ship stopped engines and went into the 'panic' routine, the crew hastily lowering the boats and pulling away with every sign of fright. The submarine, *U 36,* closed to within 300 yards, still on the surface, when the *Prince Charles* revealed her true character and the Germans, for a few brief seconds, found themselves staring down the business ends of two 6-pounders and two 3-pounder guns just before they opened an accurate and deadly fire, holing the submarine and killing two men on the conning-tower. She was unable to dive and sank stern first, the surviving three officers and twelve ratings being saved by the *Prince Charles.*

It was later claimed that Captain Robert Maxwell RNR of the Merchant Navy had actually been Master of the *Prince Charles* at the time and that Lieut. Mark-Wardlow was the RN officer in charge of fighting the ship, taking over when the U-boat was sighted.

The 'Q' ship idea, which in actual fact had only limited success, was further developed in the south and in the Western Approaches, as well as in the North Sea. One of these 'Q' ships was entrusted to Captain Moodie when his own *Sunbeam* was sunk — she was the *Probus,* renamed the *Ready,* and was the first sailing vessel to be commissioned by the Admiralty in World War I. She did, in fact, operate in the North Sea throughout the latter part of 1915 and 1916, but never caught a glimpse of a U-boat. Then she was moved to Cornwall and her luck changed. On 23 June 1917 with Captain Moodie at the helm she was escorting a convoy out of Falmouth when a U-boat, rigged as a ketch, was sighted sailing on a parallel course to that of the convoy. And there was yet another U-boat just out of range of the *Ready's* four-inch gun. So Capt. Moodie and his crew, consisting of Orcadians — Robert Walls, Finstown; James Seatter, Powdykes, Westray; George Rendall, Shoreside, Firth and John Sinclair, Shore Street, Kirkwall — opened fire on the nearer U-boat, a total of 60 or 70 rounds being exchanged before the submarine was holed and sank.

Three of the Orkney crew had been on the *Sunbeam* when she was sent to the bottom off Wick two years before — Capt. Moodie, who was awarded the Distinguished Service Cross, Peter Walls and James Seatter. They were revenged.

Capt. Moodie and his crew, incidentally, were later transferred to the 456-ton wooden three-masted schooner *Baron Rose,* armed with two six-pounders, two 4-inch guns and two bomb-throwers for operations in the North Sea but without encountering any more U-boats although they had exciting times occasionally, as when, in atrocious weather, two of the crew were washed overboard by tremendous seas — and then, happily, washed back on board again.

Between the wars, through World War II and afterwards into the uneasy peace, Captain Moodie was the highly respected Master of the ss *Amelia* carrying cargo between Leith and Kirkwall, a familiar figure on her bridge as she sailed prompt at 8 p.m. every Monday night from Kirkwall Pier.

'Q' ships, however, were not the only unconventional methods tried out to combat the U-boat menace during 1915. In July the trawler *Princess Louise* (Lieut. Morton RNR) steamed out of the Flow towing the British submarine *C 27* (Lieut. Cmdr. Dobson RN), the two vessels being linked by telephone.[16] Out at sea the trawler sighted an enemy submarine, *U 23,* one-and-a-half miles on the port bow. Her towed submarine was informed of the sighting over the phone link which then, as so often happens with phone links, broke down. But *C 27* was already submerged when the U-boat opened fire on the *Princess Louise,* having closed to 2,000 yards. The tow was slipped and the trawlermen, like the 'Q' ships crews, went into the 'abandon ship with haste' routine.

U 23 closed still further to 600 yards, by which time the British submarine had cleared the trawler and came to periscope depth, sighting the U-boat at 900 yards which was quickly reduced to 500 when the first torpedo was fired. Unfortunately it missed but the second did not, scoring a direct hit and the U-boat went down after a heavy explosion — only four officers and six men out of a total crew of 34 were picked up.

Innovations were not all on the British side, of course. *U 19,* for instance, lay off the eastern openings to the Flow for nearly a week in the middle of November 1915, watching and recording the Navy's patrol routine, for it was planned to drop 'clockwork' mines of a new type so that they would be carried through Water Sound by the tide, ending up, the Germans hoped, among the anchored ships of the Grand Fleet. Nothing seems to have come of the long reconnaissance, however, perhaps due to bad weather. But the commander of *U 19,* had he known, could have sailed into the Flow without let or hindrance at that time, for the same bad weather had so damaged the booms that the channel into the harbour was completely open for a time.

U-boats, it will be seen, were on an almost continuous prowl round Orkney in this second year of the war, but they were having to pay an increasingly heavy price for any success they achieved. Apart from these unconventional anti-submarine measures, the defence of Scapa relied heavily and mainly on the conventional defences of nets, buoys, blockships and minefields as well as shore batteries with attendant warning devices like magnetic indicator loops and, later on, hydrophones, for detecting unwelcome visitors.

The loops were cables lying on the seabed of the channels leading to the Flow, like Hoxa and Switha Sounds, and as the vessel passed over them the ship's magnetic field energised a galvanometer ashore. As soon as the intruder was indicated in this way, it was only a matter of waiting until another flick of the dial showed that he had entered the controlled minefield which could be exploded by pressing the appropriate button in the shore control room — and that was the end of that U-boat.

The hydrophones were devices which picked up the sound of a submerged submarine's engines and propellers giving warning of its approach. These came later and were sited at Stanger Head in Flotta, Hoxa Head and other points covering the approaches.

But the crucial element of the defences was eternal vigilance, an essential part of which was the patrol system for the Pentland Firth area. This comprised three armed boarding steamers, for surface craft as well as U-boats posed a potential threat, and three destroyers in addition patrolled east and north of the Pentland Firth by day, working far out to the south-east at night.

An extended patrol, usually of one light cruiser and one destroyer, worked out and north of Peterhead, with two destroyers off Noss Head in the Moray Firth at night. Destroyers were also kept at sea on constant watch off Hoy Sound and Holm Sound, while a large number of trawlers operated in and near Hoxa Sound. In bad weather, and it was not uncommon, the destroyer patrol on the east side was withdrawn to work from Swona out to the east and the north-west.[17] This was the moving seaborne screen which any marauding U-boat or surface craft had to brave and penetrate before it had any hope of getting near the harbour gates, then only to find these now securely barred and locked by nets, mines, guns and searchlights. It is not surprising that none succeeded in forcing an entry.

CHAPTER 11

Out To Battle

ALMOST AS implacable an enemy as the U-boat was the northern weather with its screaming winter gales or summer fogs. On one occasion it took the battleship *Agincourt* 36 hours to get into the safety of the Flow from Cape Wrath only about 60 miles away but they were 60 miles of dense fog in a tormented tideway — and there was no radar to help them in those days. Another battleship, *Ajax,* had to cruise around in the fog for twelve hours before it was clear enough to come through Hoxa Sound — not a very healthy way of passing the time in these U-boat-infested waters. But as 1915 shivered its way towards 1916 the main trouble was wind, including a four-day storm which played havoc with the anti-submarine defences, severely damaging many of the newly-installed steel nets. It also cut the rail communication with the south when a landslide, caused by heavy rain, carried away part of the Highland line between Thurso and Inverness.

By this time a regular special train ran nightly between London and Thurso in both directions, carrying mail and personnel. Almost inevitably it earned itself the unofficial name of the 'Jellicoe Special' — a name which stuck and was carried over to a similar train running the same service in World War II. The First War 'Special' was claimed by the railway authorities of the time as '. . . the longest distance train ever run in the British Islands and probably the most punctual'. During the Second War one of its coaches was a venerable dining-car — a real museum piece staffed by the Salvation Army providing welcome hot meals for weary and hungry Servicemen during the eighteen-hour journey to or from the ships at Scapa or the lonely windswept batteries that defended them.

After the 'Jellicoe' journey north, of course, the Service passengers, mainly navymen in World War I, had to transfer to the much more unstable ss *St Ninian,* one of the North of Scotland Orkney and Shetland Steam Navigation Company's steamers requisitioned by the Navy from her normal Leith, Aberdeen, Kirkwall and Lerwick peacetime run. Though not the acme of seagoing luxury, she carried 374,875 passengers safe if sometimes seasick across the Pentland Firth to the Flow, as well as 450,000 sacks of mail and £9 million in cash to pay the men of the Grand Fleet. Altogether between 1 August 1915 when the Navy took her over and 7 May 1919 when she was 'demobbed', she made 1002 crossings of the Firth — and she came back and did it again in the Second War.

As winter drew on and nights became longer the Navy was faced with another problem in addition to the weather and U-boat probes. The German minelayer *Meteor,* disguised as a neutral merchantman, succeeded in sowing a large and deadly minefield in the Moray Firth where it menaced ships sailing between Invergordon and Scapa. Fortunately it was discovered before it had time to do much damage and was swept without any serious casualtes. It was, however, a warning of what could happen.[1]

There were more gales for two days at the end of October and again the submarine defences suffered — it was to be a never-ending task to keep and maintain their efficiency. This time some of the blockships were shifted and damaged too.[2]

The weather was relentless. A week later during the first week of November yet another gale of westerly wind met the ebb tide in the Pentland Firth, piling up a savage sea in that stretch of perpetually troubled water.

On the night of 6/7 November at the height of the storm three battleships, *Hibernia, Zealandia* and *Albemarle,* were passing through the Firth, heading west for ports in the south of England and the Mediterranean. But they did not make it. The *Albemarle* was struck by two massive seas, one of which carried away her forebridge and everyone on it and it even displaced the armoured roof of the conning-tower. Hundreds of tons of water flooded the decks and cascaded below, washing overboard one officer and one rating, both of whom were drowned, while Captain Nugent found himself on the upper deck surrounded by wreckage. The *Hibernia* which had been leading went about to go to the *Albemarle's* assistance and in a remarkable feat of seamanship managed to take her in tow in the hostile darkness of the storm-rent night. At dawn she brought the stricken ship into Scapa through the Hoxa Boom. Jellicoe writing of the incident said — 'The ship presented a remarkable sight, the sea having made a clean sweep of her bridge and everything on it. In all our experience of the Pentland Firth, we had never witnessed such havoc before.'[3] The *Zealandia* also sustained damage which, while not so severe, forced her to turn back.

Some years later Midshipman L. Luard, who was on board

Albemarle at the time, described what he saw when he got on deck after the ship had been struck by these massive waves:

> The bridge had gone. In its place a heap of bent and twisted wreckage lay stark and naked — battered and contorted beyond belief. The beams of searchlights (from the other ships) swept the ship, picked out here the upward muzzle of a dismounted twelve pounder, there the remains of a boat, revealing a smashed-in funnel, a dented lower fighting top, huge stanchions twisted and buckled like pliable wire, searchlights smashed to smithereens.[4]

It was not only mines and submarines the Navy had to contend with.

A month later, however, the Pentland Firth, in a quieter mood, was chosen for big-gun target practice, an experiment which proved successful and which became routine not only in the First War but also in the Second. It was found to be more convenient for the Fleet than the Moray Firth and not so many escorting vessels were needed. All the same — a weather eye had always to be kept open.[5]

January 1916 was marked by almost continuous bad weather which did not, however, prevent the 4,700-ton German raider *Möwe* — like the *Meteor* previously, sailing under false neutral colours — from laying an extensive minefield in the western approaches to the Pentland Firth stretching from Cape Wrath to Strathie Point in Caithness, almost on the doormat of the Grand Fleet's wartime home. The operation was probably aided by the fact that Cape Wrath and Suleskerry lighthouses were both lit on the night of 1/2 January because of mercantile traffic in the area, so enabling the *Möwe* to get an accurate fix.

It was not long before one of these mines claimed a victim, and an important one, the pre-dreadnought battleship *King Edward VII* on passage to Belfast for a refit. Her engine-room filled and she developed a severe list to starboard but a collier, the *Melita* and the destroyer *Kempenfelt* took her in tow while other destroyers and tugs were rushed from Scapa to her aid. But the tow parted in heavy weather and Captain Maclachan decided to abandon ship as darkness fell and she was then very low in the water. Four destroyers took her crew off safely and later that night she turned over and sank. Ironically, several other ships had passed through the Firth that day without mishap, but all further movement of shipping in the area was stopped until the mines could be swept and this took some time being held up by the almost incessant bad weather.[6]

The *Möwe*, incidentally, stayed at sea for a further two months after laying the minefield, preying on shipping in the South Atlantic before returning to Germany unscathed, evading the British patrols for the second time, posing as a Swedish merchant ship.

Under her commander, Count Zu Dohna-Schlodien, she made an even more extended foray out past the north of Scotland in November of that same year, staying out in the Atlantic until March 1917, sinking or capturing 27 ships before once again slipping through the Northern Patrol back to Germany. She could carry 300 mines and was armed with four 5.9-inch guns and four 19.7-inch torpedo tubes.

The bad weather which held up the sweeping of the *Möwe's* minefield included an 80 mph north-westerly gale which caused a lot of trouble inside the Flow as well. The oiler *Prudentia* dragged her moorings, drifting across the bows of the flagship *Iron Duke* and later sinking, while an ammunition ship, a store-carrier, a tug and three trawlers all broke adrift and went ashore. Further north, three ships of the hard-worked and hard-pressed Northern Patrol were also damaged by the heavy seas on their grim beat between Shetland and Norway. The *Prudentia* still lies where she sank off Flotta, close to the pipeline across the Flow bringing North Sea oil to Occidental's oil terminal.

Jellicoe reported — 'Great injury was done to all the anti-submarine defences at Scapa, many of them being entirely destroyed.' So the Grand Fleet was once again vulnerable to U-boat attack in its base though the bad weather must also have been a big deterrent to any U-boat commander. The Fleet was directed to make and lay improvised net obstructions until the damage could be made good.[7]

The weather had at least improved slightly for the visit on 1 March of a party of distinguished Russians including Count Alexis Tolstoy. Russia, of course, was still one of the Allies and at war with Germany, although the Revolution was soon to alter all that.

By now the Grand Fleet had increased considerably in strength and numbers with the attendant problem of how to get anything up to a hundred vessels of all sizes and speeds safely and quickly to sea when the need arose. So many ships together in narrow waters presented an excellent target for U-boats, quite apart from the hazards posed by weather, tides and darkened ships at night. A drill was worked out by the C-in-C's Staff which made it possible for the whole fleet to be under way within an hour-and-a-half after the signal to proceed to sea was made. This period was increased to two hours on dark nights.

First of all a 'Prepare to leave Scapa' signal consisting of just one code word was made. On this all ships raised steam for 18 knots at two hours notice — for, of course, steam-driven vessels could not just start up at once like a motor car or a diesel-driven ship — and all preparations were made for leaving harbour. A second signal gave the order in which squadrons were to sail, speed to be maintained after clearing the booms, and the interval between squadrons, usually one mile from the rear ship of one formation to the leader of the next, but this was increased to two miles at night. Provision was also made for squadrons to pass alternately north and south of the Pentland Skerries when going east into the North Sea.

This was the tricky part of the operation. If the tide was setting west, the ships did not feel its full impact of anything up to ten knots at the Springs until they cleared Swona. After that it was quite possible for a leading division or squadron to be brought back on to the one following it. Even worse, a ship emerging from the slack water into the full strength of the tide could be, and sometimes was, caught on the bow by the force of the fast-moving water, to be swung round through 90 or even 180 degrees so that she was heading back the way she had come, an extreme danger to all following vessels as she could be nearly unmanageable. Great care was needed to avoid this danger and as Jellicoe wrote — 'Such a situation on a dark night with a large fleet showing no lights, was not pleasant and it speaks well for the skill shown in handling the ships that no accident occurred from this cause.'

Destroyers accompanying the Fleet met it just outside the booms and screened it in daylight or fell in astern at night until they could take up screening positions at dawn.

Outside the Skerries there were three well-defined routes at seven miles apart, with the strongest squadron taking the most easterly where it was anticipated the greater danger of attack lay.

Returning to Scapa the leading squadron was usually timed to pass the Skerries shortly before dawn with the Fleet normally in two lines astern five miles apart, the squadrons having three miles between them. These two lines would pass on either side of the Skerries in order to confuse any lurking U-boat and also to get the ships through the booms as quickly as possible. Once in the tideway it was believed there was little danger of attack.

If the Fleet came in at night, the ships anchored in the middle of the Flow and waited until daylight before going to their proper moorings. Later on, a system of leading lights made it possible for the ships to proceed immediately to their buoys even in the dark.

Before the Fleet entered or left the Flow an exploratory search was always made of the three main routes that might be used, one on the east side of Orkney, one running east from the Pentland Skerries and one down the east side of the Scottish coast through the Moray Firth. Normally, the one, ten miles wide running east from the Skerries was used, but in really dense fog only the direst emergency would persuade the Fleet to put to sea at all.[8]

One of these 'direst emergencies' certainly occurred towards the end of May 1916 but fortunately neither fog in the Firth nor darkness in the Flow prevented the ships from putting to sea — there is never more than twilight from mid-May to mid-July in these northern latitudes.

For nearly two years now the great ships of Britain's Grand Fleet had swung round and round their Scapa moorings waiting for their powerful adversary, the German High Seas Fleet, to come out from Kiel, the Jade and Wilhelmshaven and make a fight of it — the great clash of naval might which, it was believed, would shorten the conflict now bogged down in the static trench warfare of the Western Front. And the Grand Fleet was confident of victory, for Britain was, and always had been, a seafaring nation on which its naval tradition and supremacy had been built. Germany did not have these advantages. Her navy was new and untried, though of immense strength — the apple of the Kaiser's eye. So much so that he had issued the strictest orders that it was not to be risked unless the odds were heavily in its favour. This meant that parts only of the Grand Fleet had to be enticed into the southern area of the North Sea, with its minefields and U-boats, so that the High Seas Fleet could pounce from its lairs with more than just an even chance of reducing Britain's numerical superiority in ships.

The British, for their part, tried the same deadly game of hide and seek, trying to tempt the Germans to put to sea and come that bit too far north so that the Grand Fleet could get between them and their home ports, thus forcing a major trial of strength.

The German method of trying to draw the Grand Fleet too far south was a series of tip-and-run raids aimed at shelling east coast ports such as Yarmouth, Lowestoft and Hartlepool or by extensive mine-laying operations. The British system was to carry out offensive sweeps to the southern North Sea, using smaller vessels backed up by the heavy squadrons further north. Neither of these tactics produced the big battle that the Grand Fleet hoped would ensue. There were a few minor skirmishes and even bigger encounters such as the actions of the Heligoland Bight

and on the Dogger Bank; otherwise it was the dull grinding
monotony of long days and nights at sea patrolling to contain
the enemy, and equally monotonous periods in harbour
recovering and training to go out and do it all over again — but,
there was always the chance that one day, THE DAY, or as the
Germans called it, Der Tag, would dawn.

It did. The Day was Wednesday, 31 May, 1916. The place
was the northern part of the Skagerrak between Norway and
Denmark about a hundred miles off the Danish coast of Jutland
and the encounter which took place in these waters is known to
the British as the Battle of Jutland, and to the Germans as the
Battle of the Skagerrak. It was the last great naval battle in
history where fleet engaged fleet, ship versus ship visually.

As far as Scapa Flow was concerned it all started the day
before when Jellicoe, who was actually planning a sweep by the
Grand Fleet into that same area of sea between Norway and
Denmark in the hope of drawing the German High Seas Fleet
out to do battle, was informed through Room 40, the
Admiralty's Intelligence nerve centre, that there was an unusual
concentration of U-boats .in the North Sea and then that the
German Commander-in-Chief, von Scheer, had ordered his fleet
to assemble in the outer Jade estuary from where they could
emerge direct into the North Sea.

By 5.40 p.m. that Tuesday afternoon Room 40 had more
information and Jellicoe received a signal at Scapa from the
Admiralty which read — 'Germans intend operations commencing
tomorrow. You should concentrate to eastward of Long Forties.'
Beatty with his battlecruiser fleet in the Forth received the same
signal. At 9.30 that night the British ships began to weigh anchor
and by 11.30 the Grand Fleet had cleared the Flow and was at
sea, heading east into the long twilight of a northern summer
night. So was Beatty, further south.[9]

Altogether 72 ships sailed out through Hoxa and Switha
Sounds that night, 16 battleships, three battlecruisers, four
armoured cruisers, five light cruisers, and 44 destroyers; they
were joined at sea by another eight battleships, four cruisers and
eight destroyers from Invergordon. Together they went on to
meet Beatty with his 52 ships including the four fast new
battleships of the *Queen Elizabeth* class, and six battlecruisers.
Through the percipience of Naval Intelligence in Room 40, this
vast armada of 150 men-of-war was at sea four-and-a-half hours
before the 99 ships of the German High Seas Fleet began to
leave the shelter of their harbour at the mouth of Jade on what
their Commander-in-Chief fondly imagined was a mere raid in
force against merchant ships in the Skagerrak, though with the

H

ulterior motive of drawing a section of the Grand Fleet into a disadvantageous position. He little knew how well his ruse had succeeded, not being aware that the British were already at sea and in overwhelming strength.

Not all of them were to return to Scapa or Kiel after the confused encounter which ensued next day and during the following night of early 1 June.

Fourteen ships of the Grand Fleet's total of 150 went to the bottom including three battlecruisers; eleven of Germany's 99 including a battlecruiser and a battleship were sunk. The British fleet was manned by some 60,000 men; 6,097 lost their lives, a serious enough loss in all conscience but almost insignificant compared with the slaughter of 600,000 Allied soldiers in the Battle of the Somme which began on the Western Front just a month later. On the German side the casualties at Jutland were lighter but still grim, with 2,551 dead out of a total of 36,000.

Of those 72 ships which sailed from the Flow that night before the battle, several did not return. One of them, the 17,250 ton, 25-knot *Invincible,* flagship of Rear Admiral the Hon. H.L.A. Hood commanding the Third Battlecruiser Squadron, had come up from Rosyth to Scapa for gunnery practice and was in the Flow when the call came. She was hit by a shell from the last salvo fired by the *Derfflinger* and blew up, breaking in two amidships. The *Derfflinger* herself was damaged but managed to limp home, only to meet an ignominious end in Scapa Flow three years later when the interned German fleet was scuttled. She was the last of the big German ships to be raised in 1939 and her hulk lay bottom-up off Rysa Little throughout the whole of World War II. After the war she was towed south for breaking, still upside down.

At the other end of the size-scale another ship to leave Scapa never to return was the *Shark,* a 1000-ton, 30-knot destroyer of the Fourth Flotilla. In the thick of the close action at Jutland her captain, Commander Loftus Jones, led a division of four destroyers to counter-attack three German flotillas of torpedo-boats then engaging the *Invincible* and the Third Battlecruiser Squadron. In spite of all the numerical odds in their favour the Germans could not face the fury of Loftus Jones's onslaught with every gun he could bring to bear pumping shells at them. They turned away; but three German battlecruisers loomed out of the mist and smoke with their vastly superior fire-power and soon the *Shark* was reduced to little more than a sinking hulk, but still with her midships gun being fired by a crew reduced to two. When one of these two dropped from loss of blood the Commander, although wounded himself, took his place and continued firing until one of his legs was shot away. He was greatly distressed to find that his ship's ensign had been carried away by gunfire and he directed another to be hoisted before ordering his crew, or what remained of it, to 'Save Yourselves'. They took to the sea as two German torpedo-boats closed to administer the *coup-de-grace* and the *Shark* went down bow first, her colours still flying. A fortnight later Loftus Jones's body was washed up on the Swedish coast, to be buried in a village churchyard there. He was posthumously awarded the Victoria Cross.[10]

Licking its wounds, the Grand Fleet, led by Jellicoe in the *Iron Duke,* sailed back into Scapa on Friday 2 June. By 9.45 that night he was able to inform the Admiralty that his fleet was ready for sea again at four hours' notice.[11] And he later wrote: '. . . the Fleet under my command was the most formidable fighting machine in the world,' which was just as well for he also wrote: '. . . our Fleet was the one and only factor that was vital to the existence of the Empire'. There was no reserve outside that Battle Fleet.[12]

CHAPTER 12

Loss of the Hampshire

ARGUMENTS still go on as to who won this most decisive of indecisive battles. The answer, such as it is, probably lies in that statement by Jellicoe that on the evening of 2 June, less than two days after the battle had been fought, the Grand Fleet, refuelled and re-supplied with ammunition and stores, was ready for sea again and what was more, that sea, and all the others in the world were his and his fleet's to go where they wished almost unopposed, for the German High Seas Fleet could not, in all honesty, signal *its* Admiralty in Berlin that it was ready for sea. And then again, there is also the fact that after the confused night action of 31 May/1 June, Jellicoe and the Grand Fleet were ready and indeed eager to resume the fight as soon as daylight came but von Scheer and his fleet had just melted away. The British had lost more ships and men than the Germans but they were still in control of the North Sea; the Germans had retired to the security of their bases — and they never dared come far out again in any force with their surface vessels. Scapa Flow was still able to maintain the 'stopper in the North Sea bottle'.

Indirectly, however, a few days later the battle was to claim another British ship and the life of one of the nation's greatest military men, Lord Kitchener, as well as all but twelve of the ship's company when the cruiser *Hampshire* struck a mine off Marwick Head on the west coast of Orkney and sank. In the lead-up to the battle of Jutland the German Commander-in-Chief, von Scheer, had ordered a screen of submarines into the North Sea. One of them, *U 75*, commanded by Lieut. Commander Kurt Beitzen, laid 34 mines west of Orkney in case the Grand Fleet, on being tempted out of Scapa Flow in pursuit of the High Seas Fleet, might choose to reach the North Sea by going west-about.[1] It was known that auxiliaries and occasionally warships did use a swept channel in that area. There was a German claim after the war that four days after these mines had been laid, a 'chartered' minesweeper had been sunk by one of them but that news of this had not reached Jellicoe or was 'overlooked in the confusion after Jutland'. In any case, the Grand Fleet did not go to Jutland by that route. But a week later, on the evening of 5 June during a severe summer gale, the 11,000-ton British cruiser *Hampshire*, with the British Minister of War, Lord Kitchener, on board, did go that way *en route* for northern Russia.

He was on his way to confer with the Czar's government in an attempt to shore up its crumbling resistance to Germany on the Eastern Front. *Hampshire* paid the price of taking this fairly unusual, and as it happened, unswept channel, giving the *U 75* a belated and unexpected success in striking one of her mines — some reports say she struck two chained together — and sinking in fifteen minutes.

Kitchener, a controversial War Minister, but held in high public esteem, had arrived in Scapa earlier that day in the *Oak* from Scrabster. He lunched on board the *Iron Duke* with Jellicoe where he met many of the Grand Fleet's flag officers and heard at first hand about Jutland. Jellicoe thought he was working to a strict time schedule with not a day to lose and he asked several times about the shortest time it would take to reach Archangel, saying he could not be away from the War Office for more than three weeks.

The weather at Scapa was bad in the morning, and it became worse with a full gale blowing from the north-east by afternoon. It had originally been intended that the *Hampshire* should travel to the east of Orkney, where sweeping of the channel for mines was routine. Owing to the heavy sea raised by the north-east gale on that side of the islands, however, minesweeping in the area had been out of the question that day.

There were two routes on the west side of Orkney and Jellicoe and his staff, after discussion, decided to send the *Hampshire* on the inside route where she would get shelter from the Orkney land, rather than the channel outside and west of Suleskerry in the open sea. As the inshore route was used by auxiliaries and was also under observation from the land lookouts, it was practically impossible for the channel to have been mined by a surface vessel in the mid-summer conditions of almost continuous daylight. Submarine minelaying by the Germans had, at this time, been confined to the southern part of the North Sea and it was thought that the chance of one operating as far north as Orkney was 'very remote'. This rather complacent line of thought was similar to that of the Admiralty at the beginning of the war when it was believed that U-boats could not reach, and certainly could not penetrate, the tideways in the openings to Scapa Flow. That theory had been proved false with the ramming and subsequent sinking of *U 18* in Hoxa Sound in November 1914. The theory about minelaying submarines was to be proved even more tragically wrong with the loss of the *Hampshire*.

Owing to bad weather, minesweeping had actually not been possible on either side of Orkney for four days before the *Hampshire* sailed. Like the rest of the Fleet the cruiser had been at Jutland where she acted as a link ship between squadrons and it was even claimed that she had rammed a U-boat, though this seems unlikely in view of her being chosen to convey such an important person as Kitchener without having first been docked for inspection as to possible underwater damage.

Kitchener and his staff, Brigadier General Ellenshaw, Sir F. Donaldson, Col. Fitzgerald, Mr O'Beirne of the Foreign Office, Second Lieutenant McPherson of the Camerons and Mr Robertson of the Government's Munitions Department, boarded the cruiser in the Flow at 4 p.m. At 5.30 p.m. her commanding officer, Captain Herbert Savill RN, gave orders to weigh anchor and, escorted by the destroyers *Unity* and *Victor,* she sailed out through the Hoxa Boom.

But by now the gale had backed north-west and the western route was no longer sheltered. Quite the reverse. The *Hampshire's* top speed was 21 knots. The gale slowed her to 16 knots but even so the destroyers could not keep station. It was generally believed that high speed was the best defence against U-boat torpedo attack and so, rather than reduce speed still further to keep company with the escort when they were heading into tremendous seas off Hoy, Captain Savill ordered the destroyers to return to harbour. Less than an hour later off Marwick Head, the savage seas having slowed her down still further to 13½ knots, the *Hampshire* struck the mines. Quarter of an hour later she took her final plunge in 30 fathoms of water.

The 50 mph gale raged on unabated. No boats got away before she sank and the twelve men who did survive were all in Carley floats. Jellicoe in his book comments sadly — 'The cold water and the very heavy sea were against even the strongest swimmers surviving for any time.' Kitchener's body was never found.

Many men did get ashore on the harsh cliffs along the coast from the Bay of Skaill to Birsay, but those still alive were either killed when they were thrown against the rocks or then succumbed to exposure.

There seems no doubt that many more than the dozen men who came through the ordeal alive could have been saved had local people in the area been informed and allowed to help, for after all they knew their stark coastline better than anyone else, but Orcadians accused the naval authorities not only of failing to tell them of the emergency but also of actually preventing them going to help if and when they did know. It was stated later that many of the bodies found on the shore were still warm and might well have been saved if the potential rescuers had been allowed to reach them in time. The Stromness lifeboat was never launched in spite of strenuous attempts by the crew to get Naval permission to put to sea.

The mining of the *Hampshire* had been seen from Birsay and the HQ in Kirkwall was informed by telegraph — there were no telephones in operation from Birsay at that time. There was, apparently, some confusion over the signal sent, which caused a certain amount of delay in getting the news through to Naval Headquarters in Stromness, to Longhope and to Jellicoe on board *Iron Duke*.

In the Flow itself the gale did not seem so bad as it actually was out to the west. Jellicoe thought that Kitchener would be saved by the *Hampshire's* own boats, not realising, even though the escorting destroyers had been sent back, the strength of the heavy seas running off Birsay. Ships were sent out to search for survivors, but almost inevitably they were too late on the scene to find anyone alive either in the sea or on the shore.

Jellicoe wrote later that with the knowledge then available to him about German submarine minelaying he would have had no hesitation in taking the Grand Fleet to sea in the same conditions and by the same route. Short of postponing the departure of the *Hampshire* for several days until a minesweeper could go ahead of her, he could think of nothing that could have been done which was not done. And Kitchener would never have agreed to that amount of delay.

In his book *The Kitchener Enigma* published in 1985 Trevor Royle, in a well-documented argument, makes the point that intelligence reports that an ocean-going German minelaying submarine had been, and, in fact, still was in the area west of Orkney were available, certainly in the Admiralty, and it would seem, at Scapa.

Room 40 — the Naval Intelligence Department — having long since broken German naval cyphers had been able to decode intercepted signals from the German navy before the Battle of Jutland which indicated that U-boats capable of laying mines had been ordered to operate off the Grand Fleet's bases. One of them, Kurt Beitzen's *U 75* was ordered to lay his mines to the west of Orkney. Unfortunately liaison between Room 40 and the

Operations Branch of the Admiralty was not good. The Operations Staff tended to regard Room 40's reports with some suspicion and liked to interpret such Intelligence for themselves rather than passing it on direct to those most concerned, in this case the Grand Fleet. As a result these reports were often given a lower priority than they merited but it seems certain that information regarding *U 75's* activities had been passed to Scapa.

Quite apart from this, independent intelligence reports of a U-boat having been sighted in the Cape Wrath area on the day of the disaster were also passed to Naval Headquarters at Longhope. There were three such reports, the last of which came in after *Hampshire* had sailed but she was still in radio contact and could have been recalled. It would appear that Jellicoe and his staff either ignored these warnings or then that they had disappeared in the mass of heavy signals traffic following immediately in the aftermath of the Battle of Jutland. At all events they were not acted upon.

With the loss of such a national figure as Kitchener, the epitome of British Imperialism in the public mind and estimation no matter what reservations his political colleagues might hold regarding him, there was, not surprisingly, a tremendous outcry barely suppressed even by security measures. Indeed, lack of adequate security about the Russian visit was one of the accusations levelled against the authorities. Kitchener's visit to Russia was apparently fairly common knowledge in London long before he left.

Sir Samuel Hoare writing in his memoirs, *The Fourth Seal,* of when he was Chief of the British Secret Service Mission to Russia, says that while he knew about Kitchener's proposed visit he was very surprised to hear it being discussed quite openly at what he calls a 'cosmopolitan' dinner party in St Petersburg (now Leningrad) some time before it was due to take place.

It has been suggested that there was carelessness and negligence also in keeping the sailing arrangements secret. There seems little doubt also, that German Intelligence services intercepted radio signals from an unamed 'destroyer' on 26 May that the channel west of Orkney had been swept. This signal was said to have been repeated four times within the space of an hour, suggesting a high degree of priority which led the Germans to assume that something of considerable importance was about to happen in that area — hence the minelaying by the *U 75*.

Almost inevitably after a naval disaster of this magnitude there are stories of spies and clandestine activities by enemy agents. The loss of the *Hampshire* was no exception. There was some evidence of an IRA plot to kill Kitchener but it seems unlikely that the Irish had any direct hand in the sinking. She had had a refit in Northern Ireland in the February of that year but this was far too long before June for explosives to have been planted on board. In any case it was virtually certain that mines caused the sinking and not an internal explosion. The remainder of the special and easily recognised submarine-laid mines were swept in the area a few days later, dispelling much doubt as to the cause of the explosion which sank her.

There were also stories of a fishing-boat flying the Dutch flag and with 'elaborate radio antennae', being seen off Orkney's west coast shortly before the disaster. And, of course, there was the usual crop of rumours about mysterious strangers with peculiar accents — Irish in this instance. It might well have been, however, that these rumours, which had been circulating for some time, were the reason for the naval clamp-down on civilian, particularly Orcadian, involvement in the rescue operation — a misguided slamming of the security door after the imaginary dark horse had bolted. If so it succeeded only in spawning fresh rumours about a 'secret Admiralty inquiry' into the sinking whose findings had not been published — and which some people even today, more than half a century later, claim have never been revealed.

Its other local effect was to sour relations between the Orcadians and the shore-based naval authorities already strained by the restrictions imposed under the all-powerful Defence of the Realm Act (DORA).

A week or two after these unhappy events the Grand Fleet was in more cheerful mood to enjoy another visit from the nation's sailor king, George V, making his second wartime journey to Scapa to be with his fleet.[2] As on his first, almost a year befcre, he sailed into the Flow from Scrabster, where he had been met by his son Albert and the Chief of Staff, Admiral Brock, on board the C-in-C's despatch boat *Oak*, escorted by 16 destroyers of 11th Flotilla. After being joined by Jellicoe they steamed round the fleet lying at anchor, some ships of which still bore their honourable scars from Jutland, before the King boarded the flagship, *Iron Duke*, where he spent the night afloat — no question now as to the security of the anchorage with its great array of shore batteries, booms and minefields. He was welcomed by all the Admirals and dined with them that night. Next day, after presenting Jellicoe with the GCVO, he visited the flagships of all the squadrons in the Flow and also addressed a representative gathering of personnel from each ship on board *Iron Duke* later.

He congratulated them on the Battle of Jutland and commiserated with them that it had not been more decisive. 'But,' he told them, 'unfavourable weather conditions and approaching darkness prevented that complete result which you all expected, but you did all that was possible in the circumstances. You drove the enemy into his harbours, and inflicted on him very severe losses, and you added another page to the glorious traditions of the British Navy. You could not have done more. . .' After which he once again crossed the Pentland Firth to Scrabster with an escort of a cruiser and 16 destroyers, on his way to visit the rest of the Fleet at Invergordon.

It was, no doubt, a pleasant change for the Fleet from the stresses of battle and the strain of monotonous routine — but the war still ground on.

A week later there is the first account of a depth-charge as such being used by ships operating out of Scapa. Jellicoe wrote: '. . . on the 12th [July 1916] two divisions of destroyers were sent from Scapa to attack the submarine that had fired at the *Duke of Cornwall* — the *Musketeer* dropped a depth charge close to the periscope of the submarine and, it was thought, considerably damaged her.'[3] The *Duke of Cornwall* was an armed boarding vessel which had been missed by two torpedoes while boarding a ship south-east of the Pentland Skerries. This unsuccessful torpedo attack was probably the source of a German claim that a battleship had been hit and damaged by a U-boat off Scapa Flow.

Depth-charges were the most effective weapon against U-boats during the war, accounting for 28 in all. The first recorded use of them was on 6 July 1916 — less than a week before the one dropped by the *Musketeer* off the Pentland Skerries — when the motor boat *Salmon* destroyed the *UC 10* in the North Sea.[4] Up until then the main method of attacking U-boats had been ramming as in the case of the *U 18* in Hoxa Sound, and a total of 15 were sunk in this way. In all during the war 150 U-boats were sunk by the Navy, five of them by bombs from aircraft.

Another armed boarding vessel, the *Duke of Albany,* was not so fortunate as the *Duke of Cornwall.* She was sunk by a U-boat in much the same area not long afterwards, 20 miles east of the Pentland Skerries, with considerable loss of life. Sixteen destroyers with seaplanes and an airship were despatched from Scapa to search but found no trace of the enemy, although another boarding vessel standing by the sinking ship reported striking a submerged object.

The Pentland Firth had not been a happy area for the *Duke of Albany*. The previous summer when returning to the Flow after a sweep with the Seventh Cruiser Squadron in order to search any ships encountered, she grounded on the Lother Skerry off Burwick in South Ronaldsay at 4 a.m. on 7 June 1915 and stuck fast for seven days, suffering considerable damage before being refloated.[5]

On the last day of July 1916 the Royal Navy took a hand in the deadly minelaying game with the *Abdiel* sailing from Scapa to sow a minefield near the Horn Reef off the Jutland coast of Denmark, an area through which the German warships had to pass when on the western passage to the North Sea.[6] There was also a considerable increase in minelaying by U-boats, possibly encouraged by their success with the *Hampshire*, and the Navy was worried that this activity might be extended to the entrances to its bases. There were no new specialised minesweepers available and so, for Scapa, trawlers had to be withdrawn from patrol work to carry out this dangerous and unwelcome task. At this period Scapa's minesweeping force was two flotillas of sloops or gunboats and two flotillas each of twelve trawlers.

But Scapa's dangers were not all from enemy action. The tides and weather still took their toll as well. On 10 August 1916, for instance, the cruiser *Blonde* ran aground on the Louther Rock off the Pentland Skerries in thick weather and was lucky to be towed off next day, albeit only with considerable difficulty. It was her second encounter with these notoriously dangerous skerries, having grounded there during exercises in 1911. A fortnight after this second mishap to the *Blonde* two battleships, the *Valiant* and *Warspite,* were put out of action when they collided inside the Flow while on night-firing practice. Both had to be docked for repairs.

The Grand Fleet and its Commander-in-Chief were still very much preoccupied about ways in which the U-boat attacks could be thwarted. It was now pretty certain that while they were in the Flow itself they were secure behind the defensive system of guns, booms, nets and minefields, but there was always danger at sea. The depth-charge was now a powerful offensive weapon in their hands but avoiding-action was still a proved defence. In order to gain proficiency in this art of evading torpedoes the Navy brought its own submarines into the Flow during August 1916. In its sheltered waters they could carry out practice attacks on the Grand Fleet while it was actually under way and conversely, of course, the battleships and cruisers could counter the attacks with turning movements. The Flow was proving to be an invaluable training area for the Fleet as well as a safe operational and strategically well-placed base.

Jellicoe's time as Commander-in-Chief of the Grand Fleet was now drawing to a close. He had spent nearly two-and-a-half testing years in one of the most crucial commands in British history, not only controlling his fighting ships at sea but also building up his chosen base of Scapa Flow from virtually nothing to its new status as an almost impregnable fortress inside which his ships and crews could rest and train in safety. Now the time had come to strike his flag there on the *Iron Duke,* and, as it were, hoist it again over the Admiralty in London as First Sea Lord, another key position in his country's defence. At sea, Admiral Sir David Beatty, hero of Jutland, flamboyant and extrovert where Jellicoe was reserved and introvert, succeeded him in command of the Fleet.

CHAPTER 13

The Fleet Grows Wings

BEFORE he left Scapa on 28 November 1916, however, Jellicoe had initiated an exercise which was close to his heart, when two light cruisers sailed from the Flow to rendezvous with airships then stationed at Peterhead, in order that experience might be gained in the handling of ships and aircraft working together. The idea was to use the cruiser and airships as scouts ahead of the Fleet when it was moving south into the North Sea. That particular exercise had to be called off owing to bad weather, but it was resumed and carried out later. More airships were coming into service with the Navy at this time, though the British craft were still not as good as their German counterparts, the dreaded Zeppelins which were now frequently raiding the east coast ports and London.

While Second Sea Lord before taking command of the Grand Fleet, Jellicoe had had the Naval Air Service under his supervision and had at that time considered the building of Zeppelin-type airships for the Royal Navy. There was, however, a delay, probably because of a big debate as to whether airships or heavier-than-air machines would be of most use to the service — and, indeed, among the diehards, whether aircraft of any type should be used at all.

Jellicoe had been very much involved in this discussion and he refuted with vigour any suggestion that the Navy had not been and was not alive to the value of aircraft in naval warfare.[1] His encouragement of naval flying in and from Scapa endorses his interest in this new arm of the service although of course he, like most of his contemporaries, saw the flying machine primarily as an aid to reconnaissance and to spotting for guns rather than in an offensive role in its own right.

The first naval airship, the *Mayfly*, a rigid craft, was built by Vickers at Barrow-on-Furness in 1911. It never really flew more than a few feet before being wrecked on the ground by high winds — still, though a failure in a way, it was the first aircraft specifically built for any navy.[2] The first successful airship received by the Royal Navy was the French-built Astra

Torres in 1913, but two years later in 1915 the Submarine Searcher (SS) airship, a dirigible nicknamed the *Blimp,* was built in Britain, just three weeks from the day on which it was demanded by the ebullient septuagenarian First Sea Lord, Lord 'Jacky' Fisher, who had been recalled to the Admiralty on the resignation of Battenburg.[3]

The Royal Flying Corps was constituted by Royal Warrant in April 1913 and was divided into a military and a naval wing, the latter with naval personnel who called themselves unofficially, the Royal Naval Air Service. But even two years earlier, in 1911, four naval officers had learned to fly aeroplanes as opposed to balloons and airships — and this only eight years after the Wright brothers' historic first-ever flight by a heavier-than-air machine in the United States.

At first it was believed that in the role of supporting the Fleet, naval aircraft would have to operate from shore bases, but in 1910 an American civil pilot had succeeded — just — in taking off from the bows of a cruiser on which a wooden platform had been built. A little later he managed to land on a similar platform on the stern of the US battleship *Pennsylvania.* The age of seaborne aircraft had dawned.

The British navy was not far behind. In January 1912 a naval airman took off from the bows of the battleship *Africa* moored in Sheerness Roads. A few months later, in May, he did it again but this time from a platform on another battleship, the *Hibernia,* while at sea steaming at ten knots. But still, up until and even during World War I the Navy's attitude towards flying remained ambivalent due mainly to the ship-versus-aircraft controversy.[4]

Most naval aircraft did, in fact, operate from land bases throughout the war, although by 1913 the aircraft carrier had become an accomplished fact rather than just a pipe-dream, with the conversion of the ancient cruiser *Hermes* to this very modern role. She had a platform from which aircraft could be flown off and her total complement was just three seaplanes, though when she visited the Flow in August of that year she apparently had only two on board. She could also fly off aeroplanes but they had to be able to reach a shore station to land. *Hermes* was sunk by a torpedo early in the war.[5] By the end of 1914 the Navy had four carriers, all of them conversions from former merchant ships, and all of them small and slow.

Less than a week after the outbreak of war there were reports of enemy aircraft over Orkney on 10 August, and on the evening of the same day an airship was reported by the battleship *Centurion* north of Shetland, but 'little credence was given to these reports which in the early days of the war were very frequently received,' wrote Jellicoe. A fortnight later, however, there was a report that the uninhabited island of North Rona, west of Orkney, was possibly being used as an enemy air base and it was taken seriously enough to send the old cruiser *Sappho* out to investigate. 'She reported, after examination, that the island was, as expected, unsuitable for such a purpose,' wrote Jellicoe.[6]

On 15 August, just before the North Rona scare, the first of the Fleet's supporting aircraft, three seaplanes and two aeroplanes, had arrived at Scapa for reconnaissance work from the base. They were said to have travelled unceremoniously in a cattle boat to reach their destination, and their first air station was established by the simple expedient of dumping them in a field of still-green oats belonging to Nether Scapa on the shores of the bay, no doubt to the extreme annoyance of the farmer who owned the crop. But there the five planes stayed, the station being more or less built up round them, and it remained in use throughout the war though latterly mainly as a maintenance, repair and store base.

At first the aircraft were in the open, before getting the shelter of tents and marquees borrowed from various sources in Kirkwall. The station, such as it was, was wrecked and some of the planes damaged by a severe gale which hammered the islands from 11 to 13 November, when all work on the defences had to be suspended until it blew itself out. No sooner was the station operational again, permanent buildings having been erected after the temporary shelters had been demolished by the gale, than it was condemned as unsuitable owing to the large expanse of beach uncovered at low tide and the consequent difficulty of launching the seaplanes. It was only the first of Orkney's air stations to be found unsuitable just after they had been built.[7]

Houton, in Orphir, with its sheltered bay and easier access to open water, was now chosen as the main seaplane base. Extensive buildings, hangars, stores, repair shops with a power house and hutted accommodation as well as wide concrete aprons were erected but, once again, it did not quite fit the bill although it was operational from 1917 until the end of the war housing Short flying-boats and seaplanes. HMS *Canning,* the RFC depot ship, was anchored offshore in the Flow.

A subsidiary station constructed on the shores of the Stenness Loch just across from the prehistoric stone circle, the Ring of Brogar, was operational during 1918 with three flights of seaplanes, but the loch's shallows and difficult cross-winds meant that it was not really satisfactory either.

Although Houton remained operational, it was felt that a better site still was really needed and finally Swanbister, just along the shores of the Flow, was selected. Building began and it was still under construction at the time of the Armistice.[8] In spite of the war having ended, however, the building continued and the station, amid growing comment and criticism in the public, Press and Parliament, was duly completed—and then dismantled and sold off. Such are the inscrutable ways of Government departments.

In addition to these seaplane bases, however, it was felt that an airship station was also needed and it was described as having been 'built in a bog at Caldale,' just outside Kirkwall in the low-lying ground between the Orphir and the old Finstown roads under Burrey Brae and Keelylang where the television transmitter now looks down on the site. It does not appear to have been entirely satisfactory either, although it was used for a time to service the so-called 'kite balloons'—captive balloons with a basket carrying observers and towed aloft by merchant ships as well as naval craft for spotting enemy submarines or mines. The balloons, looking not unlike the barrage balloons of the Second World War in appearance, were maintained and inflated at Caldale, then towed by lorry to their embarkation point either in the Flow or Kirkwall Bay where they were transferred to their ship lying off. From the Flow they could travel direct but for Kirkwall Bay they had to go round to the west of Wideford Hill to avoid the town with its risks of danger to and by buildings, telegraph wires and other projecting hazards. It is said that Sion's (or Sciennes) Loan in Firth between the old and new Finstown roads was constructed to save the lorries with their towed balloons from having to go into Finstown. Below the farm of Saverock, just west of the Hatston Industrial Estate outside Kirkwall, there is a field known until comparatively recently as the 'Balloon Park' where they were held before going out to their ships.

Small dirigibles or 'Blimps' were also based at Caldale for reconnaissance purposes, although with the prevalence of gales and bad weather generally they must have had more than their fair share of problems.

In spite of all this activity over shore stations for aircraft, the Navy had by no means lost sight of the possibility that ships carrying aircraft could be sea-going mobile airfields. The first major step in this direction came in April 1915 with the commissioning of the former 18,000-ton Cunard liner *Campania* as an aircraft carrier and capable of 23 knots. At first she carried six aircraft which could be flown off from her 120-foot flight deck. She was armed with six 4.7-inch guns and one 3-inch gun. Much of her early work-up was carried out in the Flow, and on 11 June 1915 she put to sea with the Grand Fleet for exercises and gunnery practice—the first time in the history of naval warfare that seaplanes had been used at sea for observing movements by units of the fleet. From this beginning there was a big development in the work of heavier-than-air machines operating with ships at sea.[9]

The first step was the provision of a flying-off deck for seaplanes which in these early days had extreme difficulty in taking-off from the water except in very fine weather—and, in northern seas, this was rare. The next step was the substitution of aeroplanes for seaplanes working from special carriers and finally, fly-off platforms on the fighting ships themselves. Scapa Flow provided an ideal proving-ground where such experiments could be carried out in comparative shelter.

Less than a month after this initial foray to sea with the Fleet, the *Campania* was sent on her first active service mission when along with a flotilla leader, eight destroyers, four sloops and a large number of trawlers she was based on Pierowall in Westray to operate against the large number of U-boats reported to be passing between Fair Isle and Orkney.[10] This little task force operated out of the North Isles for five days at the beginning of July 1915 without, however, finding any U-boats.

Shortly after this the *Campania* went back to Liverpool for further and extensive modification in the light of experience gained during her first short tour of duty. She returned to Scapa the following April with a capacity of twelve aircraft and with her steeply inclined flight deck extended to 200 feet between her two funnels athwartships forward. She could now hoist returned seaplanes back on board without having to heave-to, so reducing the danger of U-boat attack during this operation. Following discussions with her commander, Schwann, Jellicoe pressed for the use of landplanes from ships rather than seaplanes, as the floats of the latter reduced their rate of climb, endurance and capabilities generally.[11]

Campania, incidentally, missed the Battle of Jutland. She was in the Flow but did not receive the preliminary warning signal for the Fleet's departure. She left, unescorted, some time later but was ordered back to Scapa because of the danger from U-boats reported in her area, against which she had no protection.[12]

After the RNAS merged into the RAF in 1918 Captain Schwann became an Air Vice-Marshal. He was one of the 55,000 officers and men who were transferred from the Royal Navy to the new service, along with their 3000 aircraft, this huge expansion indicating the importance the Navy had attached to its air arm. The two services separated again just before World War II, following tensions which had built up between the Navy and RAF over questions of use of planes with ships, types required and control of aircraft operating with the fleet.

The fitting out of the *Campania* was the beginning of the system which was gradually introduced providing light cruisers, battlecruisers and battleships with scouting aeroplanes capable of taking off from ships in practically all conditions although, of course, they could not land back on board and if they were too far out to reach land they had to 'ditch'. The *Campania* had also been fitted with a kite balloon for reconnaissance purposes, U-boat detection and gunnery spotting. Later these balloons were supplied to all warships, including destroyers where they proved their worth in convoy work.

At first the thought of using balloons on ships was looked on as a bit of a joke—they would blow away in anything more than a breeze, it was believed. The *Campania*, however, soon proved this to be wrong, especially when the new type of balloons came into service, in particular the French-designed three-tailed 'M' type which could be towed at speed in most weather. The metal fatigue problem of hawsers breaking was also solved. But the big trouble was fire caused by too much electricity in the atmosphere—and it did not need a thunderstorm to set them ablaze. Conditions which caused the fires were difficult to detect, the best indication being the crackles of static on the wireless sets. When that happened the observers aloft in their baskets under the balloons were hauled down as fast as possible. On one occasion no fewer than seventeen balloons burst into flames in the Flow simultaneously, fortunately without any casualties.

Thirty-two balloons could be flown at one time to supply the ships of the fleet with their own aerial protection, the balloons being stored and serviced either ashore or on the two special supply ships.

An effective anti-U-boat measure was found to be four destroyers steaming abreast with balloons and observers aloft. The first 'kill' using this method was just off the Norwegian coast by a section of destroyers led by the *Strongbow* from Scapa. A U-boat surfaced, to the surprise and delight of one of the balloon observers who alerted the destroyers, which promptly went into a complicated routine of dropping depth-charges in overlapping patterns on the position where the submarine had crash-dived. That was the end of that U-boat.[13]

Although she had been built in the 1890's, when she was the crack Cunarder on the North Atlantic run and said to be the fastest ship afloat at the time, the *Campania* was still capable of 22 knots in 1918, when a few days after the end of the war she dragged her anchor during a storm off Burntisland in the Firth of Forth, drifting across the bows of the *Royal Oak*. She was holed and sank, fortunately without any loss of life.

The next big advance in naval flying also took place in Scapa Flow. HMS *Furious*, laid down as a battlecruiser but modified before completion, was commissioned as an aircraft carrier in 1917 and capable of 30 knots, a speed which now made possible what had hitherto been impossible—landing an aeroplane on a ship under way at sea, as well as taking off from her. It was, nonetheless, still a hazardous operation as was to be all too sadly demonstrated. *Furious* was in the Flow that summer and on 5 August Commander Edwin Dunning, flying a Sopwith Pup, managed to dodge the superstructure before a last-minute turn to windward and a triumphant touch-down on the flight deck where willing hands were waiting to hold the plane back once it was on the deck, there being no arrester-wires in those days. So, Commander Dunning became the first man in aviation history to achieve the 'impossible', but unhappily he did not survive long to enjoy his success. He made a second attempt at landing on *Furious* the next day when she was again steaming in the Flow, but this time his plane overshot into the sea and he was killed.[14]

According to Brian Johnston in *Fly Navy*, Commander Dunning did actually land back on deck on his second attempt but damaged the aircraft in doing so. Not being satisfied with his performance, he got into another Sopwith Pup which was on deck with engines warmed up and took off right away to have another go, but this time when he came in the deck party, all of them flying men themselves, were unable to hold the plane as it touched down.

Although the trend was now towards heavier-than-air machines, airships and balloons were not neglected either by the British or the German navies. Houton, for instance, although primarily a seaplane station, had a balloon hangar as well as the more specialised balloon and airship station at Caldale. The Germans claimed that one of the Zeppelins commanded by von Butler made a six-day flight up the east coast of Britain on some unspecified date but probably in 1917, and that he took photographs of Scapa Flow before crossing the North Sea to Norway and back to Germany.[15]

A flight by a British airship to Scapa Flow is also recorded though again not the actual date. It lasted 61 hours, covering 1420 miles non-stop. Starting from the Forth area, probably East Fortune, it travelled up the east coast at a very sedate 23 mph. At Scapa it was ordered to escort a convoy coming through the Pentland Firth and see it safely to a port on the east side. Unfortunately the crew, at this point, found they had run out of drinking water. That problem was solved by coming down to mast height over a destroyer and getting a supply from her tanks. Then on with the escort duty. Having delivered the convoy safely into port, the airship's crew turned for home when to their dismay they were ordered to patrol north again. And by now they had run out of food. No destroyer seems to have been handy this time but after a search they found a trawler and, again coming down to mast height over the vessel, they asked if the cook could do them a fry-up. He could, and did, while they hovered overhead finally hauling the more than welcome hot meal up in a bucket.[16]

CHAPTER 14

The Long Wait

AFTER its judicious night withdrawal from the Battle of Jutland the German High Seas Fleet was still largely intact, and so remained a major threat to Britain's command of the North Sea although the battle had shown that for the Germans to come out again in force would be to court disaster. Indeed they never did emerge again, apart from small raids by a few ships, until the surrender in November 1918.

So—the Grand Fleet had still to keep 'the stopper in the North Sea bottle', with Scapa Flow retaining its strategic importance as well as its value for training purposes.

The lessons learned the hard way at Jutland were digested and as a result there were big improvements in weapons, armour, communications and training. New ships slid down the ways from yards all over the country to swell even further the Fleet's numerical superiority over that of its adversary, and this augmentation helped to some extent in relieving the stress and strain of maintaining the stranglehold of the blockade. Vigilance, of course, could never be relaxed but extra vessels meant longer periods in port, even perhaps away from the monotony of being cooped up in Scapa.

Beatty was now Commander-in-Chief Grand Fleet, based at Scapa, where he had started off the war commanding the battlecruisers before moving south with them first to Invergordon, then to Rosyth where he would be nearer the east coast ports of England which lay under the threat of bombardment from the sea by tip-and-run raids. And it was from Rosyth that he had sailed to what was, for him, the frustration and deep disappointment of Jutland. He had hoped, and expected, as indeed the British nation had, that it would be a second 'glorious Trafalgar' with himself in the role of his hero, Nelson. Such an encounter, it was hoped, would be the justification of the 'Decisive Battle' school of naval thought, an encounter which would crush the enemy, bringing victory and peace that much sooner. But it was not to be. It was, instead, an indecisive 'victory' although the Royal Navy still ruled the seas. But for a long time Beatty dreamed that his 'Trafalgar' would still come.

Mewed up in Scapa, 1917 was a frustrating year for this gregarious, thrusting, outgoing character, personified by his cap at a rakish angle over one eye and his reefer jacket with three buttons instead of the regulation four, fond of the good life, high society, polo and hunting in the Shires, all of which had been made possible by his marriage to a very wealthy American divorcée, Ethel, though this marriage had for a time caused some difficulty in their aspiration to move in the Court circles of the day.

With his nearby mansion of Aberdour House, Rosyth suited his lifestyle much better than the bleak austerity of Scapa Flow. But strategic necessity had to take precedence over personal preference and he was first and foremost a dedicated professional naval commander of the highest calibre. To make matters even more difficult he was deeply involved in a love affair with Eugénie, wife of Captain (later Sir) Bryan Godfrey-Fausett RN, Equerry-in-Ordinary to King George V. But Scapa was a very long way from London; and for Beatty, while distance might lend enchantment in one respect, it did nothing for the immediate view of grey sea, dark hills and bad weather.

In one letter to Eugénie he said the memory of being with her a fortnight earlier was helping him 'through the weary hours in this cursed region where it is blowing a gale of wind and where the sun never shines'. Hardly the sort of 'quotes by famous people' which a tourist organisation would want to use.

But in 1917 tourism for pleasure was far from anyone's thoughts. The louring threat of starvation caused by the unrestricted U-boat campaign of the enemy, the occasional raider slipping through the net of the blockade, and the urgency, as he saw it, of getting a reluctant Admiralty to introduce a convoy system for our merchant ships, was always on Beatty's mind—and there was always the chance, or hope, that the German High Seas Fleet 'might come out' and give him the opportunity for glory which he so avidly desired. And from Scapa at this time he could make the most of any such opportunity as offered, so in Scapa he had to stay.

In January of that year, Beatty concentrated the ships from all three Scottish Bases, Scapa, Rosyth and Invergordon, in the middle of the North Sea for exercises, and to carry out an offensive sweep. But nothing happened. The Germans stayed close in their ports.

Further north during this period there were always ten ships of the Northern Patrol on watch and guard and sometimes they were augmented by as many as 15 cruisers and 20 destroyers from the Grand Fleet—usually in horrible weather. Then there was constant training and exercising, both in the Flow and outside it, to perfect the Fleet's ship-handling capabilities. This constant activity and hard training along with the devotion of his crews to Beatty himself, a charismatic and popular figure, helped to maintain morale and discipline in a very trying and difficult period of the war at sea.

Rosyth and Invergordon did, however, see rather more of the Fleet during 1917 than in the previous two years. Invergordon had the nearest dockyard facilities to Scapa, including a floating dock capable of taking the largest ships. Some of these facilities were, in fact, extended to Scapa during the year, among them a smaller floating dock which could cope with minor refits and emergency repairs. Moored near Lyness it docked some 200 ships in the two years it was in the Flow.

There was more opportunity for recreation at Scapa too, and facilities, though still inadequate, were improved. Football was popular, with pitches established at various points within easy reach of the ships and there were the usual regattas, while boxing enjoyed quite a vogue. One of the Fleet tournaments attracted a 'gate' of 10,000 in an open-air arena and was attended by Prince Albert, with Beatty presenting the trophies.

The YMCA had indoor recreational facilities in its huts at Flotta and Longhope and there was a Church Army hut at Lyness.

The entry of the United States of America into the war against Germany on 6 April 1917 was naturally welcomed everywhere in the Allied camp, and its immediate effect in northern waters was an easing of the work of the Tenth Cruiser Squadron, now mainly armed merchant cruisers. Their task, often carried out in appalling weather, was to stop and investigate all neutral shipping which could be carrying contraband to beleaguered Germany. This, of course, had meant stopping American ships as well, often with diplomatic repercussions. Now these ships were no longer subject to this control, so allowing the cruisers to concentrate on the remaining neutrals with the occasional disguised enemy ship among them trying to slip through the blockade. Not many did.

This Northern Patrol had, from 1914 to 1917, guarded and quartered an 800-mile stretch of storm-rent sea from Orkney to Iceland and across the North Sea to Norway. During that period they had intercepted no fewer than 15,000 ships. Less than four percent succeeded in penetrating the blockade, which was backed, of course, by the Grand Fleet at Scapa. So effective was this ever-tightening stranglehold on Germany's economic jugular that one of the first pleas of that defeated nation after the Armistice was—'Raise the Blockade'.[1]

But it was not until late that year, December 1917, that the battleships of the United States Navy, the Sixth Battle Squadron, joined the Grand Fleet in Scapa. They included the dreadnoughts *New York, Wyoming, Florida, Delaware, Arkansas* and *Texas,* all of them becoming an integral part of the Grand Fleet under the direct operational command of its British Commander-in-Chief, Admiral Beatty.

US destroyers and other smaller craft had been operating in British waters and under British command since May 1917, within weeks of the US declaration of war on Germany. They were mostly engaged on anti-submarine operations in the Western Approaches and eastern Atlantic, based on Queenstown in southern Ireland. At the request of the British Admiralty most of the American ships were coal-burners, in order to save fuel oil supplies in Britain which were then under severe pressure due to the unrestricted U-boat warfare against our merchant ships.[2]

The US flagship *New York,* under command of Rear Admiral Hugh Rodmer, was believed to have sunk a U-boat while at Scapa, according to reports in the 'Chicago Herald' after the war. The US squadron was heading west through the Pentland Firth to meet and escort an inward-bound convoy. As they cleared the Firth and came on to a north-westerly course two bumps were felt along the bottom, one forward, one aft, the latter damaging a propeller. Three German ships had been reported at sea but were not sighted, although three torpedoes were fired at the *New York.* She retaliated with depth-charges and claimed to have sunk her assailant.[3]

At mid-summer that year of 1917 the Grand Fleet had another and rather longer visit from King George V, and the weather was still not very kind to him. It blew a full gale a good part of the time, giving him a nasty crossing of the Firth in the Flotilla leader *Castor* after he had been met at Thurso by his son Prince Albert now serving in the *Malaya* and Admiral Brock, Chief of Staff. This time there was an escort of only four destroyers.

'It was blowing very hard (Force 8) in the squalls and raining but we were pretty steady and I remained on the bridge. David Beatty met us on entering the Flow,' he wrote in his diary for 21 June.

On the flagship, *Queen Elizabeth,* where he was staying with Beatty, he met and was welcomed by all the Admirals and remarked: 'Too unlucky we should have this bad weather, also a thunderstorm this evening and heavy rain. Talked to Bertie

[Prince Albert] and Dickie Battenburg [later Earl Mountbatten] who is a Midshipman onboard here. The rain continued over an hour and was tropical. All the Admirals dined and I talked to them afterwards.'

Next morning Friday, 22 June, they had planned to go to sea with the Fleet for firing practice but: 'Still blowing and fine rain so we could not go out,' he recorded, so he spent two hours going round 'this wonderful ship', the *Queen Elizabeth*, visiting X turret, magazines, shell-room, engine-room and stoke-hole remarking that she was an oil-burner. Then he went on board *Revenge, King George V* and *Barham*, on all of which he saw all the Captains and the men marched past him on the quarter-decks. And the weather improved.

On Saturday 23 June there was no wind but the mist came up with showers. He visited *Lucia*, the submarine depot-ship, which had formerly belonged to Germany as the *Spreewald* before being captured by the British in 1914. Then luncheon in the *Hercules* with Sturdee, hero of the Falklands battle, before returning to the flagship in the afternoon to sail with her, accompanied by *Barham, Malaya, Warspite* and *Valiant*, into the Pentland Firth for firing practice—but down came the mist and heavy rain again. It cleared, however, and 'we were able to do our firing which was most interesting, we fired 7 shots a gun in double salvoes and made excellent shooting. We got in at 7.30 . . Bertie and others came to dinner. Afterwards we had a cinematograph', he wrote. Sunday brought another march-past on board involving ships' companies and detachments from the cruisers, sloops and trawlers—'of course, there were showers'.

After Divine Service at 10.30 he held an investiture and decorated over forty officers, with a GCVO for Beatty later on and the ensignia of Knight Commander of the Victorian Order for Rear Admiral O. de Brock.

After luncheon on board *King George V* he went on to the submarine *K2*, the minesweeper *Godetia* and the hospital ship *Plassy*, finishing up on his son's ship, *Malaya*. He left Scapa on Monday 25 June, steaming through the fleet in *Castor*, each ship cheering as they passed. Prince Albert and Brock, the Chief of Staff, accompanied him across the Firth where the Orkney weather did not relent for: 'It was showery and blowing a bit, a certain amount of sea in the Firth as usual,' he wrote in his diary that evening.[4]

After the Royal visit the Fleet remained at Scapa in force during early July, with the First, Second, Fourth and Fifth Battle Squadrons comprising no fewer than 28 capital ships including the *Queen Elizabeth, Marlborough, Benbow, Emperor of India,*

Iron Duke and *Canada.* The sister ships of the *Queen Elizabeth* were also there with the First Battle Squadron, *Royal Oak, Royal Sovereign* and *Resolution*, all of about 27,000 tons, armed with 15-inch guns. In the Flow, too, were nine ships of the Fourth and Sixth Cruiser Squadrons including the Australian Navy's *Sydney* which had put an end to the notoriously successful raiding career of the *Emden* off the Cocos Islan∴'s in 1914. The 57 destroyers of the Eleventh, Twelfth, Fourteenth and Fifteenth Flotillas with their respective depot ships *Blake, Diligence, Greenock* and *Sandhurst* as well as the 25 submarines of the Tenth, Eleventh, Twelfth and Fifteenth Flotillas, made a massive total of 123 fighting ships with, in addition, all their attendant auxiliaries, supply ships, hospital ships, tenders and drifters. Even so the Fleet's two battlecruiser squadrons were absent at their base in the Forth and so was the Third Battle Squadron of more elderly battleships which were refitting in the home ports.[5]

This was the force which persuaded the German High Seas Fleet, on the explicit orders of the Kaiser himself, not to risk a confrontation in the North Sea although they did carry out a successful raid by smaller surface ships on a Bergen-bound convoy and another off Berwick.

Among this mighty assemblage of ships in the Flow that summer was HMS *Vanguard* of the Fourth Battle Squadron commanded by Captain James Dick, a gunnery specialist and a former Director of Naval Ordnance at the Admiralty. With her company of over a thousand men she had been in action for just 18 minutes at Jutland the previous year.

On 8 July she slipped her moorings between the *Bellerophon* and *Neptune* to move over to the north (Orphir) shore of the Flow where she anchored for the night. Next morning the crew carried out a number of drills, including one which unhappily they would have no time to put into practice later that day—'Abandon Ship'.

At 6.30 that evening, having put ashore two dockyard civilian ordnance fitters who had been working on board, she returned to her berth in the squadron line and picked up her moorings, some two miles north of Flotta. It was a fine, calm summer evening with the Flow looking its peaceful best in the afterglow of the setting sun. Fifteen of her officers had gone across to the *Royal Oak* for a concert on board. They were the lucky ones. So were the 49 ratings on leave and the two sub-lieutenants on loan to the destroyers, the 22 of the ship's company on their way back off leave but not yet on board, and two midshipmen seconded to submarines. Not so fortunate were the two Australian stokers from the *Sydney* who were in the *Vanguard's* sick bay, or the Japanese Commander Ito, on board as observer.

A little before midnight on that 9 July, at 11.20 p.m., a few ratings on watch in some of the other ships saw a burst of flame abaft the battleship's foremast, followed by a massive ball of fire and a shattering explosion.[6]

A Flotta man who was standing outside his house enjoying the peacefulness of the summer night wrote in 'The Orcadian' after the war — 'There was a V-shaped column of flames between sea and sky, then a frightful detonation, then the spreading over the great harbour of innumerable blazing fragments of everything combustible, then the smoke and glare arising from our own hill of Golta off which the doomed ship had been lying, and the heather of which had been set on fire.' He was surprised that more houses on the island had not been damaged by fire or by the shock of the explosion. Many grim souvenirs, he said, had been picked up in Flotta, and he had, himself, found a photograph of a civilian and a small child in a sailor suit, as well as a diary which had been found three miles from the scene of the disaster.[7]

Ten miles away in Breckan Battery overlooking Holm Sound, Orkney gunners asleep in their hammocks were shaken awake with the force of the explosion; in Kirkwall, people saw a glow in the sky.[8] Some reports said there had been two explosions and that after the second there was no sign of the ship, which had disappeared below the surface in a pall of black smoke which swirled up in a dense dark column staining the northern twilight and visible for miles around.

A 30-foot slab of steel was hurled in the air to land on the upper deck of the *Bellerophon*, next ship in line, while the *Vanguard's* steam pinnace was blown clear over another ship anchored nearby and recovered almost undamaged.

Only three men emerged from this holocaust alive but one of them, Lieut. Cmdr. Duke, died next day. Stoker Cox and Pte. Williams of the Royal Marines were the only two on board to escape with their lives. The official announcement of the disaster, the third British warship to blow up at anchor during the war, was terse, merely stating — 'HMS *Vanguard* blew up at anchor on the night of 9th inst. as a result of an internal explosion. The ship sank immediately and there were only three survivors among those on board, namely one officer and two men and the officer has since died. 24 officers and 71 ratings were not on board at the time and their names will be given in a list of survivors.'[10] That was all. There was the usual tight security clamp-down after the event, so that the full extent of the disaster was not fully realised by the general public until after the war, eighteen months later.

It was the worst naval disaster ever to have happened in Scapa Flow and its full horror, with the loss of over a thousand men, was unsurpassed even by the sinking of the *Royal Oak* in the Second World War. *The Royal Oak* had, of course, been anchored close by the *Vanguard* on that tragic night. There was naturally much concern and soul-searching in naval circles. HMS *Bulwark* had blown up and sunk off Sheerness in a secure naval anchorage in November 1914; the cruiser *Natal* sank after an internal explosion in another naval base, Cromarty, just a year later—and now, the worst of all, *Vanguard* in the Navy's main strategic base, Scapa Flow itself. It was soon established that no U-boat was involved, although the Grand Fleet had naturally gone to 'Action Stations' just in case. Sabotage then?

In his book investigating the three sinkings, *They Called It Accident,* A. Cecil Hampshire hints that they could have been caused by saboteurs, possibly Sinn Fein or enemy agents. He makes the point that a dockyard chargehand, whom he does not name, referring to him merely as 'Mr Blank', had been working on both the *Vanguard* and the *Natal* immediately before they blew up—he left *Vanguard* less than seven hours before the explosion.

He also states that fragments of correspondence found among the debris which came ashore included a letter written in German, 'the contents of which could be considered incriminating'. But it is not quoted. There was also a photograph of a beautiful girl '. . . of most fascinating appearance who in style and dress appeared to be of a type much employed by the Germans in their spying system.' It had some lines in German (again not quoted) on the back. A German Bible was also found. The letter, it is stated, was passed 'in other hands for investigation'. And that seems to be the last we hear about it. The official verdicts on all three disasters were that they were caused by faulty ammunition, possibly cordite, which had become unstable while in storage. Hampshire casts some doubts on these verdicts and suggests that the official inquiry could have been more searching and thorough.

And so the *Vanguard's* rusting remains lie at the bottom of the Flow, where they were to be joined by the hulks of her erstwhile enemies two years later.

There was no question of enemy action or mysterious agents about another serious blow suffered by the Grand Fleet less than six months after the loss of the *Vanguard* when two destroyers,

Narborough and *Opal,* returning to the Flow in total darkness during a fierce gale with blizzard conditions on the night of 12/13 January 1918, struck the cliffs at Hesta Head near Windwick on the east side of South Ronaldsay. They were a total loss and only one man, who managed to scramble to a narrow ledge where he clung on for 36 desperate hours, was saved out of a total of 180 crew members. It was a grim reminder that the weather and tides were still a potent force in the Flow's defence and implacable enemies of mariners, no matter what uniform they wore.

In a private letter to George V, Beatty, who had been deeply grieved, said they had met a 'terrible end' when they 'ran full tilt' on to the rocks. Oddly enough, in his letter to the King he said the destroyers had run on to the Pentland Skerries, whereas they were several miles north of this when they struck.[11]

A week later there was a violent explosion in the area, strewing the cliffs with twisted metal and debris and even two-inch shells. It happened during the night, but earlier in the day visitors to the scene had observed a torpedo surging to and fro in the wreckage.[12] It was a tragic opening to what would prove to be the last year of the war.

CHAPTER 15

The End In Sight

MORE AND MORE, now, the Grand Fleet's centre of gravity moved almost imperceptibly further south to the Forth where the ships spent the greater part of their time in 1918, when, from April onwards, Rosyth became the main base. The Flow was still used, of course; its natural advantages made sure of that, but Rosyth was now secure and it was two hundred miles or more nearer the ports from which the German High Seas Fleet might emerge in one last desperate throw. It certainly seemed that its C-in-C, von Scheer, might risk this and he did get so far as to issue such orders to sail in April but then withdrew them.

A further last desperate attempt at forcing a confrontation with the Grand Fleet later that year was frustrated, not by the Royal Navy but by the German sailors themselves who had mutinied and had run up the Red Flag. This was largely confined to the bigger ships, the U-boat crews retaining much of their morale in spite of heavy losses. The *UB 83*, for instance, was apparently keeping an eye on Scapa in September when she had the misfortune of meeting the *Ophelia*. In 1920 the *Ophelia's* crew claimed, and was awarded, the bounty of £35 for destroying her off the Pentland Skerries.[1]

The blockade, of course, continued to tighten and it was reinforced in the summer of 1918 with a massive mine barrage between Orkney and Norway, laid mainly by the US Navy. It was completed just as the war ended.

But although the strategic centre of gravity had to some degree moved away from Scapa Flow it had by no means lost its importance in naval eyes and the base was fully maintained at its now normal pitch of security; nor, as it turned out, had the great events of history-in-the-making passed it by.

There was, for instance, the one last forlorn attempt to retrieve the honour of the German navy, now rent by mutiny and disaffection, with a lone U-boat attack on the Grand Fleet in its holiest of holies. German Intelligence was not so good either at this point in the war, less than a month before the Armistice, for the Grand Fleet had not used the Flow in any numbers since

April—just the odd ship coming in now and again. At all events the 519-ton submarine *UB 116,* with five 19.7-inch torpedo tubes carrying, it was said, eleven torpedoes and with its normal crew of 26 under the command of Lieutenant J. J. Emsmann, son of an admiral, sailed from Heligoland on 25 October 1918 with orders to penetrate the Flow's defences and sink as many ships of the Grand Fleet as possible, regardless of the risks involved.

The intention was to put as many British warships out of action as possible before the planned emergence of the High Seas Fleet for the last great battle where, it was hoped, even a Pyrrhic victory would save some remnants of German naval honour and, at the lowest estimate, might improve their nation's bargaining position at the ensuing peace conference after what they now admitted would be their inevitable defeat.

It has been frequently alleged that when the *UB 116* set out from Heligoland for Scapa Flow she was manned entirely by a volunteer crew of naval officers, pledged to redeem the reputation of their service in what would almost certainly be a suicide attack. Churchill states this in his account of the First War, *World Crisis,* and repeats it in *The Gathering Storm* dealing with the second; Gerald S. Snyder makes the same allegation in his book *The Royal Oak Disaster,* but Geoffrey Bennett, a former naval officer, discounts this story in his revised edition of *Naval Battles of World War I* published in 1974, saying that the *UB 116* was **not** manned by a 'volunteer crew of officers only, as some authorities have erroneously stated.'

The Naval Historical Branch of the Ministry of Defence confirms that the all-officer volunteer crew story is 'complete nonsense' and adds that there was, in fact, only one volunteer among the four officers and 33 ratings on board and he was a friend of the Commanding Officer who had asked to sail on the patrol as a second watchkeeping officer. The rest of the *UB 116* crew were the usual ship's company.

The 'Leader of U-boats', Commodore Michelsen, briefing Emsmann before the mission, advised him to go in through Hoxa Sound because other U-boats passing through the Pentland Firth had reported this entrance to the Flow to be in regular use by British ships so that, unlike the other entrances, it would not be blocked by nets, mines or other obstructions. He could not have been more wrong. Hoxa **was** mined—the mines being controlled from the shore from where they could be detonated electrically. Furthermore there were detector loops on the seabed, cables which caused the needle of a galvanometer to flick when an electric current was induced by the magnetic field of any vessel crossing them. And finally there were hydrophones to pick up the sound of engines from any approaching ship.

It was these hydrophones on Stanger Head, Flotta, which gave the first warning of *UB 116's* approach towards the Flow at 8.21 p.m. on 28 October. No friendly ship was expected. The loop minefield was activated, searchlights swept and probed the Sound.

Emsmann appears to have been convinced that so long as he stayed submerged he could not be detected and so he continued his stealthy approach. He was not actually sighted until 11.30 p.m. when he came to periscope depth for a few seconds apparently to check his position. He was now inside the defences and near the boom entrance, making straight for it. Two minutes later the submarine's magnetic field flicked the needles in the Flotta mining stations and 'the button was pressed.' The controlled mines were detonated and that was the end of *UB 116*. And the end of the German navy's final gesture of defiance. All that was left was a patch of oil on the surface at the mouth of Pan Hope, a mass of twisted metal on the seabed below, and no survivors.[2]

Divers went down later and were able to identify the crushed hull of the U-boat. Inside the conning-tower they found three bodies, and more inside the hull, but they were unable to penetrate to the control-room, the bulkhead door having been jammed by the explosion. The hands and forearms of an unidentified man, it was reported, were sticking out under the twisted and buckled watertight door.[3]

It has also been claimed that the *UB 116* was equipped with very accurate charts of the area—even better than our own Admiralty charts, some people said, but, if this is true, they did not apparently show the minefield which finished them off.[4] 'The Orcadian' reported some weeks later that a portion of the conning-tower had been salved and taken to St Margaret's Hope where 'it was the object of intense interest to the islanders'.[5]

UB 116 had the unhappy distinction of being the last U-boat to be sunk in World War I and also of being the only submarine to have been destroyed by a shore-controlled minefield.[6] She subsequently became the property of an Orkney man, Mr David Spence, Sandwick, a diver, and it is believed that the torpedoes destined for the Grand Fleet may still be on board.

It was not very long before the shattered hulk of the *UB 116* was joined by over seventy of her larger surface-going compatriots, the German High Seas Fleet. But there was a big difference. *UB 116* had paid the price for one last defiant but honourable gesture trying to breach Scapa's now almost

impregnable defences. Three weeks later in the uneasy peace of
the Armistice, the Kaiser's great ships, by this time ill-kempt,
dirty and rusty, slunk disarmed through those same defences in
ignominious surrender under the watchful, and it must be
admitted, scornful eyes and guns of the British navy.

True, the Germans never admitted it was surrender or defeat
and technically it was, indeed, merely internment pending the
outcome of the peace talks, but there was no doubt that the
British and Allied navies saw it for what it really was—utter,
even shameful, defeat without a single shot being fired.

When the Germans sought a cease-fire at the beginning of
October 1918 with their armies disintegrating on the Western
Front, their High Seas Fleet was physically intact. The threat
that it still seemed to pose was an important factor in the
negotiations leading up to the Armistice. In fact, even as late as
29 October, less than a fortnight before the guns fell silent, the
German naval Commander-in-Chief, Admiral Hipper, ordered
his ships to assemble ready to come out fighting in one last
throw. But his crews, already rebellious, mutinied, and this great
fleet, bigger now even than at Jutland, degenerated into an
undisciplined collection of dirty, impotent ships. There was to be
no naval *Götterdämmerung*.

But if there was anarchy in the German navy, all was not
quite sweetness and light in the Allied camp either.

As so often happens when wars come to an end, the
erstwhile bosom friends and allies began to regard each other
with some suspicion, now that the binding force of mutual
danger was relaxed. Motives and possible demands were
examined much more closely than when they all 'had their backs
to the wall.' It was generally agreed that Germany should hand
over 74 warships including ten named battleships, six named
battlecruisers, eight light cruisers and fifty destroyers. The 200 or
so U-boats were dealt with separately and without disagreement
but the surface vessels caused problems for the Allies. The
British and French Admiralties wanted them all to be surrendered
while the American Navy department wanted ten of the battleships to be interned in a neutral port. These were the sailors'
views but they were overruled by the politicians who decided that
all 74 ships should be interned, pending a final decision on their
ultimate fate being made at the peace conference.

Article XXIII of the Armistice terms stated: 'The German
surface warships, which shall be designated by the Allies and the
United States of America, shall forthwith be dismantled and
thereafter interned in neutral ports, or, failing them, Allied ports
to be designated by the Allies and the United States of America,

K

only care and maintenance parties being left on board.' And the ships were then named.

But no neutral nation wanted them. Norway and Spain were approached but turned the proposal down flat, so, on 11 November, the alternative contained in Article XXIII, 'Allied ports', was decided on by the Allied Naval Council, and Scapa Flow, where the Grand Fleet could guard them, was selected. It was to be a fateful decision.

On 20 November the Grand Fleet in all its majesty sailed out from the Forth in the dark before dawn—two squadrons of battlecruisers, five squadrons of battleships, seven squadrons of cruisers—in two columns, each fifteen miles long and separated by six miles of sullen sea. Ahead steamed a screen of 150 destroyers which, with ships from the US Navy, the Dominions and the Allies, brought the total up to some 250 ships, the largest concentration of sea power ever seen.

Operation ZZ had begun. The Grand Fleet and the *Hochseeflotte* were about to meet again in the North Sea for the first time since Jutland two-and-a-half years before. But this time not a gun was fired. The German ships had been disarmed and carried no ammunition. Just to make sure, however, the British and Allied ships were all at 'Action Stations', their guns loaded and trained on the defeated enemy which appeared in single column line ahead, like weary spectres out of the morning mist.

Nothing happened. The two columns of Allied ships carried out an impeccable 16-point outward turn in unison so that they headed the way they had come, and the once proud and formidable German ships, now dirty and dishonoured, led by the single British cruiser *Cardiff*, crept between them to be escorted into a captivity from which they would never emerge. There was no fight left in the High Seas Fleet.

They headed for Aberlady Bay in the Forth, inside May Island, bearing names to become as familiar to Orcadians as those of the British fleet—*Moltke, Seydlitz, Hindenburg, Derfflinger, von der Tann, Friedrich der Grosse, Emden* and many more, over seventy in all. Here in the Forth Beatty made his famous, and uncompromising, signal to his former foes— 'The German flag will be hauled down at sunset today and is not to be hoisted again without permission.' The German Commander-in-Chief, Rear Admiral Ludwig von Reuter, who was to command the interned fleet in Scapa, protested against this humiliation but to no avail. Beatty was adamant and did not even meet von Reuter either then or later.

Speaking to the crew of his flagship, the *Queen Elizabeth*, he rubbed salt in the wound saying without the least sign of magnanimity—'Didn't I tell you they would have to come out?'

Beatty later visited his former flagship, the *Lion,* in which he had fought at Jutland and speaking to her crew expressed in bitter words his contempt for the German navy, saying of the surrender:

It was a pitiable sight—in fact, it was a horrible sight—to see these great ships following a British light cruiser and being shepherded like a flock of sheep by the Grand Fleet. We expected them to have the courage that we look for from those whose work lies upon great waters. We expected them to do something for the honour of their country and I am sure that the sides of this gallant old ship, which has been well hammered in the past, must have ached, as I ached and as you ached, to give them another taste of what we intended for them. But I will say this, that their humiliating end was a sure end, and a proper end to an enemy who has proved himself so lacking in chivalry. At sea his strategy, his tactics and his behaviour have been beneath contempt . . .

And he added:

They are now going to be taken away and placed under the guardianship of the Grand Fleet at Scapa, where they will enjoy (laughter), as we have enjoyed, the pleasures of Scapa (laughter).[7]

These were the strong sentiments of a man denied the opportunity of 'having another go' which he so deeply wanted in spite of, or perhaps because of, having had to endure four-and-a-half years of the most horrific war the world had known up till then, and he had no scruples about heaping humiliation on a defeated enemy who had denied him the chance of the ultimate glory.

The next stage in this degradation followed almost immediately. Two days after they had been escorted into the Forth the first batch of German destroyers, twenty in all, were on their way north, escorted by an equal number of British destroyers. They arrived in Scapa Flow on Saturday morning, 23 November, to be followed next day by twenty more. On Monday 25 November, the battlecruisers *Hindenburg, Derfflinger, Seydlitz, von der Tann* and *Moltke* crept through Hoxa Sound, their shame partly hidden by a merciful mist so that they were difficult to see from the shore except that they were 'dirty, foul-smelling, and ill-found' according to a report in 'The Orcadian' and it was noted that the dense black clouds of heavy smoke from their funnels indicated the poor quality coal they were using. It was thought that this probably accounted for the fact that they were unable to maintain the 12 knots ordered by the Royal Navy escort which on this particular day included HMS *Lion,* Beatty's Jutland flagship, the First Battle Squadron and ten destroyers.

They were also given an air escort for their entry into the Flow by aircraft from Houton Air Station. The Reverend Dr T. Crouther Gordon of Helensburgh was a pilot at this time and recalls flying over the battlecruisers as they came in through the Hoxa Boom—'It was a spectacle never to be forgotten,' he wrote in 'The Orcadian' in 1983. He also remembered that the Houton aircrews had been briefed just a few days before the Armistice for a bombing raid on this same German fleet in Kiel. 'Fortunately it was not necessary. There they [now] lay surrendered and helpless with never a flag that fluttered,' he wrote. He, too, noted that 'the destroyers were in a very filthy, paintless and rusty condition'.[8]

The nine battleships followed on 26 and 27 November, *Bayern, Markgraf, Friedrich der Grosse,* von Reuter's flagship, *Grosser Kurfürst, Kaiser, Kaiserin, Kronprinz Wilhelm, König Albert* and *Prinz Regent Luitpold* with the light cruisers *Brummer, Bremse, Emden, Karlsruhe, Nürnberg* and *Frankfurt.* They were escorted by an equal number of British ships from the First Battle Squadron and accompanying cruisers.

So, exactly a week after they had surrendered to the Grand Fleet in the North Sea, all seventy ships of the Hochseeflotte were swinging unhappily at their mooring in the Scapa Flow anchorage on which they had cast so many envious but frustrated looks for four-and-a-half years of war. The capital ships were in a horseshoe formation round the north end of Cava, the destroyers in what the British navy probably considered to be the appropriately named Gutter Sound between Fara and Hoy, the coal boat anchorage for the Grand Fleet during the war. They were never to put to sea again under their own steam.

There were still four ships to come from Germany to make up the 74 required under the Armistice terms. The battleship *König* arrived on 6 December direct from Germany, after repairs, and so did the badly damaged light cruiser *Dresden* which had been hastily patched up but which was still leaking badly. A destroyer, *V 30,* had struck a mine while crossing to the surrender and had sunk. She was replaced by the *V 129*—the

German destroyers, unlike the British, did not have names, only numbers.

Finally, on 9 January 1919, the battleship *Baden*, one of the finest and newest of the High Seas Fleet, sailed into captivity in the Flow, taking the place of the newly built *Mackensen* named by the Allies but not yet ready for sea. The tally was complete.

The Germans were not impressed by the scenic beauties of their watery prison camp. 'No place could be more God-forsaken,' wrote one of them in the 'Hamburger Nachtrichten'. Another wrote home saying: 'If the English have stood this for four years, they deserve to have won the war.'

One of the German destroyer officers wrote in his diary on the day of his arrival in the Flow:

Monday, 23 November. Scapa Flow is a splendid harbour, well protected on all sides. The entrance is secured by nets and mine barriers. On shore the houses of the natives are about as high as a good German dog kennel. The English have been lying here for four years. They must have been pretty uncomfortable. It is all the stranger to see how little this naval base has been developed. There is no pier for destroyers. I am relieved by the order that only one officer and 19 men are to remain on every destroyer.[9]

Even before the ships arrived in the Flow Beatty had ordered transports from Germany to take their crews, other than those required for care and maintenance, back home to their revolution-torn Fatherland. But, of course, Germany was very short of ships. Eventually, on 3 December, two did arrive at Scapa, the ss *Sierra Ventana* and the ss *Graf Waldersee,* with supplies, for the Germans had to victual their ships themselves. These two merchant vessels were quite inadequate for the repatriation of all the German sailors who wanted to get home. About 4000 out of the 20,000 or so men who had brought the fleet across the North Sea, did get away in grossly over-crowded conditions. Three days later two more transports arrived, the ss *Pretoria* and ss *Burgermeister,* to collect some 5,500 ratings and 500 officers for Wilhelmshaven and Kiel. The third and, for the time being, final lift came on 12 December when two merchant ships, ss *Batavia* and ss *Bremen,* took a total of 4,300 men and 700 officers away to the same two ports. The Royal Navy was only too glad to see them go, even though it left a total of nearly 5000 men still in the Flow—175 to each battleship, 80 to each cruiser and 20 to a destroyer.

Von Reuter himself returned to Germany on the ss *Bremen*

for a long leave said to be on health grounds. He came back to Scapa, probably unwillingly, on 25 January, when Orkney, like the rest of Scotland, was celebrating Burns Night. It is doubtful, however, if the Rear Admiral-in-Charge, German Ships at Scapa, as the British now officially designated him, would have relished raising his glass to the Immortal Memory of a poet so imbued with egalitarian principles, especially when he saw the state of anarchy among the crew of his flagship, the *Friedrich der Grosse*. 'The ship is a madhouse,' he wrote.

To a greater or lesser extent the German ships were controlled, not by their officers, but by self-appointed Workers' and Soldiers' Councils or Soviets which had come into being as the Kaiser's Reich disintegrated in revolution and defeat. In Scapa these Councils, loosely under a Supreme Soldiers' Council of the Internment Formation, had most influence in the bigger ships and least in the destroyers and cruisers. Discipline, or the lack of it, varied from ship to ship and was almost totally absent on the flagship itself; indeed members of its particular Council had tried to kill von Reuter's deputy during his absence.

Von Reuter tried to get rid of as many as possible of the worst agitators by sending them back to Germany on the regular supply ships—the British supplied only coal, oil and water to the Germans, commodities posing too severe a logistic problem for the defeated nation itself to solve. Eventually von Reuter established some form of control over the crews, or at least a working relationship with these Councils. He also removed his flag from the tense and dissident atmosphere of the *Friedrich der Grosse* and hoisted it in the relatively calmer environment of a smaller vessel, the cruiser *Emden*. Having been in command of a reconnaissance force during the war, he said he was happier in smaller ships anyway, but both his own fleet and the British navy felt that he was lowering the dignity and prestige of his rank and appointment by the move.

As time moved on, the German sailors, already disaffected, became more and more restive. None of them was allowed ashore nor could they visit any other ship. They had no radio, no newspapers except 'The Times' and heavily censored ones from Germany, their mail in both directions was censored in London resulting in delays of ten days to a fortnight, and there was a very strict 'no fraternisation' order to British personnel with even the shaking of hands being forbidden. And their food was poor and monotonous. Moreover, their ships, even the big ones, were not designed for living on board for any length of time as the British ships were. When the German fleet was in port, and that was a great deal of the time, most of the crews were housed ashore in barracks, only going on board again when the ships were about to put to sea for a sortie which might not be of more than two or three days duration. British naval vessels, in order to protect the Empire trade routes, had had to spend much longer periods at sea and their crews' quarters were designed accordingly, although even they were by no means luxurious.

In one newspaper report it was stated that the men's quarters on the German ships were 'crude and uncomfortable. And so the German seamen are sending up howls of protest.' An officer aboard HMS *Hercules* is quoted as saying: 'If the Hun is squealing after four weeks at Scapa, I wonder what he would have done if he had had our four years of it?' To which a British staff officer who had recently visited the ships had replied dryly, 'You would howl yourself inside of four weeks if you had to stick in a Hun ship.' The pejorative use of the word 'Hun' seemed to be almost mandatory during and just after the First War.

In the Royal Navy there was a general feeling that it was 'poetic justice for the Huns having to live in their own ships in Scapa Flow'. It must have been a grim existence and it is not surprising that there was serious trouble aboard them from time to time. For instance, when two agitators who were being transferred back to Germany in March suddenly changed their minds, there was uproar on board the *Friedrich der Grosse* and a British destroyer stood by with guns trained and torpedo tubes cleared for action. The two men changed their minds again and went quietly.

The British, of course, had no illusions about Scapa Flow in peacetime either—useful it might be, and in war vital, but as a resort—well, no. Admiral Fremantle, who commanded the First Battle Squadron of battleships with 1200 men on each and wearing his flag on HMS *Revenge* in the Flow in early summer 1919 wrote in his memoirs, *My Naval Career*:

> If Scapa Flow presented few attractions in wartime, it had fewer still after the 'Cease Firing' had sounded. The stimulation of being at immediate readiness and being ready and hoping the High Seas Fleet would come out to test our efficiency and morale were gone.

The British, in strict observance of the Armistice terms that the ships were merely interned, did not have any guards or observers aboard any of them and maintained sea-borne guard with eight drifters, only three of which were on duty at any one time. They were manned by their normal civilian crews but they did carry an armed boarding party of Marines or bluejackets under a naval officer. And, of course, they were backed by the bigger craft, cruisers and destroyers, on a rota basis, as well as the capital ships using the Flow all the time.

The interned ships were naturally a continuous source of interest to the public and especially to the national press. In December 1918, for instance, the 'Daily Mail' carried a big feature on 'The Imprisoned Ships' describing 'ragged, dirty crews fishing from the side and through portholes' with no discipline and officers being ignored: 'the main impression from the collection of German sailors who fished was, first, their variegated, ragged and dirty clothing, and secondly, their extremely youthful appearance,' wrote the 'Mail'.[10]

The German sailors were apparently very surprised to find that their British counterparts had not mutinied as they had done themselves. The diarist on one of the German destroyers wrote on 'Monday 2 December—An English battleship lies not far from us. We can see the English sailors on board parading from 9 to 12. We did not do that in time of peace. Our men are astonished. These then are the sailors who, as we were told, had turned back from an undertaking against the Germans and had hoisted the Red Flag.'[11] The Germans had most certainly got it all wrong.

There was some disaffection among British sailors at one or two ports but it does not appear to have been of any significance whatsoever at Scapa. Admiral Fremantle wrote that it was known that 'Communist agitators were trying to subvert sailors but this was easy to check at Scapa Flow but not so easy at Rosyth and other bigger ports where some destroyer crews refused to sail for the Baltic'. Fremantle, in fact, was ordered south to sort the trouble out.[12]

So, the shooting and killing war was over; the weapons now were words and declarations by politicians and statesmen wrangling over the mangled carcase of Europe like pinstriped hoodie crows. It was to go on at the Palace of Versailles for six months and more while the ships lay almost derelict in Scapa. What would be their fate? Who would get them? If they were divided up equally between the victorious Allies, that would make Britain, already the strongest naval power in the world, stronger still—a state of affairs the other nations, allies though they were, did not contemplate with any enthusiasm. But if the ships were to be shared out on a differential basis—how was this to be worked out? It was a diplomatic minefield fraught with political peril. No wonder there was a British suggestion that the

A 6-inch gun in one of the open emplacements of the First War at Ness Battery covering Hoy Sound.

HMS *Vanguard* which blew up at anchor off Flotta in July 1917 — only two of the ship's company survived.

One of the Short flying-boats at Houton with some of the men who serviced it.

A kite balloon flying from a battleship in the Flow — note the basket below for the observer.

Military transport at Ness Battery in World War I.

A World War I British submarine passes one of the ubiquitous drifters in Weddel Sound.

Gardening was a welcome shore-based pastime in World War I for sailors of the Grand Fleet in Scapa Flow.

The ill-fated cruiser *Hampshire* which struck a mine off Birsay in June 1916 and sank with heavy loss of life, including that of Lord Kitchener who was travelling in her to Russia.

CITY AND ROYAL BURGH OF KIRKWALL

WARNING

The Provost, Magistrates, and Councillors of Kirkwall hereby recommend the inhabitants to vacate their homes and proceed to the country, without any delay, should the town be Bombarded by the enemy.

W. J. HEDDLE,
TOWN CLERK.

KIRKWALL, 26th April 1918.

Printed at the "Orkney Herald" Office, Kirkwall.

There were no warbling sirens in 1918.

Sphagnum moss from the hills was used for First Aid dressings in World War I.

MAKING MOSS-DRESSINGS FOR THE WOUND
AT KIRKWALL APRIL 1917.

The Kaiser's biggest battleship, the *Bayern,* creeps through the Hoxa boom to internment in November 1918.

The German sailors have opened the seacocks and as their rusty ship settles they take to the boats.

Still at its mooring, a German destroyer heels over on its final plunge.

SEA TRIPS (2 HOURS.)
"FLYING KESTREL"
"HERALD" & "EGERTON"

Princes Stage 2·45 p.m. Daily. *SUNDAYS EXCEPTED*

Fare 1/-   **Children 3ᵈ**

ALEXANDRA TOWING Cº Lᵗᵈ. LIVERPOOL

The *Flying Kestrel* was the water boat in the Flow in World War I. She took part in searching for survivors from HMS *Hampshire,* and later she was carrying a party of Stromness schoolchildren on a trip through the Flow when the Germans scuttled their ships.

Orkney Territorials guard a German destroyer which just failed to scuttle itself in 1919.

The tide races between the blockships in Holm Sound, or Kirk Sound as it was called by the Navy — ss *Thames* on the right, *Numidian* on the left, and the *Aorangi* in the middle.

BLOCK-SHIPS IN HOLM SOUND. T. KENT

whole German Fleet should be taken out of Scapa Flow and sunk in deep water somewhere.

On the other hand, Merseyside would apparently have welcomed a visit by the interned ships, at least for a short time. The 'Liverpool Echo' asked—'Why bury the surrendered German Fleet of magnificent super-Dreadnoughts and battle-cruisers in Scapa Flow? Liverpool and the other great ports which have maintained the flow of merchantmen and men-of-war through the storm and stress of five years ought to be privileged to see at least one or two of the vessels.' They could help raise money for war charities, the paper suggested. A sort of latter-day floating Roman Triumph, it would seem.

As far as the sailors, soldiers and airmen of both sides were concerned, the main thing was that the 'war to end wars' was over and all they wanted was to get home as soon as possible—perhaps even in time for Christmas—and after that, to pick up the pieces of civilian life again.

The Marines on the Fixed Defences of the Flow published a monthly magazine 'The Concentrator', which summed things up pretty succinctly for the 1200 men on these batteries at the time in its last, and Christmas, issue of December 1918.

In the Hoxa News its correspondent wrote:

Since our last notes, many interesting events have occurred. U Boat 115 [*sic*] has met her fate. Teddy has won his spoon. The Armistice has been signed. We have spliced the mainbrace. Seventy German ships have passed here for internment in the Flow. And some fortunates have been demobilised.

You can't get much terser than that even if the U-boat number is wrong—it should have been *UB 116*. A concentrator, incidently, was an internal telephone exchange through which the units' signals and messages passed—hence the name of the magazine. They were still in use round the Flow at the beginning of the Second War.

There was a verse, too, of a kind, in that issue which went—

> Are we tired, fed up with Orkney?
> With these islands of the Blessed,
> Switha, Neb, Hoy I and Clestron,
> (to say nothing of all the other Batteries, Station Huts, Patrols, Boom Defences, Drifters, Trawlers, Minesweepers, Battleships, Destroyers and umpteen other kinds of vessels).
> Answer—YES.

There was also reference to the 'flu epidemic sweeping the country at this time, including Orkney, when the magazine reported—'Monday—12 new cases; Tuesday—28 new cases; Wednesday—No new cases—all three doctors are laid up.' The rather flippant style concealed considerable anxiety, for this was a deadly epidemic which caused many deaths, both civilian and military.

But at least the horrific killing of the Western Front was ended—for a few years anyway.

CHAPTER 16

'The Suicide Navee'

IT WAS STILL, however, only a 'paper' peace—a cease-fire. Hostilities could begin again at any time for anyone who still had the will to fight. Fortunately very few did—on either side—neither the will nor, on Germany's part, the means. Now it was all up to the statesmen and politicians. A new map of Europe had to be drawn with, it was hoped, more sensible and safer frontiers. It was, unfortunately, no more than a pious hope.

And what was to happen to those seventy-four disarmed German warships sulking rustily in Scapa Flow?

In the end, of course, the problem was largely solved by the German sailors themselves. In one of the world's greatest acts of self-immolation they sank their own fleet—the most dramatic single event in Scapa Flow's already colourful history.

It began about noon on Midsummer Day, 21 June 1919—the day that Rear Admiral von Reuter, commanding the interned fleet, along with members of his staff, understood that the Armistice would come to an end, with Germany either accepting the harsh terms of the Peace Treaty or the resumption of hostilities.

The planning of the scuttle must have begun long before that—possibly when von Reuter was home on leave in December and January, or even earlier still. As far as he and his officers were concerned, the Kaiser's standing order that no German ship was to fall into the hands of the enemy still held good.

The peace terms were drawn up at Versailles by 6 May but it was the 11th before the Scapa internees knew the details of them. From the naval point of view they were harsh. All the interned ships were to be handed over to the Allies, along with a further 52 destroyers. The German navy would be cut to 15,000 men and 1,500 officers to man a maximum of six battleships of no more than 10,000 tons each, six cruisers of up to 6,000 tons, 12 destroyers only, with some smaller craft—and **no** submarines or aircraft.

The news caused deep depression and consternation among

the men of the interned ships; even the subversives felt a sense of utter humiliation.

In his writings after the war von Reuter always maintained that he received neither news of the peace terms nor any official instructions from the German Government as to what he should do in Scapa when the peace negotiations came to an end either way. So, he decided that it was up to him to take what action he thought fit and appropriate. He believed that if his Government rejected the peace terms hostilities would be resumed, the British obviously seizing his disarmed ships. There was no possibility of his making a fight of it and, with the Kaiser's standing order in mind, the only way of preventing them falling into the hands of the enemy was to sink them. The ships, of course, could be used as a bargaining counter in the peace negotiations if the German Government might just conceivably accept the peace terms as they stood and surrender the Fleet. He also pondered the problem of knowing when the Peace Treaty, if Germany signed it, would become effective—would it be on signature, or on later ratification?

Von Reuter's big fear was that the British would act pre-emptively on signature and seize the ships immediately. It was a fear that was certainly justified, for the British had foreseen the possibility of a scuttle and had prepared contingency plans accordingly.[1]

Vice-Admiral Fremantle commanding the First Battle Squadron, in overall charge of guarding the interned ships at Scapa, wrote in his autobiography *My Naval Career* that since his arrival in Scapa Flow on 18 May the German crews had been 'showing signs of truculence' and on the anniversary of the battle of Jutland they dressed their ships overall— '. . . an outburst we were compelled, of course, to suppress immediately'.

Under the terms of the Armistice Fremantle had no access to the interned ships and so had no direct information as to what preparations might have been made on board them regarding action to be taken when the Armistice ended. This was supposed to happen on 21 June but the deadline was extended by two days to 23 June when, either the Germans would sign on the dotted line, or hostilities would begin again. Fremantle himself only learned of this two-day extension from the newspapers. He received no official notification of the change of date from either his immediate superior officer, Admiral Sir Charles Madden, C-in-C Atlantic Fleet, who knew about it as early as 17 June, nor from the Admiralty, and he never received any instructions from either of them as to what was to be done with the German ships when the Armistice did end. 'A difficult situation,' he commented.[2]

It would seem that both British and German commanders at Scapa were being left to their own devices by their respective higher echelons and Governments. Fremantle wrote:

> Certain minor occurrences and movements had been observed on board the German ships which led me to suspect that some momentous action was contemplated by them. I had accordingly arranged, with Admiralty approval, that at midnight on the 21st we should board and take possession of all the ships, confining the officers and men under close confinement and using any force which might be necessary. Secret orders and preparations had been prepared to put the measure into execution.'[3]

At the same time the C-in-C Atlantic Fleet, Admiral Madden, had ordered Fremantle's First Battle Squadron to carry out certain routine exercises at sea and to finish them by 21 June. Bad weather, however, intervened and they had to be postponed. Fremantle informed Madden of the delay and suggested that the exercises should now be deferred 'until the Germans were off our hands'. Madden did not approve such a delay but ordered that the exercises should take place **on** the 21st.

'I went to sea on the morning of the 21st,' wrote Fremantle in his autobiography. 'I was very uneasy before sailing and informed von Reuter unofficially that I believed the Armistice to be still in operation.'[4] Von Reuter always maintained afterwards that he himself had no knowledge of this extension of the deadline to 23 June until after his ships were at the bottom of the Flow.

The Germans, meantime, had also made plans and preparations, starting in mid-May when they first learned the terms of the Peace Treaty. As might be expected they made a thorough job of it. Much of the planning had to be carried out under tight security for von Reuter and his staff could not entirely trust the crews, and with so many men having so little to do rumour-spreading was a universal pastime. Surprisingly enough the plans to scuttle did not become common knowledge among the ratings, generally, until 20 June, less than twenty-four hours before they were put into execution, and then the news spread through the mess-decks of at least two of the capital ships like wildfire.[5]

Just a few days earlier two transports, ss *Bedima* and ss *Schleswig,* had arrived in Scapa with stores and supplies from Germany. Von Reuter took the opportunity of getting rid of the more militant crewmen of his fleet and on 17 June embarked

2,700 men on the two ships homeward bound. They sailed out of Scapa on the morning of the 18th, leaving only 1,700 men altogether to man the 74 interned warships—75 to a battle-cruiser, 60 to a battleship and 30 to a cruiser, with only a handful to the destroyers. The British had naturally welcomed this reduction in the numbers of Germans in the Flow.

On the same day that this contingent embarked on the transports von Reuter drew up a detailed order for the scuttle, to be issued to commanders of the individual ships; only the date of execution was left blank. The destroyers had already been quietly prepared for sinking; now the commanders of the bigger ships were told to do the same. Ironically, the orders were passed secretly from ship to ship by the British patrol vessel which carried official papers to and from the ships.

Now that word had got out about the plan to scuttle the fleet, von Reuter passed another order by the same means instructing his commanding officers, at their discretion, to tell their men what was afoot. It was Friday 20 June. That evening von Reuter read in 'The Times' of London dated 16 June, which reached him four days late as usual, that the Allies had presented Germany with an ultimatum—'accept the peace terms by noon on 21 June or face a renewal of hostilities'. There was also an inference that all the German ships might be surrendered in a financial arrangement.

With a heavy heart von Reuter decided that next morning would be 'Der Tag' for his immobilised fleet. He would scuttle. What, he claimed, he did **not** know, was that on this same day, 20 June, the German Government had changed its mind. The Prime Minister, Philipp Scheidemann, who had struggled vainly to get some amelioration of the proposed peace terms, refused to sign the treaty at Versailles and had resigned. With his departure from the political scene, the Reichstag agreed by a substantial majority to accept the terms.

The Armistice was extended to Monday, 23 June, to allow further negotiations.

On Saturday morning, Midsummer Day, the British First Battle Squadron, led by Vice-Admiral Fremantle's flagship, *Revenge,* and followed by *Ramillies, Resolution, Royal Oak* and *Royal Sovereign,* sailed out through Hoxa Sound accompanied by two light cruisers and nine destroyers. Only three destroyers, *Vesper, Vega* and one other under repair, were left in the Flow along with the base ship *Victorious* at Lyness, and other auxiliary vessels. For von Reuter the coast was literally clear.

At 10 o'clock he ordered a signal 'DG' in international code flags to be hoisted on his flagship, the cruiser *Emden,* lying rather apart from the other cruisers to the north of Cava and so was one of the ships nearest to the Orphir shore. This signal meant that a close continuous watch was to be kept for further orders from the flagship—a sort of 'watch this space' instruction.

Half-an-hour later a second and equally innocuous-looking signal was hoisted—'Paragraph eleven Confirm', it read. But it was by no means innocuous. 'Paragraph eleven' was the order for the immediate scuttling of the entire fleet.[6] It was repeated by semaphore and signal lamps to be passed from ship to ship as quite a few of them, especially the destroyers in Gutter Sound, were not in visual contact with the *Emden* owing to intervening land. Oddly enough, the crew of the *Emden* herself were among the last to know what was happening. There were two British drifters and a water-boat alongside and von Reuter was afraid that the state of excitement his crew would naturally show on getting the order to scuttle would alert the British.

There was a long and pregnant pause while he waited for confirmation of his order to come in. The order had, in fact, taken nearly an hour to reach all the ships. For nearly an hour-and-a-half very little was noticeable outwardly, until about midday when the tolling of a large ship's bell sounded a sombre note across the still water. It was the 'Abandon Ship' signal from the former flagship *Friedrich der Grosse,* lying only two berths away from the *Emden*.

Slowly she settled, hung shuddering for a few minutes, then turned over and slid below the surface, two great jets of water spouting from her twin funnels as she sank. It was just a quarter-of-an-hour past noon. She was the first to go and von Reuter must have watched her demise with very mixed feelings after the difficulties he had endured while using her as flagship.

One after another these great ships settled, dipped as their bows or sterns rose in the air, rolled over and went down in clouds of steam with water gushing from the various vents, leaving nothing but oily bubbles, floating debris and sailors in boats, rafts or in the water, to mark where they had lain for seven long dreary months.

It was all over by 5 o'clock in the afternoon when the last of the big ships, the battlecruiser *Hindenburg*, pride of the fleet though never blooded in battle, settled on an even keel, her tripod mast and twin funnels clear and her deck awash, a familiar sight in the Flow for the next decade and more.

All five of the battlecruisers, *Seydlitz, Moltke, von der Tann, Derfflinger,* and *Hindenburg,* went to the bottom between ten past one that afternoon and five o'clock when the *Hindenburg* foundered. Of the big ships only the *Baden,* one of Germany's newest and most powerful battleships, did not sink and was successfully beached before she filled. She had been one of the last ships to join the interned Fleet, arriving only in January to take the place of the unfinished *Mackensen* which the Allies had originally demanded. The other battleships — *Prinzregent Luitpold, Kaiserin, König Albert, Friedrich der Grosse, König, Grosser Kurfürst, Kronprinz Wilhelm, Markgraf* and *Bayern* —all sank between 12.16 p.m. when the *Friedrich der Grosse* led the way down, and 4.45 p.m. when the *Markgraf* made her final plunge.

Of the eight light cruisers, only five succeeded in scuttling and ironically one of the three which did not make it to the bottom was von Reuter's own flagship, the *Emden,* from which the fleet order to scuttle had emanated. The *Frankfurt* was also beached and the *Nürnberg* just drifted ashore. Five destroyers were also beached.

In less than five hours of a fine summer afternoon 52 ships, including the biggest and most powerful, had foundered and now lay at the bottom of Scapa Flow under as much as 120 feet of water while the rest of the 74 were either damaged or beached or both. The vaunted German High Seas Fleet, pride of the Kaiser, had committed mass naval suicide.

So much for the cold facts. How did it look to the crowds who gathered along the Orphir shore and elsewhere round the Flow? Or to those who were at sea among the ships as they went down, such as the party of Stromness schoolchildren who were on a day trip through the fleet when everything began to happen?

But first of all, here is how it looked to trained observers led by James Mackintosh, proprietor and editor of the county newspaper 'The Orcadian,' who were on the spot as fast as they could get there and who wrote down what they had seen within hours of it happening. Their story was splashed across four columns of the paper's centre-spread in the next issue on 26 June 1919.

News that something was amiss reached Kirkwall on Saturday about one o'clock.

Representatives of 'The Orcadian' immediately proceeded by motor car to Houton Air Station overlooking the anchorage where the heavy German ships were wont to lie not a mile away.[7]

I saw several of these ships sink including the *Brummer* and the *Bremen* [*Bremse?*] which were painted black to commemorate their attack on the Norwegian convoy, and the sinking of the British destroyer, *Mary Rose;* also the beaching of three of the light cruisers.

The battleships, as a rule, gradually submerged until their decks were awash, turned turtle and quietly slipped out of sight. A slight boiling of the sea, repeated at intervals for more than an hour afterwards, and a bluish tinge on the water caused by the release of oil, were all that marked the spot where, for months before, had lain the onetime pride of a nation.

The light cruisers settled by the stern. As the afterparts of the ship disappeared, the bows and a hundred feet or more of the hull projected sheer from the sea looking like some huge whale leaping through space, for more than an hour before the final plunge. It was evident to the spectators on shore that the last of the battleships to sink was doomed. A drifter and a trawler were at work alongside; a destroyer was standing by. Evidently an attempt was being made to tow the ship, for with propellers still working she came to a dead stop. A long splash between the destroyer and the battleship showed that a tow-line had parted. Suddenly the battleship canted violently to port. The drifter and trawler moved off, and more quickly than a photographer at my side could change a plate, not a vestige of the ship remained.

A young lady told me that between 12.15 and 12.30 she saw one of the battleships take a sudden list. She called her father's attention to this but even as she spoke, masts and funnels disappeared, the hull, bottom up, lay exposed for a matter of seconds and then went out of sight. . .

A number of German sailors came alongside Houton pier early in the afternoon but were refused permission to land and directed to report to the flagship. I was told, though I was unable to obtain confirmation, that among these was the German Admiral who made an appeal for assistance to save his men.

Strong patrols of Royal Marines were landed from the battle fleet shortly after five o'clock, and these took up positions along the beach presumably to deal with any of the German seamen who may have swum ashore.

As I left Houton my attention was directed to a mooring buoy some short distance off the Houton shore to which I could clearly see a man clinging. I was told that he had been observed swimming from the direction of a sinking warship.

The late Mrs Hester Scarth of Binscarth was at Swanbister that day and she also remembered seeing survivors on the skerry, the Barrel of Butter, in the middle of the Flow, from which they were eventually picked up.

One of her strongest recollections of that eventful day, she once told me, was not so much of the German ships going down, spectacular though that was, but of the British destroyers which had been on exercise outside coming back at full speed and 'simply tearing across the Flow throwing up tremendous bow waves'.

The sight from the Orphir shore must indeed have been a compelling one. The late Mr Kenneth Flett, Mussaquoy, County Councillor for Orphir in later life, recalled that on 21 June that year there was a funeral in the Orphir kirkyard by the shore. The deceased had just been laid to rest and the minister was in the middle of the committal service when a whisper went round the mourners—'Boy, the Germans is sinking their ships.' When the minister opened his eyes he was shocked to see not a single mourner left at the graveside—they were lining the kirkyard dyke above the shore gazing out at this unique spectacle. As far as is known he joined them.

Awe-inspiring as it was, seen from the shore at least a mile away, how much more so it must have been for those schoolchildren, nearly 200 of them, on board the *Flying Kestrel* right in the middle of it all with these massive men-of-war going down all round them.

Miss Meg Yorston, who was looking after the children on board, told her brother, Frederic Yorston, editor of 'The Montreal Standard', what she had seen and he included her account in a general story about Scapa Flow which he published in his paper after the war.

Some went down with their sterns almost vertical above the water, others listed to port or starboard with vast clouds of steam and rivers of oil pouring out of their vents and bubbling to the surface after the ships had reached the bottom and there was the roaring of escaping steam and the shouts of thousands of sailors as they made off in their boats.

There was much shouting of orders from the rescue craft who were trying to get the sinking German ships ashore. Then the sea was littered for miles with all sorts of debris, boats, hammocks, lifebelts, chests, etc., bobbing along the waves.

Every sort of craft seemed to be there. There were drifters picking up German sailors from the water after they had jumped overboard, there was a pinnace towing a long string of boats. There were floats loaded with prisoners on their way to the flagship. Other craft were busy heading off German sailors who were trying to escape.[8]

Some of the debris Miss Yorston mentions travelled quite a

long way, with some very unpalatable black bread being picked up along with other flotsam some days later on the Banffshire coast.

Mrs Margaret Gibson of Kirkwall, aged ten at the time, was on the school trip and in later years gave a very vivid account on Radio Orkney of what she saw from the *Flying Kestrel* as it made its way through the stricken fleet. They had hoped to see the British fleet as well but, of course, it was at sea. While they were on their way down the Flow a trawler came up with them and one of the crew shouted across—'The German fleet is sinking. Make for the *Victorious.*' The *Victorious* was the HQ Base ship moored off Lyness.

Mrs Gibson said:

I saw twelve capital ships sinking. Some stood up on their bows, some went over on their sides and the water was boiling everywhere. Men were on rafts and in boats. We saw them landing on the island of Cava and running up from the shore. Every German boat had its flag at the top mast.

Alongside the *Victorious* she saw a trawler bringing the captains and other officers from the German ships and delivering them under armed escort. Mr J. R. T. Robertson, who was to become a Provost of Stromness in later life, was also with the school party and he recalled going back towards Stromness and seeing the ships foundering—'We saw what appeared to be hundreds of men on the surface swimming and as we got further away we heard small arms fire—machine guns—I can still hear it,' he said on Radio Orkney, adding 'and heavier guns too.'[9] Also on the excursion was the late Mrs Rosetta Groundwater, another future Provost of Stromness, who in a radio interview on the fiftieth anniversary of the scuttle remembered— 'I distinctly saw the *Seydlitz* turn turtle and the water come streaming out of the seacocks. We were only a few hundred yards away—and the activity was tremendous.

'Men were in boats and I definitely saw one man shot. He dropped right out of the stern of the boat. The other men were standing with their hands up.'[10]

The late Miss Kitty Watt was one of the senior girls at the time and she not only heard small arms fire but also saw its effect. She watched a drifter towing several boats full of German sailors, one of whom apparently tried to cut the tow-rope and free his boat whereupon one of the Marine guards on the drifter shot and killed him, she said.[11]

He was one of the total of nine Germans who lost their lives

that day, another being the officer commanding the battleship
Markgraf, who was shot as he emerged on to the deck after
completing the work of scuttling his ship. He was said to have
been carrying a white flag at the time.

'The Orkney Herald' had carried only a single-column story
of the scuttling in its next issue of 25 June under the heading
'Hun Perfidy at Scapa Flow—Greatest Sensation of the War',
and from its account does not appear to have had any of its
editorial staff on the actual scene. It tells of rafts coming ashore
in Holm with 'biscuits, bottles of light beer and signal pistols
and night lights'. In Kirkwall, it states, people did not at first
believe the story of the sinking and were 'slow to believe the
Huns would do such a dastardly trick'. And then goes on to
comment: '. . . but who can analyse the German mentality? It is
a thing apart; and savours much of the mentality of the brute
creation.' Not much sign of magnanimity there.

The 'Herald' in its next issue carried a very full account of
the scuttle as seen from the *Flying Kestrel.* She had left
Stromness at 10.30 that morning with her complement of schoolchildren, passing the *Baden, Kaiserin, Kaiser* and *König Albert*
before going on past the *Derfflinger, Hindenburg,* and *Seydlitz*
where they saw, to their great surprise, frantic preparations in
progress to launch the ship's boats—something which was strictly
forbidden. They came to the conclusion, however, that it must
be something to with a change-over of crews. The *Flying Kestrel*
went on her way to the hospital ships and the *Victorious* before
turning back.

'A sailor was seen ascending one of the masts of a destroyer
and attaching the German Imperial Ensign to the shrouds,'
stated the 'Herald' story. The crew of the *Flying Kestrel* were
doubtful about what was happening, even after a passing trawler
hailed them with the news that the Germans were sinking
themselves.

They remained incredulous until they saw a ship actually
heel over and go down a few minutes later. Then they noticed
that all the ships were flying German ensigns of the largest
possible size but they noted only one Red Flag. Pinnaces and
small boats were alongside, filled, or being filled with men. The
'Herald' description goes on—

> The ships began to sink deeper in the water, generally settling
> more quickly by the stern than by the bows. When the water
> reached the level of the deck at the stern, and was approaching
> the after turret the ship generally heeled over and turned
> bottom upwards. For some time the keel remained above the

surface with steam pouring through vents in the bottom but soon the hulls themselves disappeared.

The children were naturally very excited, especially when the returning British destroyers came up with all guns cleared for action and trained on the ships from which men were trying to get away. Machine-guns were heard firing, but not at the German sailors as far as could be seen from the *Flying Kestrel*.

'On board one of the dirty destroyers was to be seen standing on the deck a German officer dressed in his frock-coat and black gloves,' it was noted. The *Flying Kestrel* made for Stromness with all speed where anxious parents were lining the harbour front and all vantage points, relieved to see their sons and daughters safe and sound after a never-to-be-forgotten school outing.

The experience of being among these great ships as they turned over and sank left an indelible impression on the young minds of those on board the *Flying Kestrel* that day — impressions which would remain with them for the rest of their lives. Mr John Knarston was one of the party and 37 years later when he was then living in New South Wales, Australia, he recalled those impressions in 'The Orcadian' of 13 September 1956. The Stromness headmaster, Mr Hepburn, he said, accompanied them on the trip and he also remembered seeing the destroyer *Wescott* opening fire on the anchor chains of some of the German ships so that they might drift ashore. Another of his memories was of a 'puffer' steaming down among the sinking Germans and 'at the galley corner we saw a man with a rifle sniping away to his heart's content. Maybe he was just having a practice at gulls — but I "hae me doots",' commented Mr Knarston.

One man who had a ringside seat was the marine artist B. F. Gribble who had passed up the chance of going to sea with the British Battle Squadron that morning in order to sketch some of the German ships from the patrol trawler *Sochisin,* herself a former German vessel. He described what he saw in a feature published in 'The Orcadian' later.[12]

First of all he observed the cruiser, *Frankfurt,* beginning to sink although she was actually beached by the British as her decks became awash. The armed naval guard on the trawler, seeing the German sailors in her boats, ordered them back to their ship. The Germans shouted, 'We have no oars', where-upon, Gribble reports, 'a Petty Officer threw some into the sea calling out, "There you are, you swine".'

Two boats approached the trawler, the men in them asking

to be taken on board. They were refused and told to return to their ship. The British Guard Commander, Lieutenant Leeth, aboard the *Sochisin*, told them: 'Return to your ships at once. If you do not do so I will fire on you.' And he did. Gribble then records the following exchange after the Germans had put up a white flag. An officer called, 'You have killed four of my men and we have no arms. I want to look after the men.' The reply was: 'You look after them by getting them back to their ships.' To which he called back, 'We can't go back, they are sinking.' But Lieutenant Leeth was adamant, 'You must go back and prevent them from sinking.' The German's answer was 'It's not our fault. We are carrying out orders.'

Gribble also reports that some of the German officers were smoking cigars and wearing yellow kid gloves. There was, he says, 'a good deal of cross-fire which lasted for about three quarters of an hour.'

Out at sea the First Battle Squadron had ended its exercise at noon. It had included a torpedo attack by destroyers on the big ships, and twenty of the 'tin fish' were still in the water awaiting collection when an urgent radio signal from ACOS, Vice-Admiral Sir Richard Prendergast, back in Scapa reported that the Germans had hoisted their ensigns and that many of the ships were heeling over and sinking. Fremantle ordered his ships back to harbour at full speed, organising salvage operations on the way and detailing a patrol to block the entrances to the Flow in order to stop any possible attempt at escape by the Germans. Marines were to deal with any landing.[13]

On arrival back in the Flow during the afternoon, salvage parties from the Squadron boarded the ships still afloat. 'But the Bosche had been too clever for us,' wrote Fremantle in his memoirs. 'His preparations had evidently been in progress many weeks. Watertight doors were jammed open and the handles removed. Anchor chains and winding gear were wrecked.'

He goes on: 'The destroyers and drifters on guard had done their duty and as far as possible prevented lowering of boats, even inflicting a certain number of casualties in the process. But once boats were in the water they were, according to the practices of the sea, inviolable.'[14] This statement hardly accords with the description of the scene by Mrs Groundwater or Miss Watt or by the artist, Gribble.

Fremantle states that the casualty list was eight killed, eight wounded, which was true of the period during which the ships were scuttled but it rose to nine killed with the shooting that night of a German sailor, a prisoner on board the *Resolution,* for which a mentally deranged British sailor who allegedly shot him was charged with murder. The charge was found 'Not Proven' in the High Court in Edinburgh the following year.[15]

At 4 o'clock that afternoon with some of his ships still sinking, von Reuter formally surrendered on board Fremantle's flagship, the *Revenge,* where to his intense indignation he was accused by the British Admiral of treachery, a charge he strenuously denied.[16]

He was bitterly disappointed that his own flagship, the *Emden,* was one of the few ships of his fleet which had not gone to the bottom.

There are at least three versions of what happened to her and the German Admiral. Fremantle says that the RNR skipper of a drifter alongside her that morning realised what was going on when he saw the cruiser's boats being launched, for this was strictly forbidden under the internment regulations. He rounded up these boats, according to Fremantle, and took them two or three hundred yards away from the ship. 'This did not suit the Bosche at all,' wrote Fremantle, 'when he realised he would have to swim for it. The skipper of the drifter would not allow anyone to leave the *Emden,* not even von Reuter himself, until he was sure she would not sink.'[17]

The version given by Dan van der Vat in his book *The Grand Scuttle,* published in 1982, differs considerably. He writes that the order to scuttle the *Emden* herself had been delayed because of the presence of drifters alongside but when it **was** given, the crew's morale got a tremendous boost.

They abandoned their midday meal and set about the task of self-destruction with vigour. Once the nearby *Friedrich der Grosse* had gone down, van der Vat writes, the crews of the two British drifters alongside *Emden* made to cast off but were prevented from doing so by the Germans who held on to the hawsers while others tossed their gear aboard and scrambled down into the smaller vessels. The second of these was the drifter detailed for von Reuter's own use on tours of inspection.

He went ashore in her, possibly to Hoy, to try to stop the firing which could be heard. He was unsuccessful and on the way back to the *Emden,* which was still afloat, his drifter ran aground in a bay in Cava. From there he could see his Admiral's flag flying on the *Emden,* but not the ship herself as she was hidden by the intervening island. After about an hour the drifter refloated on the rising tide and by that time, 1.30 p.m. or so, the first of the British destroyers had arrived back in the Flow. One of them made for the waterlogged *Emden,* cut her mooring cable, and towed her inshore where she was beached near Smoogro in Orphir.[18]

So whatever is the true version, she did not sink and was one of the first to be salvaged; she was handed over eventually to France.

In his book *Scapa and a Camera* published in 1921, C. W. Burrows, Cashier of the Dockyard Section at Scapa from 1915 onwards, says he was on board a picket-boat which sailed through the German Fleet as it was sinking, putting boarding parties on to the ships, where possible, to haul down the German ensigns and to try to release the anchor chains so that the ships might drift ashore. They were hailed from the deck of a trawler by von Reuter, he wrote, when they were abreast of the *König Albert* some distance north of Cava.

From this it would seem that there is considerable doubt about the movements of the German Admiral between midday, after he had given the order to scuttle, and 4 p.m. when he surrendered on board the *Revenge*.

The German sailors generally were distributed among the battleships of the Squadron, '. . . where they were to be treated with no further consideration than the dictates of common humanity required,' wrote Fremantle. Von Reuter himself was isolated in Fremantle's own upper deck cabin, to which food from the Admiral's table was sent to him.[19]

The Squadron sailed for Invergordon that night with the 1774 Germans, now truly prisoners of war, to be handed over to the military escort of Seaforth Highlanders waiting for them. During the voyage south von Reuter slept peacefully and later wrote '. . . it was a long time since I spent such a restful night as this'.

But before he left the *Revenge* the following morning, he and his officers were paraded on the quarter-deck facing Fremantle and his officers, who were backed by an armed guard of Royal Marines and bluejackets in a hollow square, when the British Admiral coldly berated him, saying that by his conduct he had added one more to the breaches of faith and honour of which Germany had been guilty in the war. It had begun with a breach of military honour in the invasion of Belgium and now it was bidding fair to end with a breach of naval honour. 'You have proved to the few who doubted it that the word of the New Germany is no more to be trusted than that of the old,' said Fremantle uncompromisingly.[20]

Through an interpreter, von Reuter replied that he could not accept Fremantle's accusations and that '. . . our understanding of the matter differs. I alone carry the responsibility. I am convinced that any English naval officer placed as I was would have acted in the same way.' After this frigid exchange the

Squadron sailed again and was back in the now empty-looking Flow just before midnight.

Later Fremantle was to deny 'atrocity' accusations levelled by von Reuter regarding the British treatment of his men. Fremantle also denied allegations of the theft of personal possessions from the Germans by British sailors but he admitted rather naively that there could have been 'some souvenir hunting'. He remained convinced that von Reuter would have scuttled his fleet whatever happened, in obedience to the general orders from the Kaiser not to allow any German ship to fall into enemy hands.

He thought it 'still probable that many of our Allies believed that Britain had connived at the scuttle to obviate the distribution of the ships which would to some extent reduce Britain's naval predominance', but he denied that this was true.[21]

So ended one of the most momentous days in Scapa Flow's history. Fremantle commented: 'And so the famous High Seas Fleet, with which the Kaiser no doubt had intended to exercise his proclaimed 'Admiralty of the Atlantic' came to its appropriate end at the bottom of the great harbour which for so many dreary months had sheltered its dreaded and victorious antagonists, the Grand Fleet of Britain.'

In all, 52 ships of that High Seas Fleet had gone to the bottom—five battleships, ten battlecruisers, five light cruisers and 32 destroyers. Of those which did not sink there was one battleship, the 28,000-ton *Baden,* which was beached, as were the light cruisers *Emden* and *Frankfurt* and the *Nürnberg*, which drifted ashore herself. Of the 18 destroyers which remained above water some were beached and others settled in shallow water.

The very next day, another destroyer arrived from Wilhelmshaven with mail for the interned fleet now at the bottom of the sea. She was promptly seized by an armed boarding party which managed to prevent her commander from following the example of his compatriots in trying to scuttle her as well. One report quoted in 'The Orcadian' said that the German crew were 'very fed up about being taken off their ship and did not want to go—but they were pricked from behind with a bayonet and they soon moved on after that. It is claimed that she was looted, her crew taken prisoner and the ship herself retained as reparations.' The crew were, in fact, repatriated the next week while the Germans denounced the British action as 'pure piracy'.[22]

This was only part of the acrimonious controversy which raged among the Allies and the Germans as to how and why the High Seas Fleet had been able to commit mass suicide. Had von

Reuter acted on his own initiative as he claimed, or had he received orders to scuttle from Germany? Did he know about the extension of the Armistice or not? Did the British turn a blind 'Nelson's eye' as to what might happen?

There is no doubt that the scuttle solved a lot of problems all round, both for Germany and for the Allies, and the general feeling in Orkney itself seems to have been that, in the circumstances, it was the best thing which could have happened. But these wrangles were on an international level and did not affect Orkney directly, where the main object was to clear up the mess and celebrate with relief the signing of the Peace Treaty at Versailles just a week after the great scuttle. And, as it turned out, the sinking of the German Fleet in their midst proved to be of great benefit to Orcadians a few years later, providing plenty of employment in salvage work during the lean years of the twenties and thirties.

'The Orkney Herald' of the day broke into verse of a kind with particular reference to the reports that the German sailors had passed their time in the Flow fishing for sillocks through the portholes of their ships. It was entitled 'The Suicide Navee' and went like this—

> Tirpitz, the Kaiser's
> High Seas Fleet,
> The world mere slaves
> Beneath their feet.
>
> Admiral Jellicoe,
> Beatty and Co,
> Jutland—Silence,
> Scapa Flow.
>
> Torpedo-boats, Cruisers,
> And Battleships,
> Loaded with sillocks
> Caught by Fritz.
>
> High Seas Fishing Fleet
> Resolves to die
> Up go their heels
> Into the sky.
>
> End of Kaiser's
> Plans and tricks,
> And of his High Seas
> Suicide ships.

As might be expected the matter was treated much more seriously in the Fatherland, where the sinking of their fleet created a profound impression and was actually marked by the writing of a two-act play in blank verse by Reinhard Göringen, described as 'one of the leading lights among the newer German poets' of the time.[23]

In it, at one point, the British Admiral calls for light and a searchlight discloses the German Fleet going down. After it has disappeared beneath the waves the German Admiral is brought on board the British flagship where he exclaims: 'Somehow we erred or we should not have lost the game.'

Unlike its subject matter, which left plenty of reminders of what had happened, the play seems to have sunk without trace and no one, presumably, has thought it worth while to start salvage operations. Nor, apparently, did it receive the floral tributes accorded to some of the ships themselves. After the fleet had been on the seabed for a few days a number of wreaths floated ashore in various parts of the Flow including Cava. It was thought that they had been placed as a gesture on the quarter-deck of some of the ships before they took their final plunge. The interesting thing, however, is that they were made of flowers unobtainable in Orkney. Had they come in on one of the two transports bringing supplies from Germany two days before the scuttle? And if that is so does this imply prior knowledge of the impending 'funeral' by those in authority in the Fatherland?

At all events these flowers marked the end of, not only a chapter in the Scapa saga, but of an era in British, and indeed, world history. The spacious, leisurely days of Victoria and Edward VII were gone for ever.

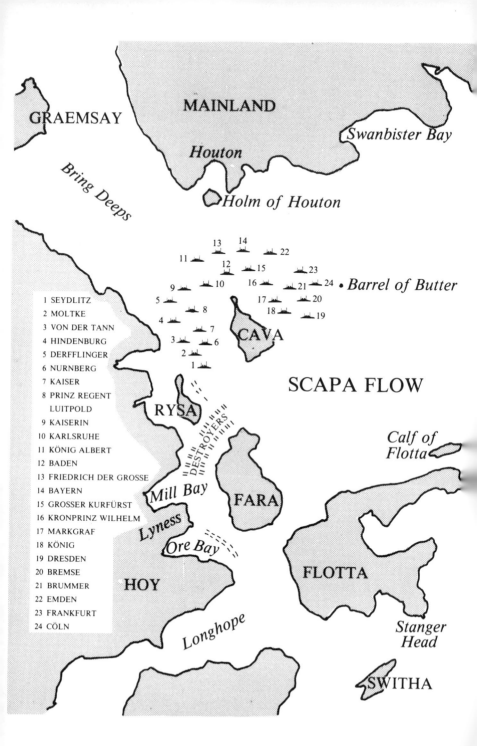

GRAEMSAY

MAINLAND

Swanbister Bay

Houton

Bring Deeps

Holm of Houton

13 14
11   22
        12   15   23
9   10   16   21   24   • Barrel of Butter
5   8   17   20
4   18   19
        7
3   6   CAVA   SCAPA FLOW
2
1

1 SEYDLITZ
2 MOLTKE
3 VON DER TANN
4 HINDENBURG   RYSA
5 DERFFLINGER   Calf of
6 NURNBERG   Flotta
7 KAISER
8 PRINZ REGENT
   LUITPOLD
9 KAISERIN
10 KARLSRUHE
11 KÖNIG ALBERT
12 BADEN
13 FRIEDRICH DER GROSSE
14 BAYERN
15 GROSSER KURFÜRST   Mill Bay   FARA
16 KRONPRINZ WILHELM
17 MARKGRAF   Lyness
18 KÖNIG   Ore Bay
19 DRESDEN
20 BREMSE   FLOTTA
21 BRUMMER   HOY
22 EMDEN
23 FRANKFURT   Stanger
24 CÖLN   Head
        Longhope
                        SWITHA

INTERNED GERMAN FLEET 1918-19

CHAPTER 17

Prosperity and Frustration

FOR THE civilian population of Orkney, numbering some 25,000 at the outbreak of hostilities, the First World War was a period of prosperity and frustration. There had never been such a concentrated influx of outsiders before; earlier 'invasions' had been by comparatively small numbers of people and their objectives had often, though not always, been peaceful settlement though with perhaps a strong element of exploitation. Certainly nothing even remotely approaching the scale of the 1914/1918 irruption had occurred within living memory or for a long time before that.

Suddenly the 25,000 native Orcadians found themselves overwhelmed by a literally 'floating' population nearly four times greater than their own. Of course, only a small proportion of these 100,000 men were stationed ashore—most of them were aboard the hundreds of ships that came and went, in and out of Orkney in a constant flowing tide; the consequent sea-borne population fluctuating accordingly.

But, land-based or afloat, they all had to be fed. As we have seen, a number of local firms and contractors had become accustomed to taking part in this great task of supplying the Fleet in the years before the war when the Navy was in Orkney waters often for quite long periods. Now however, they had to do it all the time and with reduced staffs as the call-ups took effect. The farmers were also involved, supplying the contractors with meat, and there is little doubt that money made during the war helped many of them to buy their own farms afterwards at the break-up of the big estates when sitting tenants often had the opportunity of buying at favourable prices. Merchants, too, generally did well supplying sailors coming ashore with their needs and even luxuries.

One such was the tailor Peter Shearer, a Stronsay man originally, whose shop was in Albert Street, Kirkwall. He was a go-ahead businessman as well as a highly skilled tailor and cutter who had even built up a London clientele before the war, visiting the capital and his customers there regularly. This, of course, had to stop when the war came. But in many ways it just reversed matters—now the London customers came to him as they were already in Orkney, mainly in the Navy.

He designed a special overcoat for the Services, rather shorter than the uniform greatcoat, the first one being made for ACOS himself, Admiral Colville. It was more informal than the full dress outfit and made of softer, warmer material and became famous as the 'British Warm.' The idea caught on and the design was taken up by the War Office, a battalion of the Lincolnshire Regiment in France being the first unit to be officially fitted out with it. Among Mr Shearer's other distinguished customers were the C-in-C Grand Fleet, Admiral Jellicoe, and Prince Albert.

Conditions were difficult for fishermen but they did get out, and those round the Flow found a ready market for their catches at prices which almost took their breath away. In June, 1918, for instance, the Flotta correspondent of 'The Orcadian' reported that one fisherman had got '11/7d for a cod just as it came out of the sea and there was a demand for fish at 8d a lb. 11/7 would have been what they would have got for 2 cwt of cod, headed and gutted, just before the war,' he commented—so in 1914 two hundredweight of filleted cod would have cost about 57p today.

Then again Orkney suffered no physical damage from enemy attack, not even from the Zeppelin raids such as were experienced further south along the east coast and in London.

This was the prosperity side. The frustration arose from a number of causes.

First of all, Orkney, in spite of having produced a distinguished Admiral, Alexander Graeme, born at Greenwall in Holm in 1781 and who later inherited Graemeshall, had never been really navy-oriented, even with this wonderful natural anchorage in its midst. Many Orcadians, of course, did go to sea and fine sailors they were, they could hardly be otherwise growing up with the ocean all round them, but they preferred the merchant service or the fishing fleet to the Navy, and more of them still looked to the land for their livelihood, rather than the sea.

Right from the early 19th century the Army had always attracted more interest and recruits among Orcadians than the Navy, and this interest became even more pronounced with the formation of the Artillery Volunteers in the latter half of the century. One cannot help wondering also whether this almost suspicious attitude towards the senior service may not have sprung from the activities of the Press Gangs, the frequent frustration of whose efforts are recorded with such glee in many

Orcadian tales and legends—to inflict discomfiture on the Press Gang was to become a folk-hero overnight for the individual who achieved it.

Be that as it may, Orcadians like the rest of the British public regarded the Royal Navy, especially the sea-going part of it, with pride and looked on it as the country's first line of defence. They had watched it grow, against the menace of Germany's ambitions, with interest, being keenly aware of the significance of the political wrangles over the annual Naval Estimates, growing ever more astronomical as the dangers to be faced grew greater. And, of course, they had seen for themselves this potent force on its frequent visits to the north before the war. But it is quite a different thing to entertain guests occasionally compared with having them living with you all the time—especially when the guests invite themselves and then lay down the laws of hospitality.

These rules, of course, meant restrictions which increased as the war progressed, becoming ever more irksome to a people who had never liked being pushed around in the first place, especially when the pushing came from outsiders. Most of the regulations were enforced by the Base staff ashore, composed to a great extent of retired naval pensioners of all ranks called back to the Service for the duration of hostilities. By the end of the war these 'dugouts' were operating something very near to martial law in the islands, for quite early on, Orkney and Shetland, and indeed, the north of Scotland, had been designated a 'Restricted Area', movement into and out of which required official permits. By 1916, indeed, permits were needed to visit even the north of Scotland which was part of the same Restricted Area.

These regulations were imposed with rigour but often without imagination, resulting in irritation to what remained of the travelling public. It was even claimed that on occasion they had been applied in such a way as to prevent Orcadian soldiers serving in France from getting home on leave. Nothing of this could be published at the time, of course, strict censorship having been necessarily introduced as soon as, or even before the declaration of war, but it was only a month after the Armistice when a leader in 'The Orcadian' expressed the pent-up exasperation and irritation felt by Orkney folk at these restrictions many of which were still in force.

It read:

It is an undoubted fact that the Navy has stood between this country and defeat. Yet, equally true is it that Orkney is

convinced from sad experience that in no service are to be
found so many officers in positions of authority where, with
the minimum of efficiency, they succeed in giving the
maximum of annoyance to the civilian population. There is a
whole host of subjects which require to be seriously taken in
hand—such as the measures connected with the measures to
save life after HMS *Hampshire* was mined, and many
questions affecting the public purse.

The County Council . . . will doubtless make a start in
bringing to public notice much that, for too long, has gone
under the shelter of the Defence of the Realm Act.

The unloved and unlovely lady known as DORA, while
never popular, was now positively detested especially when her
voluminous skirts continued to hide not only her unattractiveness
but also a rash of petty blemishes such as these restrictions, now
felt unnecessary when the war was over.

The leader also contains strong echoes of the resentment felt
by Orkney people that those with local knowledge had been
prevented by the authorities from going to the assistance of
survivors from the *Hampshire* when they struggled ashore—a
resentment which left a residue of prejudice against the Navy for
years to come. This attitude was summed up ten years later when
the Kitchener Memorial on Marwick Head was unveiled and
Major John Mackay, a local hotelier and Town Councillor, was
quoted as saying—'Had a little more common sense, and a little
less of the attitude of infallibility been adopted by the naval
authorities many brave lives might have been saved to the
nation.'[1] Major Mackay, a Territorial officer serving at the
Stromness Battery, had on his own initiative that night taken a
party of his troops, local men, to search the west coast for
survivors.

One local reaction at the time of the disaster in 1916 was a
surge of popular enthusiasm in Orkney for the erection of some
kind of monument to Kitchener's memory. The first idea was
that it should be in the Birsay Kirk, the nearest church to where
he had been lost. Kirkwall Town Council, however, thought it
would be more appropriate in St Magnus Cathedral and one
suggestion was a memorial window. And all this less than six
weeks after the sinking, a fact which speaks volumes, not only
about the almost religious esteem in which Kitchener was held by
the public generally, but also the feeling in Orkney about the
circumstances surrounding his death.

A week later, at the beginning of August, an appeal for
funds for the memorial was launched and within a few days

Birsay set up its own appeal fund.[2] But by now the whole idea had caught the public imagination, and the correspondence columns of both local newspapers were filled with suggestions which gradually crystallised into a general consensus of opinion that the monument should be something bigger than a window and that it should be on Marwick Head itself, looking down on where the *Hampshire* lay.

In September a public meeting in Kirkwall endorsed this suggestion, but it was to be ten years before the plaque on the tower was unveiled by General Lord Horne, former Commander of the First Army in France under Field Marshal Earl Haig.

That unveiling ceremony was attended by thousands of people from all over Orkney and beyond who flocked to Marwick Head on a hot, brilliantly sunny day, while off-shore—close to where the *Hampshire* lay—the *Royal Sovereign* fired a salute.[3]

A suggestion after the war, believed to have come from King George V himself, that a Scapa Flow Memorial should be erected somewhere on its shores to commemorate those who gave their lives either in, or sailing from the great harbour, did not catch on. The idea was bandied about for a time in the summer of 1919 with the Flotta folk saying with some justification that if it were to come about, then their island was the place where it should be sited—but nothing further happened.[4]

From quite early on in the war there had been nationwide concern over the dangers of excessive drinking, and it was not long before measures were introduced to curb this threat to the country's security and industrial output. Orkney was no worse in this respect than elsewhere—probably not so bad—but it did have many thousands of Servicemen mewed up with little to relieve the monotony of watch and ward, so when the curbs were brought in nationally they affected the islands too—sometimes, it seemed, even more severely than further south. The restrictions were not imposed on moral or health grounds but because of the fear that drinking would affect the efficiency of the fighting services and, later on, of the munitions and armament workers who were earning big money and had little else to spend it on. A measure of the anxiety caused by the problem was indicated when George V banned the consumption of all alcoholic drinks in the royal households in order to set an example to the nation.[5]

In Orkney the first indication of what was to come was when the price of a pint of beer went up to 4d (less than 2p) in November 1914, with Kirkwall and Stromness pubs being ordered to close at 6 p.m. They opened at noon. Country and island pubs, however, were given a dispensation, being allowed

M

to remain open until 8 p.m. 'The Orcadian' reported drunken scenes on the night before this early closing order came into force in December, stating that 'long before the closing hour many youths—not Territorials we were glad to notice—were in a state of hopeless intoxication', and at midday '. . . the bars were simply rushed by up to fifty men'.[6]

By May 1915 a number of cases were reported of men being jailed for supplying servicemen on duty with drink. A baker in Kirkwall, for instance, who procured a half bottle of whisky for a gunner in the Orkney RGA at the Imperial Hotel, '. . . with intent to make him drunk and so reduce his efficiency', was sent to jail for one month when he himself had sobered up sufficiently to plead guilty.[7]

These anti-drink restrictions were tightened even further at the end of 1916 when it was ordained under DORA (Liquor Control) Regulations, that no spirits were to be sold in Orkney and Shetland and that there was to be no 'treating' in pubs either—though what there was to 'treat' with was left to the imagination. As this extra twist of the screw came into operation in December—just before Christmas and New Year—'The Orcadian' recorded a big run on spirits with what it called 'Memorial Services for Johnny Walker'. By February 1917 the authorities were claiming that drunkenness had been significantly reduced in Orkney, with only two cases—one in Kirkwall, the other in Stromness—having been handled by the police since the regulations came into force.

As usual in wartime, security was the main reason given for the creeping barrage of restrictions, many of them, of course, very necessary, but not all and the nadir must have been touched when those 'drest in a little brief authority' from both the Army and the Navy turned down on 'security grounds' an offer by those two great comedians of the day, Harry (later Sir Harry) Lauder and Harry Tait, to come to Scapa and entertain the troops.[8]

In Stromness a woman was charged with having removed a 'plaque' from the window of her house. The 'plaque,' it was stated, had been placed there by the naval authorities and was emblazoned with the information that the house was 'out of bounds to servicemen', no reasons being given.[9]

A labourer who had previously been ordered to leave Orkney returned without a permit. He was sentenced to two months imprisonment with hard labour—DORA (Consolidated Regulations) 1914, again.[10]

Food for the civilian population does not seem to have caused many problems. Rationing was eventually imposed, of course, on the national scale but being a rural and sea-bounded agricultural community there was no great shortage of indigenous foodstuffs such as eggs, cheese, butter, meat and fish, especially for people who had always lived frugally in any case.

Scapa Flow was naturally closed to ordinary shipping, and the mail boat RMS *St Ola,* the first one, had to be re-routed from Stromness. Up until the outbreak of war, and again afterwards, she came through the Flow to Scapa Pier every morning to pick up passengers and mail, then out through Hoxa where a motorboat came out to her with that island's quota of mail and people before she crossed to Scrabster.

Under command of her genial Master, Captain Swanson, a superb seaman who guided her destinies through both World Wars, she returned in the afternoon by the same route. This was now stopped and she had to go west-about outside Hoy. As a result, Kirkwall and the East Mainland as well as the North Isles mail had to travel by road from Stromness instead of going the shorter route direct to and from Kirkwall—and road transport was not so fast or efficient as it is today. South Ronaldsay had to send its mail to Kirkwall by motorboat which was apparently allowed by the Navy to traverse the prohibited waters of the Flow. But it all caused delay and irritation.[11]

There were even worse delays in the North Isles mail service in 1915 when shipping regulations stipulated that there should be no movement of commercial craft during the hours of darkness. This meant that in winter the inter-island steamers such as the old *Orcadia* had to curtail their trips in order to comply.[12]

A move to cut the *St Ola's* mail service to only three crossings a week instead of the usual six was bitterly opposed by Orcadians when it was mooted in 1916 and, in fact, it never came about. There had also been suggestions that passenger sailings might be suspended altogether, but this did not happen either.

Lighting restrictions came into force in Orkney much earlier than elsewhere; a blackout was imposed in Longhope and district as early as November 1914. It was at first more as a precaution against giving away the position of places of strategic importance to enemy ships than to aircraft, so coastal areas were the first to feel its claustrophobic effect, particularly those near naval bases. Kirkwall Town Council was discussing how to darken its waterfront at the end of the month, and by the end of the year all the islands were enveloped in protective darkness after sunset. It was also one of the first restrictions to be thrown aside within days of the Armistice.

There was increased taxation on the national scale to meet

the costs of war, and powerful recruiting campaigns exhorted the
young men of Orkney as of the rest of the country to 'do their
bit', for conscription was not introduced until much later in the
war. Even as far through as 26 February 1916 there was an
appeal for recruits to swell the ranks of the Orkney Royal
Garrison Artillery, in an advertisement in 'The Orcadian' which
read—

> As there are a few vacancies for Gunners in the above branch
> [i.e. the Territorial Force ORGA] those wishing to join should
> apply to the Recruiting Officer, Kirkwall, without delay. No
> men already attested under the Group System are eligible. Age
> 19-40. Height 5ft 6 ins. Terms of Service, Duration of the
> War.

Compulsory service had yet to be introduced; even after a
year-and-a-half of war conscription was still regarded as
politically explosive, but it was obvious to most people that it
could not be long delayed.

The Group System referred to in the advertisement was part
of the 'Derby Scheme' of 1915 initiated by Lord Derby, whereby
men were asked to 'attest' their willingness to serve when
required and classified into 23 groups according to age, status
and occupation. An undertaking was given that married men
would not be called up until all the unmarried men had been
taken. It was also threatened that if insufficient bachelors came
forward voluntarily, then compulsory service would be introduced. By the end of 1915 there were still over a million
unmarried men who had not attested, and a Military Service Bill
was drafted which became law early in 1916.

The ORGA appeal contained the suggestion that Orcadians
might prefer to join the Colours among their own folk rather
than be pushed into the Forces among strangers willy-nilly.

Late in July 1916 a YMCA Hut was opened in another
group of islands far away from the cold greyness of the Atlantic
Ocean and the North Sea but also with a strong naval base
connection—Malta. And the money to put it there for the
recreation and relaxation of soldiers and sailors serving far from
home had come from the people of Orkney who had collected
£700 for this purpose—a very big sum of money in those days
when one considered that a pint of beer had just gone up to
about the equivalent of 2p.

In Kirkwall a similar amenity for sailors ashore was the
Mission to Seamen which operated a rest centre and canteen in
the Town Hall for four years.

In 1917 the United States of America, to which many Orcadians had emigrated, entered the war against Germany and one of its Battle Squadrons joined the Grand Fleet at Scapa. On Independence Day, the Fourth of July 1918, many of their crewmen were in Kirkwall to celebrate. 'The Orcadian' disregarded the censor's possible displeasure by announcing that 'citizens of the USA came to town in force'. The Stars and Stripes was flown from Kirkwall Town Hall and on the instructions of the Provost a peal of bells was rung from the Cathedral tower every hour.

But what Orcadians, like everyone else, were yearning for was peace and a return to some sort of normality with no more grim casualty lists from the battle fronts or War Office telegrams bearing grievous tidings of death. As 1918's summer dragged into autumn and the news from France and Flanders began to improve, hopes of peace began to flower and this produced an almost inevitable crop of unfounded anticipatory rumours arising out of wishful thinking.

The island of Papa Westray, in fact, acting on one of these rumours celebrated the coming of 'Peace' in October, a month before it actually happened, the school-children and the farm workers all getting a half-day holiday. The rest of Orkney was more cautious, reserving its enthusiasm for the real Armistice Day on 11 November at 11 a.m.; although in Kirkwall the news broke at 9.30 a.m., more than an hour before the Londoners heard about it. Rejoicing was intense—in both capitals. The Kirkwall streets and ships in the harbour were spontaneously dressed with flags and bunting while the steamers sounded their sirens continuously. A half-holiday was declared and a joint service of thanksgiving for all the churches was held in St Magnus Cathedral.

But the joy was shadowed with sadness in the great majority of families who remembered those who would never come back to rejoice in the victory they had given everything to win.

There was apprehension too about another and even more insidious enemy knocking at the door of many homes in Orkney and indeed throughout the land—influenza. This was no feverish cold but a remorseless killer. In the last two weeks of November alone the epidemic took a heavy toll—in at least five Kirkwall households there had been two deaths and in one instance there had been three deaths in a single family.[13] It also attacked and killed many of the servicemen, entire ships and units being immobilised with more than half of their companies going down before the onslaught.

Immediately following the Armistice there were confused

rumours as to the probable fate of the German Fleet before Orkney eventually learned that it was to be host to these rather unwelcome guests; two neutral countries, Norway and Spain, both having declined the invitation by the Allies to give the ships harbour space.

All the same Orcadians were avid with interest to see these notorious ships which had posed such a threat to Britain for so long, and most available vantage points were occupied round the Flow during the five days it took for them to creep in humiliation to their appointed moorings round Cava. But there was no contact between the Germans and the Orcadians. The Germans were not allowed ashore and the local people were not permitted to visit the ships. They remained a source of keen interest, however, and trips like the one with the Stromness schoolchildren on the day they were scuttled, were popular even though the ships could be viewed only from a distance.

There was, on the other hand, the chance to have a much closer look at some other items of German military equipment when the Government policy of showing war trophies all over the country resulted in a number of enemy field guns being displayed on the Kirk Green in front of St Magnus Cathedral.

But what Orcadians really wanted were not reminders of the war — too many of these were indelibly stamped on their minds — but to get rid of the war's irksome restraints as soon as possible in order to welcome home the returning servicemen in an atmosphere of freedom. For some of this they had to wait until after the signing of the Peace Treaty at Versailles on 28 June 1919. The signing was enthusiastically welcomed in Orkney with the burning of an effigy of the Kaiser in Kirkwall's Broad Street in front of his guns, one of which the crowd then trundled down through the main street to be dumped symbolically into the Basin.

Just a few days later it was announced that the hated permits were no longer needed and that everyone could pass freely in and out of Orkney as they wished. Censorship had, of course, gone by the board long before this—along with the lighting restrictions — so people were now able to express their strong views on what the 'occupying forces' were doing—or not doing.

In December 1918 there had been a petition by Orkney County Council to the Admiral Commanding Orkney and Shetland, who headed the naval authority.[14]

It asked—rather too politely, some people felt—for a relaxation of some of the regulations and orders still in force. For instance, it was asked that the mail boat, *St Ola*, be allowed to resume her peace-time route through the Flow from Stromness, to Scapa Pier and out through Hoxa to Scrabster; to which the Navy returned the usual official dusty answer that restrictions on the *St Ola* using Hoxa Sound would be lifted 'as soon as naval requirements permit'.

Next it was requested that Orcadians be relieved of having to obtain permits to travel in and out of their own islands. As we have seen, it took over six months for these restrictions to be withdrawn.

Then it was suggested to the Admiral that Orkney Territorial soldiers, still at that time engaged in anti-U-boat lookout duties for the Navy, should be relieved in order to return to their civilian occupations where their services were needed. A reasonable request, one would have thought, as hostilities had ended two months before and their chances of reporting an enemy submarine were consequently remote. The fourth request in the petition arose out of considerable criticism both locally and nationally.

The County Council asked that work still being carried out on the air stations at Houton, Swanbister, Stenness and Caldale and at the Lyness base by 'imported labour of a very low class at a very high rate [of pay] be meantime stopped; and in the event of it being ultimately decided to complete these works, the County Council would humbly submit that this could be done much more economically after demobilisation by the surplus local labour which will then be unemployed . . .'

But on this last request not very much happened apparently for at the end of May 1919, six months later, there was a big outcry in 'The Sunday Post' at the 'scandalous wastage of money in Orkney'. The targets for the 'Post's' attack were the air stations which, it was claimed, would never be used and which were wrongly sited in any case—the one in the Loch of Stenness being singled out in particular. In this case, the paper alleged, the Government had taken over the Standing Stones Hotel and had then spent £40,000 before finding out that the Stenness Loch was too shallow for seaplanes and that there were too many cross air currents in the area. Work on the Lyness base came in for heavy criticism, too, and there was a demand that it should be stopped at once. Millions of pounds were being wasted there, it was claimed.

Coinciding with this outburst was another kind of aviation story involving the Flow to some extent and indicating that the age of world-wide air travel was perhaps much nearer than most people imagined. Two British aviators, as they were usually termed then, Harry Hawker and Commander Kenneth Mackenzie

Grieve, attempted to fly the Atlantic from Newfoundland in a Sopwith biplane powered by Rolls Royce engines. They disappeared after take-off and were given up for lost but, in fact, they had been forced to ditch and had been picked up by a Danish cargo ship which did not carry radio. Nothing was heard of them until the ship, homeward bound, entered the Pentland Firth and signalled the shore. A destroyer was sent out from Scapa to collect them and they were taken to the flagship *Revenge*, before going south. Their aircraft was salvaged by an American ship.[15]

They hadn't made it this time but their failure did not deter others from attempting the Atlantic crossing, often using Scapa, and Houton in particular, as a staging-post.

This story did not divert the growing waves of public criticism over money wasted by the Services. The RAF caught it this time in a leader in 'The Orcadian' which commented on the extravagant use of service transport in Orkney, referring to a Parliamentary Select Committee's report on expenditure generally. The leader remarked—'From what we have seen in Orkney there is reason to fear that there is here also unwarranted extravagance in the use of mechanical transport. For one thing, the number of practically empty vehicles which are to be met with on the roads is really remarkable. May we suggest that inquiry be made whether there is any justification for the present RAF motor traffic on Berstane Road, Kirkwall?'[16] Why Berstane Road was singled out is not made clear.

RAF transport was in trouble of a different sort again as late as March of the following year, 1920, when an Air Force car was attacked in Kirkwall by local youths. They weren't so worried about the extravagance and possible waste of money as the suspicion that the RAF boys were using the transport to come to town and steal a march with the local girls. The airmen, deciding that discretion was the better part of valour, took flight, presumably leaving the locals in possession of the battlefield— and the girls.

Even later that same year, in August, the cost of what was called unnecessary RAF transport cropped up again, this time in the House of Commons, with Orkney's MP, Cathcart Wason, claiming that there was an unnecessary lorry and tender being used only for running in and out of Kirkwall from Houton. A horse and cart, he said, could do the job just as well and more cheaply. This was possibly true though the mind boggles a bit at the thought of the RAF, in spite of its versatility, using horseflesh instead of horsepower. Winston Churchill, Chancellor of the Exchequer at the time, apparently thought so too and said

'No' to the MP but added that the future of Houton 'was under review'.[17]

In the meantime things had been moving in the field of 'beating swords into ploughshares,' or perhaps in view of what was to happen a few years later with steel from the salvaged German ships, 'beating battleships into razor blades' would be a better way of putting it.

Just before the scuttling of that German Fleet the Admiralty announced that it 'had under consideration' the re-opening of Holm Sound, particularly Kirk Sound.

This would mean clearing the blockships both in Kirk Sound and in Water Sound between Burray and South Ronaldsay, to allow access to the two main pre-war fishing ports in that area. Nothing significant happened, however, for a long time and these blocked channels, with the consequent hindrance to navigation and, even worse, the eventual extinction of what had been a thriving fishing industry, was the source of further ill-feeling between Orkney and the Admiralty right through the twenties.

On 15 September 1919, the naval headquarters in Kirkwall closed down and as the naval personnel left on board the *St Rognvald* with their Commanding Officer, Commander White, they were given a great send-off, including a firework display. It seems likely that only some of the girls and quite a few shopkeepers were sorry to see them go and that most Kirkwallians were happy to have their City and Royal Burgh to themselves again.

On the other side of the Flow, however, there was still a large naval presence, with the Second Battle Squadron including *Warspite, Barham, Valiant, Revenge, Resolution, Ramillies, Royal Oak, Royal Sovereign, Queen Elizabeth* and destroyers arriving for a fortnight on exercise.

But *Victorious,* floating HQ of the Dockyard Staff since 1915, was ordered to Rosyth to pay off. She had been the flagship of Vice-Admiral Sir Robert Prendergast, Admiral Commanding Orkney and Shetland, since the departure of the other two stalwarts of wartime Scapa, *Imperieuse* and *Cyclops,* some time earlier; now her time to leave had come.

And on the first anniversary of the signing of the Armistice on 11 November, the officers and men of the Dockyards Staff at Scapa held a farewell dinner in the Masonic Hall, Kirkwall with the Dockyard Cashier, C. W. Burrows, in the chair. He was to become known to a much wider public not long afterwards with the publication of his magnificent pictorial record of the five most momentous years in the history of the Flow, *Scapa and a Camera.*

It was a little time yet before Scapa Flow reverted to the status of a peacetime base and rendezvous for the Navy but it came at last on 15 February 1920, five-and-a-half years after the outbreak of war, when Vice-Admiral Prendergast hauled down his flag as Admiral Commanding Orkney and Shetland, and Orkney could feel really free again. But even so the gate and barricade erected by the Navy at the head of Kirkwall Pier to keep civilians out was not removed until the end of 1924—six years after the war ended. Before this happened, however, there had been an interesting development in Orkney's involvement with the war at sea, which while not directly connected with Scapa Flow was nonetheless closely associated with it.

CHAPTER 18

U.S. Navy Re-opens the 'Gate'

NOT LONG AFTER the Armistice, Orkney and particularly Kirkwall experienced occupation by a foreign but friendly power—the United States of America, a land to which many Orcadians had emigrated and had acquired citizenship while still retaining emotional ties with their island homeland.

It began early in April 1919 and went on through the summer and autumn into October, involving a total of 83 ships and some 5,000 men of the US Navy. Their task was the very opposite of hostile. They were, in fact, sweeping the 56,000 or so mines which they had themselves laid across the North Sea in order to tighten the blockade on Germany and hasten her collapse. Their base for laying the mines had been Inverness; for sweeping them up again it was Kirkwall, and many of the ships employed had been engaged in both roles including USS *Black Hawk,* wearing the flag of Rear Admiral Joseph Strauss, who was in charge of the whole operation, as he had been of the laying of the mines also.

The USA declared war on Germany on 6 April 1917. The powerful USN Sixth Battle Squadron became part of the Grand Fleet under the operational orders of the British Commander-in-Chief, Beatty, and used Scapa Flow as a base. Later on the minelayers and minesweepers also used the Flow for repair facilities although the sweepers lay in Kirkwall Bay where, of course, the Royal Navy's Northern Patrol which had enforced the blockade with its 10th Cruiser Squadron had also had its base throughout the war.

It had been decided by the Naval Commands of both Britain and the USA that a barrage of mines should be laid across the 240 or so miles of the North Sea between Orkney and Udsire (Utsira) in Norway. The barrage was to be 240 miles by 25, a total of 6000 square miles. It was a colossal project involving the laying of 70,263 mines, each containing 300 lbs of high explosive—a total of some 9,500 tons.

Of this the US Navy laid the lion's share of 56,611 mines in 13 groups of varying sizes, in the western sector; the Royal Navy laid the remaining 13,652 on the eastern side nearer the Norwegian coast where, of course, a gap had to be left in the territorial waters of what, in that war, was a neutral country. The Norwegians actually closed that gap themselves with mines affecting both belligerents.

Roskill, in *The War at Sea, Vol. I* says that a similar barrage using 181,000 mines to close the North Sea at an estimated cost of £20 million, was proposed during World War II but never put into effect.

The American mines, which were set out in tiers and lines at varying depths, anchored by steel cable, were all laid in the five months of that summer and autumn of 1918 when the fate of the world hung in the balance as the German armies swept through the Western Front towards the Channel ports. The mines were brought to the Kyle of Lochalsh by sea and then transported to the US Minelaying Base No. 18 at Inverness, either by rail via Dingwall or by water through the Caledonian Canal. The Royal Naval Base for this minelaying operation was further south at Grangemouth, with Rear Admiral Lewis Clinton-Baker in command.

The Americans began laying the Barrage, using 57 vessels, on 8 June—they put the last mine in position on 26 October. The uneasy peace was declared just two weeks later. The North Sea Barrage had done its job in helping bring that peace about (two U-boats were damaged in the minefields as early as July and in September and October four were sunk in the barrage) but now the Allies were faced with the prospect of sweeping it all up again to make the North Sea safe once more for ships of all nations to go about their lawful occasions—in other words the 'gate had to be opened'.

Each navy was to sweep its own mines, but North Sea weather being what it was, still is and probably always will be, little could be done on the main task during that first winter of peace. Even so, the first experimental sweeps were tried out by the Americans using two chartered wooden sailing ships, the smacks *Red Rose* and *Red Fern,* during December. They were towed out in mist from Inverness by the tugs *Patapsco* and *Patuxent,* to test the condition of the mines after their months of immersion. The first mine was exploded by a sweep towed between the two smacks—under sail. Altogether they exploded six mines on that trip—there were still 56,605 to go!

The explosions, however, caused the smacks' timbers to spring and, taking water, they turned for home only to be caught in a northerly gale. Their tugs lost contact and the smacks disappeared. They had been more or less given up for lost when the *Red Rose* made Aberdeen and the *Red Fern* turned up in the Firth of Forth on Christmas Day. One of the tugs lost her rudder. It was a taste of things to come when the real sweeping began.

Meanwhile, in the United States, minesweepers for the job were being developed incorporating electric devices designed to make the use of steel ships possible. It was found in practice, however, that this particular gadget affected the ship's compass so badly that navigation became impossible, and it was finally abandoned after only one day's trial in the actual barrage.

Other experiments were carried out in the Forth and eventually at sea in the Barrage itself by the tug *Patapsco*. The first real sweep took place in the Barrage towards the end of March 1919 by the two tugs *Patapsco* and *Patuxent,* when they accounted for 39 mines.

The biggest danger was found to be 'counter-mining'—the exploding of one mine causing others nearby to blow up, sometimes right under a sweeper. It was dangerous work but USN personnel were detailed to carry out minesweeping duties with no extra pay, unlike the British system where the minesweepers were manned by volunteers attracted by extra pay and bonuses for mines swept.

The first US minesweepers arrived at Inverness at the end of February and by 22 March there were 12 sweepers, two tugs and 18 submarine-chasers—smaller craft which could be used for sweeping also—and the repair ships, the flagship *Black Hawk,* and *Chesapeake*. It had already been decided that Kirkwall was to be the base, and on 10 April US sailors started to erect two large YMCA huts opposite Peace's woodyard on Junction Road where the Post Office now stands. The huts were to be ready to provide recreational facilities for the main contingent when it arrived. This happened at the beginning of May and at the same time the US Navy Secretary, Josephus Daniels, visited the Grand Fleet in Scapa Flow and the hospital ships in Weddel Sound.

The 'Orkney Herald' reported that the American minesweepers were well received by the Kirkwallians, especially the younger generation who scrambled for coins thrown by libertymen off the ships. And to help cement the good relations Provost Baikie threw the first ball at the baseball match in the Bignold Park on 14 May, while a week later the Knights of Columba, a Roman Catholic administered welfare organisation, inaugurated premises open to all at No. 3 Bridge Street.

But these shore-based recreational activities, important though they were, in no way interfered with the serious business of 'opening the North Sea gate' which went on with the dedicated hustle and enthusiasm which one associates with Americans. May was still an experimental period. The mines had been in the sea for a year now, most of them, the ships' crews were new to the job, and details about the mines were woefully vague. It was found early on, however, that they were mostly still where they had been laid, which made their location that much easier.

The first operation, an experimental one, lasted two days and 221 mines were swept—one half of one per cent of the total, it was noted. This was not good enough. Admiral Strauss asked for 16 more sweepers, which he got, along with a further 20 British trawlers which were chartered and manned by US Navy personnel. This first operation had also resulted in a heavy loss of gear such as the 'kites' used for positioning the serrated steel cables used to cut the mines' moorings. The mines which did not detonate when swept by this method but which floated to the surface were then sunk or exploded by rifle fire, often from the smaller sub-chasers.

By 10 May when Operation II was due to begin there were 18 sweepers, including *Lapwing* and *Tanasea* newly arrived from the Azores, as well as nine trawlers, at Kirkwall. Many of the minesweepers were named after birds such as *Sanderling, Turkey, Teal* and *Swallow* or the more specifically American birds like *Bobolink* and *Whippoorwill*. Bad weather, however, delayed the start of the operation until 12 May.

The American met. officers developed their own theory of forecasting North Sea weather—'When the barometer falls, prepare for a blow; when it rises, expect high winds; and when it neither rises nor falls look out for a gale.' It was claimed with some justification that their forecasts were remarkably accurate.

Operation II lasted 17 days and cleared just one of the 13 groups of mines which made up the Americans' share of the Barrage and it showed clearly the possible price that might have to be paid in life and material. The minesweeping fleet suffered its first casualty just before the operation began, when Bosun's Mate William McHaskell of the *Auk* was killed in Kirkwall Bay, being involved in an accident with towing engine gear.

The tug *Patuxent* was the first ship to be badly damaged. She was hauling her gear when a mine, which had fouled the 'kite', exploded, fortunately without any casualties.

The *Bobolink* was not so lucky. Two days later she suffered a similar accident when hauling gear and was so extensively damaged that she had to be towed by the *Teal* and *Swallow* to Scapa Flow, to be patched up and sent to Devonport where she was still in dry dock when the whole sweeping job was completed in September. Her part in it had been brief indeed, but more tragically, one of her officers, Lieutenant Bruce, was killed by the explosion, becoming the fleet's first fatal casualty 'in action'. The *Teal* and *Swallow* also had trouble, but not with mines on this occasion. While towing the *Bobolink* to Scapa in fog they nearly ran aground on Fair Isle; the *Swallow,* in fact, actually grazed a reef but without serious damage.

The *Turkey* was counter-mined on 16 May and damaged, and four days later *Sanderling* was also counter-mined and damaged but managed to carry on.

Operation II ended on 29 May with one officer having been killed and five ships damaged, one of them so seriously that she was out of action for the rest of the sweeping season; sweeps had parted 200 times and thousands of fathoms of serrated steel wire had been lost. And only about eight percent of the mines had been cleared.

The arrival of the repair ship *Panther* from Brest on 2 June to act as mother ship for the trawlers and sub-chasers was very welcome. All 20 of the chartered British trawlers had also arrived and were anchored in the Bay by this time. Four new sweepers, *Chewink, Thrush, Flamingo* and *Penguin,* had come direct from the USA and after only five days in port following Operation II a fleet of 18 sweepers, nine trawlers and nine sub-chasers sailed on 5 June to begin Operation III. Their objective was to clear the mines of Group Nine in the Barrage—the biggest single group of the thirteen. This objective was achieved by 1 July after they had been at sea for 27 days, with sweeping impossible on 11 of those days due to bad weather.

This operation produced evidence pointing to the effectiveness of the Barrage when the *Heron* and *Sanderling* fouled an obstruction on the seabed and a large patch of oil came to the surface. Shortly after the mines had been laid the previous year the body of a German sailor had been found in the same area and it was believed that the obstruction encountered by the two sweepers was the hulk of the mined German submarine *U 127.* The Americans were now racing against time as they wanted to clear the Barrage before winter weather proper stopped all sweeping—and they very much wanted to be back home before that happened. So they were still not satisfied with the speed of their operation, good though it was, but they congratulated themselves that they were faster than their British colleagues working near the Norwegian coast with as many as 430 minesweepers.

While Operation III was in progress the interned German High Seas Fleet scuttled itself in the Flow. Rear Admiral Strauss and Captain Rosco C. Bulmer, Commander of Minesweeping Detachment, went immediately to Houton to see if they could offer any assistance to the British Navy, and indeed ordered two tugs and three sweepers still in Kirkwall Bay to get under way with their large pumps. But it was too late; the German ships had sunk before they could reach them.

Captain Bulmer was killed a few weeks later when he was involved in a car crash in Orphir, the most senior of the thirteen Americans of the Detachment to lose their lives in or off Orkney during the entire operation.

To speed things up, the Americans now acquired their own shore base, the old herring station near Carness on the east side of Kirkwall Bay. It had a substantial working area with a concrete sea wall and other facilities which could be pressed into service. They stationed between 50 and 75 men there, built a pier and brought in a lighter from Inverness. Here they could repair damaged gear and prepare buoys for a new system of sweeping they were about to introduce.

Up until this time most of the sweeping had been transversely across the lines of mines; now they started sweeping them longtitudinally along the lines, a faster method but one which had obvious dangers. A marking system of buoys was also introduced with a special group of vessels to carry out this 'Pathfinding' detail before the main fleet of sweepers arrived on the ground. After the sweepers proper had been along the lines, trawlers fitted with sweeping gear followed to clear any mines which might have been missed.

The buoy-laying ships sailed from Kirkwall on 2 July to mark Groups 11 and 12A in preparation for Operation IV. So far only two of the 13 groups had been swept and cleared, and time was running out. The buoy-laying crews were at sea for America's Independence Day celebrations on 4 July but the rest of the fleet had a day off with 2000 men ashore, and they made the most of it in spite of the cold cloudy weather. As the USN official record 'Sweeping the North Sea Mine Barrage' stated, Independence Day was celebrated 'in a land which our forefathers had warred with to gain their independence'. It also noted that the hospitality of the Orcadians was unstinted.

The 'Orkney Herald' reported that 'the day's celebrations passed off without any untoward incident to mar their enjoyment'—even though refreshments were handed out all evening with a generous hand. By this time, of course, the social activities ashore had become almost routine. There was a weekly dance in the Town Hall, and every Thursday evening there were entertainments in the YMCA which had been opened on 29 May with Admiral Strauss, Captain Bulmer and Provost Baikie present. The hut was named 'The Birds' Nest'.

There were dances aboard the *Panther,* and the Filipino sailors gave a ball of their own in the Town Hall. The Knights of St Columba took over the Temperance Hall, today the Orkney Arts Theatre, and opened up with a 'smoking concert' and boxing matches. The auditorium was the setting for a musical comedy 'That Long Lost Chord' by the Americans and was billed as containing 'Music, Syncopations, Melody'. It was very well received by Kirkwallians and servicemen alike—as the official record put it, 'bringing down an avalanche of applause from the people of Kirkwall'.

But the serious work went on at an ever-accelerating pace. Operation IV began on 7 July when 20 minesweepers, 10 trawlers and eight sub-chasers sailed out through the String with the Detachment Commander, Captain Bulmer, in direct control on board the *Auk,* his last active operation before he was so tragically killed on 5 August. It was to be an eventful operation. Almost right away *Oriole* and *Rail* were put out of action in the smaller minefield of Group 12A. *Lapwing* had three mines explode underneath her and *Pelican* was also damaged but managed to carry on—but not for long. A high-level mine exploded under her and five others counter-mined all round, ripping a large hole in her side and starting her seams. She took water fast and began to settle but her bulkheads held. *Auk,* with Captain Bulmer on board, and *Eider* made fast on either side of her with their wrecking pumps just holding the rising water and no more. *Teal* took her in tow, and with four other vessels she just made Tresness Bay in Sanday where she was beached on 17 July after a 23-hour tow. At one point, when the pumps failed, the crew were taken off and it was feared she would go down, but she just made it. Later she was taken to Scapa for repairs.

On the same night the *Flamingo,* which had anchored outside the minefield before beginning to sweep in the morning, dragged her anchor and drifted into it. It was not discovered that in the process her anchor had fouled a mine which exploded when the anchor was raised. She also had to be docked for repair.

But the worst disaster of all the operations had happened a few days earlier, when the chartered trawler *Richard Buckley* fouled a mine which exploded when the gear was being hauled without the danger being observed until too late. She sank in seven minutes with the loss of her captain, Commander King USN, and six members of his crew. It was the most serious loss the Detachment had suffered.

Group 11 had been cleared in seven days—they were learning fast but at a heavy cost. Of the 38 vessels which sailed on Operation IV, one had been lost with seven valuable lives, and five other ships had been damaged, two of them seriously. It was felt after this that trawlers were not entirely suitable for the task in hand and 13 were returned to the British, but at about the same time four more sweepers arrived from the States, *Woodcock, Seagull, Grebe* and *Widgeon.*

The need for a rapid clearing of the minefields was dramatically and tragically underlined on 23 July when it was learned that the Stronsay fishing boat *Olive (K76)* was missing, feared lost with all six hands. It was thought she had struck a mine on her way to the fishing grounds.

Operation V began on 22 July and cleared Group 6 minefield in the best time yet—four days—but with *Curlew* damaged and one man lost. Two more seabed obstructions were encountered and fouled the sweeps, followed by oil slicks. They were thought to be the remains of two more U-boats. All ships were back in Kirkwall Bay by 7 August, having cleared four Groups in 16 days. A week earlier Rear Admiral Strauss had decided that the North Sea Barrage **would** be cleared by September. It began to look as if his confidence would be justified. With seven Groups now cleared they were more than half-way through the task.

For Operation VI the Detachment moved to Shetland on 12 August, and the repair ship *Panther* also moved north to Lerwick. By 16 August Group 10 mines were disposed of, followed by Group 4, occupying four days during which the Detachment put into Larvik, the British minesweeping base in Norway. With the end now more clearly in sight, the Detachment was divided into two Squadrons. No. 2 Squadron continued sweeping the remainder of Group 13 while No. 1 started on the western end of Group 7 and the western part of Group 8—the last minefield left and where they had to co-ordinate with the British minesweepers.

This was a particularly dangerous operation as the mines were only six feet below the surface. *Sanderling* was disabled and *Sub chaser 38* damaged beyond repair when a mine exploded directly underneath her. She was towed to Kirkwall, while *Kingfisher* also had trouble when a mine exploded nearby but she was able to continue sweeping. The end might be in sight but the danger was ever-present.

A welcome visitor for the American sailors was the ss *Lake Freed* when she anchored in Kirkwall Bay at the end of August. She had come to load supplies to take back to the United States including 2000 buoys not now needed, and so eager were the sailors on shore to get home that they loaded her and turned her round in just one day. This was hustle with a purpose. The repair ship *Panther,* which had returned from Lerwick, left Kirkwall for Devonport with six sub-chasers on 5 September and 12 more sub chasers had gone by the 17th.

In the meantime exploratory sweeps were carried out in the areas where Groups 7, 9, 11, and 12 had been and on 13 September all the vessels engaged were back in Kirkwall after 32 days away during which time they had accounted for a total of 8,706 mines.

They desperately wanted to be away from Orkney before the dreaded equinoctial gales—and these could now come at any time. So on the day they all returned to harbour, the 13th, the flagship asked if they could be ready to leave by the 17th, just three days away. All 21 minesweepers still left in the Bay answered 'Yes' within minutes.

On that same date, 17 September, US Base 18 at Inverness, which had been operational for two years, was completely dismantled and closed down. Just before this, starting on 7 September, the minesweepers had sailed from Kirkwall on their last mission, Operation VII. They had cleared the rest of Groups 7, 8 and 9, and had then undertaken a general exploratory sweep of the entire Barrage area to make sure the job was complete.

Just to emphasise what the North Sea held in store if they delayed, a three-day gale interrupted this last operation and they were forced to shelter in Tresness Bay. On their second night sheltering there was a call for help from the British White Star liner *Vedic,* homeward bound from Northern Russia with over a thousand British troops on board, when she grounded off North Ronaldsay. The sweepers braved the gale to go to her assistance but she managed to refloat herself on the rising tide. Even in the comparative shelter of Kirkwall Bay two sub-chasers were damaged and one of the lighters foundered.

Three more sweepers left Orkney on 25 September and another three on the 27th. The numbers were thinning out. A final exploratory sweep covering 800 square miles of the Barrage area found only four mines and on 30 September Rear Admiral Strauss announced: 'Work complete.'

Next day, 1 October, the Detachment left Kirkwall for good, except for the two faithful tugs *Patapsco* and *Patuxent* and the sweepers *Heron, Lapwing* and *Teal* which left soon after. They sailed for the United States by way of Portugal, the Azores and Bermuda on 10 October, arriving in New York on 20 November.

Some measure of the magnitude of the task and the energy and determination with which the Americans tackled it can be gathered from consideration of the records of one or two individual ships. The minesweeper *Whippoorwill,* for instance, steamed a total of 8,980 miles in 63 days and accounted for 1,132 mines. Minesweeper *Lapwing* was 86 days in the minefields with a score of 2,160 mines. The tug *Patapsco* spent 111 days at sea and her sister ship *Patuxent* 75 days, and both of them had also taken part in the early experimental work as well as having been engaged in laying the Barrage the previous year.

Of the smaller craft, *Submarine Chaser No. 40* sank 866 mines but the honour of cutting and exploding the last mine of the whole operation went to the minesweeper *Chewink,* after spending a total of 11 weeks at sea in the minefields from the time she arrived direct from the States at the beginning of June.

On 1 October the Royal Navy's Base at Kirkwall also closed down and the staff moved south. The USN *Black Hawk* sailed for the United States on 2 October after a flurry of farewell dances and entertainments afloat and ashore. The YMCA 'Birds' Nest' hut in Junction Road closed down and so did the Knights of Columba in the Temperance Hall and at No. 3 Bridge Street; there were no more Masonic Banquets such as that given by the Americans on Independence Day; the baseball matches, regattas, boxing tournaments and concerts, 'smoking' or otherwise, were all over. The tennis and volleyball courts behind the YMCA in Junction Road, constructed on ground given by Meils, the fish merchants, were no longer needed and, thankfully, neither was the emergency hospital which had been established in the Paterson Kirk's Victoria Street Hall, now the Baptist Church. Even the British navymen had gone from the town.

It had been an eventful summer, both in Kirkwall and in Scapa Flow where the ships of the German navy lay scuttled on the seabed. Now it was all over, the ships and the American sailors had gone—and so had the mines. The North Sea 'gate' was open and as 'The Orkney Herald' reported—'Kirkwall Bay looks quite deserted. The town is back to its wonted quietude.'

CHAPTER 19

The Uneasy Peace

THE BRITISH, generally speaking, are not a military-minded people. True, when occasion demands they will reluctantly don uniforms and once in them will perform deeds of great valour on sea, land or in the air, showing considerable aptitude for their temporary profession of arms—but they place considerable emphasis on the 'temporary' aspect of their military service. The thing they like most about uniforms is getting out of them, sometimes with such haste after hostilities cease as to disrupt the country's smooth return to civilian life. This happened in 1919 when the sudden surge of demobilised servicemen completely upset the labour market and had to be slowed down.

Orcadians are no exception to this general rule, good volunteer soldiers though they made when war clouds gathered on their wide horizons. Now, with the Kaiser in exile, his fleet at the bottom of Scapa Flow and the map of Europe redrawn by the statesmen at Versailles, all they wanted was to resume the even tenor of their island life in peace and quiet.

Like most people in Britain and elsewhere, they still did not quite realise that the old order had not only changed but had been destroyed by the war to such an extent that there could be no going back to the atmosphere of stability which had characterised British life in the Victorian and Edwardian eras. The shaken world had entered a period of rapid and accelerating change, affecting Orkney just as much as anywhere else. National and international events had already made their significant impact on the islands, especially in the Scapa Flow area. This trend was to continue; but first of all the feeling was: 'Let's get rid of the relics of war as soon as possible.'

As we have seen, it took a little while to dispose of the paper restrictions, rules and regulations, but they did disappear in time. Next came the concrete items—literally concrete in many cases. It was March 1920 when the first sale of war surplus items was advertised in the local newspapers. These particular items were huts at Longhope and on Flotta.

A month later they were sold to various local buyers and

included the office huts of the Admiral Commanding Orkney and Shetland at the Longhope Hotel, bought for £220 on behalf of the United Free Church Home Mission by the Reverend A. B. Taylor, Minister of the Paterson Kirk (now the East Church, Kirkwall) and father of the translator of the *Orkneyinga Saga*. Nearly two years later, incidentally, 'The Orcadian' reported that the Admiral's telegraph cable connecting the hotel with Whitehall was still intact.

The hydrophone station huts at Stanger Head on Flotta, from which the German submarine *UB 116* had been tracked and sunk as it tried to penetrate the Scapa defences in the last few days of the war, were knocked down to Mrs Walter of the Albert Hotel, Kirkwall, for £140.[1] Next came the Caldale Kite Balloon Air Station just outside Kirkwall; but at the auction on 3 June there were no offers, although there seemed to be no difficulty in finding buyers for the Wireless Station at Old Head, South Ronaldsay, or the huts at Burray Ness and St Margaret's Hope.

A couple of months later the huts of the Mining Stations at Hoxa and Cantick, along with those at Roan Head and Quoyness, both on Flotta, came under the hammer. And so it went on; huts at Herston and the Hoxa Head Battery, South Ronaldsay, at Neb Battery in Flotta, and at the Holm Battery, were all sold off, the buyers having to move their purchases as soon as possible.

The steel hurdles which had closed the Hoy Sound entrance to the Flow were removed with difficulty and shipped south from Stromness; and at the end of November, James Sutherland, coal merchant, Stromness was blowing up some of the American-made coast defence guns which he had bought for scrap at one of the batteries.[2] Just before Christmas he did another deal, acquiring four 6-inch guns weighing some eight tons, for £1 each from the Hoy Batteries I and II.[3] So perhaps, with all this rapid run-down and dismantling of defences going on, it is not surprising that the Commanding Officer, North of Scotland Area, not even a flag officer now, shifted his headquarters from Lyness to Invergordon.[4]

After all this activity there was something of a pause in 1921, and then in January 1922 Houton Air Station was put up for auction 'by direction of the Disposal Board', the first of many such sales throughout the year. Among the lots on offer was a 'kite balloon hangar'. A bus was organised to take buyers from Stromness to the sale and the ss *Hoy Head* made a similar special run at 2 shillings return.

Another indication of the return to civilian life was the announcement that recruiting for the Orkney Garrison Artillery was to stop. For the first time in well over half-a-century Orkney was to have no local TA unit and this gap was to last for 18 years—a matter of considerable regret in the islands, for although not militaristic in their outlook Orcadians were intensely proud of their volunteer, part-time soldiering tradition and quite apart from its military aspect the movement had been a great influence for social good in the community.[5]

There were more sales at the Houton and Scapa Air Stations in March and April when Kirkwall Town Council took the opportunity of providing the burgh with electricity for the first time by the purchase of the Houton generating plant.[6] Orkney County Council was also in the market and bought parts of the Scapa Air Station for use as a badly-needed tuberculosis sanatorium on its existing site where the Orkney Islands Council Harbours Department HQ now stands on Scapa Bay.

By the end of April the Stromness news in 'The Orcadian' was able to report: 'The Last of Them', referring to three 4-inch guns from Hoxa which, having been dismounted and stored in the magazine at Ness Battery, had been acquired by James Sutherland for scrap. As the report noted, 'The weapons are probably the last of the Scapa Defences to be disposed of. They were among the first guns in position at the principal entrance to Scapa Flow during those fateful months of 1914 when the war hung in the balance. And now they are scrap.'[7] Even as late as August that year, 1922, Mr Sutherland was still engaged in reducing what had once been vital parts of Scapa's defence to lumps of metal by blowing to pieces the very fine 6-inch American guns at No. 2 Battery, Ness, again for scrap.[8]

The guns at No. 1 Battery were too near dwelling-houses for explosives to be used, so they were scrapped by acetylene burners. Hoy Battery (Ness) and Lyness huts were sold off, the upset price for a barrack-room hut, 178 by 25 feet, being £8.[9]

Smoogro, or Swanbister, Air Station was under construction at the end of the war and was duly completed long after the Peace Treaty was signed, in spite of strong criticism, both local and national, on the ground of waste. It was never used operationally and now in April 1923 it was sold to John Craigie, Orphir and John Tinch, Kirkwall at the last big sale in the aftermath of the war.[10] But there were still plenty of visible signs of the days when Orkney had been an armed camp—indeed, some of them were never entirely erased, like the massive concrete gun-emplacements which in some cases were used again in World War II.

But while every effort was made to efface these often unsightly relics of the war years, memories of those who had died in the service of their country remained vivid in people's minds. Memorials to their dead went up in every parish and island, sad but proud reminders not only of the loss suffered by their families and friends but by the whole nation—monuments to the memory of a 'lost generation' which could never be replaced.

Another memory which remained green was that of Lord Kitchener, lost off Marwick Head in Birsay when the cruiser *Hampshire* in which he was travelling to Russia was mined and sunk. Besides having created the armies which had fought and stemmed the onrush of German might on the Western Front, he had epitomised Britain's Imperial role in the world, and he was almost worshipped by the great majority of the British people if not always by his colleagues, especially the politicians. Within days of his death there had been a movement in Orkney to erect a memorial to him, and this continued into the days of peace so that by August 1924 the Memorial Committee which had been set up was in a position to accept a £734 tender from an Orphir contractor, W. Liddle, Cornesquoy, to build the tower, which had been considered the most appropriate monument, on Marwick Head looking out over the spot where he died.[11] It was completed in 1926 and the unveiling ceremony was performed in the presence of several thousand people from all over Orkney, and indeed the country, by General Lord Horne of Stirkoke in Caithness. The event aroused a rash of retrospective journalistic speculation as to what had 'really' happened that June night in 1916. Kitchener's body, of course, was never found but those of the ship's company were picked up—dead, except for twelve of them. It was still felt in Orkney that many more might have been saved if the local people had been allowed to go to their aid.

By 1928 many of the more bitter memories of the war had become dimmer and the German cruise liner *Orinoco* was welcomed when she dropped anchor in Kirkwall Bay, especially by the shopkeepers. She was the first of many to come to Orkney in the next decade and although they always used Kirkwall Bay, Scapa Flow was the magnet for the passengers who made the pilgrimage to the graveyard of their fleet now in process of being salved.

In the new year of 1929 came a reminder that the sea round Orkney still held dangers other than wind, wave, tide and rock, when a mine exploded on the west coast near Pallast in Sandwick. Quite a few mines had been sighted and reported from time to time, one or two in the Flow and its sounds; now it was shown that they could still be 'live' and dangerous, even after ten or more years in the sea.

A possible new use for the Flow, and especially for Stromness, was suggested later in the year. A new railway was being constructed in Canada linking the corn-rich prairies of the west with Churchill on Hudson's Bay, reducing the rail journey to the Atlantic ports of the eastern seaboard by a thousand miles. The suggestion was that big grain carriers should be used to ship the harvest out of Hudson's Bay before the ice closed it each year, and bring it to Stromness where it would be stored in huge elevators and then distributed to European ports in smaller, fast grain ships. Surveys and soundings of business opinion in Stromness were pursued with some vigour but, alas, nothing came of the project, which probably foundered in the great slump of the early thirties.[12]

That slump hit Orkney, too, especially the farmers, most of whom now owned their holdings, having bought them at the break-up of the big estates after the war. The economic climate was so severe in March 1930 that 5000 farmers attended a mass rally in Kirkwall's Broad Street, in front of the Cathedral, to protest at the grave state of agriculture. They sought import controls on what were described as 'bounty-fed' cereals from abroad, what we would now call 'subsidised crops', and not surprisingly they were particularly incensed about the dumping in this country of the so-called 'German oats'.[13]

Possible alternative industries were also examined including the manufacture of 'Scapa Flowr' from seaweed which would be pressed, dried and ground, for addition to dung or offal. It was claimed to be a deodoriser which aided fermentation but did not cause rotting so that the final product would be a valuable fertiliser. Somehow the idea did not catch on though there was plenty of the raw material readily available; and unlike several other ideas for using seaweed commercially which have surfaced from time to time, this one died the death before anyone lost money on it.

There was, however, one unusual and strictly limited export from Scapa Flow in 1931. A piece of teak from the quarter-deck of the recently salved battleship *Hindenburg* was sent to Glasgow where a firm of instrument-makers used it to make a set of bagpipes—some people said it was just going from one warlike purpose to another.

By 1933 memories of wartime Scapa Flow were fading as a new generation which did not remember the Great War grew up, while fears that it might once again have to become a strategic naval base had not yet begun to crystallise.

There was an echo of what people were now tending to call the 'last' war to differentiate it from the possible 'next' one, when flags in Kirkwall were flown at half-mast on the day of Jellicoe's funeral in London in November 1935—the prestige of the war leaders remained high in public esteem, even after 15 years. It is difficult to imagine similar veneration for any of the World War II leaders apart perhaps from Churchill himself.

With reports of a 'monster' seen in the Flow off Houton in August 1936, complete with one big fin and three smaller ones, it did look as if 'normality' was setting in over Orkney. Events in Germany, however, continued to cause rising international tension and the tendency grew of talking about 'when', rather than 'if' war came. In Orkney, air-raid precautions were discussed by Kirkwall Town Council at its April meeting in 1937 and the inevitable committee was set up to cooperate with the County Council on this matter.[14] In July the doctors and nurses attended a course on anti-gas measures, appropriately, if rather grimly, using the Balfour Hospital mortuary as a makeshift gas chamber in which to demonstrate with respirators.[15]

Hitler was still an almost comic Charlie Chaplin sort of figure to most British eyes. But they were not laughing quite so much about him by 1936, with Germany already in his grip, beginning to flex its muscles; and such announcements by the British Government that gas-masks for all would soon be ready for issue did nothing to reduce the feeling of unease. Slow though the pace of rearmament was, it was growing faster, and grim though the implications might be there was a bright side seen by the farmers in the fact that the increased industrial production which resulted meant more, and consequently cheaper, basic slag for their fields.

There was also good news that the Ministry of Transport would make a 100 per cent grant for all Class I roads in Orkney; and while this was welcomed in itself, it was generally believed to be part of that same rearmament programme to bring roads round a potential naval base up to the required military standards.

The Coronation of King George VI provided an occasion for celebrations that year and relief from the gloomy atmosphere of international affairs. There was, however, indignation in Orkney when the North of Scotland, Orkney and Shetland Steam Navigation Company in its dubious wisdom turned down an invitation to send the old mail boat, St Ola (Capt. G. Swanson), to take part in the Coronation Spithead Naval Review where she had been assured of an honoured position among the naval and merchant ships of many nations. She had, after all, played her part in one great war and was soon to do so in another. But the 'North' Company said no, they could not afford to lose her services for a mere naval review. Orkney was very angry and disappointed at this slight to one of the best-known ships round the British coast.[16] She might have given many Orkney folk a rough crossing of the Pentland Firth but they were still proud of her.

And still the German cruise liners came to Orkney—four of them in 1937, the *Milwaukee* and *General von Steuben,* both on the same day in July, to be followed a little later by the *St Louis* and the *Stuttgart,* all big ships in the 15,000 to 16,000-ton class. Some people recalling the visits of German cruise liners before 1914 wondered if all the 500 or so passengers on each of these later ships were merely on pleasure bent.

With the Territorial Army expanding elsewhere in the country there began to be rumours that Orkney, too, might be going to have its own unit again to defend the Flow as in days of yore, and these rumours were confirmed in January 1938. Orkney was to raise a troop of Gunners to man a half-battery of anti-aircraft guns to protect the Lyness oil tanks then under construction; the other half-battery was to be recruited in Caithness. Some of the Lyness tanks were, in fact, already complete and in use. The new unit was to be the 226th Heavy Anti-Aircraft Battery RA, TA, a number and name to become famous in Orkney annals. Its first Commanding Officer was from Caithness where the HQ was situated, Lieut. Col. G. D. K. Murray. To organise the recruiting drive the Orkney TA Association was reconstituted, with the Lord Lieutenant, Mr Alfred Baikie of Tankerness, as its chairman.[17]

The county's first somewhat tentative civil defence scheme had a rather muted reception compared with that for the TA unit—there were only nine volunteers for duties as anti-gas wardens and for civil defence work generally. At this time the emphasis was very much on a likelihood of gas attack.

A more comprehensive scheme was launched by the County Council at the end of March 1938, and a month later ARP ambulance classes were started. The possibility of war was now being taken very seriously and this was emphasised by the announcement that men of under 30 years of age would not be accepted for ARP duties—they were obviously being reserved for even sterner service.[18]

They got their chance in May when recruiting for the 226 HAA Battery opened in Kirkwall on Saturday the 7th. Eighty men were wanted. Seventy volunteered right away and a fortnight later recruiting closed—'226' was up to strength and had already begun drills, a fact which must have pleased the Director General of the Territorial Army, General Sir Walter

Kirke, when along with his staff in two flying-boats, he landed at Scapa and looked at possible drill hall sites. He also hinted strongly that a coast defence unit might soon be recruited in Orkney, possibly to man Ness Battery near Stromness.[19]

At the end of August after 50 drills and some predictor practice using one of Scottish Airways planes as a target, '226' went to camp. They crossed the Firth by the *St Ola* to join up with their other half in Caithness before proceeding to Burrow Head Firing Camp in Wigtownshire, where they acquitted themselves with credit as well as having a wonderful time which included a visit to the Glasgow Empire Exhibition. On their return to Orkney early in September they marched from Scapa Pier to Kirkwall, headed by the Kirkwall City Pipe Band and led by the senior officer in Orkney, Captain James M. Moar, Stromness, a First War veteran.

By the end of the month they were back in uniform again and with serious intent. The Czech crisis which had simmered all summer boiled over. It was not so much the possibility of war now as the probability of it, which faced the world. The Home Fleet arrived in Scapa Flow—in strictest secrecy.[20] The '226' stood by in their temporary drill hall behind what later became the Cosmo Ballroom, and then the Casablanca, between Junction Road and Albert Street. They waited for the call to go to their war station at Lyness but it did not come. Some 40 Naval Reservists were called up and left Orkney to join their ships, and the civilian population got its first taste of war conditions in two test blackouts between 9 p.m. and 10.30 p.m. on 28 and 29 September with naval aircraft overhead to observe its efficacy. On the first night fog made the assessment difficult, but the second test showed the islands shrouded in almost complete anonymous darkness. There were no sirens to mark these test runs, and instead the factory hooters of the Highland Park Distillery and Kirkwall Laundry on Glaitness Road were used to sound the warning.[21]

In the midst of all this warlike activity came the announcement that two coast defence units were to be raised in Orkney, bringing back memories of when the old Volunteers had been coastal gunners. In the 1938 crisis, what coast defences there were round the Flow were manned by TA soldiers from Lancashire, Cheshire and the Clyde; now, unless war actually broke out immediately, Orcadians themselves would have the chance of manning these batteries at Ness and Stanger Head in Flotta as their fathers and grandfathers had done in the past.[22] Early in October the tension eased: the Prime Minister, Neville Chamberlain, along with other leaders at Munich, had signed the bit of paper with Hitler which, he told a relieved nation when he flew back from Germany, meant 'peace in our time'. Whether he **really** believed that or not probably no one will ever know. But, at least, it did give Britain breathing space to get ready in case 'our time' was to be short. And it was.

In Orkney there was a big recruiting drive for the two new units, the Orkney Heavy Regiment RA, TA, to man the guns of the coastal batteries with ten officers and 208 other ranks, and the Orkney (Fortress) Company RE (T) with seven officers and 110 men to operate the searchlights for them. There were recruiting meetings in Kirkwall, Stromness, Dounby and many other centres, addressed by the Lord Lieutenant, former TA officers and some of the regular army soldiers posted north to train the embryo units.

The Lord Lieutentant told one such meeting in Stromness that when negotiations regarding the formation of TA units in Orkney were in progress at the War Office, local representatives had insisted on two conditions which had been accepted by the 'top brass'. The first was that in the event of war the Orkney men were to be retained as a unit and not put under the command of 'dugout' Marine officers as had happened in the First War, and secondly that annual camps should be held outside Orkney. The trip south for these camps was looked on as being an incentive to join the TA. In fact, one camp in every four had to be held on the unit's war station and this was agreed, though in the event the whole question became academic. The matter of the Royal Marine command over the Scapa defences in the First War had been a very sore point with Orcadians but it very nearly happened again in the Second as we shall see.

By the beginning of November, 264 out of the 399 men required for all three Orkney units had been enrolled.

The year ended in a more relaxed frame of mind with only make-believe war in Scapa Flow, when the film producer Michael Powell arrived to shoot scenes on location in Longhope for the film *The Spy in Black*, starring Conrad Veidt and Valerie Hobson and based on a novel by J. Storer Clouston, Orkney's County Convener and historian.[23]

The new year, 1939, came in with the usual celebrations in Orkney. Welcoming lights from houses round the Flow as elsewhere guided the sometimes unsteady footsteps of over-enthusiastic first-footers to hospitable doors—it would be the last lamplit Hogmanay for many years to come and the traditional greeting of 'Happy New Year' was perhaps an expression of hope rather than conviction, and for many the new year brought no happiness at all. World events were moving to a grim climax with all the inevitability of a Greek tragedy, but most people tried to pretend that they could not read the writing on the wall. But it was there writ large all the same, and there was plenty going on in Orkney alone to spell out those words of doom. Some of them were small things in themselves like the issue of steel helmets to Special Constables in January, the beginning of a ten-week course for air-raid wardens covering their duties if, or perhaps now, **when** an air attack came, and the first meeting of the County National Service Committee to coordinate all these civilian efforts.

All this pointed in only one sinister direction, the apparent inevitability of war which no one wanted to admit. The local TA units were already in training and on the civil side 322 ARP wardens had already been enrolled, 72 people had joined the First Aid Groups, while Report Centre and Communications recruits numbered 140 and a dozen or so had joined the Auxiliary Fire Service.

At the beginning of March there was an even stronger pointer to what was happening when it was announced that Hatston farm and some nearby holdings just outside Kirkwall had been chosen as the site for a Fleet Air Arm aerodrome at an estimated cost of £130,000, probably more like £30 million today (1985).[24] It was the same site suggested by Captain E. E. Fresson of Highland Airways six years earlier as a civil airport for Kirkwall. The scheme now involved the diversion of the main Kirkwall-Stromness road to its present route by the golf course going round the perimeter fence, instead of across the flat ground lower down where the old road now became part of the main runway. It also meant closing the Oyce by which the sea ebbed and flowed into and out of the Peerie Sea through the bridge known as The Eye close by the Ayre Mill.

Although it was all supposed to be rather hush-hush, it was known that tunnelling was going on into the hills behind Lyness and it was generally believed that this was for underground fuel tanks for the Fleet. A Glasgow firm employing workers from the south had been engaged on this work since September 1938. It began to look as if the drilling of the TA and the training of the Civil Defence might be all too necessary.

As very often happens in such times of growing tension there were spy scares. Strange and unexplained lights were said to have been seen in the Flow—but the Fleet was not there. Was it perhaps potentially hostile submarines spying out the anchorage and even laying 'sleeping' mines? No mines were ever found and the lights, if they existed, remained unexplained.

Other rumours circulated to the effect that camera owners had been questioned by 'secret police' and their equipment confiscated. Again these rumours proved to be unfounded and 'The Orcadian' went so far as to claim that amateur photographers were able to take pictures of subjects that the newspaper was not even allowed to mention.

There **was** a 'spy' in Orkney at this time but he was as insubstantial as the rumours, being confined to celluloid. The Albert Kinema in Kirkwall on 8 April screened the world premiere of the film, *The Spy in Black*. This midnight matinee was a big social occasion with the producer, Michael Powell, present as well as the author of the novel on which the film was based, Storer Clouston, Orkney's County Convener. 'Based' is the operative word, for the author must have had considerable difficulty in recognising his own brain-child after the script writers had finished with it—still, the title was the same and some of the scenes had been shot on location in Orkney.

By the end of April local authorities were being urged by Government to give Civil Defence priority over all other matters, and this was followed by the announcement that conscription was to be introduced for men aged 20 and 21—an unprecedented step for Britain to take in what was still only just peacetime. The 'Militiamen', as they were called, would undergo six months training and then go into the TA or the Army Reserve.

It caused quite a surge of recruiting for the TA further south, but not in Orkney where the three units were already nearly up to strength.

In Orphir the conscription measure caused something of a flurry when the Church of Scotland missionary, Quintin Findlay, himself an ex-serviceman, condemned it during a sermon in the presence of the County Convener, J. Storer Clouston, at the normal morning service. The Convener, however, could only take so much and rose to his feet saying: 'This is a most disgraceful and unpatriotic sermon. I leave the church,' and he walked out. An uneasy congregation remained to hear Mr Findlay later say that the excuse given by the Government for introducing conscription was the defence of small countries and he was then reported to have said: 'To my mind beggars cannot be choosers . . . the weak nations must take their chance and we should mind our own business.' Most of the congregation were said to have been 'uncomfortable' during the sermon and the Convener's denunciation but it was also said that later many of them agreed with Mr Findlay to some extent while condemning his attack on conscription itself.

Another angle on the general atmosphere of public opinion

in Orkney at the time was revealed a few days later when an anonymous writer of a 'Letter to the Editor' of 'The Orcadian' took him to task for having allowed one of the advertisements for printing in his paper to be decorated with a swastika and asked: 'Is it evidence of the bond between Hitler, Chamberlain, the Tory Party and The Orcadian?' which was pitching it rather high and suggests the motivation behind the letter was party political rather than purely patriotic. In any case, as the Editor pointed out, 'The Orcadian's' swastika hooked the other way from the Nazi symbol and had been a venerated sign of good fortune with religious significance for many centuries before it was degraded by Hitler.[25]

Although war was still a few weeks away wartime-type restrictions were already being imposed in Orkney. The Labour Party's prospective Parliamentary candidate, J. J. Robertson, was one of the people to be caught up in them. During May he was campaigning in the county, using a van equipped with loudspeakers. He chose at one point to address the workers engaged on building the new aerodrome at Hatston by delivering his speech from the van parked on the main Kirkwall-Stromness Road. He was promptly moved on. The road by this time had merged with what was to be the main runway and, although still in use as a public road, stopping on it was forbidden.

By 1 June there were 449 men and 165 women enrolled in Orkney's various Civil Defence services—341 men and seven women were ARP Wardens, for instance, and still more were needed.[26]

The registration of the 'Militiamen' on 8 June in Kirkwall again showed the Orkney bias in favour of the Army, when 25 men out of the 38 registered asked to be soldiers compared with eight for the RAF and only five for the Navy.

Orkney now seemed to be full of 'eens fae aff', workers from the south being carried all over the place in RAF or Army transport. Local people found them pretty tight-lipped as to what they were actually doing; but whatever it was, the correspondence columns of the two local papers resounded to condemnations of Sabbath-breaking by men working on defence projects on Sundays with particular reference to Hatston—but time was short and it was running out fast.

It looked as if Orkney was indeed to become an armed camp, war or no war. The camp for workers of Baldry, Yerburgh & Hutchison, contractors at Lyness, was described in one newspaper report as 'Utopia' with its comfortable huts, separate married quarters and welfare club getting special mention, suggesting that the firm would be in Orkney for many years. There was something of a crisis in Orkney's labour market in July. Many workers, skilled and unskilled, had left local employers for the very much higher wages which the big contractors on defence work could offer. It was the old, old story, to be repeated again after the war in the oil boom. Now the problem was aggravated—temporarily, it was vainly hoped—by the three local Territorial Army units going to camp at much the same time; the '226' would be away for a complete month, in fact, two weeks at Burrow Head and two more weeks on their war station at Lyness. The two coast defence units went to the Forth for a fortnight, the gunners to Kinghorn and the sappers to North Queensferry. They were given a great reception on their return from Leith in the old *St Rognvald*, with crush barriers having to be erected on Kirkwall Pier to hold back the crowd of around 700 who came to welcome them home.

By the end of August all Orkney's part-time soldiers were back in uniform again and now their profession of arms was to become full-time for the next six years or so.

There was a warning to shipping that Kirk Sound, East Weddel Sound and Water Sound on the east side of the Flow, and Burra Sound on the west, were closed by 'obstructions'. Unhappily, one at least, Kirk Sound, was only partially obstructed, with dire consequences.[27]

War had come, not only to soldiers, sailors and airmen, but to civilians as well, with the so-called 'warbling note' of the air-raid siren becoming an all-too-familiar sound throughout the land.

CHAPTER 20

Blocked Channels

DURING THE 20-year interregnum between the two world conflicts, one subject with its centre in Scapa Flow was of supreme interest in the islands—salvage. Many ships of all kinds had been sunk in and around the Flow for a variety of reasons, ranging from the massive battleships of the German navy scuttled by their own crews, to the smaller merchantmen sunk across the channels to keep that same navy out. Now, following the signing of the Versailles Peace Treaty, the problem was—how to get them up again and out of the way of ordinary peacetime shipping. There is an old anti-aircraft gunners' maxim about planes, bombs and shell splinters that 'what goes up must come down', but that by no means holds good in reverse when applied to ships that have sunk. What has gone down most certainly does not come up again automatically, but only after the application of great skill, much money and hard work, often in dangerous conditions.

Orkney before the war had enjoyed a thriving fishing industry, with special emphasis on the seasonal herring catch each summer as the shoals moved south through the North Sea, passing close to the east of the islands on their way. Stronsay was probably the biggest herring station along with Holm, while Burray which had thirty boats fishing out of it, sixteen of them locally owned, claimed to be the oldest in Orkney. Before 1914 these Burray boats had brought an income of £6000 a year to the island, probably equal to something in the region of £¼ million by 1980s standards.

That was before the war. By 1923 only seven boats sailed from Burray and even so they had to land their catches in Stronsay, there being no shore stations left in their own island.[1] There were several reasons for this decline. The advent of the steam drifter with its increased catching capacity and the ability to deliver its fish direct to mainland ports was an important factor, but so was the closure of channels leading in to Scapa Flow by blockships, which also closed in the Burray and Holm piers and herring stations.

Before 1914 the Admiralty had not considered it worthwhile to close these channels against submarine or destroyer attack on the Flow, relying on the swirling tides and rocky shores to deter an enemy from making the attempt, even if, as was thought unlikely, they had the range. Then it was found that U-boats *could* reach the Flow; and the Navy, with some justification, got the wind up. Something had to be done to protect the Grand Fleet in its chosen base—and done quickly. So with all haste they sank commandeered merchant ships across the five most vulnerable channels. In all, 19 such ships were sunk for this purpose across Kirk Sound, Skerry Sound, East Weddel Sound and Water Sound, all on the east side of the Flow, and across Burra Sound on the west.

After the war it was Kirk Sound—usually referred to locally in those days just as Holm Sound—and Water Sound which became the main bones of contention between Orkney and the Admiralty for, in both instances, the ships had blocked the channels between the fishing stations of Holm and Burray and the grounds on which their boats normally fished in the open North Sea. It was a long way round for the boats of those days, often using sail only, to go out through Hoxa Sound, quite apart from having to cope with the dangerous tides of the Pentland Firth. In addition, these channels, especially Holm Sound, had been regularly used by merchant vessels such as the 'North' Company ships and coal boats. Now they could no longer take these routes.

As early as June 1919 the Admiralty had apparently accepted that it had a responsibility and an obligation in this matter when it was announced that the re-opening of Kirk Sound was 'under consideration'. But nothing happened. Then, in March 1920, there was a tragic accident when three Orcadians who were travelling from Burray to Holm in a small sailing boat were drowned. When they were in the middle of Skerry Sound between Glims Holm and Lamb Holm the wind suddenly dropped, leaving them at the mercy of the very fast tide which smashed their boat against the blockship *Rheinfeld,* throwing them into the water, where they died. There was naturally a great public outcry and a reinforced demand that these obstructions be removed for safety reasons as well as for purely navigational needs.

In August of that year removal operations began. The East Coast Wrecking Company of Dundee was doing the job of salvage and removal of the Kirk Sound blockships on behalf of the Admiralty. There were four of them in this Sound between Lamb Holm and Holm: the *Numidian,* a former Allan Line

Trans-Atlantic passenger ship, nearest the Holm land; the *Aorangi* of the New Zealand Line next to her; then *Minieh,* entirely submerged except for her mast; and finally, nearest Lamb Holm, the graceful three-masted, two-funnel steamer of the Royal Mail Steam Packet Company, the *Thames.* All of them had been sunk by the simple expedient of blowing their bottoms out.

Main salvage operations were on the *Aorangi* in mid-channel, and to facilitate work a suspension bridge was constructed between her, the *Numidian* and the Holm shore. Three divers worked on her and although at first she refused to budge, she eventually came up at the beginning of September. She was taken down through Holm Sound and finally grounded near the Auld Kirk just short of Roseness. And there she stayed and mouldered away. In the meantime there had been another boating accident involving a blockship, this time in East Weddel Sound, fortunately without loss of life. Again the boat had been swept by the fierce tide on to the hulk, an urgent reminder of the need to get these wrecks away. But still nothing happened.

Next year, in July 1921, the MP, Sir Malcolm Smith, raised the question in the House of Commons, quoting the inconvenience and danger to fishermen caused by these obstructions. He received the surprising reply from the First Lord that the Admiralty did not admit liability to pay compensation. Their Lordships took an even stronger line a few months later in January 1922 when they said 'the Admiralty is not responsible for removing the blockships in Holm Sound'.[2] They had, however, been responsible for putting them there. The MP had a stand-up row with the Admiralty and issued an ultimatum in September saying: 'Move these ships—or else', but what the 'or else' implied is not clear. Nonetheless by mid-October the Admiralty did go so far as to say they would engage a salvage company to remove them.

By now the blockships had become an issue in the impending General Election, and under pressure the Admiralty agreed to move the *Numidian* and also the *Lorne* in Water Sound. So far, so good, but Sir Malcolm Smith was defeated in the election and his place as MP for Orkney and Shetland taken by Sir Robert Hamilton, who continued, however, to maintain the pressure.

Work did begin on the *Numidian* in January 1923 when the salvage ship, *Ixion,* of the East Coast Salvage Company arrived and began taking stones out of the hulk. These had been put in to hold her in position when she was sunk. An attempt was made to slew her round out of the navigable channel and in March they succeeded in swinging her more or less parallel with the Holm shore, and that was as far as they went.

The Burray people were now desperate, and a big protest meeting on the island in April 1924 told the authorities exactly what the islanders thought about it all. A petition was signed asking for the removal of the blockships, and this had the support of the County Council. [3] After all, the Burray boats had by this time lost at least ten years' fishing, counting the war years. The channel through Kirk Sound might now be partially clear—no more than that—but nothing had been done about Water Sound at all.

The Admiralty stalled and continued to do so quite successfully from its own point of view for several more years in a classic example of stonewalling and procrastination by a Government department. And all this time one of the greatest salvage operations in history was going on only a few miles away across the Flow, where the scuttled German ships were being raised almost like shelling peas.

Orkney County Council had also been pressing the Admiralty without success and they had even set up a special 'Blockship Committee' to deal with the matter in 1925. But it too came up against the brick wall of officialdom.

In July 1927 the Council discussed the matter at length once again and there was a division of opinion as to whether Kirk Sound or Water Sound was the more important channel. The Admiralty had by this time agreed to accept an offer from a salvage company of about £7000 to remove the *Lorne* from Water Sound, but only on condition that there would be no further claims or demands on them by the Council to remove any other blockships. It was a good delaying tactic if nothing else.

In October of that year the MP, Sir Robert Hamilton, explained the current position to his constituents. At first, he said, the Admiralty had been uncooperative but had then moved the *Numidian* saying that they could do no more. When pressed, however, they had sent an 'expert' up to Orkney and he had confirmed that nothing more could be done. More pressure was applied politically whereupon the Admiralty said that the County Council could have one of the blockships for nothing and remove it themselves if they so wished.

The Council had decided that this was not good enough. It was a question of cost and who was going to pay, so the MP kept up the pressure. Fortunately the Admiralty had given way to the extent of offering to stump up £7,500, probably equal to about £¾ million by 1980s' standards, for the removal of the

Lorne on condition that there would be no further demands on them. At this point, reported the MP, the County Council itself had entered the negotiations and he had withdrawn on the grounds that there was no point in having two negotiating bodies on the one side. The Council was now pressing that the Admiralty's condition of 'no further demands' should be withdrawn and had, in fact, demanded that the Admiralty should remove the Holm Sound obstructions as well as the *Lorne* in Water Sound.

In November the County Clerk, Duncan J. Robertson, a Kirkwall solicitor, sent a long detailed argument setting out the County Council's case in a letter to the Secretary of State for Scotland. In it he demanded that the Admiralty should remove the blockships as the blocking of the channels had been 'undertaken in the interests of the nation and not for any local benefit to the County of Orkney'.

He argued that with this being the case it was inequitable that Orkney should have to bear the cost of removing the obstructions. The Admiralty, after having said it was impossible to move the blockships, had changed its mind several times and did, in fact, achieve that 'impossible' by moving the *Numidian* in Kirk Sound. But this, continued the County Clerk's letter, had, along with the other ships which had not been moved, diverted the currents in Holm Sound to such an extent that the sea was now undermining and damaging the roadway, 20 feet of ground between the sea and the road having been washed away. There were similar problems in Burray and South Ronaldsay. It was pointed out that after considerable procrastination the Admiralty had, in fact, agreed to foot the entire cost of removing the *Lorne* but had not agreed to pay for moving the *Thames* in Holm Sound. The Council's argument was that having blocked these channels and eventually having agreed to pay for the clearance of one of them, Water Sound, the Admiralty had, in fact, admitted responsibility. It was a well-argued case but the Admiralty, having backed down over the *Lorne,* would still not entertain any further claim, nor would it accept liability.[4]

So matters again hung fire for 18 months until in September 1929 the Admiralty did give the go-ahead to remove the *Thames* and so clear the navigable channel of Kirk Sound. Their Lordships were, ten years after the war had ended, to hand over ownership rights to the ships to the County Council, for James Mitchell & Son, Dundee to attempt their removal on a 'no cure, no pay' basis. Within days the company had a salvage vessel on the scene, the *Ceto,* formerly a yacht belonging to the Guinness family which during the previous year had been chartered by the

'Daily Mail' and fitted with powerful loudspeakers to dispense music while moored off seaside resorts—it could be danced to at a range of four miles, it was claimed. She had a much more utilitarian job now, and by the beginning of October the firm reported that there should be no trouble in removing the *Thames,* or at least moving her out of the navigable channel. But there was an ominously familiar ring to the further statement that the operation would be delayed until the better weather of spring the following year.

And still the scuttled German warships were coming up with almost monotonous regularity on the other side of the Flow.

It was actually the following summer of 1930 before work started on plugging the holes in the hull of the *Thames,* two salvage ships being engaged in this operation, the *Ceto* and the *Nornord,* but the salvage company reported in mid-September that she was still not ready to lift. By mid-October bad weather was hampering operations and once again work was stopped for the winter. And that was that, apart from a controversy over the depth of water to be acceptable over the *Lorne,* should she be moved, the Council eventually agreeing to ten feet compared with the twelve feet previously stipulated.

Work began on the *Thames* again in May 1931, but at the beginning of July the final blow fell when the company announced that it was abandoning salvage on both the *Thames* and the *Lorne.* It had now been found, after nearly two years' work, that it would be impossible to refloat the *Thames* owing to the condition of her hull which was, they stated, 'as thin as a sixpence'.

As for the *Lorne,* she would have to be blown up and removed piecemeal. They had found when attempting to pump out the *Thames* that the water level just would not drop, owing to seepage through the hull. They had lost a lot of money over these preliminary examinations, they said. And Holm and Burray had lost the chance of starting up again as fishing stations. No wonder the Admiralty was regarded with something less than affection in Orkney.

That was nearly the end of the blockship saga for that war, but at least it closed with a bang and not a whimper—two bangs, in fact. In August they blew the stern off the *Lorne* with 300 lbs of gelignite and a few days later the rest of her was 'dispersed', as they termed it, in the same way.

The old *Thames* with her 'sixpence-thin' hull remained a prominent feature of the East Mainland scene for the best part of another decade, but was not quite sufficient an obstruction to prevent Prien and the *U 47* from escaping from the Flow after sinking the *Royal Oak* in 1939.

CHAPTER 21

Raising the German Fleet

IF THE SALVAGE SAGA on the east side of the Flow was one dominated by frustration and the intransigence of officialdom, it was a very different story on the other side where the scuttled German fleet lay in anything up to 130 feet of water. Many of them, however, especially the destroyers, were much shallower than that, and quite a few appraising and acquisitive eyes had cast glances in their direction. There should be plenty of good scrap metal there, and pickings generally, if only they were accessible. As early as August 1919 it was stated in the House of Commons that 19 of the German ships, including the battleship *Bayern,* three light cruisers and 15 destroyers, all of which had drifted ashore instead of sinking, had been salved by the Admiralty itself, and work was reported to be proceeding on others. There was even a suggestion that one of the battleships might be raised, filled with cement, and then sunk again across the Bay of Skaill to make a breakwater for fishing-boats, but nothing came of the idea—scrap metal became too valuable in its own right for a time.

In February 1920, ten British destroyers arrived in Scapa to tow some of the salvaged German ships south. It was not a very successful operation. Seven of these German destroyers were under tow on their way to Rosyth when the almost inevitable gale sprang up and caught them in the Pentland Firth. There was considerable naval secrecy and embarrassment over the incident, as might be expected. One of them got back into the Flow but then sank, apparently somewhere off Flotta in the Pan Hope area, only its mast showing above water. Another ran aground in Lopness Bay, Sanday with one of the 'North' boats, the *St Fergus,* standing by. The rest were reported as lost. The other eight destroyers had left Scapa a week earlier, so missing the gale but arriving in Rosyth looking 'very dirty and worse for wear'. Along with other German ships they were still lying in the Forth as late as May, waiting to be allocated to the various Allied countries. A French commission of naval officers had visited Scapa earlier in the year, to see which of the scuttled ships still above water were worth having.

After all this the Admiralty seemed to lose interest in Scapa Flow salvage. Others did not. Among them was a group of Stromness men who formed themselves into a syndicate to buy one of the German destroyers, the G 89, lying in shallow water off Fara. How many were involved in the operation is not clear nor is it known now who they all were, although one leading member appears to have been Jack Moar, a North Hoy man who was in charge of one of the forges in the Stromness smiddy. His skills would have been vital to the enterprise, for it would seem that individual members of the syndicate all buckled to and took an active as well as financial interest in the salvage work. The price paid for the destroyer is believed to have been in the £200-£250 region, perhaps equal to somewhere about £10,000 by 1980s prices. By mid-August 1922 they were ready to lift, but it was not until the middle of December that G 89 was actually refloated and towed to Stromness—on a Sunday. Two salvage vessels owned by J. W. Robertson, County Convener of Shetland County Council, had come down from Lerwick to assist the syndicate's own ship, the *Campania*—a very different sort of vessel from her namesake the crack Cunarder-cum-aircraft-carrier of the war.

Bad weather had held them up for several weeks, but the final tow was accomplished without trouble, under the watchful and expert eye of Captain George Porteous of Stromness, directing operations from the bridge of the destroyer herself. It was a tricky tow, but she was beached successfully on a sandbank in Stromness harbour and subsequently moved further up towards the North End and finally hauled ashore on what was known as the 'Reclamation'.[1] Here she lay, a familiar sight, while the syndicate, which seems to have been variously named Stromness Wrecking Company or Stromness Salvage Company, broke her up. It was said that some of her boiler tubes, polished and cut into suitable lengths, graced many houses in Stromness and round about as very elegant curtain rods. The G 89 was the first German ship to be raised by a civilian company and towed away from her resting-place in the Flow. The Stromness men pointed the way which many others would later follow on a much bigger scale.

During 1923 while the Stromness syndicate was 'digesting' its destroyer there was much speculation as to the fate of the other German vessels, but the only 'hard' news was that the Shetland Convener, J. W. Robertson, had bought four destroyers for breaking, and in June he formed the Scapa Flow Salvage and Shipbreaking Company Ltd in Lerwick with a capital of £7,000 to carry out the work.[2]

The really big Scapa salvage news came early in 1924 when the firm of Cox and Danks, steel and iron merchants in London and engineers and shipbreakers at Queenborough in Kent, bought 26 of the destroyers and two of the big ships—one of which was the huge battlecruiser, *Hindenburg*, of 26,180 tons—for an undisclosed price stated in Parliament 15 years later to have been £24,000. It was the beginning of the greatest salvage feat ever attempted and at this time Ernest Cox, sole partner in the firm — having bought out his sleeping partner, Tommy Danks, a wealthy cousin of his wife — had no experience whatsoever of salvage work, brilliant engineer though he was.[3] He did have, however, knowledge of shipbreaking, having previously bought two paid-off British battleships, *Orion* and *Erin*, for £25,000 apiece after the war, disposing of them profitably as scrap from his Queenborough yard. But they had both been floating when he bought them—the ships in Scapa Flow were on the bottom, and at some very awkward angles as well as being mostly deep and upside-down. Only the *Hindenburg* was on an even keel, and, oddly enough, she proved to be one of the most difficult of all to raise.

Besides being an autocratic engineer of genius, Cox also had the happy talent of being able to pick the right men for the job in hand. He chose two who were to become his joint Chief Salvage Officers on the Scapa project, Ernest McKeown, a former Engineroom Artificer in the Navy, and Thomas McKenzie, a foreman diver with the Clyde Trust, who joined Cox and Danks at Queenborough, proving himself to be an outstanding engineer. They were both to work with Cox right through his part in raising the German ships, and McKenzie continued with Metal Industries Ltd as their Chief Salvage Officer when they took over from Cox and Danks in the 1930s. He stayed on in Orkney when the war came as Chief Salvage Officer for the Navy's Northern Area, his bailiwick stretching as far north as Faroe.

During March 1924 Cox came north to inspect his purchases in the Flow, having already bought the huge floating dock which had been seized by Britain as part of the reparations for the scuttling of the German High Seas Fleet. It was to play a big part in bringing those same ships up to the surface again. By 25 May it was already in the Flow, having been towed north from Queenborough by the two ex-Admiralty sea-going tugs *Ferrodanks* and *Sidonian*, which Cox had also bought for his Scapa enterprise. They had been held up in the Pentland Firth but had come in through Switha Sound piloted by William Mowat, coxwain of the Longhope Lifeboat, for the last part of the ten-day-long 700-mile voyage. The dock went to Mill Bay to be near Cox's headquarters at Lyness.

The completely submerged 924-ton destroyer *V 70*, the one nearest to Lyness, was to be its first lift; but in the meantime more detailed surveys of the other sunken ships were carried out, including a close look at the *Hindenburg,* lying right way up in 11 fathoms of water but with her tripod mast, twin funnels and part of her superstructure above the surface. When the divers went down on her and the other ships they confirmed what had been discovered on the *Baden* which had not sunk but been beached—the portholes were all open or smashed, toilet and water pipes were cut, the watertight doors in the bulkheads were all jammed open and the seacocks appeared to have been treated with acid to prevent their being closed. The ships themselves were covered in marine growth although there was little or none elsewhere round the hulks. They found the engines intact and reported that glasses and champagne bottles were strewn around, while in the cabins mattresses were still in the bunks. There were not many fish about but plenty of lobsters and crabs. For one of the divers on this preliminary inspection it was his second time down on the *Hindenburg.* He had previously been down on her only three weeks after the scuttle, in search of documents for the Navy.

While all this was going on, the floating dock had been cut in two along its length to provide two lifting platforms, L-shaped in section. The main salvage party arrived and was housed in the former naval base complex at Lyness with its piers, wharfs and other equipment. Cox himself lodged at Haybrake nearby.

So now for the *V 70* lying upright in 60 feet of water. Cox's plan was to position the two halves of the floating dock on either side of the destroyer and pass chain loops underneath her keel, with both ends of the bight attached to winches on the dock sections. This was done at low water. The chains were then tautened by the winches and as the tide rose, so would the destroyer. Other chain loops would then be passed under the vessel until there were ten in all, forming a cradle. On 5 July, a Sunday, all was ready to lift and although the two Chief Salvage Officers, McKenzie and McKeown, had misgivings as to the wisdom of using chains rather than wire cables, they had been over-ruled by Cox who gave the order to winch in. But they were right and he was wrong. After several turns on the winches as the tide rose there was an explosive crack like a gun going off and one of the chains parted, its massive links flailing through the air in a deadly whiplash. Almost immediately the other chains also parted, like a gigantic zip-fastener being opened. The air was full of flying menace but miraculously not one of the 25 men working on each platform was injured, although the two docks presented a scene of utter chaos.

Cox had learned an expensive lesson, and within days the nine-inch wire cables had arrived. Each loop, weighing 250 tons, was passed under the *V 70* in the same way as that used for the chains and on 1 August, less than a month after the earlier fiasco, they were ready to lift again on the rising tide. This time there were no problems, and by high tide *V 70* was ready to be towed into shallower water, hanging between two dock sections in her wire hawser cradle. It took four lifts by dock and tide to get her to Mill Bay where she was beached. *V 70* was the first of many and, in fact, she was not broken up but pumped out, patched up and converted into what was called *Salvage Unit No. 3,* a sort of floating carpenter's shop and something of a good luck symbol in Cox's eyes.[4]

Eleven days after the *V 70* Cox had his second destroyer up, the *S 53*—and then they began to come up almost like clockwork. The dock and cable method had proved highly successful, but as the destroyers came up the price of scrap went down nearly as fast, dropping from £5 a ton to less than £2. But Cox carried on.

There was a record for the Flow on 29 August when two destroyers were brought to the surface in one day—Cox's third and Robertson's Scapa Flow Salvage Company's first. The Robertson company was cooperating with another firm, UK Salvage Ltd, and on 11 September they were delighted to find that their second prize, the *S 141,* was completely watertight, ready to be towed away as soon as she was pumped out. Cox raised his fourth destroyer the following day. They found, incidentally, that all the instrument panels and especially instruction plates in the ships, particularly those referring to the operation of valves, had been removed with typical Teutonic efficiency to make things more difficult for would-be salvors.

Robertson's method of raising his destroyers differed from that employed by Cox. In the first place he did not own a floating dock. He had two ex-Admiralty concrete barges with a 1000-ton lifting capacity each and with a capability of lifting 3000 tons between them. They were moored 30 feet apart over a destroyer, with an elaborate system of girders, blocks, pulleys, wide belts and hawsers between them. This complex was then submerged over the hulk and with a complicated arrangement of spanners the lift was aided by the rising tide and the inflation of four 'camels' or balloons. Each balloon had a lifting capacity of 150 tons.

On 16 October Cox raised his sixth destroyer in which one of the finds was a cat-o'-nine-tails complete with a petty officer's name on it. But winter was beginning to close in and gales lashed the Flow with more ferocity than any 'cat'. One of his tugs foundered at Lyness Pier and so, on 20 November, Cox decided to call a halt to salvage work for 1924 and to concentrate on getting the shore establishments, including a shipbreaking yard, ready for next year's lifting season.

At the same time Robertson brought his third destroyer ashore. Before the year ended, however, one of Cox's destroyers was towed south for breaking at Granton on the Forth and another was being broken at Lyness.

The Cox and Danks winter did not last long. By 19 March the firm had raised its seventh destroyer, the first for 1925. Robertson's company had now completed its stint and was closing down in the Flow, its associate company, UK Salvage, towing the S 20 to the Clyde for subsequent breaking at Stranraer. Cox now had Scapa to himself as far as salvage was concerned.

He went ahead with almost monotonous regularity raising destroyer after destroyer, apart from two slight hiccups when a labour dispute, one of the few in the firm, had to be settled and a fire on one of the dock sections had to be dealt with. Neither caused serious delay and by Midsummer Day, just six years after they were scuttled, up came destroyer No. 13. Cox had reached the half-way stage for the smaller vessels of which he had acquired 26. He had been on the actual job for less than a year—an average of roughly one a month. There was, in fact, a bit of a problem in that Mill Bay was now getting rather cluttered up with salvaged destroyers.

Another record was established on 6 July when the 15th destroyer was raised after only three days' work on her—the salvors had by now established a routine.

The means of speeding up operations still more came on 18 September with the arrival in the Flow of a second huge ex-German floating dock for the firm. It was to be used for raising the bigger destroyers and flotilla leaders, but it did not prove too successful for this particular task so they reverted to their original wire hawser cradle system which, with modifications, was capable of lifting even these bigger ships. And indeed, the flotilla leader B 110 came up this way just before Christmas—the 14th for 1925.

They were now getting the salved destroyers away as fast as opportunity and price allowed, but there was one unfortunate mishap early in December when the 1116-ton flotilla leader

G 103 broke adrift in snow squalls 20 miles off Rattray Head in Aberdeenshire, and drifted ashore near Rosehearty close by Fraserburgh, where she broke in two.

The year 1926 proved to be one of mixed triumph, frustration and finally disappointment for Cox. The triumph came on 1 May when the last of the 26 destroyers, the 1116-ton *G 104* came up. In 20 months he had raised 23,000 tons of shipping with a market value of some £50,000, probably equal to about £1 million today (1985), and although he had not made the fortune he had hoped for he had at least recovered his original risk capital of £40,000 and, perhaps more important, he and his team had gained experience of inestimable value. They were ready for the big ships now.

Almost inevitably, Cox being the man he was, they went for the really big one. The *Hindenburg* had been one of the largest ships of the Kaiser's navy, at just over 26,000 tons only surpassed in tonnage by the *Baden*. She had sunk on an even keel in comparatively shallow water about 70 feet deep with her superstructure above the surface, a prominent seamark for miles around. Her tonnage was more than that of all the destroyers the team had already raised put together, and it was obvious that the steel-hawser and pontoon system of raising them could not be applied to this monster.

A quite different technique would have to be adopted. By great good fortune, divers found a previously undiscovered complete plan of the ship aboard her while Cox himself was actually in Berlin to see if he could locate one there. The scheme now was to patch every opening in the vessel of whatever size—and there were about 800 of them varying from portholes and severed wastepipes to hatches and companionways. After this vast operation requiring at least 16 divers—in the copper helmets and waterproof suits with air lines to the surface of those days—the floating docks, both now cut into huge L-shaped sections, would be stationed round the ship and, the holes having been plugged with quick-hardening cement, the water would be pumped out, letting her float to the surface to be towed away. That was the plan.

There were many problems. One was a shortage of coal to keep the various steam engines going. This was 1926 when the General Strike brought the country more or less to a standstill for a week during May, just when work was about to start on the *Hindenburg*. The Cox and Danks workers themselves did not strike, but a shortage of fuel threatened to hold up the job. Surveys had, however, been carried out on some of the other big ships of the scuttled fleet and these had revealed that one at least, the *Seydlitz,* had gone down with full bunkers. Better still, part of her hull was above water and it did not take long to cut away the armour-plating; and there, so to speak, was a custom-built mine with plenty of coal and much cheaper than that which might, or might not, be available commercially, for it had rocketed from £1 a ton to £5 while the miners remained out even after the General Strike was over.

By mid-August Cox was ready to try and lift the *Hindenburg.* But she proved awkward. Although on an even keel while resting on the bottom, she started to list as soon as she began to gain buoyancy with the water being pumped out at anything up to 3,600 tons an hour. An attempt to keep her upright during one of the trial lifts was made by attaching steel cables from her mast to a salved destroyer sunk off Cava—but these snapped like cotton thread though much more dangerously. Another destroyer was lashed to the side of the bigger ship to correct the balance but this, too, failed to hold her upright.

After seesawing up and down in attempts to control the list, the crowning disaster came in the form of a northwesterly equinoctial gale in September during which one of the main boilers on the floating dock failed, reducing available power, and Cox had no choice other than to let the *Hindenburg* go back to the bottom again. He was £30,000 the poorer after five months of grinding, dangerous work with nothing to show for it but experience. He had, however, by no means abandoned the idea of raising *Hindenburg* one day. The time would come when she would obey his commands, but that was not to be for another four years.

Preliminary survey work had been going on all this time on the 22,640-ton battlecruiser *Moltke,* not far away but upside down in 70 feet of water off Cava. Like most of the big ships her heavy top-hamper of gun turrets, masts, and funnels had caused her to turn turtle as she went down. She was a danger to navigation as parts of her hull were barely covered at low water, but these conditions demanded yet another salvage technique to get her up again.

Within hours of the *Hindenburg* failure Cox and his team were working full blast on this next project. Secretly he hoped to have her up and beached by Christmas but this was expecting too much, especially in what was now Orkney's winter weather. The first big obstacle was the incredibly tough marine growth on the hull, which needed specially sharpened axes to cut it. Then there was the new technique—new to the team, that is, but one which had been used elsewhere, notably by the Italians. This was to plug all the holes and then fill the hull with compressed air, causing it to rise from the sea floor of its own volition. It had worked well in the Mediterranean but it had never been attempted on such a big ship before, nor in such adverse conditions.

Fortunately, with the hull upside down and not too deep, the openings were comparatively easy to find and seal without divers having to go inside the vessel.

By mid-October they were ready to fill her with compressed air. Early in December the bow started to lift but with a pronounced list. Furthermore, the bulkheads inside the ship did not prevent the compressed air from travelling right through the hull as it lifted. As the bow came up there was a rush of air to that part of the ship, upsetting the stability still further. The bow was allowed to settle again.

It was obvious now that the hull would have to be divided up into airtight compartments in order to control the buoyancy. This meant sealing openings inside the hull itself—a difficult and dangerous task.

The solution was to use airlocks, steel cylinders bolted on to the hull, the upper opening of them being well above the high-water mark. An airtight trapdoor was fitted to this top and the section of the hull inside the cylinder was cut out by an acetylene burner, compressed air previously pumped into the hull having forced the water level down inside. Another airtight trapdoor was then fitted there at the bottom of the airlock shaft. As the water was forced down still further inside the hull workers without diving suits could enter the ship through the airlocks, preceded by divers operating at a lower level still under water. The men entered at the top, shut the upper hatch, went down to the second trapdoor by way of steel ladders and opened it, the pressure inside the hull and the air-lock being equalised. To get out, the reverse order was adopted so that little or no compressed air escaped.

It was dark, dirty, dangerous work but this was just accepted as part of the job, and the pay was appropriately good. It also meant that work could go on inside the hull more or less regardless of weather conditions on the surface, always provided the men could be safely delivered to the airlock and recovered from it after their shifts. It was also remarkable that although working under considerable air pressure there was no incidence of the dreaded 'bends', the affliction which affects deep-sea divers who come to the surface too quickly after working under pressure. The airlocks, incidentally, had been constructed at the firm's Lyness workshops out of old and disused boiler sections welded together. The first was operational on the *Moltke* early in

1927. It was comparatively short, the *Moltke* being in fairly shallow water, but on some of the later and deeper jobs the airlocks were over 100 feet in length.

By the beginning of May the various internal compartments had been sealed off and could be filled independently with compressed air. There was a trial lift of bow and stern alternately, but once again a serious list to port developed. Cox ordered one of the salvaged destroyers to be grappled to the starboard side to counter-balance this tendency, and giant hawsers from the two pontoons moored on the other side were passed under the hull, secured to the gun turrets under water, and tightened to provide a stabilising pull. As the tide rose the *Moltke* lifted with a much reduced list; then it happened again, just as with the very first destroyer—the hawsers began to part. By good fortune it was not found to be so serious a problem as had at first been feared. The cables had not parted because of over-strain but because they were resting on the edge of the deck, and it proved to be a cutting edge. All the same, *Moltke* had to be allowed to sink again until those cutting edges could be 'blunted', and to wait for another suitable tide. The tide was right on 13th June and she came up with very little trouble and hardly any list at all—still upside-down, of course, and in a very spectacular flurry of escaping compressed air.

The tow to Lyness between the two floating docks began at once but there was, quite literally, a snag. Her superstructure was now hanging down below the hull, but rather than hold up operations Cox decided to get her into shallow water as soon as possible. Unfortunately one of the big gun barrels dropped still further and stuck fast on the bottom during the tow, bringing the whole complex of hulk, pontoon and tugs to a halt. Cox had hoped that the gun barrel might just carry away if it snagged but this did not happen, according to what the salvors described as the 'Law of Cussedness'. Divers had to go down to blast it free, a difficult and chancy task. It was the end of August 1927 before she finally reached Lyness.

The *Moltke* was the firm's first really big prize—all 22,000 tons of her. The story was not quite finished, however. She still had to get to the breakers' yard at Rosyth, where the Alloa Shipbreaking Company, which had bought her, was waiting to finish her off. This Company, incidentally, later became Metal Industries Ltd, succeeding Cox and Danks in the Scapa salvage enterprise during the 1930s.

Already some 3,000 tons of scrap had been brought out of her at Lyness but it was a difficult operation with the limited facilities available there, and it could be done much more

Q

efficiently in a properly-equipped dry dock. Further breaking was stopped and a complex of steel buildings such as a power-house with generating plant, compressors to maintain air pressure, a bunk-house and kitchens, was erected on the broad bottom where the crew would live during the trip south. Nothing quite like it had ever been attempted before—towing an upside-down battleship through 230 miles or so of potentially stormy sea held every promise of being a navigational nightmare. It was.

She left Lyness on 18 May 1928, towed ironically enough, by three sea-going German tugs: *Seefalke*, said to be the most powerful in the world, *Simson* and *Pontos*. No British tugs were prepared to take on the job and the Dutch, who were the recognised masters in this difficult art, wanted too much money. But although under way the problems were by no means solved. Once out in the Pentland Firth the cavalcade was hit by an easterly gale, so that with an ebb tide the *Moltke* started towing the tugs instead of the other way round. They had been about to round Duncansby Head into the Moray Firth when the blow began but soon found themselves with Dunnet Head abeam, 15 miles west in the wrong direction, and she was rolling badly, causing some of the compressed air which was all that was keeping her afloat, to spill out. There were some very nasty moments and then, almost as dramatically as it had begun, the gale blew itself out and soon they were up with Duncansby Head again. And so, round the corner and south-east across the Moray Firth and down the east coast to the Firth of Forth.

Even then all was not sweetness and light when rival claims as to who should pilot her into Rosyth itself resulted in her drifting apparently under no one's control at all, and only narrowly avoiding collision with one of the piers of the Forth Bridge. And, when all was said and done, Cox did not make much money out of her, in spite of scrap prices having improved.

Now came the turn of the *Seydlitz*, a 25,000-tonner and a big sister ship of the *Moltke*, lying on her starboard side in 70 feet of water. With a beam of 93 feet, this meant that a large proportion of her 656-feet length was as much as 20 feet above the surface, looking for all the world like an additional small island in the Flow. She had been a tough nut to crack at Jutland, having taken 28 direct hits from the British guns but still managing to struggle back to port. She had also been in the Dogger Bank action and had taken part in the shelling of Yarmouth and Scarborough. She was to prove just as tough a proposition for the salvors.

True to type, Cox decided to attempt the impossible—to

raise *Seydlitz* in her side-up position. Work had, in fact, begun on her before the *Moltke* was secure. She had already yielded a badly-needed coal supply during the General Strike, and now she gave up nearly 2,000 tons of 12-inch-thick armour-plating from her exposed port side to provide equally badly-needed money for the firm, although the excuse for taking it off was that it would lighten her, which was true, of course—up to a point. She, as *Moltke* had been, was divided off internally into six compartments which were then sealed and made air-tight so that they could be pressurised individually to control buoyancy. All was ready to lift, port side up. But it did not work out like that. The absence of the armour-plating, which had been removed and sold to America to raise funds, caused an imbalance as she rose with compressed air being pumped into her, and one of the bulkheads gave way. Others followed. A surge of air right through the hull brought the bow up with a rush. She rolled over, showing her keel before going down again in a cataclysm of exploding air pressure which threw water and spume in all directions.

It took four more months of grinding underwater labour, cutting away the superstructure, now underneath and compacted, to get her back to the state of readiness to lift again. She was now 70 feet down, and Cox regretfully decided to float her bottom-up like the *Moltke*. She lifted early in October but still the list was excessive, so down she went again. Altogether there were 40 of these trial lifts before it was thought the list had been largely cured. On 1 November she finally came to the surface in a text-book lift, apart from ten supporting cables which parted, but now she had her own buoyancy and could float safely on her own. Within hours she was on her way to Lyness only five miles away, towed by *Ferrodanks, Sidonian* and *Lyness,* but even so she took a week to get there as she too grounded on the way and had to wait until the tides were right again. At Lyness she was lightened by the removal of machinery, plating and one of the forward turrets, but it was not until May 1929 that she was ready for her final voyage to Rosyth.

Even then she gave trouble, grounding on the way out of the Flow when one of her guns snagged the bottom; but worse was to follow. Like the *Moltke* before her she hit a gale, a worse one, and she was not even as stable as her sister ship had been. The journey took seven long days and nights with the maintenance crew housed on her bottom suffering acute discomfort, not to mention danger from being swept overboard or worse still, of her foundering. But she made it.

By now Cox and Danks had raised 25 destroyers, the *Moltke* and the *Seydlitz,* the *Moltke* alone yielding 15,000 tons of scrap metal. They had spent some £300,000 so far and still had the *Hindenburg, Kaiser, Bremse* and one destroyer of their purchase to come. The destroyer was actually up but being used as a workshop. The rest of the scuttled fleet—two battleships, nine battlecruisers and seven light cruisers—would go out for tender when the first lot were all salved.

Work on the 24,380-ton battleship *Kaiser* had actually been going on simultaneously with that on the *Seydlitz* and she came up without trouble from close on 100 feet, the deepest yet, at the very first attempt in March 1929. She was towed south to Rosyth at the end of July, only a few weeks after the *Seydlitz*.

A problem-free lift it may have been, but working conditions in her were no better than in any of the others. They were, in fact, typical of what men had to endure to retrieve these prizes from the sea. A representative of 'The Orcadian', probably J. G. Marwick, a future Provost of Stromness, visited the *Kaiser* when her bow first came above water on 7 February, a fortnight before the rest of her left the bottom and floated free. Describing the scene he wrote:

> . . . it was just knocking-off time. A couple of divers had just come up and were giving their report that the *Kaiser* was well clear of the bottom forward but vast quantities of material hung down from her decks . . . A hiss of escaping air was caused by the deflating of the three air-locks and presently from each of them emerged half-a-dozen grimy men in overalls. Some of them strode into the sea up to the waist in order to wash off the greasy slime which covered everything, while others emptied muddy water out of their long rubber boots. 'It's none too clean a job inside her,' one of them remarked smilingly as we put a cigarette in his mouth and lit it. His hat, overalls, gloves and boots were simply smeared with slimy grease.[5]

Once there was enough room inside the hull, the compressed air having forced the water level lower, these men had to go down the airlock under pressure, enter the hull itself, and work standing on an often tilted, slime-covered, slippery black ceiling—for the ship was bottom-up, with equipment which should be standing on the floor hanging from the 'roof'. It was often pitch dark so that they had to work by feel with torches as much as by sight at times and always in the vile stench of rotting sea-growth, oil and coal dust which could easily conceal an explosive quantity of methane gas. It was no job for the faint-hearted. The pay might be what was considered good at that time, the equivalent of 5p an hour and a 40-hour week, but it was a hard way to earn it.

The *Kaiser,* too, grounded on her way to Lyness when the conning-tower, part of the 'material' hanging from her decks as reported by the divers, stuck on a sandbank just three miles short of the pier. This time they did not try to cut or blast it free. They just allowed air pressure inside the hull to drop, letting her settle until the sheer weight of the ship forced the conning-tower up into the hull; then they refloated her and went on their way without the hindrance of these dangling obstructions. It was a method they used on several subsequent operations.

Next on the list came the only cruiser to be raised, the *Bremse* (4,400 tons), lying on her side in Swanbister Bay. She was refloated and turned bottom up. After burning off what remained of her fuel oil and blasting off her mast, she was towed stern-first to Lyness at the beginning of December. Now Cox turned his attention back to the big one, the *Hindenburg,* which had beaten him in the first round. This time he was determined that *he* would win.

Work began on her early in January 1930, with some time in July as a possible target date for raising. At the same time the *Bremse* was being broken up at Lyness, and guns and turrets which had been cut off the earlier ships to lighten them and which, weighing anything up to 500 tons, still lay on the bottom of Mill Bay, were retrieved using caissons and compressed air for lifting. Altogether he had three separate squads working at Lyness, Mill Bay and on the *Hindenburg*—and this in the middle of winter.

It was found that about 500 of the 800 sealing patches put in four years earlier on the *Hindenburg* were still sound, but the other 300 meant a lot of hard work. One big problem during the 1926 attempt to raise her had been the list to port as she came clear of the bottom. To correct this, Cox designed a huge wedge from one of the salved destroyers and sank it under her port quarter. This was then filled with 600 tons of cement. The mast, funnels and some of the turrets which had become an almost integral part of Scapa scenery for more than a decade were now removed to lighten the ship, prevent the tendency to roll over and, perhaps most important of all, to provide money to complete the main job, scrap metal commanding a good price at this time.

By June shifts were working round the clock on her, night and day, while pumps were taking 150 tons of water out of her every minute. Cox was on the scene all the time, very much in charge of operations—the *Hindenburg* was very much his baby, all 26,000 tons of her. At the beginning of July all seemed ready to lift on schedule. The pumps were put on to full power and gradually the seaweed-encrusted leviathan rose ponderously from the depths. Her bow came clear and still showed no sign of listing. The wedge was doing its job. She rose still higher, 16 feet above the water. All seemed set for a copybook salvage operation when suddenly and without warning the dreaded list developed—but on the starboard side this time. It grew worse as the water still remaining in the hull sluiced across to that lower side. There was nothing for it but to let her go back to the bottom again. Now an equally large wedge was needed for that side as well, costing a further £2000. And as all this was happening, another German ship of a very different kind appeared on the scene—the airship *Graf Zeppelin* cruised sedately up Hoy sound, just level with the top of the Ward Hill at 1,500 feet, dipped gracefully in salute over her marine ex-compatriot and then flew on across the Flow and down the east coast.

The second wedge was built at break-neck speed by double shifts mixing the quick-hardening cement and sending it down in jute bags to the diving teams working below the surface. Having given his orders, Cox disappeared for a three-week break. By the time he returned the wedge was in position, the pumping system had been checked over and improved. They were ready to lift again. This time it went according to plan, the two wedges holding the hull upright until enough water had been pumped out to prevent it swilling from side to side as she floated clear of the bottom. By the end of July the *Hindenburg* was afloat fore and aft and on an even keel. Cox and his team of salvors had won.

With pumps still taking 50 tons of water out of her every minute, the tow to Mill Bay where she was beached began, stern first and with the Union Jack fluttering over her in the summer breeze, the first and only one of the big ships to make the trip the right way up. A month later she was on her way to Rosyth with the three German tugs, including the *Seefalke* again doing the honours, and the Second Coxwain of the Longhope Lifeboat, William Mowat, acting as pilot as he had on the other big tows. The weather was perfect, the *Hindenburg* behaved beautifully, and they made the voyage in the record time of just three days, the best yet.

It had been thought that with this victory over the *Hindenburg* Cox might well bow out after his seven years of unremitting, and for that matter, financially unrewarding, toil.

He was, in fact, £20,000 out of pocket although he still had his expanding and profitable scrap metal business in the south. But no: he decided to give it one more year.

Work was started early in October on the 19,400-ton battlecruiser *von der Tann,* bottom up in 20 fathoms of water not far from where the *Hindenburg* had been lying. Very long airlocks were needed for this depth, of course, but the ship presented few difficulties which had not already been overcome in the others, although she still posed problems. The autumn weather worsened into winter gales which sheered off and damaged one airlock, and operations were occasionally held up with men being marooned for several hours if the relief boat could not get alongside the airlock. The hull also held extra risks with the presence of excessive quantities of gas, which besides its foul stench was potentially explosive.

All due precautions were taken to avoid igniting any gas which might be present but flame-cutters always posed problems, and in November disaster struck. Four men, including McKenzie the Chief Salvage Officer, were trapped inside the ship for three hours when the flame of a cutter bit through into a pocket of gas, exploding it. The rising water was up to their chins before they were rescued—a nerve-shattering experience. Amazingly, none of them was seriously injured although they all needed hospital treatment.

In spite of this setback and the winter gales the *von der Tann* was afloat on 8 December after only eight weeks work on her. She was towed to shallower water half-a-mile off Cava just before Christmas, being moved on to Lyness early in February 1931.

There were still 290,000 tons of German ships waiting to be raised, and work began on the *Prinzregent Luitpold* as soon as the *von der Tann* was at Lyness. She was lying deeper than the others in the Bring Deeps.

By this time the bottom had fallen out of the scrap metal market again, so Cox decided to leave the *von der Tann* beached at Lyness and to concentrate on the *Prinzregent* in the hope that the market would pick up again by the time he got her up. One of the first jobs was fitting the longest airlocks yet used. To clear the surface with adequate freeboard they had to be 60 feet high and a dozen of them were needed. The first was bolted on to the hull at the beginning of April. All went well and Cox, always very much alive to the dangers which his men faced, especially in the early stages of an operation under water, and with the memory of the unnerving experience of the explosion on the *von der Tann* very vividly in mind, had insisted on all safety precautions being strictly observed. This ship, like the *von der Tann,* contained particular hazards due to the collection of inflammable gases as the water level dropped. Her bunkers were full and the water during work became black as ink with a mixture of oil and coal dust leaving a filthy stinking residue as it receded.

With the intense heat of the flame-cutters several small fires had been started from time to time, but this was not unusual and they had quickly been put out. Then at the end of May real tragedy struck. The hull had been blown through several times to clear any gases and tests had been taken to ensure that the work area was gas-free, but with no warning there was a shattering explosion followed by an inferno of roaring flame just where a carpenter, Wilfred Tait of Thurso, had been working. His three mates were blown off their feet and dazed but they lived to tell the tale. Two of them were Orcadians, Robert Johnston, Longhope, and Robert Mowat from Flotta. But in spite of every possible effort to save him Tait died in that awful blackness as the bulkhead collapsed and water poured through. Other men working in the hull were ordered to the surface and safety through the airlocks. Chief Salvage Officer McKenzie and three volunteers went down to try and bring Tait out but they were driven back by thick smoke from the explosion. It was only on their third trip back inside the ship that they found him, dead. He had been knocked unconscious by the explosion and had then drowned in the inrush of water.

The cause of the explosion was never discovered. The torpedo flat in which they were working had been tested and was known to be free from gas. None of the men was using a flame-cutter. It was just one of those lurking hazards that these men faced and accepted as part of the job every minute of their working day. The unexpected was always more likely to happen than not.

Cox, tough and hardbitten though he was outwardly—he had not been called 'Britain's brainiest bulldog' for nothing—was deeply affected by the tragedy, for his team, both individually and collectively, meant much to him. He laid the entire work-force off on full pay while the matter was fully investigated. When the men went back below into the ship again, no flame-cutters were permitted, even though they had not, apparently, been the cause of the blast. There is not much doubt that this disaster did a lot to influence Cox's decision to call it a day at Scapa. The *Prinzregent* duly came up without further trouble on 6 July to be hailed as 'the greatest salvage feat in history'.

NOTICE.

On 9th April 1918, a German submarine grounded on the island of Sanda, Orkney. She was seen by some of the inhabitants of the island, yet no steps were taken by them to ascertain whether the vessel was friendly or hostile, nor was she reported to the look-out station or Naval Authorities.

The result of this was that the submarine was left undisturbed and was able to discharge some stores and re-float, and a means of causing considerable losses in shipping and valuable lives has thus been allowed to escape.

It is pointed out that, apart from the national interest in destroying hostile submarines a reward of ONE HUNDRED POUNDS is payable to any person or persons giving information leading to the destruction of a hostile submarine.

H. G. KING HALL,

Vice-admiral.

Commanding Orkneys and Shetlands.

There were several stories of U-boats being ashore in the North Isles during World War I. This one seems founded on fact, judging by the Navy's reaction.

Part of the US minesweeping fleet seen from the tower of St Magnus Cathedral while they used Kirkwall Bay as a base during 1919.

At last the *Hindenburg* — once pride of the Kaiser's navy — comes to the surface.

Getting to and from work could be a hazardous business for the salvage men of Cox & Danks — and the work itself was even more hazardous at times.

IMS *Iron Duke*, Jellicoe's flagship in World War I, was back in the Flow again in the Second War — this time as a Base flagship.

HMS *Royal Oak* at speed in the Flow with guns cleared for action.

A 4.5-inch HAA gun such as those of 226 HAA Battery at Lyness, which shot down the first enemy bomber over the Flow in October 1939.

Cox claimed she could have been righted, cleaned up, fitted out and re-commissioned as an operational warship without difficulty, but this was forbidden under the conditions of the Versailles Treaty and so she had to be scrapped. She had been completely submerged at a depth of over 100 feet at high water, with 40 feet over the keel at her stern. It had needed two floating docks and 11 airlocks of 60 feet in height to get her off the muddy bottom, the largest ship ever to be raised from such a depth by compressed air. A film was made of the operation and just before she came up the *Graf Zeppelin,* making a second flight across the Flow within a year, had a good look at her from 800 feet before going on to Iceland.

Soon afterwards Cox and his family left Orkney. It might have been the 'greatest salvage feat in history', but it had left a sour taste in his mouth. The *von der Tann* was still lying unsold at Lyness; now the *Prinzregent Luitpold* joined her there.

The slump was hitting trade and industry badly everywhere; no one wanted scrap metal. Cox and Danks had employed 150 men on the Scapa salvage enterprise but now it seemed work would be suspended. Just in time for Christmas, however, there was better news. Salvage at Scapa would continue, said Cox. Prices for scrap metal had picked up just as he had decided to pack it in with another 13 ships still on the bottom. He had raised 32 including eight of over 20,000 tons since August 1924, before which time he had never salved a single ship of any size. He still had 70 men working for him at Scapa though his normal work force in good times had numbered anything between 100 and 200, half of them local men.

But the mood of optimism did not last even a month. Early in 1932 Cox decided to stop further salvage work in the Flow, bowing his head to the economic blizzard then sweeping the world. Orkney hurricanes he had coped with, but this freezing blast beat him. Since 1924 he had spent £450,000 on Scapa alone, probably equal to some £10 million at 1980 prices—a very big boost to the Orkney economy, especially in a time of deep recession. Of this total, £180,000 had gone in wages alone.[6] He reckoned he had lost £30,000 on one single ship, the *Hindenburg,* although he calculated that over the entire eight-year enterprise his total out-of-pocket losses amounted to only £10,000.[7] He was now 47 and still had his profitable scrap metal businesses in the south to run but he did not give up salvage work entirely, as his efforts in World War II showed. He remained active until 1959 when he died, still in harness, at the age of 76, one of the greatest salvage experts who has ever lived.

No ships were salvaged in Scapa Flow in 1932 although

maintenance work was carried on with clearing-up operations at Lyness, and in March 1933 a few extra hands were taken on by the firm. The local manager, Firmstone, said however that it was really nothing more than the 'beginning of the end'. Moreover, the last two ships to be raised, *von der Tann* and *Prinzregent Luitpoid,* were still lying rusting and unsold at Lyness. The prospects for starting up again looked pretty forlorn and remote. In May, however, the *Prinzregent* was sold for £33,000 and towed away to Rosyth after her 22 months on the beach. Again the tugs were from Germany and the *Seefalke* was on the job once more. There was fog in the Firth as she left which must have caused problems for the local pilot, Captain Dunnet of Greenhill, but she made the passage safely.

Two months later, in July, the *von der Tann* followed her on the same final trip and again the tow was by the German tugs but now, for the first time, flying the swastika flag of the Nazi state, a straw in the cold wind which was beginning to blow through European affairs.

This was the last ship salved by Cox and Danks to go south and she was broken up by a firm on the Firth of Forth whose name would soon become as familiar to Orcadian ears as Scapa Flow itself, Metal Industries Ltd which had merged with the Alloa Shipbreaking Company, buyers and breakers of the previous German ships.

Within a week of the *von der Tann's* departure, the new firm announced the acquisition of the Cox and Danks plant at Lyness and the good news for Orkney that salvage of some of the remaining 13 German ships would begin as soon as possible. Thomas McKenzie was appointed Chief Salvage Officer, the same post he had held with Cox and Danks, and there could have been no more appropriate appointment, for no one knew the bottom of Scapa Flow and its contents better than he did. In October the huge 28,000-ton *Bayern* was being surveyed with a view to raising her the following year. No time was being wasted.

Early in 1934 Metal Industries acquired and converted the Southern Railway ship, *Bertha,* for use as a salvage vessel. She became a familiar sight in the Flow as did the new *Metinda* which joined her in 1935. It was all part of the modernisation plan by the new owners, for there was no doubt that much of Cox's gear was obsolescent and worn out. Badly-needed new and improved management practices were also introduced; for Cox had been primarily an engineer, and a brilliant one, but business management had not been his strong suit.

It was ironic, however, that almost as soon as Metal

Industries took over, the price of scrap metal rose sharply with the prospect of an accelerating rearmament programme and so the new salvors, unlike Cox, were able to raise their ships at a profit. By April four 100-foot airlocks had been fitted to the *Bayern* and another three were added in June. She was lying in 120 feet of water between Cava and Houton, with 90 men working on her in shifts round the clock. On 1 September she surfaced rather abruptly in a 30-second surge of spilling compressed air, the biggest ship ever to be raised by this method—Metal Industries' first and with McKenzie very much in charge.

From then on the firm raised one big ship each year until 1939; the 25,000-ton *König Albert* in 1935; *Kaiserin* in May 1936; the one-time flagship, *Friedrich der Grosse* in March 1937 after only nine months' work on her; the *Grosser Kurfürst* on 26 September 1938 amidst all the sabre-rattling of the Munich crisis; and last but by no means least, the 26,700-ton *Derfflinger* from the greatest depth of all, 140 feet, on 27 July 1939, just before the outbreak of war.

She had been the most difficult lift of all and she was the last of these great ships to be refloated in more or less one piece. The remaining seven, the battleships *Kronprinz Wilhelm*, *Markgraf* and *König* with the cruisers *Dresden*, *Cöln*, *Karlsruhe* and *Brummer*, are still on the bottom lying at awkward angles, too deep for refloating to be economic, and although attempts have been made to take some of them up piecemeal their main interest now appears to be for skin-divers going down on them just for the fun of it.

It would be wrong to suggest that from 1934 onwards when Metal Industries took over, the raising of a battleship each year became just routine. Each one had its own special problems as well as all the usual imponderables connected with salvage, but work did progress to a pattern using techniques which had been evolved by Cox, McKenzie, and at first McKeown, on the *Moltke*, the first of the big ones.

With the exception of *Derfflinger*, all the ships had been towed to the Forth for breaking with the price of scrap booming as war drew nearer. The *Derfflinger*, however, was caught by the war. She was towed keel-up to shallow water off Rysa where she stayed, afloat, with a maintenance crew aboard in temporary accommodation built on the bottom, right through the war, unharmed by the Luftwaffe raiders which passed over her in 1939 and 1940. Her turn for the breakers came in September 1946 and she went, not to Rosyth as the others had, but to Faslane on the Clyde, where she yielded over 20,000 tons of scrap metal. And preceding her by only a fortnight on a similar last voyage was her erstwhile adversary at Jutland, the *Iron Duke*.

And so the great salvage saga of Scapa came to an end. The raising of these ships of the German High Seas Fleet remains the greatest feat of salvage ever attempted and what is more important, brought to a succesful conclusion, while in its story is enshrined the memory of two men of undoubted genius, Ernest Frank Cox and Thomas McKenzie, not forgetting the others who laboured long and dangerously under the cold, menacing waters of Scapa Flow.

CHAPTER 22

New Aerial Horizons

THESE MASSIVE salvage operations were the dominant feature of the Scapa story between the wars but the activity was by no means all under, or even on the surface of its grey-green waters. There was quite a lot going on above it in the air as well.

During the war Orcadians had become accustomed — almost blasé — about aircraft, both land and seaplanes as well as airships, throbbing across the islands' skies from air stations round the Flow and from the ships themselves. With the coming of peace, however, aerial activity dwindled and then ceased altogether. It was to be more than a dozen years before aircraft once again became an everyday sight over the islands, with the coming of Orkney's own commercial air services in the early 1930s.

There had, it is true, been a flurry of interest when the two intrepid aviators, Harry Hawker and Commander Kenneth McKenzie Grieve, tried to fly the Atlantic from west to east in a twin-engined bomber during 1919; they had to ditch in mid-ocean and were lucky to be picked up by a merchant ship which, because it did not carry radio, had been unable to tell the world of their safety until they were duly delivered to the Navy in Scapa Flow. But that hardly counts as air activity over Orkney.

It did, however, indicate how trans-ocean travel might develop, while emphasising that the Atlantic was still a very long direct hop for the aircraft of the day. Aviation eyes turned northwards. A series of comparatively short hops from Britain to, say, Faroe, Iceland, Greenland and on to Canada brought the New World much closer to the Old by a more practicable air route. And as seaplanes or flying-boats were thought, quite logically at that time, by far the most appropriate aircraft to fly over the sea, where better to find a suitable jumping-off place in the east than the sheltered water of Scapa Flow? From wartime experience quite a lot was known about its potential and the first hop to Faroe was only a little more than 200 miles.

The first people to try it were the Americans on a round-the-world flight in three seaplanes during the summer of 1924, coinciding incidentally with the start of Cox and Danks' salvage operation on the German Fleet. There was quite a build-up of interest in Orkney over this flight, which had started from the United States earlier in the year, flying west-about across the Pacific. They arrived in Britain from the east early in July. Great preparations were put in train in Orkney where they were to use what had been the wartime air station at Houton on the northern shore of the Flow, now, of course, more or less dismantled. Fuel supplies were organised and waiting for the planes, US Embassy officials came north to smooth their diplomatic path and the US cruiser, *Richmond,* anchored in the Flow, ready for any emergencies which might arise.

The three aircraft took off from Hull at 10.20 a.m. on 30 July 1924, and less than six hours later they touched down without trouble off Houton, watched by the biggest crowd to gather there since the German Fleet scuttled itself, five years before. They intended flying on to Iceland next day but, as so often happens in Orkney, the weather took a hand and thick fog prevented any further movement for three days. Then, rested, they took off again from the Flow just outside Houton on 2 August.

The weather was still not too good but one of the aircraft, piloted by a man with a famous name, Nelson, did manage to reach Iceland, the other two being forced to return to Orkney. An official of the US Embassy was still in Kirkwall after having seen them off, and one of the pilots forced to return, Wade, wanting to inform him as soon as possible that they had lost contact with Nelson's aircraft, 25 miles west of Orkney, flew low over the town and dropped a message in a weighted bag which landed neatly at the Kiln Corner and was duly delivered—an early example of 'air mail' in Orkney, and one which had been used by Naval airmen during the war.

The two remaining aircraft took off again from Houton the following morning, 3 July. Wade was not so lucky this time. He got into trouble about 115 miles out and had to come down in the sea, but happily he and his crew were rescued unharmed.

Less than a week later, another round-the-world flight used the Flow as the starting-off point for the Atlantic crossing. This time it was an Italian crew of four, including two engineers, in a Dornier WAL flying-boat. The leader and chief pilot was Captain Antonio Locatelli, who was to be killed some years later in Mussolini's ill-conceived invasion of what was then called Abyssinia, now Ethiopia. He, too, used Houton as a landing place, arriving there on 9 August. It was not quite what he wanted, however, so he took off again for Stromness where the big flying-boat anchored in the harbour aroused great public interest. Locatelli, too, was held up by bad weather and spent some time sight-seeing, becoming very popular with the local people.

He took off for Iceland on 13 August but, running into rain and fog, was forced, like the Americans Wade and Smith, to turn back to Stromness for another two-day wait. The weather cleared and on 15 August he tried again, this time successfully reaching Iceland by way of Faroe. He joined up with the American flyers already there but crashed the Dornier near Reykjavik and had to give up his round-the-world bid.

After this flurry of air activity Orcadian skies were quiet again for several years, although there was a German scheme proposed for using the islands in a trans-Atlantic link in a commercial air service from Hamburg to New York via Scapa, Faroe, Iceland and Cape Farewell in Greenland, but it never got further than the paper-work. A similar proposal that Scapa should be a staging-post in a UK/Canada air service, made in 1930, also came to nothing.

It was still thought at this time that the future of trans-Atlantic air services probably lay with the airship and, of course, the *Graf Zeppelin,* one of the first successful commercial airships, made two trips across the Flow, first in 1930 and again in 1931; but then came the series of disasters to airships, both British and German, which sounded the knell for lighter-than-air trans-Atlantic flying and brought nearer the day of the aeroplane, both sea and land craft, on this ocean crossing, especially by the northern route.

As the 1930s opened, however, it was no great commercial airliner which took up this challenge of the northern passage, but a minute single-engined monoplane with a mere 40-foot wing-span. Its crew of two, both Germans, Wolfram Hirth and Oscar Weller, had been expected to bring it down in Kirkwall's Bignold Park where a white sheet had been pegged out as an indicator. It was on Sunday, 28 July 1930, when they arrived over Kirkwall but failed to see the white sheet in the park and so landed in a field, alongside Old Scapa Road, on the farm of Corse where they were met by the German Vice-Consul, Fred Buchanan, a Kirkwall solicitor, who was later to command the Orkney Coast Defence gunners in Flotta at the beginning of World War II. He was accompanied by about half the population of the town, for a generation had grown up to which an aeroplane was an unfamiliar sight. The Germans were re-directed to the Bignold Park only about a mile or so away, so they took off and landed again there—just. It was far too small even for a tiny plane like this. It was parked there overnight with a guard of Boy Scouts to deter souvenir hunters, and on the following day the two airmen surveyed other possible landing-fields from the ground. Among the possible places were the Kirkwall golf course and a field at Swanbister in Orphir on the shores of the Flow not far from Houton and where the last—and unused—wartime air station had been constructed. They settled for this and flew there on the Tuesday with the aircraft unladen in order to facilitate take-off from the cramped confines of the Bignold Park.

Next morning, early, 1 August, they made a hair-raising departure with their heavy fuel load, only just clearing the dyke, after which they clawed themselves into the sky over the Flow and headed for Iceland which, for them, was nearly 12 hours flying time away. They made it, but then abandoned the attempt to fly on to the United States, putting their plane on a steamer bound for Greenland and subsequently North America.

Early in September of that same year, Orkney and the Flow had a very distinguished aeronautical visitor when Squadron Leader Orlebar touched down in Kirkwall Bay and Stromness Harbour in his RAF Southampton flying-boat with a crew of four. He was not engaged on any world-shattering record attempt but just carrying out a routine survey of possible emergency landing-places for RAF flying-boats including some in the Flow. He did not need records in any case—he already had some, including the world air-speed record, as well as being one of the pilots who won the Schneider Trophy for Britain, flying a Supermarine seaplane from which the famous wartime Spitfire was developed. Unfortunately his flying-boat sustained damage while surveying Scrabster and it had to be beached for temporary repairs on the sand at Scapa Beach. More extensive repairs were needed, so, with its survey mission in the north uncompleted, it was flown back to base at Felixstowe. The survey was completed the following year when four RAF flying-boats were engaged in the Flow though anchored at Kirkwall overnight.

Shortly after Orlebar's visit, four more RAF flying-boats were in Orkney on a training flight from the south of England.

In 1931 Orkney's air age really did take off when Captain E. E. Fresson, piloting a Gypsy Moth single-engined biplane and accompanied by a Miss Pauer, arrived in the islands for the first time on 19 April, landing incidentally in the same field at Corse which the Germans, Hirth and Weller, had used the year before.

With its isolated geographical position, separated from the rest of Britain by the notoriously storm- and tide-riven Pentland Firth, and also with the difficulty of access to islands even within the group itself, Orkney was ripe for the development of an internal air service. Fresson realised this potential and wasted no time in getting one started. He was back in Orkney that September to provide Orcadians with a taste for air travel by giving five-shilling trips round the islands or taking on air-taxi runs when chartered, going wherever he was asked to go and using whatever fields might present themselves for landing purposes. Less than two years later, on 8 May 1933, his company, Highland Airways, opened the first scheduled air service between Kirkwall and Inverness.

It was in 1933 also that the first British attempt to reach America by air using the northern route took place. John Grierson, on what he called the 'First British Atlantic Air Route (Experimental) Flight', touched down off Scapa Pier in a single-engined DH Moth seaplane on 5 August, having taken off from the Humber. He was not at all pleased with his reception in Orkney. His fuel and oil had been sent to Kirkwall instead of Scapa, and he refused to take off again for the one-and-a-half mile trip to fill up there. Instead, it had to be brought across to Scapa in spite of waste of time and transport. As 'The Orcadian' reported, 'everyone was wrong except John Grierson' and he 'played war' with everybody. He then found that there was 'no room at the inn', nor at any of the hotels for that matter, and he was lucky to get a bed for the night with the Muir family at Scapa Pier.

He left Scapa the following morning at 10.35, arriving at Torshavn in Faroe just over three hours later at 1.45 p.m. From there he flew on to Reykjavik in Iceland, but on taking off from there on 24 August he damaged his plane, and that was the end of the 'First British Atlantic Air Route (Experimental) Flight'.

The next year, 1934, besides seeing the start of Britain's first internal air mail service between Orkney and the south by Highland Airways, also brought the first trans-Atlantic 'air tourists', Dr Richard Light and Robert Wilson who arrived from the United States via Faroe after a successful negotiation of the northern route in their second-hand, single-engined high-wing monoplane, a Skyrocket seaplane. They were doing the trip 'just for the hell of it' and not with any idea of pioneering an air route. They just wanted to 'do' Europe, they said.

Aircraft, especially the DH Dragons and Rapides of the commercial air services, were now becoming as familiar sights in Orkney skies as the whitemaas or rooks, scarcely meriting an upward glance, although five flying-boats from Calshot on a training flight over the Flow and Kirkwall Bay occasioned quite a lot of interest in March 1935. And so did the 16-ton Blackburn

R

Perth flying-boat which carried out anchor tests in the Flow and elsewhere during June 1936, which must have brought back memories for one of her crew who had served on the Houton station during the war.

When the Home Fleet was in Scapa later that year, the aircraft carrier *Courageous* flew her planes off while steaming in the Flow, so that they could carry out formation flying training over the islands.

Orkney still had no military or naval aerodrome so it was learned with interest in 1937 that Wick would have an RAF station, presumably to provide fighter cover for the Fleet in Scapa, but few people at the time could have guessed that the time was not far off when Orkney itself would have no fewer than four aerodromes for that same purpose, two Naval and two RAF. Even as late as 1938 the RAF's main interest in Orkney seemed to be concentrated on possible flying-boat bases, and in June that year what was described as a 'very large flying boat' flew around the Flow and touched down in landlocked Widewall Bay under Hoxa Head and also, oddly enough, on the Stenness Loch where it 'taxied around'.

There were more than a few raised eyebrows that same June of 1938 with the Munich crisis coming to the boil, when two young Germans arrived at the civil airfield at Wideford in a 190 mph Messerschmitt monoplane, to 'do' Orkney in two hours, they said. It was felt that our relations with Germany just then were a bit too strained to welcome its airmen flying over a sensitive area like Scapa Flow.

There was an even more sinister aerial visitation the next year in August 1939 within days of the outbreak of war, when the Air Attaché at the German Embassy in London, Captain Spiller, also flew over Orkney in a private aircraft, carefully avoiding, it was claimed, 'prohibited areas'. Did any of them return in the ensuing years on even shorter and certainly less friendly visits, one wonders?[20]

On the same day as Captain Spiller, the British Prime Minister, Neville Chamberlain, also flew over Orkney and Scapa Flow in an RAF plane at the end of his Scottish holiday— presumably he did not avoid the 'prohibited areas'. Neither did the Luftwaffe's Junkers, Heinkels and Dorniers a few weeks later.

CHAPTER 23

Count-down to War

IN THE 1920s and '30s, backed up by its economy-conscious political masters, the Admiralty reverted to its love-hate attitude towards Scapa Flow. Of course, as the shadows of war retreated after the signing of the Peace Treaty in 1919, so the importance of the Flow as a naval base diminished, but it did not entirely disappear. During the Budget debate in the House of Commons in June 1920, for instance, it was stated that the Flow would be used as an exercise-ground for Royal Navy ships but it was 'very improbable it would again serve the purpose of a naval base'. How wrong can politicians be? ACOS HQ had, in fact, already closed down by this time, reducing Scapa to the status of a 'Secondary Base', and by November 1920 the HQ of the Commanding Officer, North of Scotland Area, which appointment had taken the place of ACOS, moved from Lyness to Invergordon.[1]

The sea-going navy, however, still appreciated Scapa's value for training purposes, and on 8 July that year 11 big ships—including the flagship *Queen Elizabeth*, the seaplane carrier *Argus,* 25 destroyers, 16 submarines and six depot ships of what was now called the Atlantic Fleet—anchored in Scapa on a four-day visit, the battleships and battlecruisers in the wartime anchorage off Flotta, the destroyers off Scapa Pier. The two famous battlecruisers *Hood* and *Tiger* stayed on in the Flow for exercises.

Shortly afterwards the training ship *Temeraire* also lay in the Flow for several days. On board was Prince George, later to be the Duke of Kent, who lost his life during the war in a Sunderland flying-boat which crashed not far away in the Sutherland hills. The Prince visited Kirkwall every day during the visit, lunching in the Kirkwall Hotel as his father, King George V, had done before him. He was taken for a drive round the West Mainland by Peter Shearer, Cedar Lea, Kirkwall, the designer of the 'British Warm'.[2]

The Atlantic Fleet was back in force in October 1921 and included *Hood, Repulse,* the seaplane carrier *Argus* and 'a string of submarines' which lay in Longhope. Gunnery practice went on all the time, even at night, and the ships also carried out torpedo attacks on Stack Skerry near Sule Skerry off the west coast of Orkney. Altogether the Fleet was in and out of Scapa for over a month all told, even holding a regatta, late in the year though it was. They finally departed on 3 November.

The Fleet was late in the Flow again in 1922, with the C-in-C, Admiral Sir John de Roebeck, taking time off to look at the scuttled German ships at the end of October. They came earlier in 1924, arriving for a short stay at the beginning of June, and included the flagship *Queen Elizabeth*, the aircraft carrier *Hermes*, and *Malaya, Barham* and *Warspite*.

The War Graves Commission's War Service Cross in Lyness Cemetery was unveiled at the end of September 1925 by Surgeon Rear Admiral Sir William Watson Cheyne, HM Lord Lieutenant of Orkney and Shetland (it was a joint appointment in those days). The C-in-C of the Atlantic Fleet, Admiral Sir Henry Oliver, was also present, his flagship *Revenge* lying off in the Flow and a flotilla of destroyers being anchored in Longhope.[3]

So it went on with units of the fleet visiting Scapa nearly every year. *Iron Duke, Benbow, Marlborough* and *Empress of India* were all off Flotta in June 1927, and the flagship *Revenge*, with Admiral Oliver on board, paid a visit to Kirkwall at the same time.

The ships' companies were given plenty of shore leave, the narrow streets of Kirkwall being packed with bluejackets, reminding townspeople of less happy days in wartime, reviving memories that were fading with the passing of the years and the growing up of a new generation who could listen to the band of the *Revenge* quite happily, as it paraded and played in front of the Cathedral, without the sadness of recollection or the apprehension of anticipation.

Many of the navy men did, however, look back, taking the opportunity of visiting the relics of their estwhile adversary, the scuttled German fleet, including that year the *Moltke* which had just been raised by Cox and Danks while the British Fleet was actually in the Flow.

In September the minelayer *Adventure*, with her drifter, *Mist*, anchored off Scapa Pier for a month while engaged in 'experimental work' of an undisclosed nature. She was to become a familiar sight to Orcadians, spending several weeks each autumn in the Flow over a period of several years.

And so there was a naval presence in the Flow throughout the 1920s and '30s, either with single units like the *Adventure* or more often with the full panoply of the Atlantic Fleet numbering as many as 36 ships on occasion. This fleet, which in 1932 was re-named once again, this time the Home Fleet, was in the Flow for at least a week and sometimes more every year between 1927 and the Second World War, except for 1937 when it was engaged in Coronation ceremonial, but even so both *Revenge* and *Ramillies* managed a visit at the end of that summer. Until 1932 the big ships normally used the wartime anchorage off Flotta, with some of the smaller vessels, the cruisers and destroyers, lying further north near Scapa Pier; but later in the 1930s they all used the northern anchorage except for special purposes, probably because it was easier to re-victual when nearer Kirkwall, and also it gave the ships' companies more opportunity for recreation such as football matches, dances and concert parties, all of which caused a big stir in the town. The time was fast coming, however, when they would be based permanently in the Flow and the name 'wartime anchorage' would mean just that. But that was still a few years away, although swastika-shaped war clouds were already beginning to gather over Central Europe.

These visits of the Fleet could also mean a mini-boom for local merchants and contractors, not to mention the pubs, for, although with refrigeration and big supply ships the Navy could be largely self-supporting, fresh food was always welcome. In 1931, for instance, J. & W. Tait, the old-established Kirkwall merchants, who then had a shop on Broad Street, and John T. Flett, butcher, also of Kirkwall, supplied the 21 ships of the Fleet which spent a month in the Flow that year, with 55 tons of vegetables and 15 tons of meat respectively.[4] The following year when over 30 ships lay off Scapa Pier for 12 days, it was calculated that the 12,000 men on board had accounted for 8000 pints of beer and 2000 glasses of whisky in Kirkwall's half-dozen pubs during their days, or perhaps nights, ashore. On that occasion the Fleet arrived on 28 May 1932 and included the then new flagship HMS *Nelson, Hood, Malaya, Rodney* and *Valiant* along with cruisers and destroyers, the two aircaft carriers *Furious* and *Courageous* arriving later.[5] The two 34,000-ton battleships *Nelson* and *Rodney*, with their peculiar sawn-off appearance aft and their nine 16-inch guns, were to become familiar sights in the Flow for the next decade and more.

During these summer visits the fleet rowing regattas were usually held between the lines of anchored ships with a great display of enthusiasm, cheering and expenditure of energy which no doubt helped to generate that 8000-pint thirst.

Kirkwall Bay was not entirely neglected either, although the main naval interest was concentrated in Scapa; but, for instance, while the main fleet was in the Flow in 1931, five minesweepers of the 1st Flotilla—*Sutton, Pangbourne, Albury, Dundalk* and *Dunoon*—lay off Kirkwall where they, too, held their pulling regatta.

In 1934 the German tanker *Kattegat* stranded on Torness in Hoy and after being refloated was brought in and moored off Longhope, where the crew celebrated Hitler's birthday by parading and visiting the German graves in Lyness Cemetery.[6] In Berlin itself ex-servicemen paraded to celebrate, or at least mark the anniversary of, the scuttling of their fleet in Scapa fifteen years earlier—apparently regarding it still as a kind of victory.

More pragmatically the British, in the shape of Metal Industries' salvage team, marked the occasion a little later by bringing one of these same ships, the mighty *Bayern*, back up to the surface again, a mass of rusting metal due to be scrapped. It was the firm's first victory and a big one in every way.

The Home Fleet of five battleships, one battlecruiser, five cruisers, 18 destroyers, five submarines and an aircraft carrier spent nine days in the Flow that year. It was still very much a peacetime summer cruise type of visit with the regatta and the usual social and sporting activities, but already the danger signals were beginning to flicker in the Chancellories of Europe as the now Nazi Germany started to flex its sinews.

Was it going to happen all over again—the war to end wars? And if war did come, would Scapa Flow be better prepared for defence this time? Was there any truth in the rumour that a regular artillery unit was to be stationed in Orkney? And, if so, what kind of guns would it have and why not a Territorial Army unit of local men to man them?

After 1918, economy, retrenchment, and reform had brought about what was known as the 'Ten Year Rule' in British defence: an assumption that there would be no attacks on the United Kingdom for at least a decade. Moreover it was a 'rolling' rule—in other words, in 1919 it was assumed there would be no war before 1929, and in 1921 that there would be peace until at least 1931; and so on. This meant a run-down in both coastal and air defence. There was also considerable controversy as to whether coast defence artillery was now obsolete or not, and this naturally delayed improvement or even adequate maintenance of coast defence establishments to such an extent that by 1930 it was considered there was not a port in the UK or the Empire whose guns were not outranged by those of a modern cruiser armed with 6-inch guns. Scapa was no exception: it had no guns at all. The Navy after the London Treaty of 1930 was also inadequate, its 50 permitted cruisers being 20 short of the number needed merely to safeguard the international trade routes. There were similar inadequacies in the field army and the air force; any crisis overseas would have meant denuding the defence of the UK itself to meet it.[7]

As the German menace grew in the 1930s with the rising tide of Hitlerism, defence thinking in Britain changed and the Ten Year Rule was dropped in 1932; but even so it took a long time for the change to become effective in the shape of rearmament. The country as a whole, and consequently most of its politicians, could not bring themselves to believe that the unthinkable could really happen again. Only in the last years of the decade was it realised that war was probably inevitable, given the continued manic government by Hitler in Germany. Only then was rearmament reluctantly begun.

Scapa Flow was one of 19 ports which in theory were to have defences installed before the outbreak of war, and schemes to implement this policy were drawn up or were under revision; but they were still only on paper.[8] It was not, in fact, until the spring of 1939 that the Admiralty actually informed the Home Defence Committee of its intention to use both Scapa and Rosyth as bases for the Home Fleet in the event of war.[9]

The Admiralty 'War Memorandum (Germany)' of May 1937 had designated Rosyth as the Main Fleet Base, with Scapa Flow as a base for three battlecruisers and two aircraft carriers.

Supplement No. 1 to this Memorandum, issued in August 1938 to cover a situation where both Germany *and* Italy were involved, stated that 'North Sea Force' was to have its battleships at Rosyth and its battlecruisers at Scapa.

Supplement No. 2, issued a few weeks later in September 1938, just before the Munich crisis, left the choice of bases for 'North Sea Force' to C-in-C Home Fleet, and he chose Scapa. This was confirmed in the Admiralty's 'War Memorandum' of January 1939, with Scapa Flow designated 'Fleet Base'.[10]

By 1939 the Air Staff, too, had reconsidered an earlier estimate of the Luftwaffe's capacity to bomb the Fleet in Scapa which had suggested that such a danger was not excessive. Now it was their revised belief that the German Air Force **could** drop as much as 446 tons of bombs in one day on the Flow or, in a longer and more sustained effort, about half that weight every day.

And just after war broke out it was considered that, while Scapa was 'submarine-proof', a 36-gun density was needed to cover the area from air attack and that this would best be provided by a land-based 'AA umbrella'. A 72-gun density had already been approved for the air defence of the Navy's Malta base.[11]

It was the accepted view that the Fleet was capable of defending itself with its own guns against air attack, both at sea and in harbour, but that attendant tankers, store ships and auxiliaries were not so well off. So the experts calculated that 24 HAA guns would be needed at Scapa, rather than the eight which had originally been allotted to it as a mere 'naval port of secondary importance'. In addition, two fighter squadrons were to be stationed at Wick.[12]

A rather primitive radar set was moved from Ravenscar in Yorkshire to Orkney until such time as the east coast radar screen would be complete, a necessary precaution in view of the German reconnaissance flights over the North Sea which began as early as June 1939 and which caused considerable apprehension, although they did not actually enter British air space.[13]

What was known as the 'Lyness Scheme', providing for 650 officers, ratings and civilians to be accommodated ashore at Scapa Flow, had been drawn up by 22 July 1939, but until such time as the hutments could be built they were to live and work aboard a depot ship, probably the *Iron Duke*.[14]

Surveys had been made for the underground fuel oil tanks near Lyness in 1936, and in September that year the Home Fleet, led by HMS *Nelson* and *Rodney,* with the cruisers *Orion* and *Cairo,* the carrier *Courageous* and a flotilla of destroyers, was in the Flow for a week and with them a film crew from the Herbert Wilcox Company aboard the flagship taking shots for a film to be called *The Navy Eternal,* scripted by the popular naval writer Bartimeus.[15]

By April of the following year, 1937, work had begun on the 100,000-ton-capacity above-ground oil tanks being erected by Balfour Beatty Ltd at Lyness, some of which were completed by the end of the year, with the first tanker-load of oil being discharged into them before Christmas.

During the summer of 1936 a survey of the channels leading into the Flow had been undertaken by the Admiralty, and in 1937 the position of the three main anti-submarine booms had been fixed for Hoxa Sound, Switha Sound and Hoy Sound, the Flow by this time having been designated a Category A Defended Port on 21 October. There was still, however, uncertainty and indecision as to how the other smaller channels such as Holm Sound and Water Sound should be made secure.

The actual laying of the booms did not begin until June 1938, when Commander Hopkins was appointed Boom Defence Officer Scapa, based on Rysa Lodge in Hoy. He had two boom defence vessels and the netlayer *Guardian* to do the job, but at the time of the Munich crisis that autumn only the Hoxa Boom, admittedly the most important, had been laid between Hoxa Head in South Ronaldsay and Quoyness in Flotta.[16] Had war come in 1938 the C-in-C Home Fleet, Admiral Forbes, would have had just the same anxieties as Jellicoe, the C-in-C Grand Fleet, had had quarter-of-a-century before—a vitally important concentration of ships in a confined area open to submarine attack, but with now the potential danger from the air as well. He did get the breathing-space of a year, but even that proved all too tragically short.

Even as it was, Forbes was a very worried man—so much so that on 4 October at the height of the Munich crisis when the Fleet was in Scapa, he personally ordered the purchase of the concrete barge, *Zata* or *Majda*, from James Anderson, Victoria Street, Stromness for £100, which was considered a bargain. It was towed away from Stromness by one of the Metal Industries tugs, with the idea of sinking it in Kirk Sound as a blockship.[17] In fact, it was not sunk then but five months later, and then not in Kirk Sound but in Water Sound between Burray and South Ronaldsay, the operation being carried out under the watchful eye of McKenzie of Metal Industries, who for once, was putting a vessel down instead of his more accustomed task of bringing them up.

As the Munich crisis was coming to the boil in the autumn of 1938 the possibility of closing Water Sound with concrete blocks had been considered by the Admiralty. A detailed survey estimated the cost at about £21,000, whereas blocking by steel hurdles with connecting chains would be much cheaper at £5,500, but would need replacing every five years as well as having an annual upkeep cost of £2000.[18]

Earlier that year it had been reported to the Admiralty that East Weddel and Skerry Sounds were still effectively obstructed by the First War blockships, that Water Sound needed attention which it subsequently got with the concrete barge, but that action was definitely needed to make Kirk Sound impassable. A further survey, made by the Commander-in-Charge Boom Defence, Firth of Forth, resulted in a report dated 1 March 1938 which stated: 'There is a perfectly clear and deep passage through Kirk Sound 300 to 400 feet wide. A 2000-ton vessel is said to have made it in 1932.'[19] It was also suggested that the barge subsequently acquired by Admiral Forbes was available 'almost as a gift' and could be sunk to block this gap. But nothing was done about the barge at this time.

In September of the same year, with the Home Fleet already at war stations in the Flow, the Military Branch of the Admiralty got so far as to state that 'it was considered a matter of urgency to provide greater security for HM ships lying in the Scapa anchorage. It must be blocked to prevent, at all states of tide, the passage of a small submarine drawing 10 feet and of 13 foot beam.' But being still in the days of comparative peace, all the various interested parties had to be consulted first, the Ministry of Agriculture and Fisheries, the Board of Trade, the Scottish Office and the Fishery Board being the main ones mentioned.[20]

The Munich crisis passed. Britain and France got their breathing-space to rearm in some degreee.

On 24 March 1939 the Commanding Officer Coast of Scotland (COCOS) wrote to the Secretary of the Admiralty reporting that the old merchant ship *Seriano* had been sunk as a blockship in Kirk Sound on 15 March. He had considered that along with the *Thames,* already there from the First War, the main channel in Kirk Sound and the eastern channels generally had been effectively blocked but, he went on, 'It is now disclosed for the first time navigable channels still exist through Kirk Sound between the broken-up blockship south of the *Thames* and Lamb Holm and through Skerry Sound.' COCOS wanted a comprehensive survey of these channels to be carried out.[21] It was, in fact, through Kirk Sound that Prien crept in *U 47* on the night he sank the *Royal Oak.*

On 26 May 1939, less than four months before war broke out, the Admiralty informed the C-in-C Home Fleet and COCOS that the investigation carried out earlier in the month by the survey vessel HMS *Scott* 'indicates no risk at present exists of submerged entry by Holm or Water Sound and that entry on the surface will be extremely hazardous'. Unfortunately for the *Royal Oak* there was a U-boat commander not only ready to face those hazards but also capable of overcoming them. The survey vessel *Scott,* incidentally, had reported navigable channels in these sounds of up to 400 feet wide with a depth of two fathoms at low water.

In their wisdom, Their Lordships went on to say that they 'doubted if the further proposed measures would be found to provide 100 percent security against a determined attempt at entry by enemy craft on the surface though such an attempt is considered extremely unlikely'. Finally it all came back to money again and they decided 'that further expenditure on blocking cannot be justified'. But they did go so far as to provide three more patrol boats for the booms and agreed that the Hoxa Boom should be a double one, though they doubted the effectiveness of such booms in preventing entry by surface vessels bigger than launches. The C-in-C, however, felt that **all** booms should be double.[22]

But in any case, so far as blocking was concerned, the Treasury had put a limit of £10,000 each on the purchase of old ships for this purpose, one very suitable vessel priced at £12,000 having to be turned down because of this edict, while the Senior Naval Officer, Scapa (SNO), Commander O. M. Frewin, a cousin of Winston Churchill, who had been appointed in February that year, was told on 27 May: 'Not another penny to be spent on blockships for Scapa Flow.'[23]

Admiral Forbes, the C-in-C of the Home Fleet who would have to use the Flow, was, not surprisingly, less than happy about Their Lordships' decisions. He wrote to the Admiralty quoting a letter written to him by Admiral Sir William French, the Admiral Commanding Orkney and Shetland (ACOS) designate who visited Scapa in June. French had written:—

. . . I went in and out of both Sounds [i.e. Kirk and Skerry Sounds] on a young west-going tide in a picket boat. I would have no hesitation in doing either of them in a submarine or a destroyer provided I could see and could select slack water to do it in . . . It's complete rot about the swirl and eddies putting you on the beach of the sunken ships. The sunken ships provide you with an excellent beacon.

He considered it essential to sink blockships in these two channels, and to get it done by Metal Industries as soon as possible because they intended to pull out of Orkney by October.

The C-in-C asked for urgent reconsideration of the Admiralty's decision not to block the channels. Large charts of Kirk and Skerry Sounds, he pointed out, showed 'that three straight channels exist through which enemy submarines or destroyers could enter Scapa Flow and attack the fleet . . . Unless these channels are effectively blocked,' he wrote, 'the C-in-C at Scapa cannot be free from constant anxiety as to the safety of his ships from submarine or destroyer attack' — a strong echo of Jellicoe's anxiety at the beginning of World War I. Just to rub it in, Forbes added that he could not understand the Admiralty's reference to anti-submarine (A/S) booms not being capable of preventing entry by surface vessels larger than Motor Torpedo Boats (MTBs) — 'The A/S boom at Hoxa brought HMS *Resolution* [a 28,000-ton battleship] to rest in September 1938 when steaming at 7 to 8 knots,' he commented drily.[24]

This broadside from two such senior flag officers had the desired effect. The Admiralty wrote to COCOS and Forbes on 4 July that in view of these representations Their Lordships had modified their views on blocking and had decided that three more ships should be sunk in Kirk and Water Sounds — but not at more than a total cost of £30,000.[25] A long haggle over costs and availability of suitable ships ensued but it was not until 5 September, with actual war providing the impetus, that the Admiralty finally agreed that the blocking of these channels should go ahead 'without prejudice to price'. But it was too late to save the *Royal Oak.* The 4896-ton *Cape Ortegal* was sunk three days later in Skerry Sound; but the 3859-ton *Lake Neuchatel,* destined for Kirk Sound, was still afloat on the night of 13/14 October at high water when *U 47* slipped through the channel where she should have been sunk and over 800 men died in the *Royal Oak. Lake Neuchatel* was sunk in position a week later on 21 October.[26]

In February 1939 work had begun on the Fleet Air Arm aerodrome at Hatston, and such was the drive engendered by impending war in this case that the first aircraft were able to land there towards the end of May, just four months after work had begun. The runways were usable even if the hangars and other buildings were not complete.[27]

The boom across Switha Sound was laid in April that year, followed by the Hoy Sound boom between Scad Head and Houton, completed in May, while Boom Defence HQ at Lyness was ready in July at the same time that permanent fleet mooring buoys were laid off Flotta and in Gutter Sound. Commander Frewin, the SNO who was also King's Harbour Master, had arrived in Lyness in April, but as there was no accommodation available he established his office in the more congenial surroundings of the Kirkwall Hotel. Owing to the cheeseparing attitude of the Treasury, however, he did not even have a boat in which to visit his bailiwick and, worse still, he had to suffer the mortification of having to borrow a launch from the RAF in order to pay an official visit to the French Navy when the battleship *Dunquerque,* the battlecruiser *Admiral Gensoul* and the three cruisers *George Lerques, Montcalm* and *Gloire* came into the Flow in June. He was equally incensed when the 'top brass' of the Army, including General Sir Alan Brooke, carried out a reconnaissance of Orkney from the anti-aircraft point of view, also in June, without his being notified.[28] They looked at possible gun positions round the Flow, and especially at Lyness, without ever contacting him. When he did find out they had been in Orkney he pursued them by air to Scrabster, as they were heading south, to talk things over.

The 1938 crisis had speeded things up round the Flow but even so the defences were still woefully inadequate in 1939.

There were the eight 4.5-inch HAA guns, four on either side of the Lyness oil tanks, the two 6-inch coast defence guns at each of Ness and Stanger Head, as well as a 4.7-inch gun on temporary mountings at Stanger which was to be moved to Neb, also in Flotta. These coast defence guns were of rather ancient vintage, but any suspicion that they might prove more lethal to their own gun crews than the enemy was disposed of when the veteran of them all, the 4.7, was fired by mistake in a moment of enthusiastic aberration shortly after the outbreak of war — they were, in fact, surprisingly accurate and, like the HAA guns at Lyness, manned by the Orkney TA gunners. The accidental firing occurred during gun drill when the examination drifter in Switha Sound had been used for laying practice. Fortunately she had moved slightly and the round struck the water just astern of her, causing no more damage than a nasty fright and ruffled feelings among the crew. The round itself, being solid, did not explode, and finished up somewhere near Cantick Lighthouse.

With the definite designation of Scapa as 'Main War Base' for the Fleet, preparations for that war gathered momentum. Teleprinter communication with Rosyth was established, the radar station — called RDF (Radio Direction Finding) in those days — became operational at Netherbutton in Holm, telephone and teleprinter circuits were laid round the Flow, work on Hatston aerodrome was speeded up, and the Navy's Port War Signal Station (PWSS), already under construction just along from the coast battery overlooking the two main entrances to the anchorage from Stanger Head in Flotta, was ready in August for its signallers — it did not have long to wait.

Already much of the Home Fleet was in or around Scapa. HMS *Nelson,* wearing the flag of the Commander-in-Chief Admiral Sir Charles Forbes, slipped quietly through Hoxa boom at about 4 p.m. on the afternoon of 11 August and secured to 'A' Buoy off Flotta at 5 p.m.[29] 'A' Buoy had a direct phone line to the shore and to Whitehall. This was no summer cruise with regattas, football matches and social gatherings. Next day, 12 August, was no 'Glorious Twelfth' on the moors either — quite a different sort of shooting was in prospect as the cruiser *Aurora* with the 8th Destroyer Flotilla arrived at 8.30 a.m., followed half-an-hour later by the carrier *Ark Royal. Ark Royal* was soon to become almost a household name in the news stories of both Britain and Germany as the Nazi propaganda machine in both newspapers and on radio 'sank' her regularly, much to the amusement of Orcadians and Servicemen on the Scapa defences who could see her very solidly afloat with equal regularity.

Another carrier, *Furious,* was already in the Flow along

with *Royal Sovereign, Jersey* and the big Tribal class destroyer *Ashanti.* HMS *Hood,* the biggest ship in the Royal Navy, arrived two days later on 14 August. They all went to sea again on the 15th, not returning till ten days later, when *Nelson, Hood, Repulse, Ark Royal* and the cruisers *Southampton, Glasgow, Effingham* and *Enterprise* entered harbour through Hoxa Sound. The *Nelson's* log for that day carries the laconic but sinister entry: 'Hands preparing for war.'

Last-minute preparations for war were going ahead on shore also, where the pressures were building up to the climax. At 6.15 p.m. on 22 August the codeword 'Hastings' was flashed to all three Orkney TA units, in common with others all over the country. 'Hastings' meant the detailing of duty officers and continuous manning of telephones at unit headquarters. A few hours later saw a quickening of the pace as the codeword 'Byng' came out from the War Office, with key parties being called out in the early hours of 23 August; guns and searchlights were manned to 60 percent strength by Orkney Heavy Regiment and Orkney (Fortress) Company at Ness and Stanger Head, 226 HAA Battery being already at its war station in Hoy. The '226' gunners went to Lyness by naval craft, the Caithness troop coming across the Firth to join them by the specially chartered *St Ola.* The coast defence units travelled in two War Department vessels from Stromness and Scapa to Flotta. Then at 4.30 p.m. that afternoon of 23 August came the final codeword, 'Plumer' — general mobilisation — on which several hundred Orcadians like their TA comrades throughout the country ceased at one stroke to be civilians, a status they would not regain for another six years.[30]

In Orkney mobilisation had gone smoothly in beautiful summer weather — war still seemed unthinkable in spite of the fearsome news bulletins and the brooding grey shapes of the men-of-war in the Flow, constantly on the move in and out of the anchorage.

Rodney, almost indistinguishable from her sister ship *Nelson,* came in. *Ramillies* and *Royal Oak* had also been ordered north, and on 26 August the veteran battleship *Iron Duke* steamed sedately into the harbour she knew so well from that earlier war when she had proudly worn Jellicoe's flag as she carried him to Jutland and back. Now, no longer a fighting ship, she returned to Scapa once again as a flagship, but not in a sea-going role. She was to be the HQ of the Admiral Commanding Orkney and Shetland and would act as an accommodation ship and communications centre off Lyness. The shortage of accommodation was already causing acute problems as the Base began belatedly to build up, and the old 12,000-ton liner *Voltaire* was a very welcome addition when she also took up her moorings nearby, helping to relieve some of the congestion.[31]

Naval reservists under a retired Captain with his Yeoman of Signals, all recalled for war service, took up quarters with the Army on Stanger Head and went on continuous watch from the PWSS with its direct lines to the flagship and ACOS; they were in constant touch with the movement of ships in and out through the Hoxa and Switha booms, as well as providing very welcome navy cocoa to gunners and searchlight men in the long and still unfamiliar watches of the night.

These watches were carried out in makeshift draughty Battery Observation Posts (BOPs), gun shelters and searchlight emplacements thrown together out of corrugated iron and now being rapidly, if inadequately, strengthened by sandbags. At least they kept some of the wind out; but they were cold, rattled in the merest breeze and would probably have been ineffective against anything more lethal than an airgun pellet. The gunners were at one end, the sappers controlling the lights for them at the other, divided from each other by yet more corrugated iron. There was a flap in front, again of corrugated iron on wooden battens, hinged at the top, which when pushed out gave unimpeded vision over the possible target area of Hoxa Sound and the Pentland Firth; it also allowed unimpeded ingress for the wind, the rain and, eventually, sleet.

On 25 August, 771 Squadron of the Fleet Air Arm arrived at Hatston and there also was 700 Squadron, formed of venerable Walrus amphibians disembarked from the capital ships; the Walruses were to become an almost integral part of the Orkney skies in the early days of the war as they chuntered around in front of their pusher airscrews on surveillance and anti-submarine patrols. Gladiator biplane fighters came later from 804 Squadron. They, like the other Fleet Air Arm fighters, were under the operational control of the RAF at Wick with its operations room in a school until the permanent one was established near Kirkwall.

On the last day of August with the sands of peace fast running out, there were 44 ships of the Home Fleet in Scapa Flow, six battleships of 2nd Battle Squadron, two battlecruisers, one aircraft carrier, four cruisers each of 7th, 12th and 18th Squadrons, 17 destroyers of 6th and 8th Flotillas, seven minesweepers of 1st Minesweeping Flotilla, as well as the *Iron Duke, Voltaire* and other auxiliaries and boom defence vessels.[32]

The batteries at the main entrance to the anchorage were manned and so were the HAA guns at Lyness. An officer and 20 men were detached from 226 Bty there and sent to Netherbutton with four very inadequate First World War Lewis guns, to protect the radar establishment against low-flying air attack until such time as a troop from 39 LAA Bty with its Bofors guns could get to Orkney from the Forth. Machine-guns were also landed from the Fleet for the Royal Marines to take up an LAA role at the Lyness oil tanks.

The Scapa Flow defences, insofar as they had been provided, were manned and ready for action. Everyone waited apprehensively for 'the balloon to go up' for now war **did** seem inevitable — and it was. The pale blue skies and sunlit days of the lovely late summer slipped away while the news from Europe grew ever darker. Poland was invaded by Germany on 1 September and, with Britain's pledge to that unhappy country, war was only a matter of hours away. The Home Fleet put to sea in all its majesty, to patrol between Shetland and Norway, it was said. RAF Coastal Command aircraft were also patrolling over the North Sea. Round the now rather empty Flow we could only watch and wait. We did not have long to wait.

CHAPTER 24

At War Again

THE COUNT-DOWN to war ticked away like a time-bomb and, just as in August 1914, the British Fleet was not in its chosen base of Scapa Flow on 3 September 1939 when threat became reality. But, as before, the ships were not very far away on that fine, if misty, Sunday morning when the Prime Minister, Neville Chamberlain, told the British people over the radio that they were once again at war with Germany. The Orkney gunners and sappers in their three main battery positions at Ness, Stanger Head and Lyness stood guard over a rather deserted-looking Scapa Flow glinting in the autumn sunlight as they listened to the news that would take a large slice out of their lives and, in some cases, life itself. These four hundred or so men from the islands and parishes and the two towns of Kirkwall and Stromness, along with the Caithness half-battery, constituted virtually the entire land-based military presence round the anchorage when war actually came. They were the first of the many who would come later.

The bulk of the Home Fleet was at sea some 500 miles west of Orkney at midday that Sunday when peace finally came to an end, but on information that units of the German Navy had left harbour the British ships altered course, heading east at 16 knots to pass between Fair Isle and North Ronaldsay in thick fog. They carried out a sweep in the North Sea, zig-zagging as an anti-submarine precaution and only returning to Scapa shortly after dawn on the 6th. Even then it was for only a few hours and the flagship *Nelson* passed through the Hoxa boom again, outward bound, at 6.25 the following morning.[1]

On that same morning, 7 September, the Flow had its first visit of the war by a submarine, the British *Swordfish* coming in through the Switha gate. Two weeks later the first foreign submarine came in the same way, the Polish *Wilk* which had made good her escape from the Baltic. The main fleet which accompanied the *Nelson* out into the North Sea that morning — including the battleships *Rodney* and *Repulse*, the aircraft carrier *Ark Royal*, and the two cruisers *Aurora* and *Sheffield* with ten

S

destroyers — went north-east to patrol off the Norwegian coast and did not return until the 10th, by which time *Hood* and *Renown* had left to patrol between Faroe and Iceland. *Royal Oak* and *Royal Sovereign* had also sailed, while *Norfolk* had come in to join the 18th Cruiser Squadron, *Newcastle* and *Suffolk* arriving later.[2]

The first reported enemy air activity over or near the Flow came on 5 September when it was noted in the War Diary of Orkney Fixed Defences, the HQ of the coastal batteries, that the Fleet had opened fire during a general air alert but had not scored any hits. The Navy base records themselves do not mention this but do record an enemy reconnaissance flight east of the Flow on the 6th.[3] Strangely enough, the '226' War Diary does not mention either occurrence.

At the time, there was no central operations room or similar organisation to plot the approach of possibly hostile aircraft and pass on warnings to gun sites and ships. In fact, the air-raid warning system, such as it was, could best be described as 'Gilbertian', and that would be a very polite way of putting it.

No one, of course, knew what would happen when war came. Massive bombing of big cities had been anticipated. It did not come — not then. Nor did the air attacks on military and naval centres which had also been expected.

Warning systems were, to a large extent, still in the development stage and although there was an attitude of groundless hope that Scapa, lying at the extreme range of bombers operating from German airfields, would be unlikely to suffer heavy attacks, it was a hope not shared by the Air Staff, where informed opinion now believed that sustained attacks on the anchorage were at least a possibility and perhaps a probability. Nobody really knew, and the result was an edgy 'finger-on-the-button' atmosphere.

ACOS, Admiral French, on board the *Iron Duke,* had a direct phone line to an RAF radar corporal at Netherbutton. He also had a close personal relationship with the Officer Commanding 226 HAA Battery at Lyness and, in fact, tended to regard the Battery's two troops as extra turrets of his flagship. He alone could issue air-raid warnings and this he did only after a telephone conversation and consultation with the RAF corporal. As a result some of the warnings were often a little late in coming through to those who needed to act on them, as might be expected.[4]

It is not therefore surprising that the first weeks of the war had a rather unreal feeling about them, with 'alerts', air-raid warnings and 'all clears' followed by more warnings and 'all clears' in bewildering succession, with gun crews 'Standing to' then 'Standing down' only to be called out again, while off-duty personnel were ordered to the slit trenches, or to disperse in the case of Stanger Head where the ground was so rocky that trenches could not be dug. Sometimes there was the throb of distant, high-flying aircraft but more often than not, 'the rest was silence'.

In the gun positions themselves the Orkney troops were carrying out the normal soldiers' routine of digging and sandbagging themselves in, laying water supply pipes, and at Stanger Head constructing what its architect designer, one of the Fortress Company Engineer officers, proudly described as a 'sanitary escapement for the rapid disposal of refuse etc' over the cliff and directly into the sea below. The troops who translated this ingenious chute into reality had a shorter, more expressive name for it.

The coast gunners were fortunate. Their more or less permanent hutted camps had already been built for them by contractors; but the '226' troops were not so lucky, being accommodated in tents to begin with.

There were drills, drills and more drills both on guns and searchlights, for the handling of equipment had to become second nature in daylight, darkness, sunshine or rain—not forgetting Orkney's almost incessant wind. Lifelines and paths down the cliffs at Stanger Head were laid to make access to the searchlight emplacements near sea level safer on dark and stormy nights now that they were getting longer, and now that the searchlights themselves, officially known by the Army as Defence Electric Lights (DEL), were being exposed more frequently to carry out sweeps and searches at irregular intervals through the hours of darkness. The process of settling in to an entirely new kind of life was under way.

Water was a problem on Flotta, the large artificial catchment near Stanger Head being a quite inadequate source of supply for the sudden influx of troops, which even at this early date more than doubled the native population of the island.

Food supplies from the Navy, Army and Air Force Institute (NAAFI), to supplement the standard rations, were not all they might have been and, in fact, were described in the Fixed Defences War Diary as 'appalling, putrid and short' on 13 September when the Stanger Head Battery was visited by the General Officer Commanding (GOC) Scottish Command, who was doubtless told all about it in no uncertain terms.

Three days after the war started, on 6 September, the Chiefs of Staff, having reviewed the Scapa Flow defences, reported to the War Cabinet. They pointed out that material and extra equipment for these defences had to be provided by Services other than the Navy itself, in other words by the Army and Air Force. Many interests, and many pressures, were involved in maintaining security of the Fleet. The War Office had to provide the guns, but could not consider weakening the air defence of the rest of the country which already employed all the 3.7 AA artillery available. Equally, equipment for a balloon barrage was not available because of demands elsewhere, although it was possible that 20 balloons might be supplied by taking them from the London defences. Recommendations had been made by the Committee of Imperial Defence (CID) that two fighter squadrons which could be increased to five, should be made available, but the Chiefs of Staff did not agree, saying: 'We cannot, however, recommend that the air defence of Great Britain, which is still short of 15 squadrons, should be further depleted by taking two for Scapa. No organisation exists at present for the effective cooperation of fighters at the latter place, and it would not be sound to rob an organisation at full working order to place squadrons where they can only operate at reduced efficiency.'[5]

In his book *Churchill at War — Alone 1939-40,* Patrick Cosgrove writes that Churchill, now once again First Lord of the Admiralty, as he had been in World War I, following his invariable principle of not demanding for the Admiralty anything which it would be too difficult for the other Services to provide, was subdued if not actually worried in the deliberations which followed the Chiefs' of Staff review when on 7 September the War Cabinet approved the whole 'ideal' programme for Scapa — 'subject to other priorities and the establishment of adequate facilities at the Base'. Churchill, Kingsley Wood the Air Minister and Hore-Belisha, War Minister, met for discussion after the Cabinet meeting to see what could actually be done in practice — 'Little of substance was achieved,' comments Cosgrove.

On 16 September Churchill visited the Flow to assess its defence needs for himself. One gets the impression that while he could appreciate the strategic importance of Scapa as a naval base, he never really favoured it one hundred percent, preferring somewhere a little nearer the enemy, such as Rosyth or even the Humber; but in both wars he took, however reluctantly, the professional advice of the Naval Commanders-in-Chief who would have to use it — Jellicoe in the First War, Forbes in the Second, and once having accepted that advice threw all his weight into making it the strongest and safest base possible.

He stayed on board the *Nelson* during the visit and actually went to sea with her when he left to visit the rest of the Fleet at

Loch Ewe on the west coast. *Nelson* left Scapa, incidentally, without a destroyer escort owing to the shortage of escort vessels, a point not lost on the First Lord.[6]

Forbes must have impressed him with the need for more and stronger defences for the Flow, both anti-aircraft and coastal, quite apart from increasing the actual base facilities themselves. During that first September of the war the War Office produced a scheme for strengthened land-based defence of Scapa called the 'Q' Plan, which emerged following the inevitable reconnaissance carried out by a party drawn from all three Services. It recommended that the Flow should have 80 heavy anti-aircraft guns, 40 light anti-aircraft, 108 searchlights and 40 barrage balloons.[7] The extension of the coast defence system with new batteries and equipment was dealt with separately a little later on in December 1939, following yet another reconnaissance, survey and report ordered by the War Office.[8] The defence of Scapa Flow was at last being taken very seriously.

But Churchill did not like 'Q' Plan. He had other ideas which he thought would produce the same result quicker, with less equipment, fewer men and at a lower cost. After his return to the Admiralty from Scapa he wrote a Minute dated 20 September in which he criticised the War Office recommendations in 'Q' Plan for 80 HAA guns as excessive.

'It is altogether out of proportion to lock three Regiments AA (6,200 men) for the whole war in Scapa,' he wrote, adding: "Scapa Flow is no longer the base for the Grand Fleet but only for three or four principal vessels and alternative harbours can be used for these. We must be careful not to dissipate our strength unduly in passive defence.' But he did approve 16 extra 3.7-inch HAA guns as a matter of highest urgency.[9]

Three days later on 23 September, he was in the chair at a meeting in the Admiralty and approved (a) the existing eight 4.5-inch guns at Lyness, (b) 16 extra 3.7-inch guns to be deployed within a fortnight, (c) 20 more 3.7's and nine LAA guns to be mounted by the end of 1939.[10]

A further Minute by the First Lord dated 23 September shows that he had even more radical ideas on the defence of Scapa Flow — he wanted the Army out and the Navy, in the form of the Royal Marines, in. This, of course, is what happened in the First War, when the Navy preferred to defend its own bases itself both on land and sea — and the resultant change-over from the Army to Marines then had caused considerable ill-feeling among Orcadian soldiers. There were obviously indications that it would do so again.

In the Minute of that meeting on 23 September Churchill is
quoted as saying:—

> I am not seeking to lay down general principles for the
> organisation of the Royal Marines in any future war; but only
> what ought to be done at Scapa this winter.
>   At present the Army are building villages to put up
> batteries; and you will find that their programme extends over
> many months and costs too much. Let me see at your
> convenience their time-schedule.

He went on:—

> It would be better that the Royal Marines should take over at
> once from the Army the responsibility for erecting the reduced
> batteries at Scapa. They should mount the first sixteen 3.7
> guns on the best selected sites themselves. The Army should
> get right out of Scapa as soon as the transference can be
> made. In six weeks (25 days) from the delivery of these 16
> guns the Marines would have them up. This must be regarded
> as a field operation and not as a matter of coast fortification
> on a peace-time basis.

The '(25 days)' in parenthesis is a pencilled interpolation.[11]
    At a meeting in the Admiralty on 26 September the First
Lord announced that the Secretary of State for War, Hore
Belisha, had agreed with him the previous day that the Navy
should take over 'straight away' the defence of Scapa and get the
Army out of it. He asked for reports from the various
departmental heads as to the earliest date on which this could be
achieved.[12] In the meantime the 8000-ton British India liner
Mashroba had been taken over and was being fitted out for just
such gun-mounting operations by the Marines as he had been
suggesting.
    Churchill had obviously been largely influenced by his naval
experiences in the First War and perhaps even more by a report
from the Admiralty's Director of Local Defence, Captain RM
Servaes RN, which stated:—

> It has been ascertained that it is most improbable that
> personnel at present serving on the Coast and AA Defences
> would transfer to the Royal Marines on a 'hostilities only'
> basis. They cannot be compelled to do so. It is understood
> that there are strong parochial objections to their becoming
> anything other than what they are at present viz., independent

and somewhat insular units of Coast Defence and AA
Territorial Army. So the whole of the defences will have to be
taken over by the Royal Marines.[13]

It is just as well that the 'independent and somewhat insular'
Orkney units of the Territorial Army knew nothing of this
patronising report at the time, or the 'objections' might well
have been more than just 'parochial'.

For once Churchill did not get his own way, although he
fought a characteristically vigorous rearguard action right into
1940, by which time the Army was pretty strongly entrenched, if
that is the appropriate word, round the Flow.

At one Admiralty meeting when he was in the chair,
Churchill said he felt guilty at asking the War Office to under-
take a commitment on behalf of the Navy which would 'lock
away between 9,000 and 10,000 men in such an isolated fastness
in the North of Scotland'. He deplored the universal dispersal of
defensive effort: we had to take some risks. He suggested
'putting in a General and giving him, say, 5,000 men and telling
him to get on with it'. The meeting not surprisingly felt that this
would be unfair to that local commander. Churchill did not give
up easily. He said he still thought that this valuable formation of
men might well be locked away and might never fire a shot —
which brought a rejoinder from Major General K. L. Loch,
Director of AA & CD at the War Office, that should that be the
case then they would have achieved their aim.[14]

The First Lord did not, in fact, receive a great deal of
support for the Marine change-over idea, even from his own
department in the Admiralty, although the War Office and the
Admiralty had actually come to an arrangement whereby the
Marines would take over the Scapa defences at the beginning of
July 1940 — but much was to happen before that.

Vice-Admiral T. H. Binney, who took over from Admiral
French as ACOS in December, wrote a personal letter to
Churchill, with copies to the First Sea Lord, Third Sea Lord and
others in high places at the Admiralty in which he said:

> Orkney Heavy Regiment were recruited on the distinct
> understanding that they would not be absorbed into any other
> unit. To absorb these men into the Royal Marines would
> produce great dissatisfaction in the islands. Not to do so
> would lose the services of many valuable men whose local
> knowlege and keen eyesight should not be neglected.

> There would be no advantage to be gained from a change-

over from the Army to a Royal Marine organisation, he pointed out, and concluded:

> There may be reasons for the change of which I know nothing but my impression is that we shall be trying to substitute an amateur force for an efficient professional one.

He was backed up by a new Director of Local Defence at the Admiralty, J. M. Fuller, who Minuted on 26 December 1939 that the Marines had neither personnel, material nor the administrative capacity for the defence of Scapa Flow: 'The Army are getting on with the job and it would only cause delay to 'swop horses' at this juncture.' The Army had established that 10,000 to 11,000 men would be needed and petrol for at least 500 vehicles, as well as stores and ammunition for 140 HAA guns, 108 LAA guns, 108 searchlights, 17 coast defence guns and 17 coast defence searchlights. It would need in addition the equivalent of an infantry division's staff to administer the defences rather than the existing brigade staff standard. The change-over to Royal Marines could not take place without loss of efficiency, the Director stated.

Once again, broadsides from two such experienced officers had their effect. The Chiefs of Staff decided on 25 January 1940 that the Coast Defence and AA Defence of Scapa should remain an Army commitment.[15] It was noted with satisfaction in an Admiralty Special Secret Branch 'Acquaint', however, that the Army had agreed to the installation of AA guns being carried out by the Royal Marines, commenting that this 'would more than halve the time taken to instal them'.[16]

Sir Archibald Sinclair, who later became Air Minister and whose home was just across the Pentland Firth in Caithness, also had a considerable influence on the final decision to leave things as they were. He visited Orkney at the beginning of the new year for two days during which he studied the implications of the proposed change-over. He reported that he had found the understanding and cooperation between the Army and the Navy in Orkney was complete, and he came down firmly in favour of maintaining the status quo.[17] The Army progress in Orkney was, in fact, already gathering momentum by this time.

CHAPTER 25

OSDef is Born

AT THE OUTBREAK of war there had been no unified Army command in Orkney. For administrative purposes 226 HAA Bty had come under 36 AA Brigade which had its HQ in Edinburgh; the coast defence units were loosely under Scottish Command, also in Edinburgh. Both the coast and AA gunners in Orkney were under the Navy's operational control to a large extent, and that meant ACOS. Obviously a tighter system of control, both administrative and operational, was needed, especially in view of the 'Q' Plan for more guns, equipment and troops to man them.

So, on 29 September 1939, Brigadier Geoffrey Kemp MC RA, who had commanded the parent 36 AA Brigade in Edinburgh, arrived in Orkney to take over and build up what came to be known as OSDef, Orkney and Shetland Defences.[1] He was 48 and had been wounded twice in the First War while serving in the field artillery when he won the Military Cross. After the war, as a Major, he had been an Instructor in Gunnery at the School of Artillery, a background which was to stand him in good stead as Commander of the Scapa Defences.

OSDef had a very modest beginning. Brigadier Kemp's Staff and equipment amounted to one Sergeant Clerk (Royal Artillery), one driver, one car and a typewriter and no headquarters accommodation.[2] Operationally he had eight 4.5 HAA guns at Lyness, manned by the 226 Battery, four six-inch guns for coast defence — two each at Stanger Head in Flotta and at Ness just outside Stromness — and a very old 4.7-inch coast gun also at Stanger Head but due to be moved to Neb, also in Flotta, as well as five 90 cm coast defence searchlights; all manned by the Orkney Heavy Regiment and Orkney (Fortress) Company RE. There was also a troop of the 39 LAA Battery from Linlithgow with its three Bofors guns for the defence of the Netherbutton radar station in Holm, 275 Field Company RE and one Company of the 5th Battalion Seaforth Highlanders providing guards for Stanger Head and Ness batteries. And that was just about all the military presence in Orkney when OSDef was born.

Two days after the Brigadier landed in Orkney, the first of his staff officers arrived on 2 October: Lieut. Col. S. O. Jones of the Welsh Fusiliers to be AA & QMG and Major G. N. Tuck, later promoted Lieutenant Colonel, to be GSO I.

The Navy had already taken over most of the available accommodation in Kirkwall, where Vice-Admiral Max Horton had established his HQ for the Northern Patrol and Contraband Control in the Kirkwall Hotel, now re-named HMS *Pyramus,* so it was decided Stromness should be the Army base and headquarters. Brigadier Kemp borrowed an office from Coast Defence HQ which was already established in the town and on 2 October decided that the Stromness Hotel, or Mackay's Hotel as it was known then, would house OSDef HQ. Accommodation there was duly requisitioned. And just to underline the urgent need for increased defences at Scapa, there was an air-raid warning for a single enemy reconnaissance aircraft that same day. It was not engaged by any of the guns, either Navy or Army.

On 4 October Kemp worked out priorities for gun and searchlight sites and next day called on ACOS, Admiral French, on board the *Iron Duke* off Lyness, where they agreed that any aircraft flying at over 4,000 feet and within a six-mile radius of 'A' Buoy, the Home Fleet flagship's mooring off Flotta, would be engaged. This decision embodied in OSDef's Operation Instruction No.1, dated 10 October 1939 and signed by Major Tuck, had a distribution list of just three — 226 HAA Bty, ACOS and File.[3]

The new OSDef staff was not given long to settle down before they were involved in a very royal occasion with the visit to his fleet of King George VI who had, of course, served in Scapa Flow in the First War aboard both the battleships *Collingwood* and *Malaya.*

He arrived during the afternoon of 6 October in the cruiser *Aurora* with an escort of Tribal class destroyers passing through Hoxa boom at high speed, something that lesser mortals in other ships were never allowed to do for fear of damaging the nets; but in this instance the main object was to get him out of more or less open sea, where anything might happen, into what was thought to be the safety of the Flow.[4]

When he landed next day at Scapa Pier on his way to visit HMS *Sparrowhawk* (Hatston aerodrome), the Army provided the Guard of Honour from the Orkney Heavy Regiment, under 2nd Lieut. Macrae, a Highlander who had been in the First War but who owned and ran the Stronsay Hotel until he was caught up in the Second War. Also on the Guard were men from Orkney

(Fortress) Company, 5th Seaforths and 7th Gordons who had been earmarked for guard duties at key points such as cable terminals throughtout Orkney.

The flag officers of the Fleet dined aboard HMS *Nelson* with the King that night and he duly recorded in his diary:—

> Not quite such a number as there were in the Great War, when Papa came to visit the Grand Fleet . . . I was very interested to see things as they are at the beginning of a war. In rather a muddle, but it is amazing how the Services put up with things and carry on under trying conditions.[5]

There were certainly some very trying conditions lying ahead for those Services round the Flow, and the 'muddle' was to have dreadful consequences within days of his visit.

There was at least one lighter moment during the King's tour of inspection. The old steam drifters and trawlers of the East Coast fishing fleets were found to be still the best vessels to maintain base patrols and communications, just as they had been in the First War, and accordingly a pool of them was being built up at Scapa. The King inspected a parade of the hardy fishermen who manned them, among whom was Skipper J. Watt RNR, of the *Flora Fraser*. He had won the Victoria Cross in 1917, and not surprisingly the King spotted the douce but distinctive medal ribbon.

'Where did you get the Victoria Cross?' he asked and received the reply: 'Buckingham Palace, Sir.'[6]

The King, incidentally, landed for this parade at Lyness where he was also to visit 226 Bty, using the only jetty available — and it had been condemned as 'unsafe' five years previously. But it was not only the Lyness jetty which was unsafe — it was the anchorage itself.

Two days after the Royal visit the OSDef War Diary records for 9 October: 'Severe gale.' It was to become a frequent entry during the next few months — a taste of what was to come.

The 7th Gordons took over the manning of Vital Points (VP) on the 13th and these included mounting guards on cable huts at Tarracliffe Bay, Roan Head and Neb in Flotta, Hacksness in South Walls and North Ness in North Walls, Green Head, Ore Bay, Houton, the C-in-C Home Fleet's 'A' Buoy off Flotta, the RDF Station at Kirkwall, the radio masts on Wideford Hill, and the Wireless/Telegraph (W/T) station for Hatston at Mayfield near the Highland Park Distillery.[7]

OSDef staff officers were also discussing with the Navy the establishment of a Gun Operations Room (GOR) for the centralised control of all the AA guns round the Flow when they arrived.

The Commander OSDef had already noted what he saw as the main deficiencies in the Scapa defences, in addition to the woeful shortage of guns. Communications were bad. The telephone and teleprinter circuits round the Flow had only a limited capacity and were subject to frequent damage — by ships' anchors among other things.

The RAF radar set at Netherbutton was restricted in the arc it could cover and it was not in good condition in any case, quite apart from the 'Gilbertian' method of issuing air-raid warnings through ACOS and the RAF corporal. As a result of its deficiencies the radar warning was untrustworthy, and enemy aircraft made frequent reconnaissance flights over the Flow often without any warning at all. Moreover, the Netherbutton station was virtually unprotected.

Brigadier Kemp also noted that the one HAA Battery (226) gave an eight-gun density only over Lyness and that the gun crews worked and lived under extreme difficulties. There was no gun-laying radar (GL) equipment whereby the guns could be trained on to their targets in darkness or thick weather when the aircraft themselves would be invisible, there being no AA searchlights either, apart from those on such HM ships as might happen to be in the Flow at the time.

The Garrison Engineer was not a regular soldier — he was, in fact, a Territorial Army Officer, Major Gibson, OC Orkney (Fortress) Company RE — and he had no staff to put the War Office 'Q' Plan into effect. There was no Royal Army Service Corps (RASC) nor Royal Army Ordnance Corps (RAOC), and no NAAFI in the Area.

Port facilities, Kemp noted, were poor, with only two main harbours, Kirkwall and Stromness, already being stretched to capacity; while for transportation he still had only two or three cars and one unseaworthy speedboat.[8] There was a lot to be done, and Brigadier Kemp wanted it done quickly.

By mid-October his staff had begun to build up with four more staff officers, a Deputy Assistant Quartermaster General (DAQMG), a staff captain, a Commander Royal Engineers (CRE) and a Senior Medical Officer (SMO).

Two Field Companies of Royal Engineers had arrived to start work on the vital hutting needed to implement 'Q' Plan, and liaison and 'good relations' with Kirkwall Town Council had been established.[9]

Then came two shattering events which jeopardised the whole future of Scapa Flow as a major naval base — the sinking of the *Royal Oak* at anchor in the Flow itself, and the bombing and holing of the *Iron Duke* also at anchor off Lyness just two days later.

War had come to Scapa and had found it more vulnerable than even the pessimists had feared.

CHAPTER 26

Baptism of Fire

ON 8 OCTOBER reports were received that ships of the German Navy had been seen off the south of Norway, steering north. The battlecruisers *Hood* and *Repulse* with two cruisers, *Aurora* and *Sheffield,* and four destroyers, sailed at once for the Bergen area to head them off should they be making for the Atlantic on a commerce-raiding expedition. The old and slower *Royal Oak* with two destroyers left Scapa to patrol the area west of the channel between Fair Isle and Orkney as a back-up force. An intensive search was carried out but failed to find the enemy ships, which had, in fact, turned south again.[1]

It looked like a repeat performance of so many similar operations in that earlier war, with the harbour-bound Germans making a sally out into the North Sea in an attempt to entice the British Fleet to come a little too far south so that they could be attacked more easily. This time, however, the idea was to draw them well within the range of the Luftwaffe bombers poised to strike from airfields round the Heligoland Bight. And it succeeded. The British ships were attacked from the air but suffered no damage.

Two days later, on the 11th, the Fleet returned to Scapa and the C-in-C left again for Loch Ewe on the west coast of Sutherland. By that time, plans laid by Admiral Dönitz (Flag Officer U-boats) for a submarine attack on the Home Fleet in Scapa Flow itself were already in train, and the *U 47* commanded by the resourceful and courageous Lieut. Cmdr. Günther Prien with his crew of 40 was already at sea heading north-west.[2]

Another submarine, *U 16* (Lieut. Cmdr. Welner), had been operating in the Orkney area for some little time previously and had supplied Dönitz and Prien with valuable intelligence as to possible ways into the Flow. It would seem that as a result both Dönitz and Prien were able to make an accurate assessment of the weak points in the defences. Four other U-boats in the Orkney area were withdrawn to give Prien a clear run in and also to avoid arousing British suspicions that something special might be afoot.[3]

Dönitz ordered an aerial reconnaissance of the Flow on the 12th when aircraft from Group A reported having sighted an aircraft carrier, five heavy ships and ten cruisers at anchor there.[4] Oddly enough, only the Orkney Fixed Defences War Diary records having seen an enemy aircraft that day. It was reported to be over South Ronaldsay, presumably being seen from Stanger Head Battery. Neither OSDef nor 226 Battery diaries mention it and no one at all recorded a flight, stated by Dönitz in his memoirs to have been made low over the Flow by two other aircraft of No. 2 Luftflotte, three days earlier on the 9th. It was a flight he did not want, in case it caused the defences to take extra precautions against a possible attack. Whether the flight, against his wishes, actually took place is not clear. It may be that the Netherbutton radar failed to pick up the planes, or it could be that they never actually came over the Flow in what the OSDef War Diary recorded as a 'severe gale' that day. It also seems a little odd that the reconnaissance on the 12th was carried out, for there was no way of telling Prien what it had observed — he was lying on the bottom of the North Sea waiting his chance to go in. Nor was there any chance of informing him that the German monitoring stations had detected considerable radio traffic from the Orkney area possibly indicating the departure of the British Fleet, perhaps as a result of the reconnaissance flights.[5]

Indeed the greater part of the Fleet did leave the Flow, but there were still quite a few naval craft left there on Friday, 13 October, including the *Royal Oak, Repulse, Pegasus,* an old seaplane carrier, and several cruisers, *Cardiff, Delhi* and *Calypso* among them, as well as a number of destroyers such as the Tribal Class *Somali, Ashanti, Mashona, Tartar* and *Eskimo.* There were auxiliaries too like the Destroyer Depot and Repair ship *Greenwich,* the net-layer *Guardian* and, of course, the *Iron Duke* herself — about fifty vessels in all, but not the big concentration of capital ships for which Dönitz and Prien had hoped. The numbers were reduced still further that evening.[6] *Repulse, Royal Oak* and *Pegasus* had been anchored on the north side of the Flow under the Gaitnip Banks not far from Scapa Pier. *Royal Oak* and *Repulse* both had powerful anti-aircraft armament and from this position could provide extra cover over the main anchorage, standing in for the Army's AA batteries which still had to be mounted. The *Repulse* actually sailed on the afternoon of the 13th, leaving the *Royal Oak* and *Pegasus* isolated from the other ships in the anchorage.

They felt quite safe. Were they not, after all, in the Navy's main northern base? And was it not good to be tucked up safe and sound in harbour after taking quite a hammering from the gale while patrolling to the west of Fair Isle? They were lulled into a false but understandable sense of security.

It was a calm, dark night with no moon but according to most witnesses, including Prien himself, there was at least a glow from the aurora borealis in the northern sky, the 'fearful lights that never beckon save when kings and heroes die' according to the poet W. E. Aytoun, and which Orcadians call the 'Merry Dancers', but there was nothing 'Merry' about them that night.

High water on the eastern side of the Flow was at 11.38 p.m. Prien timed his arrival well. He had been helped to fix his position very accurately as the Pentland Skerries lighthouse, and, it is said, the Roseness light at the entrance to Holm Sound, had been switched on between 10 and 10.30 the previous night for ships leaving the Flow.

At 27 minutes past midnight on the morning of 14 October, at slack water, he manoeuvred his 66.5-metre-long *U 47* drawing 9.5 metres aft, past the blockships in Kirk Sound, hugging the northern shore close to the Holm land. He was on the surface but no one saw the sinister shadow of the U-boat as it crept towards its target, edging past the rusty hulk of the old *Numidian* which had blocked the channel in the earlier war but not now; on past the sleeping village of St Mary's — well, not quite all sleeping for there was a dance on in the hall that night and a car, probably coming down to the shore road from it, gave him a nasty moment when its dimmed headlights flicked across the water. But the danger passed; apparently no one had spotted the dark invader as it made its way across the Bay of Ayre and rounded the Point of Skeldaquoy and Howequoy Head to open up the Flow. Dönitz had been quite right when he said during the planning of the attack: 'I hold that a penetration at this point on the surface at the turn of the tide would be possible without further ceremony.'[7]

He had picked his night well; conditions could hardly have been better for him. Mr Alfie Flett of Dunerne, in Holm, remembers it well. He had served as a gunner in the Holm Battery in World War I and in the Second War he was air-raid warden for the area. There had been reports of possible mine-laying by aircraft off the east side and Mr Flett was asked by Kirkwall headquarters to investigate. So he was out and about but neither saw nor heard any aircraft and, of course, *U 47* had still not come in at this time. He remembers it as a very dark night apart from the 'Merry Dancers' and there was a very high tide. On returning home he recalls saying to his wife: 'If anyone wanted to get into the Flow, this is the night for it.' He did not know until next morning that someone had not only wanted to get in but had done so.[8]

Prien had done something that no U-boat commander had ever done successfully before. He had found the gap in Scapa's defence, its Achilles heel, and he was in the Royal Navy's 'holy of holies'. Then bitter disappointment: the British Fleet was not there.

He headed out into the Flow towards the main anchorage to make sure — but no; nothing there worthy of his metal. Just a few smaller ships, destroyers and the like.

Then, joy: what he took to be two battleships or battlecruisers much nearer at hand. He had found the *Royal Oak* and, he believed, the *Repulse*. It was not all he had hoped for, but it was most certainly better than just a destroyer or two. Time was running out if he were to make a successful exit the way he had come, for the slackish water at the top of the tide would not last for ever.

Just before 1 a.m. he closed to 4,000 yards and fired three torpedoes from his bow tubes. There should have been four but one misfired. Nothing much happened as seen from the *U 47,* but on board the *Royal Oak* there was a small explosion forward. It may have been that one torpedo scored a minor hit, possibly on the anchor chain. An investigation in the ship itself resulted in a conclusion that there had been an internal explosion, possibly in one of the storage rooms forward.

Prien put the *U 47* about and fired his stern tubes. Again he missed. But the bow tubes were now reloaded and he came in again for another attack, firing three more torpedoes. This time two found their mark, and 13 minutes later at 1.30 a.m. the *Royal Oak* rolled over and went to the bottom, taking with her the lives of 24 officers and 809 men out of a ship's company of some 1400.

An hour later *U 47* was out and clear of the Flow, heading back for Germany. Her commander had successfully negotiated the other unblocked channel on the south side of Kirk Sound, passing close to the uninhabited island of Lamb Holm and almost scraping the barnacles off the other First War blockship, the *Thames,* a prominent and well-known seamark with her two funnels, three masts and clipper bow. In his log Prien seems to have recorded her as a 'schooner' — there was certainly no schooner in Holm Sound that night.[9]

Behind him Prien left a scene of chaos. The impossible had happened: a capital ship of the Royal Navy had been sunk in its own harbour. Many of the crew were fighting for their lives in the thick viscous scum of oil which gushed out of the stricken ship as she went down and some of which still seeps out of her hull from time to time nearly half-a-century later. The shore was not far away — about half-a-mile or so — but the oil made swimming almost impossible, even though the night was calm.

Many were saved by the courageous action and superb seamanship of John Gatt, skipper of the Royal Oak's drifter *Daisy II* which had been moored alongside. He had been roused by the first explosion and must have sensed that something was seriously wrong, for he did not go back to his bunk. When the fatal torpedoes struck, he was in the wheelhouse and the drifter had steam up. As the great ship lurched in her death throes the drifter was literally being dragged up her side by the hawsers as the list increased. They were slashed and the drifter slid back into the water, steaming the length of the *Royal Oak* as she went down, collecting as many of the crew as she could take, and more. It was said that she had oil stains right up her funnel where the survivors had clambered up to make room for others on the deck or who had jumped down as the battleship heeled over.[10]

Pegasus, too, was picking up survivors in her boats, and the destroyers still in the anchorage were on the scene with their searchlights sweeping the surface to locate the men struggling in the oily water while others searched for the submarine itself which had caused the horror — if it was a submarine. There were some doubts about it for quite a time. The ugly word 'sabotage' began to be heard. But to the Navy that was even more unthinkable than a torpedo attack inside the anchorage — still, it was recalled, the *Royal Oak* had taken on stores at Invergordon only a few days before. Some people still believe it was sabotage in spite of the conclusive evidence to the contrary from Prien's own log, the reports of many divers who have been down on what is now classed as an official war grave, and the discovery under water of parts of a German torpedo motor — not to mention the official Court of Inquiry which accepted as correct a report by one of the survivors that when he was in the water he had seen the conning-tower of a submarine.[11]

Ashore, the coastal defence guns were manned all night after the alarm had been raised and on into the next day. At Stanger Head Battery a mysterious fire broke out in the BOP at 5.30 that morning, destroying range-finders and other instruments and putting the battery temporarily out of action for accurate shooting, but by this time *U 47* was well beyond the range of any guns in Orkney. The mystery of the fire was to some extent cleared up at the inevitable Court of Inquiry, which established that it had been caused by a paraffin stove used to take some of the chill out of the Flotta night air.[12] What had made it flare up at the back of the OP, where it had been left unattended while the watch were all on lookout at the front, was never officially found out although it was commonly believed that someone from the Army may have replenished the stove by 'borrowing' fuel from the nearby naval store — and had 'borrowed' petrol in mistake for paraffin. No one was badly injured although one man got his hands burnt.

For weeks, even months, after the *Royal Oak* went down the shores of the Flow were stained with the black scum of her oil, a constant reminder, as if that were needed, of the terror which had struck by night — a terror which had robbed the Navy of a powerful, even if old, fighting ship and much worse, had taken so many irreplaceable and valuable lives. And hanging over the whole ghastly episode was the now proven certainty that the Fleet's main strategic base was not safe from submarine attack.

The Navy's problems were to multiply two days later when there was to be a harsh reminder that it was not secure from above the sea either, any more than from under it. Even before *U 47* and her crew got back to the heroes' welcome in Germany and personal commendation from the Führer himself, their compatriots in the Luftwaffe were attacking British warships, too, and like Prien doing it in the Navy's own harbours.

The first raid came just two days after the *Royal Oak* was sunk, when nine of the new and so-far untried Junkers 88 bombers from Kampfgeschwader 30 based at Westerland on the island of Sylt, led by Kapitän Pohle, attacked the Fleet in the Firth of Forth. They did little real damage to the ships, being hampered by what was almost a convention accepted by both sides at that time — that no bombs would be dropped by either Air Force on enemy soil; only ships at sea were to be attacked, those tied up alongside quays were to be left alone, as were merchant ships. Neither side at this juncture wanted to be blamed for starting indiscriminate bombing involving civilians, and Hitler believed apparently that by showing restraint on his part the British would soon 'see reason' and negotiate a peace settlement.[13] It was, in a way, an extension of the argument used by certain British appeasement circles in the mid-1930s against rearming, on the grounds that to do so would annoy Hitler and make things worse.

The Forth raid produced a British success. Spitfires of the Royal Auxiliary Air Force from 603 (City of Edinburgh) Squadron and 602 (City of Glasgow) Squadron shot down the leading German aircraft piloted by Kapitän Pohle, the first enemy plane to be brought down on British soil by fighters in World War II.

Scapa Flow did not have long to wait for its turn. An armed reconnaissance over it had been ordered for the next day and on the morning of 17 October four Ju 88 bombers from the same group, now led by Kapitän Dönch, took off from Sylt, Orkney-bound. The guns received a 'Red Alert' and at 10.20 the raiders were spotted by 226 Bty as they came in out of the sun at 11,000 feet in arrowhead formation.[14] They were wrongly identified as Heinkel 111s, probably because these were the best-known German bombers, the Ju 88s being relatively new and unknown at the time. Two of them dived to 700 feet and dropped four bombs round the *Iron Duke*. The Orkney gunners engaged with all eight 4.5s. The Fleet as a whole was not in the Flow, having stayed away after the sinking of the *Royal Oak,* but the ships which were still in the anchorage opened fire with everything they had got. There is little doubt, however, that the Orkney battery drew first blood although one of the destroyers also put in a claim. One of the bombers appeared to stagger slightly as shells burst round it, then, quite slowly it seemed, a wing dipped steeply, and trailing black smoke it plunged earthwards to crash on the banks of Pegal Burn in Hoy.

Those of us at Stanger Head watched it go down and then, strangely enough, there was not so much a cheer from the troops but a clapping of hands like applause for a good act on the stage. There was a ripple of white not far away and one of the air crew, the gunner, swayed to the heather in his parachute. His companions died, but he escaped with severe burns and was taken prisoner. Another Ju 88 making its getaway over South Ronaldsay was thought to have been hit by gunfire from the Tribal Class destroyer *Ashanti* which was steaming in Hoxa Sound. It was seen from Stanger Head flying low and very erratically out to sea over the land, losing height as it went. No wreckage could be found, however, and so the second 'kill' could not be claimed.[15]

It was all over by 11 a.m. And it was almost quite literally 'all over' for the *Iron Duke* which had opened up with her own guns too. The bombers had scored two hits and several very near misses, and the old veteran of Jutland suffered considerable damage, listed 25 degrees to port and began to founder. Many of the *Royal Oak* survivors were on board and on the depot ship *Voltaire* nearby, which also had a narrow escape later in the day. One man was killed in *Iron Duke* and 25 slightly injured. The Admiralty tug *St Martin* got a line aboard and towed her to Ore Bay where she was successfully beached.

Another Tribal Class destroyer, the *Eskimo,* went alongside to provide the *Duke's* pumps with power; her own engine-room being flooded and the generators out of action, but at 1.40 p.m. the destroyer had to leave the old ship to her fate as another wave of bombers came in over the Flow at between 16,000 and 18,000 feet.[16] There were 15 of them this time in formations of four, seven and four and they stayed high. None of the unit War Diaries record what types of aircraft were engaged but some of them were almost certainly the slim Dornier 17s — nicknamed 'Flying Pencils'.

The 226 guns opened up again and so did the ships, but conditions were not so good in the afternoon with cloud building up and no hits were scored.

According to OSDef and 226 Bty War Diaries they dropped at least 12 bombs, six of which fell in the sea near the *Voltaire,* five in Longhope Bay and one, significantly, on land at Ore near Lyness, so that Scapa Flow had two more 'firsts' to notch up on its record: the first enemy aircraft to be shot down by British anti-aircraft guns and the first German bomb of the war to fall on British soil — fortunately it did little more damage than making a big hole in the ground. There were probably a good few more dropped further out in the Flow and in Hoxa Sound as soldiers on Stanger Head, myself among them, have vivid recollections of seeing *Ashanti,* her guns blazing defiance, steaming zig-zag through huge columns of dirty, grey water towering well above mast height before they subsided, almost like a slow motion film, back into the sea.

The second 'Red Alert' had gone out at 12.47 p.m., and the first two formations of aircraft came in nearly three-quarters-of-an-hour later when they were first sighted and engaged by 226 Bty. The bomb at Ore exploded at 1.45 p.m. and the third formation was reported approaching half-an-hour later. The 'All Clear' sounded at 2.33 p.m. and the gun teams stood down, having fired their first shots in anger and scored their first 'kill'.

A few hours after, in the late afternoon, one solitary enemy aircraft flew very high round the Flow, presumably on reconnaissance to see what damage, if any, the earlier raiders had done. No bombs were dropped. There was another reconnaissance flight the next day at 15,000 feet when 226 Bty again went into action as the plane made off to the south-ward.[17]

Scapa Flow had had its baptism of fire.

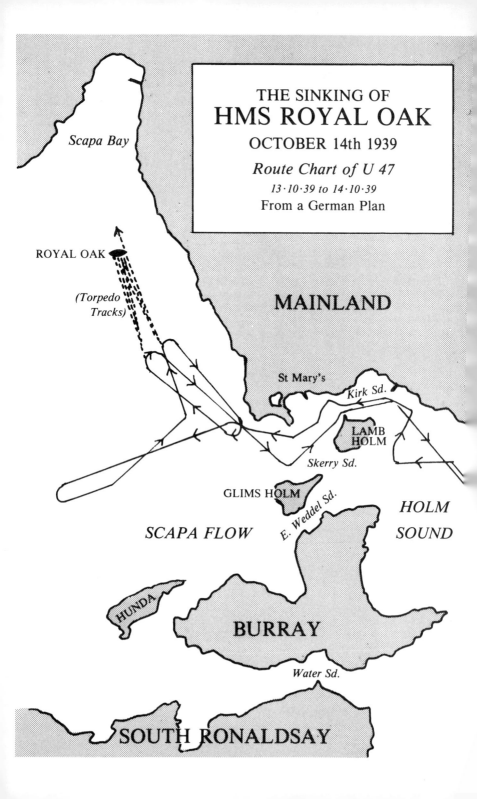

THE SINKING OF
HMS ROYAL OAK
OCTOBER 14th 1939

Route Chart of U 47
13·10·39 to 14·10·39
From a German Plan

Scapa Bay

ROYAL OAK

(Torpedo Tracks)

MAINLAND

St Mary's

Kirk Sd.

LAMB HOLM

Skerry Sd.

GLIMS HOLM

E. Weddel Sd.

SCAPA FLOW

HOLM SOUND

HUNDA

BURRAY

Water Sd.

SOUTH RONALDSAY

CHAPTER 27

Empty Harbour

PRIEN'S *U 47* and the Ju 88s of Kampfgeschwader 30 had got the best of these first encounters — one capital ship with the loss of 800 lives, another badly damaged and a hole in the ground to their credit, while on the British side there was just one bomber shot down. But the debit balance against the Flow itself was more serious than appeared on the surface, bad though that was. The Admiralty and the defence chiefs were in disarray. There was consternation in high places — very high places indeed, the War Cabinet. The defences of the Navy's chosen and cherished base had been effectively pierced both from above and below the sea. The Fleet, just as at the beginning of the First War, felt very insecure, and with even better reason than in 1914. Now it was known for certain that ships could be attacked and sunk in the Flow; in 1914 there had only been the fear that it **could** happen.

As a result, the first move was the evacuation of Scapa by the Fleet which departed in haste, dispersing to various other harbours not so well suited as naval bases but further away, it was hoped, from danger of attack.[1] Loch Ewe on the West Coast was one of them, Sullom Voe in Shetland was another, the latter being used mainly by the Northern Patrol cruisers; the Clyde was yet another and the Forth was also used. But all these harbours had defences which were, if anything, more inadequate than those at Scapa, and the flagship *Nelson* was damaged by a mine at Loch Ewe on December 4; and one of the Navy's newest cruisers, the *Belfast,* suffered a similar fate in the Forth about the same time, being seriously damaged.[2] Up until the 1938 crisis it had looked as if Rosyth on the Forth might become the main Home Fleet war base, but the C-in-C, Admiral Forbes, opted for Scapa which he had personally favoured right from the beginning. Now, the problem was — could Scapa Flow be made sufficiently secure for it to be used again as the Fleet's main base?

Following a study of air attacks made so far on his ships, Forbes noted that these had caused little damage either at sea or in harbour, and similar attacks by the RAF on the German Navy did not appear to have been particularly effective either. From this he came to the conclusion that the air menace to naval ships had been exaggerated. Given adequate, properly organised and controlled defences, both fighters and AA guns, the ships would be reasonably safe in harbour, he concluded, provided the harbour was also made safe from surface and submarine attack. Scapa at that moment did not meet any of these requirements.[3]

One of the first things to do was to find out where and how the *U 47* had got through the defences. There was much confused thinking about this even in the War Cabinet itself, where the Naval Chief of Staff told members on the day after the disaster that the U-boat was still in the Flow and that the location of the sinking had not been disclosed to the British Press in order to see what the Germans would say. It was believed, he said, that the submarine had been in the Flow for 24 hours before the attack, having got in through the open gate in one of the anti-submarine nets, presumably Hoxa.[4] Churchill told the Cabinet that the Navy was convinced that this was how it had happened, the gate having been open for an unusually long period as the ships, for which it had been opened, were two to four hours later than expected.[5]

The Minister for the Co-ordination of Defence, Lord Chatfield, himself a former First Sea Lord, thought rafts or floats might have been used to get heavy torpedoes in through the blockships to sink the *Royal Oak*. Or perhaps a small submarine which could get through the nets — maybe even two submarines with one waiting outside to take the crew off the one which did get in and which was scuttled after the attack.[6]

At a subsequent War Cabinet these flights of fancy were given their quietus by the First Lord, Churchill, who told his colleagues that:

> It appeared that certain recommendations had been made in the early part of the year [1939] as to the Scapa Defences, but it had not been considered necessary to take steps to improve them. Some of the drifters which had been picketing the entrances to the Flow had been withdrawn for use at other anchorages which had been taken into use in view of the threat of air attack. There could be no doubt that the U-boat in question had passed through one of the unguarded entrances. It was obvious that the possibility of submarine attack had never entered the minds of those on board the *Royal Oak*. The lesson was clear that we could not take anything for granted, but must be continually on the watch and guarding against every conceivable contingency in our defences.[7]

Later still, Churchill reported to the War Cabinet that the nets at Scapa Flow did not extend beyond the five-fathom line, and an entrance 'near Kirkwall' (presumably Kirk Sound) which had been closed in the last war had not yet been closed in this war. A small merchant ship had come through this entrance a week or so previously, he said.[8] This may well have been true, for the 135-foot-long 231-ton *St Ola* on her daily mail and passenger run through the Flow and across the Pentland Firth early in the war regularly went round the ends of the booms in Hoy Sound and at Hoxa, rather than having to wait for the gates to be opened.

The Cabinet also discussed the movement of the Fleet to the Clyde for safety, and the relative merits of Rosyth and Scapa on a long-term basis were also considered. Churchill said that it would be at least six weeks before the underwater defences at Scapa would be ready. The present intention was to make it a safe anchorage from the point of view of submarine attack, and to prepare emplacements so that a large number of guns could be deployed at short notice when required.

The Naval Chief of Staff said he did not think that Scapa Flow was as well placed as in the last war when they had known from the Admiralty's Intelligence centre, Room 40, when the German Fleet was coming out. This was not so this time, and without such information ships working from a base as far north as Scapa could hardly hope to intercept any ships which did come out. The Chief of the Air Staff, Air Chief Marshal C. Newhall, was also unenthusiastic about Scapa as a base. He could supply extra fighter cover for the Forth or Clyde at short notice but this would not be possible at Scapa, he told the Cabinet. Churchill stated that his view had always been in favour of basing the Fleet at Rosyth and making the anchorage there as safe as possible.[9]

On the last day of October Churchill, along with the First Sea Lord, Admiral Sir Dudley Pound and the Deputy Chief of Air Staff, visited the C-in-C Home Fleet at his temporary refuge in the Clyde, although in Volume I of *The Second World War: The Gathering Storm* Churchill states that the conference took place on board Forbes's flagship in 'Scapa'. The flagship was not in Scapa at this time.

Reporting to the Cabinet the following day, 1 November, Churchill said that Forbes had stressed a preference for Scapa Flow as his base and accepted that it could not be provided with air cover so easily as the Clyde or Forth. He had also pointed out that the Clyde had a difficult entrance and was not suitable as a permanent naval base for this reason, besides being too far from the most likely area of operations, the North Sea. Rosyth had better anti-submarine defences but it too had entrance problems, being very vulnerable to mining and it was difficult from a navigational point of view in thick weather. The Cabinet accepted this and it was decided that of the capital ships *Hood* should go to Devonport and *Rodney* and *Nelson* to Rosyth, after a period at sea and until such time as Scapa was secure.[10]

Forbes had convinced Churchill that 'the proper base for the Fleet was Scapa and that the defence must be pressed ahead as fast as possible'. It was agreed that the AA gun density must be greatly increased. Heavy nets must be placed round the anchorage so that torpedo bombers would be forced to close to point-blank range before dropping their torpedoes.

Two squadrons of high-performance RAF fighters should be stationed at Wick and all unused entrances to Scapa Flow were to be **permanently and totally blocked.** The main entrance at Hoxa was to be strengthened, booms were to be extended to the shores, and controlled minefields and indicator loops were to be laid. In the meantime the Clyde was to be used as a temporary base, in spite of its being a long distance from the North Sea.

In a Minute to the Deputy Chief of Naval Staff on the same day, 1 November, arising out of the Clyde conference with the C-in-C Home Fleet, and the War Cabinet's decision to strengthen the defences, Churchill points out:

> Scapa cannot be available, except as a momentary refuelling base for the Fleet before Spring. Work is, however, to proceed with all possible speed upon — (a) blockships in exposed channels, (b) doubling the nets and a study made on the 'gate' routine to ensure briefer openings and greater security, (c) trawler and drifter fleet to be brought up to numbers equal to those in the first war, (d) work on hutments to proceed without intermission, (e) concrete emplacements for all 80 AA guns contemplated for the defence of Scapa, work on these to proceed throughout the winter but the guns themselves should be moved there only in the Spring when all should be ready to receive them, (f) Wick aerodrome to be extended to take four squadrons of fighters, (g) RDF [Radar] work to be carried on but must take its turn with more urgent work.[11]

Meanwhile Scapa was to be used as a destroyer refuelling base, although later on cruisers also used it occasionally with suitable precautions, long before the defences were anywhere near complete. The famous 'K' Class destroyer *Kelly* of the 5th Flotilla, with her even more famous Captain (D) Lord Louis

Mountbatten in command, arrived in the Flow on 5 November and was in and out all through the winter and indeed took part in the Norwegian campaign from the Flow.[12]

Another distinguished though ill-fated visitor that winter was the armed merchant cruiser *Rawalpindi* commanded by Captain E. C. Kennedy, which carried out gunnery calibration and practice with her four old six-inch guns in the Flow before she sailed to meet her tragic but honourable end between Faroe and Iceland under the vastly superior gun power of the German battlecruiser *Scharnhorst,* in a gallant action for which Captain Kennedy was awarded a posthumous Victoria Cross.[13]

But the Fleet as a whole dared not use the Flow. In Volume I of his official history of *The War at Sea* Captain S. W. Roskill RN comments: 'Had the enemy realised the full weakness of the Home Fleet's position and exploited it with U-boat attack and magnetic mining on a bigger scale or put some of his capital ships into the Atlantic, the situation could have been serious.'

A Court of Inquiry was held to investigate the technical features concerning the sinking of the *Royal Oak,* but Churchill afterwards told the War Cabinet that he did not intend to hold a similar inquiry to apportion blame. He did feel, however, that the matter could not be allowed to drop without the observations of the Board of Admiralty being conveyed to the officers concerned, who were, he said, the Commander-in-Chief Home Fleet, the Senior Naval Officer Scotland, and the Assistant Chief of Naval Staff.

According to the Cabinet Papers Churchill reported that:

Examination of the Admiralty file had shown that when the C-in-C had decided to make Scapa Flow his base and had written to the Admiralty for the necessary measures to be taken, the matter had not been brought before the Board of Admiralty. The Chief of Naval Staff at this time was ill, a change was taking place in the office of the Deputy Chief of Naval Staff, and the matter had been dealt with by the Assistant Chief of Naval Staff who in peace time was not a member of the Board of Admiralty. A reply had therefore been sent to the C-in-C's letter without the authority of the Board of Admiralty. The Senior Naval Officer at Scapa was also at fault in not having taken action to impress on patrol vessels, as a matter of urgency, the need for special vigilance in view of the gaps in the defences.[14]

But as Roskill points out in *The War at Sea,* the true causes of the loss go much deeper than this when he writes: 'Loss of the

Royal Oak was the result not so much of a failure by the officers on the spot, who had, in fact, reported these weaknesses for which they were concerned and had done their best to remedy this, as of the policy of the Government of the day and the failure of the Admiralty to obtain in times of peace for the defences of the fleet's chosen base.' This failure had resulted in the loss of one battleship, damage to another and damage to a valuable new cruiser — and even worse, had vitiated the ability of the Fleet to perform its proper functions through the temporary loss of its main strategic base, Scapa Flow.

As Churchill himself put it to Admiral of the Fleet, Sir Dudley Pound, the First Sea Lord: 'We were driven out of Scapa through pre-war neglect of its defences against air and U-boat attack.'[15]

The years that the locusts had eaten now had to be restored in a few short months of northern winter before the next big testing time.

CHAPTER 28

Closing The Gaps

WHEN THE Navy abandoned Scapa Flow in mid-October after the *Royal Oak* had been sunk, doubt as to its future as a main naval base resulted in a slowing down, almost a cessation, of work on the Army's 'Q' Plan of reinforcement. The Navy's own expansion schemes also came to a halt.

The old *Iron Duke,* left to her own devices during the afternoon raid, had no power for her pumps and gradually settled fore and aft. Nothing could be done without salvage plant, so she was secured by anchors to prevent her from slipping into deeper water. But she was now useless as flagship and HQ for ACOS who moved ashore to Lyness, where he and his staff took over a small concrete building originally intended to be the Boom Defence HQ. ACOS's office itself was just 14 feet square, and it had to accommodate not only him but his Chief of Staff and Flag Lieutenant as well. The other officers were in the Longhope Hotel eight miles away, and his writers (office staff) were in the boiler house. As a flag officer's headquarters the arrangement was less than ideal, and later Rysa Lodge was requisitioned for ACOS himself and Orgil Lodge for his staff.

The fate of Scapa hung in the balance for several weeks until the War Cabinet, following the outcome of discussions between the First Lord and the C-in-C Home Fleet in the Clyde, gave the go-ahead signal to build up the Flow's defences as quickly as possible.

The Lyness Base had by this time been renamed, Navy fashion, HMS *Proserpine* after the King's Harbour Master's launch which later sank in Gutter Sound. It was the first of Scapa's 'stone frigates', two of the others being HMS *Pomona* (Boom Defence HQ) and HMS *Pleiades* (Drifter Pool), where rooms in huts became 'cabins', the floor was the 'deck', latrines were the 'heads' and anyone going outside the perimeter of the camp was deemed to have 'gone ashore'.

Proserpine's first commanding officer was Captain T. H. Jermain, who took over in November with Commander (Acting

Captain) O. M. Frewin as Captain of Dockyard as well as King's Harbour Master. The number of communications ratings had now risen to 80, most of them living on board *Greenwich,* the submarine and communications depot ship, one of the first of HM ships to come into the Flow just before the outbreak of war.[1]

Captain R. D. Oliver RN, former Commander of the now beached *Iron Duke,* was appointed head of a Committee for the Defence of the Fleet Anchorage of Scapa Flow on which all three Services were represented — Brigadier Kemp, Commander OSDef, for the Army and Wing Commander Tucker for the RAF Balloon Command. In December they produced their 'R' Plan which complemented and incorporated the Army's 'Q' Plan and at an estimated cost of £500,000 provided for defence against underwater, surface or air attack on the Flow itself and against U-boat attack only on the Kirkwall Northern Patrol Base. The underwater defences would be minefields and indicator loops laid at the entrances to Stromness, Hoxa, Switha, Kirkwall and Shapinsay, with indicator loops also at the eastern entrances to the Flow, especially in Holm Sound — a 3,800-ton blockship, the *Lake Neuchatel,* had already been sunk across the Kirk Sound section of Holm Sound used by the *U 47* when it sank the *Royal Oak,* and others were to follow. Accommodation for personnel operating these often remote minefields and loops would in the early stages have to be in 'garden sheds and caravans', it was noted.

Coastal artillery would be provided at each entrance, some of which was already in position, and the Navy commented that although 'the vintage of some of these pieces was "somewhat hoary" the Artillery had great faith in their performance'. Balloons were to be sited round Lyness, on Flotta and Fara, and on trawlers anchored on the east side of the Flow. For all practical purposes it was the Plan which was implemented and became fully operational in 1943 when the need for it was perhaps not so pressing and, apart from the anti-aircraft defences which had not been needed then, it was remarkably similar to the defences finally deployed during the First War.[2]

Also in December when 'R' Plan was adopted, Vice-Admiral T. H. Binney relieved Admiral French as ACOS, and Rear Admiral A. L. St G. Lyster was appointed Rear Admiral Scapa whose responsibilities were 'to carry out the duties of flag officer-in-charge of the Port of Scapa and of Admiral Superintendent, Lyness and to organise and supervise the construction of the naval defences of Scapa and Lyness Naval Base'. He had a big job on his hands.

Admiral Binney was no stranger to Scapa. He had served as gunnery officer in Beatty's flagship, *Queen Elizabeth,* in the First War and had been on his staff in 1918. Later he had been Flag Captain of the *Nelson* and had commanded *Hood* from 1932-33, two old commands of which he would see quite a lot when the Fleet came back to Scapa, but that was still a few months away.

From the end of November until late summer 1940, as well as the actual defence work of the Navy, there was very intensified road and hut-building activity in and around Lyness, in addition to what the Army and Air Force were doing. None of them had their troubles to seek. At Lyness itself, during 1939, hutted camps for contractors' men had proliferated, springing up all over the place with no hint of rational layout. It was a planner's nightmare to try and fit in an integrated naval base complex as well. And then there was the Orkney weather which proved a major obstacle to rapid progress, not to mention such matters as labour problems and shortage of accommodation.

On 21 November Orkney and Shetland became the country's first 'Protected Area' under Regulation 13 of the Defence Regulations 1939, which meant, among other things, that all civilians — including Orcadians themselves — resident in the islands, had to obtain a permit to enter or leave the county. In all, the Security Unit, which had to deal with anything up to 200 civilians on the move every day, issued some 67,000 of these permits during the war and they turned down only 1,400 applications.[3]

One of their big problems was the civilian labour force engaged on the ever-growing number of defence contracts for the Army and Navy. Orkney was not popular with these workers who had to be housed in hutted camps often in isolated areas, and even when they were persuaded to come north by the big money being offered, there was often difficulty in getting them to stay. They missed the amenities of city life, hated the weather, did not like the isolation and were scared by the air-raids — in fact, after each raid quite substantial numbers downed tools, left the job and headed south again.

A fairly large proportion of this labour force, which reached a peak of 3,700, came direct from Southern Ireland and was joined by Liverpool and Glasgow Irish workers. It was known that quite a few of them had IRA sympathies, and this made them a constant source of anxiety to the Security forces in this very sensitive area. When finally an anti-British slogan was found in one of the huts, no more direct labour from Ireland was permitted to enter Protected Areas.

Eventually, to hold workers on vital defence projects in the islands for a reasonable time, the Ministry of Labour made the 'Orkney and Shetland Labour Agreement' whereby the Ministry itself recruited workmen and compelled them to stay at least six months on the job under the 'Essential Workers Order', with National Service Officers sent north to enforce it.

But progress was still desperately slow. It was intended that the Scapa anchorage should be operational again as the Fleet's main base by the beginning of March 1940, a deadline which was set early in the new year. Now it looked doubtful if that target could be achieved. The C-in-C was worried about the slow progress and, commenting on the bad conditions which many of the workmen were having to endure, he suggested a weekly bonus of £1 as 'hard-lying money'. His further suggestion of recruiting a labour battalion did not find favour at first, although a personal Minute by Churchill read: '. . . I share the Commander-in-Chief's anxiety about the slow progress of this indispensable work.'[4]

There were at this time, 5 January, 1,100 men, all civilians, working on the Base for Balfour Beatty.

The C-in-C's idea of a labour battalion did, however, bear fruit later when a Royal Marine Labour Battalion arrived in Orkney on 8 March. It became the RM Auxiliary Battalion, carrying out building, stevedoring, and other work until in 1942 it replaced civilian labour at the Base. Among its many varied jobs were the building of the Flotta canteen and cinema, collecting hay for a cargo of starving mules evacuated from Norway, salvaging the cargo of the ss *Tennessee* aground near Kirkwall, and on one occasion providing two lighthouse-keepers. It also provided guards for surrendered U-boat crews, and once it salvaged a Walrus amphibian aircraft.[5]

Elsewhere in Orkney the Navy was having other and more physical problems, especially with blockships and the weather. The *Majda* and *Seriano* had already been sunk in Water Sound and Kirk Sound respectively, early in 1939 before the war started, and the 4,896-ton *Cape Ortegal* was put down in Skerry Sound a week after the declaration of war. The *Lake Neuchatel* was sunk in Kirk Sound just a week after the *Royal Oak* was torpedoed, a tragic slamming of the stable door after the horse had bolted. Two ships selected to block these channels still further, the *Pandora* and the 8,000-ton Union Castle liner *Durham Castle,* never reached Scapa at all, the latter being sunk by a magnetic mine off Invergordon while on the voyage north.[6] 'The misfortune was one of a series which affected the blockships destined for Scapa Flow,' it was noted in the Cabinet Papers of 27 January 1940.

Even those which did arrive at their final destination did not always stay put. The *Cape Ortegal,* for instance, rolled over and broke up during a gale, leaving a navigable channel open once again through Skerry Sound. Forbes suggested that one answer might be to resink the salved German battleship *Derfflinger,* then lying keel-up off Rysa, as a blockship owing to the trouble being experienced with the smaller ships shifting in gales. During one storm in February 1940 for instance, one blockship already in position was swept away and yet another was lost on passage to the Flow.

The 5,000-ton *Gambhira* joined the *Lake Neuchatel* in the vulnerable Kirk Sound in December, to be followed by the smaller *Busk* two months later and the 3,000-ton *Redstone* later still that year, in May. The biggest blockship of all for these eastern channels was the 8,212-ton *Ilsenstein* put down across the troublesome Skerry Sound to replace the broken-up *Cape Ortegal.* Water Sound was not trouble-free either, where the *Gondolier* also rolled over and sank in deep water during a storm and she had to be replaced by the *Collingdoc.*

The sinking of all these ships was carried out by Metal Industries Ltd, which took over all the Admiralty salvage work in the area in June 1940 but which retained its civilian status. Altogether, 19 blockships totalling some 70,000 tons were sunk during World War II across the Flow's minor entrances, the largest of all, and one of the last to be sunk, being the 9,141-ton *Inverlane* in Burra Sound between Graemsay and Hoy where she was joined as late in the war as 27 July 1944 — less than a year before VE Day — by the 2,624-ton *Tabarka* which had the doubtful distinction of being sunk twice as a blockship, first in Kirk Sound on the east in March 1941, only to be raised and resunk in the west over three years later when the need for blocking the channels would seem to have passed.[7]

More active blocking measures for the main entrances were envisaged under 'R' Plan — as well as doubling up the booms there were to be indicator loops and controlled minefields.

The Controlled Mining Base ships *Madula City* and *Ringdove* arrived in Scapa soon after the 'R' Plan was adopted in December 1939, and towards the end of that month the Hoxa minefield was laid by the *Manchester City, Miner* and *Ringdove,* and it consisted of two guard loops and eight mine loops set in echelon, each buoyant mine containing 500 lbs of high explosive. They were operated from a portable control system at Quoyness in Flotta and became operational on 21 January 1940. The Switha and Cantick minefields followed quickly, being operational by 22 February. They each consisted of guard indicator loops and three loops of mines controlled from Stanger Head. The *Manchester City* went on to lay similar minefields in Hoy Sound and in the approaches to Kirkwall harbour while another vessel, the *Atrens,* arrived later to lay a second system of minefields in Hoxa, Switha and Cantick.

The Navy was taking no chances this time and indeed a U-boat was reported in Holm Sound on 21 April, and there were also definite indications of a hostile crossing of the Switha guard loops about the same time when the in-shore minefield was fired but there was no confirmation of a 'kill'. In May the Controlled Mining Base was opened in St Margaret's Hope.[8]

At Lyness construction work on the Base accommodation, though still slower than the First Lord and the C-in-C would have liked, did gather momentum and in February 1940 ACOS, Rear Admiral Scapa, and the Commanding Officer *Proserpine* were able to move into newly constructed and more commodious office accommodation at Head of Right, and the communications ratings could be brought ashore from the *Greenwich* to be housed in three huts next door to ACOS. In March, Haybrake Camp (just up from Lyness) opened with ten huts immediately referred to, of course, as 'mess decks', but it was not until May that *Proserpine's* 'wardroom' was functioning for officers of the Staff, by which time the Lyness Cinema had been operating in the Metal Industries building for some weeks — a small but badly needed source of recreation for those living in conditions which at best could only be described as primitive. The Navy was used to coping with wind and water, and in large quantities as a matter of course — mud was a different matter.

CHAPTER 29

The Army Digs In

ALL THAT DARK winter of 1939/40 the Army's reinforcement of the Scapa defences was also gathering pace, against a background of gales, blizzards, blackout, horrible living and working conditions, air-raid warnings — and mud.

'Q' Plan was in train, mainly concerned with anti-aircraft measures, but 'R' Plan had demanded a further strengthening of coastal defences by more guns and searchlights at entrances other than those covered by the existing batteries at Stanger Head and Ness. Inevitably there was another reconnaissance and survey ordered by the War Office on 27 November 1939, which was duly carried out at Holm, Houton, Hoxa, Cara, Burray, Neb, Scad and Carness.[1] More detailed surveys of Neb, Gate and Buchanan in Flotta, Scad in Hoy, and Burray were made early in the new year, and work on the huts for Holm battery began on 21 January, the day that Lieut. Col. W. E. Walter-Symond MC RA arrived to take over command of all the coastal batteries in what was now termed Orkney Fixed Defences, which had its HQ at 33 Alfred Street, Stromness, since demolished for street widening.[2]

His command was divided into three batteries — 191 Heavy Bty which included Stromness, Carness near Kirkwall, Houton, Holm, Wasswick in Rendall, and Galtness in Shapinsay; 198 Heavy Bty which comprised Stanger Head, Neb, Buchanan, Gate in Flotta and Scad in Hoy; and 199 Heavy Bty which administered Hoxa in South Ronaldsay, Balfour, Cara and Burray. The name Orkney Heavy Regiment disappeared and with it quite a lot of its local identity, as officers and NCOs from outside, mainly regular soldiers, took over commands.

Many of the individual gun positions within the Command structure were still names only, the men and the guns having yet to arrive. But at Holm on 22 January the 'holdfast' construction was begun, and its 12-pounder gun was ready to be mounted on it 24 hours later. It was in position on 5 February and Holm Battery at Breckness was 'ready for action' by 10 March. No time was being wasted. Two officers and 22 other ranks had been on the site from mid-February and they had their first shoot, along with the Burray Battery, at a derelict barge in Holm Sound on 21 May. Twenty-one rounds of HE shells were fired and the barge was duly sunk. Holm had a full establishment of four officers and 123 other ranks, and was the first of the new batteries to be constructed and to become ready for action, the comparatively short time taken to achieve this illustrating the urgency with which the coast defence build-up was regarded. The others followed in quick succession and Holm itself was further strengthened with the addition of a second 12-pounder and a twin six-pounder later on in the same year.[3]

In addition to the Holm Battery the overall recommendations of the War Office survey party included two six-inch guns at Hoxa, opposite the two on Stanger Head from which the 4.7-inch gun was to be moved along the coast to Neb where, in addition, there was to be a 12-pounder. Twelve-pounders were also recommended for Hoxa (2), Houton or Scad (2), Lamb Holm/Holm (2), Burray/Lamb Holm (1), Burray/South Ronaldsay (1), Graemsay (2). Two more 4.7s were suggested for the Head of Work to cover the entrance to Kirkwall Harbour, but Carness was the position finally chosen. Searchlights were to be installed at all the batteries.[4]

As shown by the speed of installation at Holm, work on landing and mounting the guns went on at an almost frenzied pace in the new year, a special *ad hoc* unit formed by members of the old Orkney Heavy Regiment carrying out much of this arduous work. They were all big powerful men with that instinctive Orcadian knack of being able to move heavy and awkward objects with comparative ease and an almost complete lack of shouted orders or fuss — admirable qualifications for the tasks which faced them in difficult situations. Fortunately the 'top brass' for once had the good sense to leave them alone to get on with the job in their own way — a law more or less unto themselves, but they got things done.

As a result, by 3 June 1940 OSDef Operation Order No.22 was able to list 19 coast defence guns in action on 14 battery positions including six 6-inch guns, two each at Ness, Stanger and Hoxa; three 4.7s, one from Stanger now at Neb, and two at Rerwick Head in Tankerness, to cover the approaches to the String; and ten 12-pounders, one each at Galtness in Shapinsay, Wasswick in Rendall, both also for the Kirkwall harbour defences; as well as Buchanan, Balfour, Holm, Scad, Gate and two at Houton for Scapa — quite an improvement on the four 6-inch and one obsolete 4.7 of a year previously; more were to follow, mainly twin six-pounders for close defence of the booms.

The decision to increase the anti-MTB defences was taken on 11 April just after the invasion of Norway. It involved extra guns at Holm, Burray and Buchanan with the addition of two more batteries, one at Stromness Golf Course below the six-inch battery, and one in Hoy, both to cover Hoymouth. Extra searchlights were also planned and the reconnaissance duly carried out, including a light on Graemsay.[5] Later still the Black Craig area (outside Stromness) and St John's Head in Hoy were also surveyed for a possible radar station, possibly of the CHL type.

To man these new batteries, troops were brought in from the South-West Defences, in the Plymouth area, and from other south of England defended ports where the need of them was thought not to be so pressing at this time as at Scapa.[6]

By 6 February the OC and HQ party of the newly formed 191 Heavy Battery had arrived to take over at Ness, and three days later the OC of the entirely new 199 Heavy Battery which would include Hoxa's 6-inch guns had set up his HQ in St Margaret's Hope, ready for the six officers and 75 men, all trained on 12-pounders, who arrived from Devon on 14 February to man the new batteries at Cara and in Burray, which was also part of his command. Ten RE Fortress searchlight officers were added to the strength on the 17th, and the two 12-pounders were mounted at Houton on the 29th. The first week of March saw the 12-pounders ready at Buchanan and Gate in Flotta and at Cara on the South Ronaldsay side of Water Sound, while another detachment arrived at Scad in Hoy on 7 March to take over a very different type of gun position from what they were used to in 'glorious Devon'. But at that time of year they were at least spared the misery of air attack by Hoy's ferocious midges which afflicted this battery in summer and autumn, making the use of mosquito-netting masks for sentries essential items of wear.

The detachments for Buchanan and Gate came on the 16th in time for the bigger air attacks of the Luftwaffe, and Houton's gun teams from Plymouth came in on 28 March before their camp was ready, so that they had to be quartered in Stenness at first. And on 13 April three officers and 74 gunners from the Forth Defences occupied Hoxa Battery, recalling the days of 1914-18. Throughout the summer, reinforcements came from Dover, Portsmouth and Plymouth to bring Orkney Fixed Defences up to full strength by 17 August although they had, of course, been fully operational long before that. Many had been in action of a kind, firing at suspicious objects which could have been U-boat periscopes, or firing bring-to rounds to stop unauthorised vessels from approaching the anchorage. On one occasion, Ness Battery even had to put a round across the bows of the mail boat *St Ola* to stop her from entering her home port of Stromness. On 21 August enemy aircraft had dropped mines by parachute in Hoy Sound, and the gunners at Ness Battery, many of them Stromnessians, had taken a very accurate 'fix'. The *Ola* was heading into the danger zone and had to be stopped. The Navy later cleared the mines which were exactly as plotted from the battery. Several of the batteries also sank drifting mines.[7]

The Navy was very pleased with the build-up. In a dossier of information — produced by the Secretary's Department of the Admiralty after the war — on how the Flow was developed as a naval base, the anonymous compiler comments that by the middle of 1940 the defences of Scapa were 'very considerable'. He goes on: 'The Military had installed Coastal Artillery and searchlights at each entrance and although not up to the high standard of efficiency as at the end of hostilities they originally formed the basis of the major defence of this Base against submarines, MTBs and E-boats throughout the whole period of the war.' He adds, rather unfairly, 'The Fleet was protected by several batteries of AA guns, pretty raw but did good work.'[8] By that time there were, in fact, three regiments of HAA artillery totalling ten batteries with over 80 guns in action, as well as two LAA batteries, and searchlights by the score. And they had quite a respectable tally of enemy aircraft shot down to their credit.

But the Army's most vital role was in warding off air attacks on the Fleet and its Base, as once the underwater and surface defences were reasonably secure the main threat would come from the sky, a threat which grew ever greater in 1940 as Germany invaded Denmark and Norway, bringing the Luftwaffe airfields to within 300 miles of Scapa.

To meet that threat, 'Q' Plan had stipulated that 80 HAA and 40 LAA guns were needed, as well as 108 searchlights and 40 balloons — a tall order and a far cry from the eight guns of the 226 HAA Battery which were all that was on the ground in September 1939, but after the slow-down in October 1939, 'Q' Plan was given the green light on 5 November, and, appropriately, it went off like a rocket.[9]

The aim was to have the guns and lights ready by March, when it was hoped the Fleet would be able to return to a secure Base. That meant four, or at most five, months of short days, long nights, gales, rain, possibly snow, in which to build camps, bring in the guns by sea, mount them and have the administrative services to supply them and the troops who would man them in a jigsaw of scattered islands, with poor roads, poor drainage, and difficult sea communications. Or, in today's terminology, inadequate infrastructure and always the possibility of commando-type or paratroop landings, so that ground defensive positions had to be prepared at the same time and sometimes manned. There were also the mine-laying forays by German aircraft round about, and even in, the Flow which had to be guarded against and reported when they did occur so that the Navy could deal with them.

The weather aspect of the problems involved is illustrated by two entries in the OSDef A & Q War Diary for November that year. For the 11th it reads: 'First consignment of gum boots received from Stirling.' Many more were required — Stirling in central Scotland was the main Ordnance supply depot. On the 26th the entry was: 'Westerly gale. Much damage to huts. One of the masts at Netherbutton partially blown down. All masts at Wideford Hill down. Hutting at dumps blown in all directions.'

It was a daunting prospect, involving the establishment of ten HAA gun-sites on the Mainland, six in Hoy, two on Flotta, three on South Ronaldsay and one in Burray, and there was no road link between the Mainland, Burray and South Ronaldsay as there is now across the Churchill Causeways — they were still to come as part of the overall defence scheme. Then there were to be LAA gun positions at Netherbutton, Hatston and Stromness on the Mainland, and in Hoy, Burray, Flotta, Fara and Cava in the islands, some 35 individual gun positions all requiring accommodation for the gun crews and emplacements for the guns.

The searchlight situation was even more demanding with 41 individual and isolated positions on the Mainland, 18 on Hoy, six on Flotta and seven in South Ronaldsay. Each of these also required hutted accommodation. The need for a central Gun Operation Room (GOR) to control all this weaponry was urgent and high on the list of priorities when Brigadier Kemp and Major Tuck attended a conference with the C-in-C Home Fleet and his Staff aboard the flagship in the Clyde on 21 November. It was confirmed that the GOR should be near Kirkwall and it was, in fact, already in the course of construction, near where the North of Scotland Milk Marketing Board 'Cheese Factory' now stands. It became operational on 10 February 1940.[10]

The scheme proposed at the Admiralty for mounting the new guns was now put in operation — the Royal Marines installed the guns on the islands and the Army put them in on the Mainland. The Marines came from No.1 RMNBDO on board the specially converted and equipped liner *Mashroba,* which dropped anchor in the Flow in mid-November.[11]They did magnificent work often in very adverse conditions, such as on the night when a 100 mph gale broke the *Mashroba's* anchor cables and she had to spend the entire night steaming round and round the Flow in total darkness.

By January, AA units were beginning to arrive at the rate of about one a week, the guns and searchlights being brought in by the ships *Cyprian Prince* and *Rutland.* Other ships bringing army supplies were *Kyle Castle, Kylebrook, Britannia, Ford Fisher, Welsh Rose, Sir Walter Campbell, Malplaquet, Jorse, Gannet* and *Bullfinch.*[12]

The state of the roads and the congestion on the piers was causing considerable anxiety, as might be expected. The roads had, in fact, been much improved just before the war, but even so they had never been designed to cope with the volume and weight of traffic they now had to carry.

There had been a lot of head-scratching at AA Command as to where the units needed to reinforce the Scapa defences under 'Q' Plan were to come from. Time was running short if the Scapa base was to be secure by spring, so defences elsewhere had to be reduced to provide the men and material to bring it up to strength. It was apparently decided that those in the north of England and the Midlands could best spare them, not being under immediate threat themselves.

The first reinforcements had, in fact, arrived in Orkney two days before war broke out — the three Bofors guns of 39 LAA Battery from Linlithgow sent north to cover the Netherbutton radar station against low-flying attack. Another troop of this battery arrived later in the year and established its Battery HQ in Finstown and then in the Apostolic Hall in Stromness. The battery also covered Hatston and Lyness and, for a time, provided anti-torpedo-boat defence in Hoy Sound. It was joined still later by 42 LAA Battery.

The heavy anti-aircraft guns were manned by 64 HAA Regiment from Tyneside; 70 HAA Regt from Merseyside, where its sites included Seaforth, Walton and Widnes; and 95 HAA Regt whose home ground was the Midlands, occupying positions round Birmingham, Castle Bromwich and Coventry. The ancient oak tree traditionally marking the 'heart of England', the point furthest from the sea in 'this sceptred isle', grows on the edge of the 95 HAA Regt's recruiting area — now, like the other two Regiments, it would find itself much more closely associated with the ocean, and not a tree, oak or otherwise, in sight.

The searchlights came from the north of England, 62 (The Loyal) Searchlight Regiment RA from the Preston area in

Lancashire and 61 Searchlight Regt which had had its Regimental HQ in St Helens and sites in the Kingsley and Widnes areas. In the Movement Orders and the War Diaries of these units, the posting north was usually referred to as 'to join 'Q' Force', presumably a reference to the 'Q' Plan.[13]

The first progress report in OSDef A & Q War Diary on 6 February 1940 stated that there were still only the eight HAA guns of the Orkney 226 Battery in action but that another 12 were already emplaced on the Mainland and another eight in Hoy, while four more had been landed in Orkney but were not yet deployed. None of these were ready for action yet, nor were the 15 LAA guns which had been landed but which were still not on site.

As far as personnel was concerned, some 4,000 men from 70 HAA Regt, 64 HAA Regt, 39 LAA Bty and 142 LAA Bty had landed in Orkney and had already been deployed to their various regimental areas, as had two batteries of 62 Searchlight Regt.

Accommodation was a major problem, and shelter was vitally necessary in the hard conditions of that first winter which only slowly gave way to a reluctant spring and tardy summer. For the LAA men 36 huts had been put up, representing about half the requirement on the Mainland and Hoy but only five percent of what was needed for Flotta. The searchlight men had 92 huts up, only a tenth of the Mainland and South Ronaldsay needs but nearly the full quota for Hoy and Flotta — 80 percent, in fact.

On the weapon side, things were looking up by 1 March when it was reported that the 226 Battery's eight 4.5 guns had been joined by another 16, as well as 15 3.7s, 13 LAA guns and 28 searchlights — all ready for action, and only just in time for the first raids on the Flow.

Six weeks later still on 15 April, the day before the Luftwaffe's last big attack on the anchorage and the ships engaged in the Norwegian campaign, the OSDef A & Q War Diary issued its fifth progress report on 'Q' Plan. It painted a very different picture from that of the second report less than two months before.

All 88 HAA guns had been landed and emplaced, although eight were still not in action while they awaited the arrival of vital stores and spares; 32 of the 36 LAA guns were ashore and ready for action, apart from four which were also awaiting stores and spares. Six more were still to come.

Eighty-eight AA searchlights were in action, with 14 more on site awaiting stores, while six more had been landed but were not yet deployed. Troops to man all this equipment were now in

Orkney, numbering about 10,160 men, the total for whom emergency rations were held at this time, no doubt the responsibility of 908 Company RASC with its HQ in Stromness.

In addition to the HE ammunition for the bigger guns, there were 30,000 rounds of ball and 9,000 rounds of tracer for 98 Lewis guns of ancient but fairly reliable vintage; but still more were needed.

The report described the accommodation situation as 'satisfactory' but whether some of the troops who had to live in it would have agreed is open to question. But there is no doubt whatsoever about the achievement of those who built the huts, for there was now a total of 877 — 93 for coast defence; 458 for HAA; 119 for LAA and 207 for searchlight crews, an increase of 749 in just ten weeks. This meant an average of ten a day, mainly wooden Jayne huts and the ubiquitous corrugated-iron humps of the Nissens, remains of which disfigure the Orkney landscape still, even after half-a-century. They were, nonetheless, a very welcome and necessary sight at the time, with conditions emphasised by the report which said 'gum boots and oilskins still short of requirements', and the War Diary which recorded for 16 January: 'Gales snow etc', and for the 18th: 'Blizzard continues.'

Much of the building work on these huts had been carried out by the units which were to occupy them, by men whose civilian skills were many and varied but which did not normally include hut-building. It was a skill they very soon acquired.

Throughout this build-up period there was almost constant enemy air activity. The Luftwaffe was keeping a watchful eye on progress, too. Between 5 November when 'Q' Plan got the final go-ahead and the end of the year there were at least 20 air-raid alerts, and January 1940 saw almost daily reconnaissance flights from Germany over the area whenever weather conditions permitted.

A fairly typical example of this harassing activity — which, quite apart from its direct military implications, severely hampered construction work — occurred on 22 November 1939 when, shortly before 10 a.m., the 39 LAA troop at Hatston heard a plane diving over the airfield. They tried to engage but their gun jammed. This aircraft had come in over Rousay flying south. Five minutes later the other 39 LAA troop at Netherbutton had a go at extreme range on a plane to the east flying north-east. Another plane crossed Orphir and came low over Stromness where, of course, at this stage there were no AA guns — only OSDef HQ. At 10.13 a.m. 226 HAA Bty at Rysa engaged an enemy plane which made off north-east, and at 10.25

a.m. what seemed to be the same aircraft appeared over Netherbutton where both the 39 LAA troop and a destroyer in the Flow opened fire on it. It seemed that two or three aircraft had taken part in this confused and confusing foray, and they had probably carried out a pretty detailed land survey in spite of poor visibility with a low cloud ceiling. They dropped no bombs and the guns did not seem to have scored any hits.

Things quietened down after that but there was another alert later that afternoon and everyone stood-to again; but as so often happened this proved to be a friendly aircraft from 803 Squadron FAA based at Wick. It was just one of those all-too-common frustrating days with a lot of to-ing and fro-ing and nothing much to show for it.[14]

Nor, of course, could the threat of possible enemy landings by ground forces be ignored. In its Operation Order No. 2, dated as early as 22 October 1939, OSDef stated that Inganess Bay, east of Kirkwall, was a possible target for a sea landing and that parachute drops might be expected in the East Mainland, the northern part of the West Mainland or in Hoy. Royal Marines were preparing an inner line of defence round Lyness, and the Army would establish defensive positions on the Hill of Heddle above Finstown, at Towerhill overlooking Kirkwall and Inganess Bay, at Netherbutton in Holm, and in Hoy at Wee Fea above Lyness and at Rysa. These positions were to be made ready at once.

The coast gunners at Stanger Head would be responsible for the ground defence of Flotta, and mobile reserves were to be held at Holm and Stromness to deal with paratroop drops. All positions would be manned from dawn to dusk and would be at 15 minutes readiness during the night. Barbed wire trips were to be used, and there would be 360 rounds per automatic weapon and 30 rounds for each rifle available.

Not all the air activity was from the German side — British air forces were busy too; offensively with RAF fighters from Wick, and with the Fleet Air Arm at Hatston, while on the more passive side, the balloon barrage was growing. The Flow had seen plenty of balloons in the First War but those were mainly to be towed by ships and were manned by observers to spot enemy submarines and to report fall of shot for the ship's gunners. Now a new sort of balloon was needed for this new war — an unmanned balloon, or rather balloons, whose purpose was to force enemy aircraft to fly higher and render their bomb-aiming less accurate, and possibly also to damage any plane which tried to fly through their cables.

For the defence of Scapa, 950 Squadron was created and

assembled in Glasgow at No. 18 Balloon Centre RAF towards the end of 1939. It was composed mainly of volunteers from the three Glasgow Auxiliary Squadrons, and its advance party arrived in Orkney during January 1940 when Squadron HQ was set up in huts on the top of Ore Hill near Lyness. Originally the balloon barrage defence plan was for 12 sites on the east coast of Hoy, four each on Flotta and Fara, and eight on trawlers on the east side of the Flow. The trawlers, based on St Mary's in Holm, were to be manned by the Navy to work the ship, with four RAF men to handle the balloon.

The main body of the squadron arrived in Orkney on 2 February, and less than three weeks later the first balloons made their debut in Orkney skies, flown from Hoy and Flotta.

A second squadron was formed during the summer of 1940, and the Lyness HQ was upgraded to become No. 20 Balloon Centre controlling a maximum of 56 balloons, restricted to 40 actually flying at one time. On the day this 'target' was achieved, with 40 balloons actually in the air, the Orkney weather did it again. There was a sudden gale and 39 of them were 'gone with the wind', an experience that was to become not altogether uncommon during their stay in the islands. But within hours, 15 sites had balloons aloft again and the full 40 were airborne once more soon after.

The Orkney gales were a constant source of trouble — and loss. In the bad winter of 1943/44, for instance, over 350 balloons were lost or damaged and the WAAFs, who had arrived in Orkney that summer, had plenty to keep them busy on repair work. But not too busy to enjoy themselves as a letter home from one of the girls shows, although there is a *cri de coeur* at the end. She wrote: 'We are terribly hard-worked but I have managed to get to four dances. Please send me a picture with some trees.'

During one 90 mph gale one of the balloons on Cava carried its winch across the island and out over the Flow where it eventually broke free and plunged to the bottom, the balloon itself carrying on out to sea. Divers went down but were unable to locate the winch, and it was written off. But it did turn up again, hooked by a ship's anchor which brought it to the surface when she weighed.

There were supply problems too. Sometimes there was a shortage of gas which had to be shipped from Leith or Aberdeen, and to overcome this a hydrogen factory was planned and laid out at Rinnigal in Hoy; but it took so long to build that it did not become operational until quite late in the war, and the small portable hydrogen-producing plant which had been brought in as a temporary measure could hardly meet the demand.

The prime purpose of the balloons, of course, was to keep aircraft away or destroy them, but they could, on occasion, save them as well. One British plane made a forced landing in South Walls and ended up stuck in a bog. In the soft ground no vehicle could get near enough to tow it clear so they borrowed one of the balloons and attached it to the plane, which then became airborne in a most unusual way as the balloon lifted it and deposited it on firm ground.

In January 1941 there were administrative changes and the whole Scapa Flow Balloon Barrage became No. 950 Squadron, expanding operationally to a total of 81 balloons, the biggest squadron in Britain, with 19 on Hoy, eight on South Walls, 19 on Flotta, six on Fara, two on Cava, one on Rysa Little and 26 seaborne on trawlers.

By June 1944 the need for a balloon barrage round the Flow had diminished with the changing pattern of the war, but the increasing number of flying-bomb attacks on London and the south-east made their presence round the capital of vital importance, and so the balloons and their crews embarked from Lyness in two Liberty ships and sailed away after nearly five years' arduous service in the north, leaving Orcadian skies to the whitemaas, the Spitfires, the Hurricanes — both man-controlled and climatic — and even an occasional Dornier or Junkers taking a chance.[15]

The more aggressive air defence measures for the defence of Scapa were actually outside its periphery at Hatston, the Fleet Air Arm base, and at Wick where the RAF fighters were stationed. Hatston, now HMS *Sparrowhawk,* had, of course, been operational since before the outbreak of war — but only just before. It was intended that Castletown in Caithness should be the main RAF fighter base but until it was ready two Hurricane squadrons were to be operated from the Coastal Command station at Wick. By the end of February 1940 three RAF squadrons were at Wick, Nos. 43, 111 and 605, two of them, at least, equipped with Hurricanes. No. 111 Squadron, in fact, shot down a Heinkel 111 while on routine patrol as early as 2 March, and on 25 March fighters from Wick chased off German aircraft attacking a convoy 20 miles south of Start Point in Sanday.[16]

Hatston had been selected as a naval air station on the advice of Captain E. E. Fresson of Highland Airways, although he stressed that tarmac runways would be essential there. This was a revolutionary idea in those days, when aircraft of all sizes normally operated out of grass fields, but the authorities accepted his recommendations and so Hatston became, almost certainly, the first airfield in Britain with hard runways. As a confidential report on the construction of the airfield states, 'the making of runways [was] necessitated by the geological structure of the Orkneys, which is very favourable to the formation of large pools of water.'

The first Fleet Air Arm unit, No. 771 Squadron was already there when war broke out, and it was joined in November by a newly-formed 804 Squadron equipped with the biplane fighter, the Gladiator, and also Martlets, all coming under RAF operational control from Wick.[17] There were, too, those workhorses of the sky, the old amphibious Walruses with their open cockpits and pusher airscrews to carry out routine anti-submarine patrols. During the Norwegian campaign RAF Blenheims acting as long-range fighters for operations over the North Sea were also based for a time at Hatston.

Later still, the RAF Fighter Sector Control combined with the Gun Operations Room at Kirkwall for the overall co-ordination of fighters, guns and searchlights against any enemy attack — and ACOS was at last persuaded to delegate responsibility for the issue of air-raid warnings to the officers in charge at GOR.[18] Even so he retained his direct phone link with Netherbutton radar station and had to be consulted before warnings were issued for quite some time still.

The defences were getting stronger every day, and friendlier eyes than those of the Luftwaffe were keeping an even closer and more anxious watch on the progress — those of the Navy who could hardly wait to get back to its chosen base from where it could operate at maximum efficiency.

The hopeful deadline had been 1 March and they very nearly made it. A signal from the C-in-C Home Fleet to the First Sea Lord read: 'It is intended to make Scapa the main base of the Home Fleet from 7 March and I suggest fleet tenders arrive there 1 March.'[19]

ACOS signalled the Admiralty on 22 February that on 1 March it was expected that 36 HAA guns could be in action, and another 16 as soon as stores became available. Two Hurricane squadrons were expected at Wick on 27 February and should be operating by 1 March. Twelve balloons would be flying, and the Navy's own underwater defences were well in hand with minefields and guard loops operational at Hoxa, Switha and Cantick. The doubling of the Hoy boom was 40 percent complete, and the guard loops there should also be ready by the target date. On the east side, anti-submarine blocking in Kirk Sound and Skerry Sound was complete but four more blockships

were needed for East Weddel Sound and Water Sound, and
ACOS anticipated that two would be sunk there during the neap
tides at the beginning of March. He concluded: 'I should have
preferred a week's delay before the big test but in view of the
arrival of the fleet about 7 March I consider that this is
unacceptable and am sure the defences will be able to give the
enemy a hot reception on 1 March 1940.'[20]

The defences were not, in fact, asked to provide that hot
reception for more than a fortnight after 1 March, by which time
they were still better equipped numerically to give an even
warmer welcome than ACOS envisaged, having by this time 52
HAA guns ready for action. And by that time the Fleet was back
in its Scapa home, well able to add its own measure of 'heat' to
the reception.

CHAPTER 30

The Bombers Come At Dusk

TWO OF THE FLEET tenders mentioned in the C-in-C's signal to the First Sea Lord did arrive on the suggested date, 1 March — hardly an aggressive show of strength, one might think, but it looked very different, which was what the Navy wanted. *Fleet Tender B* was, in fact, the 30-year-old steamship *Waimana* of the New Zealand Shipping Company, rebuilt in wood above the upper deck to a five-sixths scale resemblance to the battleship *Resolution,* complete with dummy guns. She carried 5,000 tons of rock in her holds to reduce her freeboard, and 10,000 empty oil drums to keep her afloat should she be hit. She was, like the nearby dummy *Revenge,* completely unarmed and on receipt of an air-raid alert the crews had orders to abandon ship and pull for the nearest shore, which happened to be Flotta. Another ship which looked like the aircraft carrier *Hermes,* was added to this 'dummy fleet' later.[1]

The Germans certainly seem to have responded to these imitation 'warships' staked out like decoy ducks in the Flow, for they had several good hard looks at them from the air, and the week after they arrived a plane, said to be a Heinkel of unusual design, dived over the Flow and dropped an unidentified object by parachute. No mines were found nor was the mysterious 'object', but the Heinkel was shot down by RAF fighters from Wick.[2]

The old Union Castle liner *Dunluce Castle* also arrived at the beginning of March, having been saved from the breakers' yard.[3] She had undergone a six-months conversion to her new role of depot ship to act as the terminus of the Scrabster-Scapa ferry operated by the old *St Ninian* and the *Marialta,* as well as being holding ship for navymen awaiting their own ships. She also held stores for the re-kitting of men who had lost their gear when their ships had been sunk and, very important, she became the HQ of the ever-growing 'Drifter Pool'. She provided facilities for entertainment in a 250-seat theatre in No.2 Hold which was eventually fitted out with seats and dressing-room accommodation from one of the blitzed London theatres. In addition she housed the Fleet's photographic department which recorded, among other things, some 1500 shoots by the Navy's low-angle guns. The Fleet Mail Office was on board and so were the dental surgeries. Moored off Lyness near the *Voltaire* — another ex-liner converted to be a depot ship — she was a valuable asset to Scapa's still rather sparse base facilities. The victualling ship *Boniface* had arrived off Lyness some months earlier.[4]

Now, with the defences very much strengthened and growing stronger by the day, the scene was set for the return of the Home Fleet, which, of course, was the object of the entire exercise. It was an important turning-point in the history of the Flow and with his instinctive feeling for a great occasion, Winston Churchill as First Lord of the Admiralty was determined to be there — and in any case, he wanted to see for himself just how good the defences he had asked for really were, as well as tying up a few loose ends such as the permanent blocking of the eastern entrances. As he wrote in *The Gathering Storm:* '12 March was the long-desired date for the re-occupation and use of Scapa as the main base of the Home Fleet. I thought I would give myself the treat of being present on this occasion in our naval affairs.'[5]

In actual fact he made the trip several days earlier than this, and according to the Cabinet papers in the Public Record Office he was on board HMS *Hood* in Scapa Flow on 8 March, and back in London three days later on the 11th when he reported on his visit to the War Cabinet.[6]

He had embarked in Admiral Forbes' flagship, HMS *Rodney,* in the Clyde on 7 March, and 24 hours later was off the west coast of Orkney. About midday when the fleet of five capital ships, including the *Renown* and *Repulse* as well as the *Rodney* and accompanied by a squadron of cruisers and a score of destroyers, was half-an-hour's steaming time from the Hoxa boom, warning was received that enemy aircraft had been active in the area and it was suspected that mines had been dropped at the entrances to the anchorage. The C-in-C decided to stand off for 24 hours until the channels could be swept, but knowing that his distinguished guest had allowed himself only three days away from the Admiralty and War Cabinet meetings and also that patience was not one of the more notable Churchillian virtues, he suggested that the First Lord should transfer to a destroyer which could take him safely into the Flow where he could stay aboard the *Hood* which had come up the previous day and was already in the anchorage.

He was duly rowed across to the destroyer which took him

in through the 'Tradesmen's Entrance', Switha Sound, and so to *Hood* from where he could carry out his inspection. Next day he was happy to note that 'more than six months of constant exertion and the highest priorities had repaired the peace-time neglect' of the base. He went on: 'At last the Home Fleet had a home. It was the famous home from which in the previous war the Royal Navy had ruled the seas.'[7]

But, of course, more still had to be done, and it would seem that the final decision to block the eastern channels leading into the Flow by the permanent causeways which bear his name to this day, was taken during this visit. Reporting to the War Cabinet on his return to London on 11 March he said he had found the Fleet in good heart, and a lot of work had been done to make it a safe harbour, but there was still more to be done. It could now be considered 80 percent secure, he said. The risks of using it were acceptable. Owing to the good strategic position of Scapa, it would not be necessary for the ships to spend so much time at sea, and this would ease conditions for personnel.[8]

It was not long before the reinforced defences received their first real test. The Luftwaffe had sown the wind in autumn; now it returned to reap its fiery whirlwind in the spring.

The enemy bombers came in from the east as darkness began to fall on Saturday evening, 16 March. Intelligence reports later put the number at 14 or 15 although some estimates were as high as 35 — it was difficult to make an accurate count as some of them dived out of the twilight while others made high-level attacks. It was thought they were mainly Heinkel 111s but two Ju 89Ks were identified and several Ju 88s, some of them from what was known as the 'Lion' or 'Red Lion' Squadron. Their targets were the Fleet in Scapa and Hatston airfield (HMS *Sparrowhawk*) on Kirkwall Bay, with the attack starting at 7.45 p.m. and lasting a noisy, confused and hectic three-quarters-of-an-hour.

The main attack on the Fleet was by eight aircraft in line-astern but breaking formation over the Flow itself as they selected their individual targets. The raid on Hatston was by five or six bombers flying fairly low. A total of nearly 100 HE and incendiary bombs were dropped on land, quite apart from those which fell in the sea, and there was no question this time of the German bomb-aimers forbearing to unleash their missiles at land-based targets. Thirty bombs were dropped round Hatston where they did little damage and another 50 at the completely innocuous Brig of Waithe where they demolished several houses, killing James Isbister, who thus gained the melancholy distinction of being the first British civilian to be killed by enemy action in World War II. Five other people were injured. Why they bombed the Brig of Waithe is a mystery. There were no military targets anywhere near the area at that time. It may have been that in the failing light they mistook it for Hatston, or again it may have been because on some maps the Allied Airways landing strip nearby at Howe was marked as an aerodrome.

There was some indiscriminate machine-gun fire from a few of the bombers, as well as firing down searchlight beams. The blockships in Holm Sound were also bombed and machine-gunned, apparently in the mistaken belief that they were anchored merchant ships. Here the planes were identified as Heinkels which had apparently gone out to the west before turning back over the Flow to attack the blockships while heading east. Another Heinkel went out low through Water Sound where the Cara Coast Battery opened fire on it with rifles. Troops in the Stanger Head Battery also had a go with their light machine-guns at two bombers making their way seaward, low through Hoxa Sound.[9]

And once again the old *Iron Duke,* having been patched up and moved to Longhope, was bombed for the second time with, however, little damage. Much more serious was the attack on the cruiser *Norfolk* which was hit and also holed by a near miss.[10] Three of her officers were killed and six ratings injured. This was presumably part of the 'acceptable risk' of using the Flow which the First Lord had mentioned to the Cabinet.

The Home Secretary, Sir John Anderson, reported to the Cabinet on the raid the following week and said that 120 HE and 500 incendiary bombs had been dropped deliberately on land, a considerably higher figure than the total of 100 estimated in the OSDef Intelligence Report. Ten per cent of the incendiaries had failed to ignite, said the Home Secretary, and added that the total damage from the rest had been one haystack burned. The targets, according to Sir John, were the Brig of Waithe and two landing grounds east of Kirkwall — 'Craigiefield and Crossiecroon'.[11] Bombs certainly fell near Craigiefield, causing quite a lot of damage to the house and injuring a man nearby, but there had never been a landing field there of any kind, and Crossiecroon used to be a small farm near Crowness not far from Hatston, so that may have been the 'landing ground', although it is hardly to the east of Kirkwall: it is almost due west, in fact.

The response from the defences on this their first major ordeal under fire was spectacular and noisy, the gun flashes from the 44 HAA guns in action lighting up the darkening sky as searchlights criss-crossed the area, sometimes holding in the apex of their beams the glint of a fast-moving speck of silver as a bomber dived and weaved in its avoiding action, but the firing was erratic and no hits were seen although there were unconfirmed reports of planes crashing in the Pentland Firth and off Noup Head in Westray, while others were said to have been damaged over Kirkwall and Finstown, but no wreckage was ever found. It seems almost certain that the honour of firing the first rounds went to 142 LAA Battery in Hoy, but the heavy guns were not far behind.

The Navy itself had quite an evening, firing 1100 rounds of two-pounder ammunition from its multiple pompoms and 120 rounds of heavier calibre shells. There was only one barrage balloon flying during the raid, the others having been grounded due to weather damage.

The RAF carried out a reprisal raid on various installations on the island of Sylt three days later but without apparently causing much damage either, although they dropped 15 tons of bombs.

The Admiralty had become increasingly sensitive to the threat of bombing attacks on the Fleet, so much so, in fact, that Admiral Forbes was told to take the Home Fleet to sea, out of the Scapa base to which it had only just returned, during the next period of the full moon on 19 and 20 March.[12] There were presumably still some doubts as to the effectiveness of even the strengthened defences.

Judging by the very detailed Intelligence Reports, compiled by Brigadier Kemp, Commander OSDef, for AA Command and above, the Army possibly shared some of these doubts and was certainly disappointed over the performance of the defences generally that night. Kemp's previous misgivings as to the effectiveness of the Netherbutton radar had been amply justified. He wrote:

. . . the attack was beautifully timed and executed. There is no doubt that our failure was due to lack of early information. I do not see under present circumstances that it will be any better in the future until quick and efficient steps are taken to improve our warning system.

The first four radar plots of the bombers' approach had actually come from Sumburgh in Shetland at 33, 35, 37 and 39 minutes past 7 p.m. The first attack of the raid, on HMS *Rodney,* was delivered unopposed, just 11 minutes later, at 7.50 p.m.

Netherbutton radar was obsolete and comparatively useless, wrote Kemp, and as a result the RAF fighters could not intercept, the guns were not given enough warning which meant that the crews were flurried, GL (gun-position radar) did not have a chance to get on target, and the telephone lines became 'red hot' with jammed calls. He suggested that one of the Navy's ships fitted with efficient radar should be stationed in the Flow and coordinated with the land-based defences until such time as Netherbutton was sorted out and became efficient.

He went on to report that of his 68 HAA guns which were mounted only 52 could fire, the others being out of action due to lack of essential spare parts, gun dials, cables and the like. Only 17 of the 28 LAA guns mounted were operational, again due to lack of spare parts. Those 17 did all fire — but three of them jammed. One HAA battery in 'a key position could not get its predictor dials to settle and so did not engage', said the Intelligence Report.

Of the searchlights, Kemp wrote that there were 30 in action — 61 Regiment was admirable but 62 Regiment was 'comparatively useless and need a vast amount of training. I am doubtful if they are sufficiently efficient to protect an area of this importance,' was his harsh criticism.[13] Churchill on the other hand, at the War Cabinet meeting after the raid, said that while the AA fire had not been very effective the C-in-C Home Fleet had remarked on the efficiency of the searchlights, and the First Lord added that it was hoped to give the German aircraft 'a much warmer reception the next time they came'.[14] With the shortage of GL radar sets for direct control of the guns at individual sites, especially in darkness or cloud, visual contact was essential for the engagement of targets at night or even, as in this raid, dusk, so searchlights were of vital importance at this stage in the war.

Kemp and his staff had, however, been contemplating for some time the introduction of barrage fire to overcome this visual handicap, and also to deter dive-bomb attacks on the Fleet. The idea was to put up a curtain of bursting shells in the sky on a fixed line and bearing, covering the direction of an expected attack. Such a barrage would last for three minutes, after which the guns would revert to predictor-controlled firing at selected targets when they could be seen. This idea went completely against the accepted precepts of anti-aircraft gunnery at this time, where it was believed that only aimed fire, controlled by predictors, would be effective. The conventional gunnery theories asserted that the sky was a very big space to cover against attack and so barrage firing would be prohibitively expensive without any compensatory effectiveness. Kemp was not so sure.

As this had been the first raid of any size on a British target by the Luftwaffe, Lieut. Col. Tuck, GSO I of OSDef, went south to report on it in detail and in person to AA Command, while Kemp went to visit ACOS at Lyness on 23 March to discuss the possibility of a Scapa barrage.

ACOS, Admiral Binney, was enthusiastic and the C-in-C, Admiral Forbes, agreed to having a trial shoot. No time was wasted. Indeed it would seem obvious tht OSDef already had the details of such a barrage worked out. Methods were developed of using what GL equipment was available to initiate barrage firing, and arcs of fire for the batteries were allocated. Three days later on 26 March a two-minute trial barrage was fired over the eastern perimeter of the Flow. It was a great success. Naval observers on the *Rodney* reported: 'the barrage appeared to form a complete curtain.' The barrage system was adopted — just in time.[15]

The next three days were relatively peaceful except climatically for there was a gale from the north-west bringing snow and blizzard conditions; but this kept the Luftwaffe at home until the last day of March when an enemy aircraft made a reconnaissance flight over the Flow and was met by 200 rounds of HAA fire.[16]

But as darkness fell on the evening of 2 April the bombers came back out of the east again in the half light. This time there were 12 aircraft on the GOR plot at 8.22 p.m., but only eight of them actually penetrated to the Flow itself. This time the guns and searchlights were already manned when the warning came, a dawn and dusk stand-to having been adopted throughout OSDef after the 16 March raid.

Again the planes came in line-astern but on meeting the controlled and intense barrage from the Army guns, thickened up by the Navy, they dispersed, split up and made only ineffective dive attacks towards the ships, even missing the *Iron Duke* this time. It was a half-hearted attack, the aircrews having obviously been deterred by the intensity of the barrage during which the HAA guns fired 360 rounds, with another 90 on predictor control.[17] The LAA guns and the light machine-guns on various sites, including the coast defence batteries at Stanger and Ness, also went into action, the gunners at Ness seeing their tracer bullets hitting a He 111 flying west through Hoy Sound at about 500 feet. The starboard engine emitted smoke and a dull red glow, it was claimed, and the aircraft disappeared out to sea after giving the battery a burst of its own machine-gun fire which caused no damage beyond leaving pit marks on a latrine wall.[18]

As in previous raids the Germans, when making for home and flying very low, had tended to follow the same channels as those used by shipping, doubtless finding them useful for navigation purposes in the semi-darkness which Orcadians call the 'grimlings'.

On one such occasion an Orcadian officer, Captain John Sabiston MC, was returning to Ness Battery on foot after a day's leave on his nearby farm of Arion when the raid caught him in the open, midway between farm and battery. On arrival back at Ness as the 'All Clear' sounded one of his fellow officers said to him:

'Did you see the German planes, John? They were right low, weren't they?'

'Aye, I saa them aal right,' replied John, 'Yaas, they were most aaful low. Man, Ah hed to boo the heid to let them by.'

A slight exaggeration maybe, but an indication of how they made their way out of the Scapa barrage.

This time they scored no hits on any ship and no damage was done on land. The raid lasted little more than ten minutes, and the defences had shown themselves well able to cope with it. But more was to come. 'Lion' Kampsgeschwader 26 of the Luftwaffe did not give up as easily as that. There was, however, a slight lull in enemy air activity for nearly a week with only occasional reconnaissance flights, although these were of particular significance at this time for much was happening at sea off Norway and Denmark as well as in the Flow — the German invasion of the Scandinavian countries was imminent, even if, on the British side, the actual date was still unknown.

One particular activity on the Norwegian coast had been causing Britain and her allies much concern. This was the supply of iron ore from the north of Sweden which was continuously reaching the German war factories through Narvik in Northern Norway when the Baltic froze and where it arrived by rail to be loaded and shipped south through the always ice-free Leads, the sheltered channels between the outlying islands and the Norwegian coast proper.

Using this route, the blockade runners and the ore carriers could reach German ports, sailing in neutral waters all the way. The Admiralty, and especially its First Lord, Churchill, dearly wanted to do something aggressive to stop this traffic, as they had done in a different context during February by sending the destroyer *Cossack* into the neutral water of Jøsing Fjord in southern Norway to rescue 300 British seamen being transported to German prison camps by this same route in the *Altmark,* supply ship of the now scuttled pocket battleship *Graf Spee.* But to suggestions of any further incursions into neutral territorial water, the British Foreign Office said a definite 'No' on diplomatic grounds.

Churchill, however, did not give up and continued to press for some action. At last the Foreign Office gave way and 'Operation Wilfred', codename for laying mines in these neutral channels, was scheduled for 5 April but then postponed until the 8th. In the meantime, however, the minelayer *Teviotdale* and what was called 'WS Force' had sailed from Scapa to be ready to lay the mines off Standlandet, just south of Aalesund, accompanied by the battleship *Renown* and four destroyers. Two other mine-laying forces also sailed for different locations off Norway.[19]

On Sunday, 7 April, Admiral Forbes in *Rodney,* with *Valiant, Repulse,* the cruisers *Sheffield* and *Penelope* and ten destroyers, was still in the Flow where the Fleet was joined by the French cruiser *Emile Bertin* and two French destroyers. At 8.15 that evening this Fleet, after receiving conflicting reports regarding movement of the German Navy, put to sea on information from an RAF reconnaissance flight that a German battleship, two cruisers, 14 destroyers and a transport had been sighted in the Skagerrak. The opening moves in the Norwegian campaign had begun, and in addition to the ships from Scapa, units of the Home Fleet from the Forth and the Clyde also put to sea.[20]

The following evening, Monday 8 April, once again at dusk, the German bombers struck again, launching their heaviest attack yet on the big assemblage of ships still anchored in the Flow in anticipation of trouble across the North Sea. And they met the most intense barrage to date from the 81 land-based guns now in action, as well as those of the Fleet.

They came in to the attack in what the Intelligence Reports described as 'penny numbers' of three or four aircraft either in 'V' formation or in line-astern at heights varying from 12,000 to 20,000 feet, very difficult to pick out visually in the half-light, but apparently in five waves. There was ample warning this time, originating from the radar of the AA cruiser *Curlew* stationed in the Flow on Kemp's suggestion and co-operating with the Army's GOR. The *Curlew* picked the raiders up very accurately when they were still 80 miles out, at which point they were intercepted by RAF Hurricanes from Wick. Six were turned away before they got anywhere near the Flow but twelve certainly, and possibly as many as 18, pressed home their attack. The *Curlew* estimated the total number of attacking aircraft at 24, but other observers put it much higher. About 15 bombs of between 750 lbs and 1000 lbs as well as incendiaries were dropped, the two main targets apparently being the Hoxa and Switha booms. The attack was ineffective.

The Scapa Barrage opens up. A County Class cruiser in dazzle paint in the foreground.

A Bofors LAA gun prepares for action near Stromness.

ORKNEY PERSONALITIES—1

HEATH

W^E intend to publish from time to time, in our columns, cartoons of celebrities in Orkney. Our first is that of our General Officer Commanding—Major General G. C. Kemp, M.C.

'The Orkney Blast' — Friday, February 21, 1941 — published this cartoon Major General G. C. Kemp MC, man who built up OSDef.

Major General Slater, the second Commander of OSDef.

An 90-cm coast defence searchlight in its emplacement on the shore.

One of the 6-inch coast defence guns at Ness Battery during World War II.

Fleet Air Arm Swordfish torpedo-bombers ('Stringbags') on the apron at Hatston (HMS *Sparrowhawk*) with Kirkwall in the background.

King George VI relaxes at an ENSA show on Flotta, when the comedian Leslie Henson made him laugh.

Booms sealed the main entrances to the Flow in both World Wars. They were opened and closed by vessels like these.

The trench round the Ring of Brogar provides an obstacle for the Bren carriers during anti-invasion exercises.

Before the building of the Churchill Barriers, merchant ships were sunk to block a number of the channels leading into the Flow. The blockships were sunk by controlled explosions.

Permits to enter or leave Orkney were needed in both wars.

Page 2

PERMIT issued to *(Insert name, address, nationality and occupation)*

Mrs Margaret Mowatt,
Graemsay, Stromness,
Orkney

for No TWO Protected Area for the purpose

Visiting Relatives

to enter Area on or after 6.8.43.

to leave Area on or before

a which date the validity of this Permit expires unless it is previously withdrawn or extended by adorsement on page 4.

Issued at MILITARY PERMIT OFFICE, EDINBURGH.

behalf of

21 JUL 1943

PERMIT No. P 70312 3

British

(Office Stamp)

This Permit is valid only if signed by the and if he produces the following Docum Identity on demand:

National Registration Identity Card No.

SEWT 141

1 August 1945

Signature of Bearer Mrs Margaret Mow

Looking across Skerry Sound to Glims Holm from the top of the Lamb Holm cableway as the causeway emerges above the surface to take the place of the blockships in the foreground.

An aerial view of No. 1 Barrier nearing completion, to take the place of the line of blockships behind it. This was the channel that earlier in the war had been used by the *U 47* when she sank the Royal Oak.

A German U-boat passes the Pentland Skerries on its way to surrender in Scapa Flow in May 1945.

The last battleship of the Royal Navy to visit Scapa Flow, HMS *Vanguard*. Her namesake, the previous *Vanguard,* lies on the bottom of the Flow — she blew up in 1917.

Three heavy HE bombs fell on the Buchanan coastal battery at the end of the Hoxa boom in Flotta and incendiaries set the heather alight round about, but it was still not operational at this point and so unmanned. There were no casualties and no damage. The only actual damage reported in the entire raid was to a house in South Walls and that was said to be slight.

Heavy anti-aircraft fire had been opened by the guns at 8.22 p.m., using both barrage and predictor control. A few LAA guns also loosed off in the excitement of the moment, but for the most part the raiders stayed too high for such fire to be effective. Searchlights were also in action and with better results, several aircraft being held in their beams for considerable periods — long enough, in fact, to allow guns to be laid visually by predictor control and to good effect, for the OSDef Intelligence Report on this raid stated: 'At least 4 aircraft can be claimed as destroyed.' One Heinkel 111 hit by gunfire over the Flow made a forced landing at Wick airfield with two of its crew dead and the pilot badly shocked.[21]

The RAF Squdrons at Wick claimed three more shot down over the sea, and damaged rubber dinghies from German aircraft were later found off Fair Isle and Start Point in Sanday and two German aircrew were picked up off Burray. They said that their targets had been Lyness and the booms at the main entrances. These two prisoners had been on the last three raids on Scapa — on 16 March, they said, they had found the AA fire of little consequence but by 2 April things had changed and the barrage had been bad, causing them a lot of trouble.[22] Now on 8 April it had been so effective that they had been forced to stay high — but not high enough to escape being hit; their plane had crashed and for them the war was over.

There were other claims that the fighters had shot down five planes for certain with two more probables, but these figures were not confirmed. Quite apart from the naval contribution, the OSDef guns fired in all 2,743 rounds of HAA ammunition — 1843 of it in the barrage. There was no doubt as to its effectiveness; almost certainly seven enemy aircraft had been shot down and the others driven off without hitting a single target.

OSDef was raised to the status of an infantry division in spite of being composed almost entirely of gunners and Kemp was accordingly promoted to the rank of Major General and given the appropriate staff establishment. A little later, during May, OSDef was divided into two AA Brigades, the 58th under Brigadier Hancock MC, with its HQ at Lynnfield just outside Kirkwall, and the 59th, commanded by Brig. Peck DSO MC, with its HQ in Hoy. By this time OSDef as a whole numbered about 11,000 men and was still growing. Its HQ remained in Stromness.[23]

On the morning after this raid the Orkney defences realised what it had been all about when they heard the news that Denmark was occupied and that the invasion of Norway had begun. The German troop transports and warships had actually been at sea while their aircraft were attacking the Flow in what was presumably meant to be a diversionary operation to keep the Home Fleet quiet and, if possible, immobilise it by destroying the booms. What proved to be the final and certainly the biggest test of the defences was, however, still to come — and there was not long to wait.

With Norway now a theatre of war only 300 miles away, Scapa became more important strategically overnight. It would obviously be a key point for the naval direction of any campaign across the North Sea. Equally obviously the Germans would want more than ever to neutralise it, at least to such an extent that the Navy could not use it with any degree of security. The defences realised only too well that they would be subjected to heavy, and perhaps sustained, attack. The only question in most minds as they stood to their guns and searchlights on that fateful night for the Norwegians, 9 April, was — when, and from where? Darkness fell gently over the islands but no bombers came in the grimlings this time. Nor did they in the morning when the teams closed up to their guns again before dawn. Nerves were at full stretch of anticipation, for the Flow was full of shipping from many nations including warships from France, Norway itself, and Britain, along with transports carrying troops and supplies including two ships with the famous French mountain troops, the Chasseurs Alpins, the Blue Devils.

Radar beams scanned the skies, finding nothing until about 3.30 in the afternoon, but from then on there was considerable enemy air activity all round Orkney with reconnaissance flights over South Walls, Flotta and South Ronaldsay, some of them as low as 3,500 feet when they machine-gunned sites. There was one peculiar report of what were described as 'fluted nails' being dropped on Flotta but what these were and what was their function was never discovered. Radio signals from another German aircraft off Wick were intercepted, revealing that it was sending back weather reports.

The bombers themselves came, as usual, just before dark at 8.45 p.m. and in the greatest force yet, determined to deny the Navy the use of the Flow. They came in several waves from the east and south-east at heights varying from 7,000 to 10,000 feet.

The radar plots which had given the defences ample warning showed that about 60 aircraft, He 111s and Ju 88s, were involved. Two waves circled east of the Flow, well out to sea, and apparently did not come in to attack at all, but at least 20 planes did brave the intense barrage which was now not so much a 'curtain of fire' as an impenetrable wall of flashing shell bursts across their path.

Meeting this aerial holocaust the formations split up, diving and weaving as they took violent avoiding action, although some stayed high, hoping to clear the gunfire. For those on the ground amidst the thunder and crash of the barrage, it was difficult if not impossible to keep track of the attackers; but again the booms seem to have been the main targets, along with such ships as might present themselves to the bomb-aimers. The unfortunate Buchanan coast battery at the end of the boom on Flotta was hit for the second time but again without casualties or damage, being still unoccupied. No damage was caused to the booms although 500 lb and 1000 lb bombs were dropped round them. Both the coastal batteries at Stanger Head and Ness opened up with light machine-gun fire which was returned by the planes as they made out to sea.

In the engagement, which lasted for nearly an hour, OSDef guns fired a total of 1,700 rounds of HAA ammunition, 1,400 of them in the barrage and the remaining 300 under predictor control, and also 150 rounds of LAA. There is no record of how many rounds the naval ships put up. The resultant screen of what looked almost like twinkling fairylights against the darkening sky was described rather flippantly by some naval observers as ' a real Brock's Benefit', but the continuous roar of the guns and the crump of bombs gave ample proof that these 'fireworks' were deadly, not decorative. The guns certainly broke up the attack, and were credited with three planes destroyed, while the RAF Hurricanes shot down another two for certain and probably seriously damaged at least another four. The naval compiler of the Scapa dossier in the Public Record Office, written after the war, goes even further when he says: 'And it is understood that the Germans lost most of their attacking force in this raid.'

On the debit side, the cruiser *Suffolk* was hit but not apparently badly damaged, for she was in action off Norway a few days later. No bomb damage on land was reported, but two men were killed and three slightly injured in an explosion at one of the gun sites in South Ronaldsay.[24]

The raiders again made their escape by the usual getaway routes, Holm Sound, Hoy Sound, over Kirkwall, Finstown and

South Walls, machine-gunning indiscriminately as they went.

Commenting on the raid, the compiler of the Scapa base dossier makes the point that the Germans never made another serious attack on Scapa Flow, and describing the action he wrote:

> A defensive victory of considerable importance was scored. Kemp's initiative and courage in adopting barrage against approved AA practice and ammunition shortage deserves high praise. Co-operation between him and Admiral Binney [ACOS] was excellent — a close relationship. **On no subsequent occasion did the raiders get within striking distance of the fleet.**[25]

It was an early example of what was really an *ad hoc* 'Combined Operation' for defence.

When he arrived in Orkney a few days later for a routine tour of inspection, General Sir Freddie Pile, GOC-in-C AA Command, must have been well pleased with his most northerly contingents which had emerged so triumphantly from their baptism of fire.

An Admiralty paper of 14 April summed up the lessons learned from the first two April raids on the Flow. In the attack of 2 April dive-bombing tactics had been used and were countered by a barrage at 2,500 feet, 2,000 yards to the eastward of the anchored ships. At least four determined raiders continued their dive through the barrage and one ship was hit, but three planes failed to drop bombs and one other bomb was nowhere near target. Several other planes turned away from the barrage, stated the paper. On 8 April only one or two of 60 aircraft dared to dive through the barrage and they did not drop any bombs near the target, the paper said, putting the estimated total of raiders much higher than had the OSDef Intelligence Report.

The study paper went on to say that while HAA fire against diving targets was ineffective the barrage firing was a strong deterrent but that it could not be put up right round the target area, nor kept up for more than a few minutes, for economic reasons.

Night bombing of airfields had caused little damage so far, it was claimed, though it very nearly had done so at Hatston where incendiaries were used to light up the target.

Attacks on the Flow had seen considerable use of tracer by the German air gunners but it had not been very effective and had, in fact, shown up the position of the aircraft. There had been deliberate machine-gunning of isolated searchlight positions and Shapinsay was picked out for special mention in the paper, the site there having no AALMG with which to return the fire. The GL radar on gun positions had been useful for fixing the timing for opening barrage fire. It was also noted that the planes dived very low to get away from the Flow and had obviously prepared their escape routes beforehand.[26]

As far as the defences were concerned, the weary months of unremitting toil in horrible weather and worse living conditions had paid off decisively, although the troops and even the command were not to realise it at the time.

The disastrous Norwegian campaign had only just begun and there was no way of telling if, or when, another and perhaps even more massive attack might come. There was, in fact, a haphazard, half-hearted raid a fortnight later on 24 April with 23 enemy aircraft on the radar plots; only five of them, however, actually came in, and even they did not press home any attack on the anchorage itself, being met, as was now usual, by a savage volume of barrage fire, in which 414 HAA rounds were used, along with 61 aimed rounds under predictor control. The weather was bad and visibility very poor when the raid started at a few minutes before 10 p.m., the raiders' tactics this time being an approach from the west. Two heavy bombs fell harmlessly in the Hoy hills, two in Holm Sound apparently aimed at the blockships again, two in Hoxa Sound and two off Burwick at the south end of South Ronaldsay. No damage was caused by the bombs nor was the sporadic machine-gun fire effective.[27]

The repulse of the 10 April raid, by far the most determined so far, marked a watershed in the reputation of Scapa Flow's defences. They had proved themselves capable of keeping enemy bombers at bay and, in fact, destroying a fair proportion of the attackers so that the Fleet now felt it could use the base at will in reasonable safety — and it did so from then on. The ships, both naval and transports, came and went without molestation during the vicissitudes of the Norwegian campaign — only at sea were they subjected to vicious attack by the Luftwaffe. Scapa was a place of refuge and comparative calm where they could prepare for the next sortie.

The cruiser *Suffolk,* for example, heavily attacked from the air and badly damaged while bombarding Stavanger airfield, limped in through the Hoxa boom one morning, her quarter-deck awash after being bombed continuously for seven hours on the way back — but her assailants did not follow her into the Flow where she found sanctuary.

And so this vital phase in the defence of the Scapa Flow Base drew to a close. There had been convincing proof as to its effectiveness, and although much more remained to be done in the months and years ahead to make the Base even more secure, it was never again seriously tested. The sheer strength of the defence had meant that the danger peak had actually passed, but no one knew that for certain and in any case the threat still remained for a long time to come.

The position is perhaps best summed up by the anonymous writer of the preface to the chapter on the part played by the army units of the Orkney and Shetland Defences, compiled, it is understood, by the Historical Section of the Tactical and Staff Duties Division of the Admiralty just after the war; in it the development of the base is discussed at considerable length. He wrote:

> The really important defeat of the Luftwaffe on 10 April never seems to me to have obtained a fraction of the recognition it deserved. The Germans never again attacked the fleet base seriously. Had they done so with success before the *Bismarck* and other operations, who can tell the result for the Battle of the Atlantic.[28]

CHAPTER 31

Building The Barriers

IT WAS, however, no time to rest on whatever laurels had been won. The war was moving fast and accelerating to a dangerous pace with, first, the fall of Norway and Denmark just across the North Sea, followed into the abyss by the Low Countries and France. The Flow's defences, although so much stronger and of proven worth, were by no means impregnable, especially, it was feared, from the sea now that Norway's fjords could provide excellent shelter for possible surface raiders as well as the air cover that such ships would have from Scandinavian air bases now in German hands. And the same shelter was available for U-boats, too. The ghost of the *Royal Oak* haunted the Navy. Those eastern approaches to the Flow, though blocked by more ships and more adequately covered by new coastal batteries, were still felt to be vulnerable.

On 11 April the Army decided to increase the anti-MTB defences with additional 12-pounders and searchlights at Holm, Burray and Buchanan, and with two new batteries at Links below Ness Battery and on Hoy to cover that approach.[1] And, in fact, on 9 May enemy MTBs or E-boats were reported only 50 miles away from Orkney.[2] Reinforcement went on apace. Hoxa Battery was fully manned by gunners from the Forth defences; Houton's two 12-pounders were ready for action on 11 May; dazzle lights were operational in Holm, Graemsay and Burray on 15 May, the same day that Galtness Battery in Shapinsay became operational.

To keep the pot boiling there had been an indication of a submarine crossing the Switha entrance to the Flow in the early hours of 21 April. The mine loops were fired, but no evidence of a 'kill' was found.[3] Then there was a bleep on an indicator loop in Holm Sound on the evening of 13 May, and five minutes afterwards a periscope was reported as being seen. An anti-submarine patrol vessel dropped depth-charges but no results were observed. Three days later another possible periscope was reported from Wasswick in Rendall going towards Kirkwall. Nothing more was seen of it either.[4] Cara Battery in South

Ronaldsay opened fire on 20 May at an 'object' seen passing through the blockships in Water Sound, and the Fleet stood to.[5] It turned out to be a float for measuring tides. Next day Holm and Burray Batteries engaged a derelict barge and sank it.

The extra guns were ready for action at Holm and Burray by 4 July, and on that same day it is recorded that four gunners from the Burray Battery saved some contractors' men who were drifting seaward on a raft. These men were engaged on what was to be the biggest Scapa Flow defence scheme of all — the building of the Churchill Barriers or Causeways.

Even before the First War the possibility of blocking the channels permanently had been considered, but nothing had been done.[6] Then in 1915 a distinguished engineer, Sir William Halcrow, had been sent to Scapa by the Admiralty to plan and carry out such a scheme for blocking the eastern channels. He had estimated that the job would take 18 months to complete, and as the hopeful powers-that-were at this time thought the war would be over in six months the scheme was dropped. Blockships were sunk across the Sounds instead.

The idea of permanent blocking, however, had not been forgotten. It cropped up again just before World War II but once again did not get the go-ahead, mainly on account of cost. The *Royal Oak* disaster concentrated many people's minds on the blocking problem, not least that of Winston Churchill, now First Lord of the Admiralty. He asked the Civil Engineer-in-Chief to the Admiralty, Sir Arthur Whitaker, KCB, M.Eng, MICE, whether it was feasible to block these channels permanently once and for all. He was told that it certainly could be done — at a cost.[7] But in wartime, costs tend to become of secondary importance, especially when set against national security and the safety of men and ships. It would seem that Churchill probably gave final approval for the Barriers during his visit to the Flow when the Fleet returned there in March 1940, after its enforced sojourn in other harbours. At all events, preliminary work was certainly in hand by the summer of 1940, though actual construction work on the Barriers themselves did not begin until August 1941.

The physical problems which faced the planners and engineers were how to close four very tidal channels — three of which, Kirk Sound, Skerry Sound and Water Sound, were just over 2,000 feet across, and the other, East Weddel Sound, 1,400 feet wide — with maximum depths varying from 59 feet at high water in Kirk Sound to 38½ feet in East Weddel. The main causes for concern, however, were the tides with a rise and fall of anything up to 12 feet and a maximum current of 12 knots under constriction, although the top velocity was usually said to be lower than this, at about nine knots.

To study these tides and the effects of various kinds of obstruction possible, such as more blockships, embankments built out from the shores, and so on, two scale models were constructed in the Whitworth Engineering Laboratories at Manchester University under the direction of Professor A. H. Gibson, DSc, Ll.D, MICE.

One model was of the three most northerly channels, Kirk Sound, Skerry Sound and East Weddel Sound, and the other was of Water Sound alone. The coastline and islands were made of wood treated with paraffin wax and the blockships were of lead, while a circulating pump with pipes and valves reproduced to order the east and west-going tides, along with a wave-producing mechanism to simulate gale conditions. These models provided information on the channels as they were before work began and then, by the addition of more ships and embankments, what could be expected when the job actually started. The engineers would, ideally, have liked a scale model of the whole of the Flow area, but with pressures of war there was no time for this to be made. An even more difficult problem was the fact that they were unable, because of the tides, to make an accurate underwater survey in the channels themselves until the barriers had been largely constructed, although a survey ship, HMS *Franklin,* took soundings and obtained other vital information during the summer of 1940.

These two models, however, provided valuable data from which to work and the University also carried out experiments as to the most suitable materials to use and how to get them into the right position. As the channels were gradually closed there would be an ever-narrowing gap through which it was thought the constricted water would gush at accelerating velocity, perhaps carrying away such rock or blocks as had already been laid. Certainly many, if not most, local people as well as a large proportion of the labour force itself, believed that the blocking process would fail due to these very strong tides. The designers and engineers were able to prove them wrong, as can be seen to this day across the four sounds.

Labour and accommodation for the men on the job was a major problem. Orkney was not popular with the type of labour needed, and in any case the other defence projects already in hand round the Flow were absorbing all that was available. In addition, the air-raids had done nothing to popularise the area in the minds of potential workers, in spite of big money incentives.

The solution hit upon in order to save time was to bring up

W

a 28-year-old 16,000-ton Royal Mail liner, the *Almanzora,* and anchor her on the east side of the Flow. She was loaded with stores, supplies, machinery, plant and everything needed by the 230 men and 20 Admiralty and contractors' staff living on board to begin work when she arrived to start discharging on 10 May 1940.

The contractors were Balfour Beatty & Company Ltd, who already had defence contracts in other parts of Orkney. For the next four months they battled with the Orkney weather and tides to maintain the flow of materials and men from the ship to the shores. At first some of the men were housed in tents on Lamb Holm and Glims Holm until more permanent hutted accommodation could be built. By September camps were ready: the headquarters, known as Rockworks, in Holm, on Lamb Holm, and at Warebanks in Burray, with another camp on the south side of Burray.

This was a considerable construction feat in itself, providing accommodation for a peak labour force of 1,720 in 1943 which included 1,200 Italian Prisoners of War. The normal strength at any one time was 1,270 — 920 Italians and 350 British workmen, the Italians leaving their mark on Lamb Holm in the shape of the PoW Chapel made out of Nissen huts and what scrap happened to be available, with *coup d'oeil* murals painted by Domenico Chiochetti from Trento.[8] Not surprisingly, Lamb Holm did not much appeal to the Italians' Mediterranean temperament, and there was at least one unsuccessful attempt to escape in a hijacked drifter.

It is said that the Italians objected to being made to work on the 'Barriers', claiming that this was constructing defences and thus a breach of the Hague Convention. So the 'Barriers' were re-named 'Causeways' to connect up the islands by road. Whether this is true or not, it appears that latterly the Italians were not employed on the actual Barrier-building.

In addition there were three piers of stone and timber to be built in order to facilitate landing of stores and equipment, one each in Lamb Holm, Glims Holm and Burray, the existing piers in Holm and Burray also being used. To supply power three generating stations were built, one at Lamb Holm with two 325 kilowatt sets, and two in Burray with a 260 kw set each. Later another two were installed at St Mary's and Grimsetter Quarry for the two block-making yards.

All this was quite apart from the construction of the actual Barriers themselves.

Experiments had shown that loose rubble in shallow water might have better holding qualities than had been originally thought but even so it was decided that although the embankments would employ rubble, it would be contained in steel wire 'bolsters' roughly 6 feet 6 inches by 4 feet by 4 feet 7 ins. As these would be flexible it would make for better cohesion. Altogether some 117,700 of them were actually used in the four causeways. The idea was that these 'bolsters' would subsequently be protected by massive concrete blocks, of which it was estimated about 66,000, each of five tons or the equivalent, would be needed. Tipping from barges had been considered but the tides ruled this out as the operation would have to be largely confined to the period of slack water, which surveys had shown lasted no longer than 20 minutes. Some building out from the shores could be used, but the main work would have to be carried out from overhead cableways from which the materials used would be dropped into position.

Time again was of the essence and although such cableways should ideally have been specially designed and built, the urgency of defence needs made this impossible.

A search around revealed that four such cableways had been used before the war during the construction of the Kut barrage across the river Tigris in Iraq. They were not ideal but could be modified to suit the Scapa conditions. Unfortunately the entry of Italy into the war on the side of Germany meant that there was a considerable delay in getting them back to this country but it was finally achieved, and the first one was erected across Weddel Sound between Burray and Glims Holm in June 1941. Kirk Sound had its cableway up in March 1942 — in fact, it had two cableways eventually, while those across Skerry Sound and Water Sound were up by July and September 1942 respectively. All the cableways from Iraq were electrically driven, and had been constructed by Henderson of Aberdeen; the fifth, built for a bridge across the river Dornie in Sutherland, was steam driven and was used on the Weddel Sound causeway.

The two Kirk Sound cableways had spans of 2,400 feet each between the masts, which for the westerly cable were 180 feet high, and ten feet lower for the easterly cable. The Water Sound cableway had the biggest span of 2,550 feet between its 172-feet masts, and Skerry Sound had the highest masts of all at 190 feet with a span of 2,500 feet between them. The cables themselves were of 2½-inch diameter and could take loads of up to 10¾ tons. It was calculated that some 125,000 dumpings of 'bolsters' and rubble took place from these cableways and their skips.

To supply material for the 'bolsters' and the huge five and ten-ton concrete blocks which are still so much a feature of the Causeways today, new quarries to supplement the existing ones were opened quite early on; there was Moss in Holm, Lamb Holm which was the largest, Glims Holm which was abandoned as unsuitable in October 1942, and one at Warebanks in Burray with another at Links later on. The Water Sound causeway was supplied from Housebreck quarry and from another at Hoxa, the stone of which was said to be excellent. Moss supplied Kirk Sound and the Holm block-making yard; Lamb Holm, the south end of Kirk Sound causeway and Skerry Sound, while material for the Weddel causeway came from Warebanks. For the most part the stone quarried was Rousay flags which, while not ideal for the job, was at least readily available and near at hand. Altogether a total of 492,829 cubic yards of 'bolsters' and loose rock was used and 521,980 cubic yards of rockfill.

Block-making yards were established at St Mary's in November 1942 along with Warebanks in Burray at about the same time; Lamb Holm and another yard in Burray were producing blocks in March 1943. For six months from July 1942 there was also a yard at the Grimsetter Quarry after which it closed down, but the others were in operation until the middle of 1944 by which time they had produced totals of 34,384 five-ton, 15,036 ten-ton and 2,206 of the 4.8-ton blocks. At the peak production phase 30 blocks were being produced every hour. Except for Weddel which was not so exposed to weather as the other channels, the central rubble bank is protected by five-ton blocks below low-water mark and ten-ton blocks above that.

The underwater embankments were built up until what the engineers called the 'knife-edge' appeared above water, and then the 'bolsters' were dropped on either side of it to complete the top on which the roadway was eventually constructed. Storms broke down some of these 'knife-edges' after they emerged above water and became vulnerable to wave action, but this merely helped to broaden the top. By the end of 1942 these 'knife-edges' were sufficiently high to ensure that no submarine could ever again pass that way, and by early 1943 they were proof against surface craft as well. So in less than three years the prime purpose of the causeways, the total blocking of the eastern channels leading to Scapa Flow, had been achieved.

By 1944 road traffic was using the causeways. Connecting roads were built across Lamb Holm and Glims Holm and on Burray, a total of three-and-a-quarter miles of new roadway in all being constructed, including that on top of the causeways themselves.

The time taken over the whole of this massive enterprise was four-and-a-half years from the beginning until the roadways, now part of the Orkney Islands Council road network, were officially opened by the then First Lord of the Admiralty, Mr A. V. Alexander, on 12 May 1945 just after VE Day, when the need to keep enemy ships out of the Flow was over. The total cost was put at between £2 million and £2½ million, of which £750,000 went on plant and equipment including 24 cranes, 58 locomotives for two-foot and three-foot gauge railways, 260 wagons of all types, 19 excavators, 16 crushers, 51 lorries, 12 dumper trucks and 10 miles of railway track. Afloat there were two steam tugs, two steam drifters, a diesel tanker, four launches, a 350-ton steel hulk and eleven barges. It took nearly a year to clear the sites after the job was finished.

The causeways were designed and work on them supervised by Sir Arthur Whitaker, and the work was carried out under the direction of H. B. Hurst MICE, who was succeeded by C. K. Johnstone-Burt MICE, Dr H. Chatley MICE and J. A. Seath BSc, MICE. E. K. Adamson MICE was Resident Superintending Civil Engineer until 1941 when he was succeeded by G. G. Nicol, DSO, MICE until completion after which John L. King took over.

It was a tremendous feat of engineering, carried out in the face of very adverse conditions — wartime shortages of men, material and equipment, with plant which was not designed for the job and which had to be adapted, not to mention the Orkney weather. Over all these difficulties they triumphed magnificently. But, in the end, was it worth all that money and effort? People in Burray and South Ronaldsay would unhesitatingly say 'Yes' for they no longer live in isolation but in islands which have become, for all intents and purposes, part of the Orkney Mainland, and certainly had it not been for the pressures of war no Government would have backed such a scheme in peacetime.

But from the defence point of view — and that, after all, was the real reason for their construction — their value may be questioned although no ship, enemy or otherwise, has passed through these channels since 1943 and probably never will again.

In the Admiralty dossier on the development of Scapa Flow as a naval base it is stated: 'Before the completion of the Churchill Causeways every responsible officer was satisfied that the risk of attack through these entrances was negligible.' It goes on to say that they took so long to build that blockships had to be sunk and certainly at least ten were put down during 1940, three more in 1941 and a couple in 1942, but had some firm decisions about the defence of Scapa Flow been taken earlier, in peacetime, this might not have been necessary and the loss of a battleship and 800 lives might have been avoided.

The Admiralty dossier goes on to say, however: 'The

causeways are a magnificent engineering feat; but it may be considered that their construction proved, due to the large amount of wartime labour and shipping required, an uneconomical scheme of defence.'[9]

Hindsight is a wonderful thing.

CHAPTER 32

Pinprick Attacks

IMMEDIATELY following the raids of spring 1940, however, there was still a lot to be done to make Scapa really secure for, after all, the Churchill Causeways would not seal its eastern sounds for another three years and while the defences against air attack were now considered at least adequate, these eastern channels still caused concern. Coastal artillery was still needed there and, as we have seen, the batteries in Holm, Burray and South Ronaldsay were strengthened and the Hoxa and Hoy booms were given extra protection. By the beginning of June 1940 there were, in all, 14 coastal batteries in Orkney with a total of 19 guns of various calibres from six-inch to 12-pounders. Twin six-pounders were brought in later to provide added protection against MTBs at the main booms. In mid-August the War Diary of HQ Fixed Defences duly recorded that with the arrival of over a hundred gunners from Portsmouth and Plymouth the coastal artillery units in Orkney were up to full strength. This was followed by a general reorganisation in the Fixed Defences set-up.

Because of the big increase in numbers of men and the proliferation of gun sites the old Orkney Heavy Regiment of 191, 198 and 199 Batteries ceased to exist as such, becoming 533 (Orkney) Coast Regiment RA — the Flotta Fire Command covering Hoxa, Switha, Holm and Water Sounds with its HQ at Stanger Head in Flotta itself; 534 (Orkney) Coast Regiment — the Stromness Fire Command covering Hoymouth and Bring Deeps with batteries at Ness, Links, just below Ness, Houton in Orphir, Scad and Skerry in Hoy; and 535 (Orkney) Coast Regiment — the Kirkwall Fire Command defending Shapinsay Sound, The String, Gairsay Sound and Deer Sound with batteries at Rerwick Head, Carness at the mouth of Kirkwall Bay, Wasswick in Rendall, Galtness in Shapinsay and Deerness covering the inner part of Deer Sound from Northquoy Head. The Flotta Command batteries were at Stanger Head, Neb and Buchanan in Flotta, Hoxa, Gate and Cara in South Ronaldsay and Burray.

Kirkwall Fire Command was not, strictly speaking, part of the Scapa defence system as its primary function was the protection of the Contraband Control anchorage in Kirkwall Bay and Wide Firth on the north side of the Mainland, but it came under OSDef for administrative purposes. Carness and Rerwick Head started off with smaller calibre guns but eventually mounted six-inch armament which had been taken off the *Iron Duke* now beached at Longhope.

At the end of 1941 Orkney Fixed Defence HQ itself disappeared as a separate entity, coming under HQ RA OSDef with the Brigadier RA in overall command of both AA and Coast Defence Units in Orkney. The total strength of coast gunners in OSDef at its peak was just under 900 men, spread over 20 gun positions and batteries. Fom time to time they were relieved by other coast gunners from the south, as in May 1941 when batteries from the Isle of Wight, Dover, the Forth, Milford Haven, Mumbles, Hartlepool, Bovis and Felixstowe took over at Balfour, Cara, Holm, Buchanan, Scad, Rerwick Head, Houton and Carness.

Although they never had to engage a truly hostile target on the sea, they were frequently called upon to destroy drifting mines or to fire bring-to rounds across the bows of ships entering prohibited areas by mistake. And there was always the chance of a shot or two with light machine-guns at a prowling enemy aircraft which came too near and too low. But for the most part it was a monotonous routine of watch and ward.

By mid-April 1940 the last of the AA defence reinforcements had arrived in Orkney and were in position bringing the units embodied in 'Q' Plan up to full strength. Now it was a case of training, training and more training to achieve that peak of readiness to cope with what might well be no more than a fleeting glimpse of a silver dot in a darkening sky. The battery sites and positions themselves had also to be improved, in order to make living and working conditions at least bearable. Welfare and other ancillary services had to be up-graded, entertainment and recreational facilities had to be organised and developed — it was a process of consolidation, with the more insidious enemies, boredom and apathy, to be fought as relentlessly as the Germans.

The general war situation did not help this settling-in phase for the garrison not only had to be ready to perform its primary function of engaging enemy aircraft, warships or U-boats — now it might have to fight units of the Wehrmacht itself, or the SS, and in common with other Commands in Britain after the fall of Norway and France, OSDef had to re-train and prepare ground defences against an invasion which now seemed not only possible but all too probable.

This meant re-thinking the defences, with coast and AA gunners having to re-train for field gunnery or even infantry roles while service units, not normally thought of as fighting troops, found themselves suddenly equipped with rifles and Bren guns and given defensive positions to man if, or as now seemed likely, *when* the time came to 'repel boarders'.

To thicken up these hastily devised defence schemes a new organisation came into being — the Local Defence Volunteers (LDV), soon to be renamed, more imaginatively, the Home Guard.

By 19 May, only 24 hours after the radio appeal by Mr Anthony Eden, then Secretary of State for War, for such volunteers, 50 recruits had signed on in Orkney, most of them farmers who at least often had their own shotguns, for there were few weapons available from military sources.[1] A week later and there were 200 Orkney volunteers forward, and already their defence posts had been allocated throughout the county. Many of them, of course, were soldiers and sailors of the First World War now considered too old for full active service in the current conflict. They were to show that on their home ground, at least, they could give the professionals a good run for their money, and that would probably have applied to the German professionals as well, had the test come.

Within about ten days it was announced in 'The Orcadian' that the Orkney volunteers were about to go on 'active service' — the first group in Scotland to do so. But then, Orkney was a very special place, the base of a fleet which was still engaged in the last phases of the Army's sad withdrawal from Norway. Further south, Holland, Belgium and finally France capitulated and a beleaguered Britain stood alone. We needed that fleet and we needed a safe place to keep it in.

By the first week in June the Orkney Home Guard strength had risen to 300 and continued to rise until there were two battalions and an independent company poised ready all over the islands, only Papay, North Ronaldsay and Graemsay being without a separate unit. Volunteering had always been a popular feature of Orkney life right from the days of the 'old Volunteers' in Victorian times — in the invasion-threatened summer of 1940 it was no different. By the end of July there were 529 Home Guardsmen in Orkney armed with 490 rifles and 25,000 rounds of ammunition, and they were described in a report to the War Office by a Captain W. B. Salitt as being of 'considerable value'.[2]

Orkney's overall ground defence scheme was contained in OSDef Operation Order No. 22, dated 3 June 1940, and involved a change of role by AA personnel in particular to meet the emergency — or it might be more accurate to say that they had to prepare for a dual role, their own and an infantry one. It was now the Orkney summer of light nights with late sunsets and long twilights merging into early dawns. Searchlights were not really needed in these conditions, it was thought, so their crews could be trained as infantrymen, and with their small detachments of about platoon strength dotted about all over the islands in isolated positions they were specially adaptable for rapid deployment.

There was, unfortunately, a shortage of infantry instructors, who were needed even more urgently further south to re-train the BEF now back from Dunkirk, and to make up this deficiency in Orkney ex-stalkers and ghillies from the deer forests and grouse moors of Caithness and Sutherland, who were already serving in some of the AA units, were used to impart their specialised knowledge of fieldcraft.

The HAA gunners were trained to use their guns as field or medium artillery, especially those batteries equipped with mobile 3.7s. With their long range and great accuracy, they were particularly effective in this ground role when tried out firing shrapnel over the Orphir hills and moors and also out to sea from Carness.[3]

Concrete pill-boxes were constructed covering vital points in the road system and possible landing places on the beaches where anti-tank 'dragons teeth' were also established at places like Dingieshowe in the East Mainland, while plans were made to blow up bridges at the Brig of Waithe and the Oyce in Finstown.

Mobile reserve forces were to be maintained at Kirkwall, where Lynnfield was the HQ, and in Stromness to reinforce the troops on the ground when needed. The Kirkwall force consisted of three companies from the 61st and 62nd Searchlight Regiments and from the 7th Gordons. In Stromness the reserve force was from 908 Company RASC and 435 Searchlight Bty.

The need for such a co-ordinated ground defence of Orkney was underlined in a rather bizarre fashion — the invasion that never was.

It happened about half-an-hour after midnight on 28 May 1940 — a thick, foggy night but with still a hint of some lingering light in the sky: the sort of dank, drear night when the defences hoped the Germans would have more sense than try an attack. But no, Netherbutton radar put out an air-raid warning 'Red' — full alert. Still, this often happened and as frequently, just one plane or none at all turned up.

Troops resignedly donned their tin hats and respirators and took post. Suddenly pandemonium broke loose. Netherbutton reported 300 — some reports said 400 — unidentified aircraft on the plot, 150 miles east of Kinnaird Head in Aberdeenshire. Was this IT? Unpleasant reminders of Nazi atrocities in Holland where disguised paratroops had descended from the skies dressed as nuns, so the newspapers said, flashed through more than one mind round Scapa Flow as the 'whistle blew' and the 'balloon went up'. The defence plan went into top gear though admittedly with a few cogs missing.

I remember being called out by the Naval HQ in Kirkwall. I was stationed at Wasswick in Rendall at this time and we came directly under the Navy operationally, not Army HQ in Stromness. I was ordered to take a foot patrol along the coast to Woodwick and Aikerness. We did the Navy's bidding, though what we were supposed to see in the fog and deep twilight I never found out, but I have no doubt the rest of the Orkney defences were doing the same sort of thing.

Being away from our battery, armed to the teeth, for the Navy had been able to supply us with plenty of small arms ammunition — something the Army had been unable to do — but with no radio, we were, of course, unable to hear what happened next on the 'invasion' front. At four minutes past one in the morning, more than 50 unidentified aircraft were plotted by Netherbutton east of Fair Isle and even though they were reported as going north, this was much too close for comfort. Then a quarter-of-an-hour later most of them 'disappeared from the plot' but tension remained high in the defences, and just before 2 a.m. another 50 aircraft turned up on the radar screen south-east of Orkney.

It really looked like something nasty this time, but at 2.12 a.m. they all vanished too — not a plane was to be seen on the plot and nothing was heard either, down in the south-east corner of the Flow. It all began to seem a bit doubtful — especially when the 'All Clear' came at 3.19 a.m.[4]

The defences stood down or staggered back wet-footed from patrol through the damp light of dawn, all a bit worried and rather bad-tempered. What had happened? No one knew. Were there really all those planes heading our way? No one seemed to know that for certain either. But some time later a rather sheepish Netherbutton reported that 'it was possible that electrical disturbances off the east coast might have been responsible for the large number of plots'. They were nothing to the disturbances experienced by the troops, especially those on patrol in the 'foggy, foggy dew', but at least the 'invasion that never was' did provide experience for the real invasion which mercifully never came either but which might have done if the defences had not kept on their toes.

Real air attacks continued but on a much reduced scale, as Hitler's interest focused on Western Europe and France but with acquisitive eyes already turning east towards Russia. Northern Europe, or at least the Scandinavian part of it, tended to become rather a backwater in the German scheme of things, although Scapa Flow remained of crucial interest because that was where the British Fleet operated from in maintaining and increasing the stranglehold of the Continental blockade.

May and June were relatively quiet over the Flow itself although the sirens wailed their warning nearly every day it seemed — some members of the public estimated that the so-called 'warbling note' had sounded well over a hundred times since the outbreak of war, though in actual fact the number was less than that. Often the cause of the alert was neither seen nor heard, but not all were false alarms.

On 16 July, for instance, 20 small bombs were dropped in the Widewall district of South Ronaldsay and four nights later on 20/21 July several enemy aircraft approached Orkney from the south-east, splitting up when they were about 50 miles off. RAF fighters from Wick went up to intercept and chased one German plane, which proved to be a decoy to draw them off while two others slipped through the radar screen unplotted in cloud at about 2,000 feet. They were, however, apparently unsure of their position and circled north and north-east before coming in low again from the east. One was flicked by a searchlight following it by sound locator. They bombed another searchlight site and also one of the eastern entrances to the Flow, dropping eleven 250 lb bombs from 1,500 feet, damaging an Army hut and a farm house at Ness in Burray where a civilian was injured.[5]

On another occasion the RAF chased a Heinkel 111 across the Flow and shot it down over the North Isles. One survivor was picked up by a destroyer.

On the night of 2/3 August, RAF Fighter Command became very worried about possible large-scale operations against Orkney. Four groups of hostile aircraft were plotted approaching the islands from the north and north-west.

Visibility was bad, with mist and low cloud, as they crossed the West Mainland and spent some time apparently searching for a target, although it was not clear to those on the ground what their objective might be. One group circled Stromness and then headed west out to sea. There were unconfirmed reports of bombs falling in Hoy and in the West Mainland, then a second group came over Stromness and went away over South Walls, while yet a third group flew east across the southern part of the Flow and circled over South Ronaldsay before splitting up. One of these turned south and dropped bombs harmlessly near Burwick, also giving the area a burst of machine-gun fire. No damage was done. The rest of this group went over Burray where they were engaged by HAA guns using 'Unseen Target procedure'. Yet another group was heard approaching Kirkwall from the west, but it turned and went back the way it had come without attacking anything.[6]

It was all very confusing. Nobody knew what was really happening, either on the ground or even in the bombers at the time, it seemed, and the narrative was only pieced together from Intelligence Reports later on, but apparently not more than 12 aircraft were involved. Only nine rounds of HAA ammunition (4.5) were fired, owing to the very bad visibility. This was the first time that a raid had come in from the west and north-west, although reconnaissance flights had sometimes used that approach.

These apparently aimless enemy sorties continued as the nights grew longer once again, towards autumn. On the night of 19/20 August, for example, several aircraft appeared to be looking for Hatston but were once more frustrated by bad weather, although what was later thought to have been a magnetic mine fell near the airfield, exploding on land but doing no damage.

A week later there was an intrusion by two aircraft, and two mines were dropped just north of Flotta about midnight. Two more planes came in from the west a couple of hours later and a third circled Burray, dropping mines by parachute; one of the mines landed in Burray itself, exploding only 30 yards away from the farmhouse of Ladywater, which lost its roof and had its doors and windows blown out, but the five occupants miraculously suffered only minor injuries. There was a lull for about an hour and then yet another German aircraft arrived about 3 a.m. to drop a mine in Water Sound. It was engaged by three troops of guns which fired 28 rounds.

The mine-layers were back again the following night with single aircraft at intervals of about five miles and this time their targets were the western approaches through Hoy Sound, where they dropped their loads from about 600 feet. The weather was bad again and although they were engaged no hits were scored, but their mines did not claim any victims either, being swept very promptly by the Navy. Holm Sound and Water Sound were the next to receive attention, followed by more mines in Switha and Cantick Sounds and Longhope.

These pin-pricking operations went on into the winter, with 15 bombs being dropped near a CHL (Chain Home Low) radar station in Deerness, causing no damage, and on the same night of bright moonlight another aircraft dropped 14 bombs in Shapinsay, none of which exploded, but the plane was seen to be hit by LMG fire.[7] The CHL station was part of a radar system which could detect the low-flying aircraft and surface vessels which ordinary radar had been unable to pick up.

In November it was Burray's turn again with four 500 lb bombs dropped, damaging a cottage.

One Dornier 17 on reconnaissance which did manage to get into the Flow about this time was heard on the radio sending back very accurate counts of the ships actually in the anchorage.

But perhaps the choicest action of 1940 came right at the end of the year, on Christmas Day. The Luftwaffe apparently thought that the British would be too busy with turkey and plum pudding to be keeping as good a look-out as they should. The Luftwaffe was very wrong.

They had sent out a Junkers 88 to have a look round for shipping over the North Sea. The pilot must also have decided to have a quick look over the Flow and possibly even at the new airfields under construction at Skeabrae and Twatt in the West Mainland. Or he may just have lost his bearings, for at about 1.30 p.m. the plane suddenly appeared without warning over Stromness, coming in low from the south-west at about 600 feet. Feeling perhaps that he was not in too healthy a situation, he turned smartly north and headed along the west coast towards Skaill. It was not a good move. Unfortunately for the Germans, Fleet Air Arm Grumman fighters were just landing at Skeabrae and, hardly believing their luck at getting a Christmas present of this magnitude, they took off again having barely touched the tarmac. They opened up on the Junkers, putting one engine out of action. He took avoiding action, flying south-east round the West Mainland, hotly pursued by the naval fighters who finally got in a long burst over the Loch of Skaill. The Junkers, which had no bombs on board, crashed near the loch but was not seriously damaged, only one of the crew being injured.[8]

The three crew members were about to try and destroy the plane when they found themselves confronted by two determined and fully armed farmers from nearby who were on the scene in minutes, Captain Thomas Harcus of Flotterston and his son Leslie who was about to join the RAF. They were both in the

Home Guard and were not going to stand for any Teutonic nonsense like burning or blowing up aeroplanes. Captain Harcus, a native of Faray in the North Isles, now uninhabited, had gone to sea as a young man and had risen to command in the Merchant Navy, from which he retired to take up farming. He had been waiting for just such a meeting with the Germans for close on quarter-of-a-century.

During the First War he had been bringing his ship back to Britain from West Africa with a cargo of groundnuts, when he encountered a German submarine. The U-boat was about to sink his ship, but Captain Harcus took over the gun with which she was armed and opened fire first, registering a hit on the submarine which made off without any attempt to prolong the engagement. Captain Harcus went on his way, only to be sunk by another U-boat several days later.

He was taken prisoner aboard the submarine and was interested to find that the two U-boats had been working together, the commander who had captured him expressing anxiety as he had not heard from his opposite number for several days. Captain Harcus said nothing but secretly hoped that his gunnery had been even more effective than he had expected. He was prisoner in the U-boat for some time and eventually it made for Germany round the north of Scotland. As they came in sight of Orkney, the commander invited Captain Harcus to come up into the conning-tower to see the homeland to which he would be unable to return until the end of the war — a kind act, or a cruel one? During his two years or so in a prison camp he learned to speak German and always nursed the hope that one day he would be able to use it while getting his own back. And so he did. He could not have wanted a better Christmas present.

He held the Ju 88's crew at gunpoint while a lorryload of Home Guard, armed to the teeth and led by Captain Pat Scott of nearby Kierfiold House — formerly of 226 HAA Bty but now a Staff Officer at OSDef HQ with special responsibility for Home Guard affairs — accompanied by Section Leader Willie Ritch, hurried to the scene with anything but a message of 'peace on earth and goodwill towards all men' as far as German airmen who disturbed Christmas dinners were concerned. They took over from where the Harcuses left off and the Germans spent the next few Yuletides a long way from the Fatherland.

It is said that there was a lady with a shotgun also on her way to the crashed plane but seeing the matter was in good hands she did not proceed with her patrol.[9]

It was an excellent example of what, later on in the war, would become known as 'Combined Operations', including an

American-built fighter, flown by Royal Navy aircrew, directed by the RAF Sector Control at the Operations Room, along with the Merchant Navy and the indigenous army, not forgetting the female of the species, quite ready to have a go. In a slightly different version of the air engagement given in Vol. 7 of *Action Stations — Military Air Stations of Scotland, the North-east and Ireland* by David J. Smith, it is stated that it was an FAA Martlet from Skeabrae crewed by Lieut. Carver and Sub-Lieut. Parke which shot the Junkers down. At all events, it was the first German aircraft to be shot down by an American-built fighter in World War II.

CHAPTER 33

In The Air

THESE LUFTWAFFE probes were not just for the nuisance and harassment they might cause, nor only for the possibility that some of their mines might claim an unsuspecting victim — they did not do so in any case — nor were they just to see what ships might be in the Flow although that was perhaps the main reason for most of the reconnaissance flights. But in addition they very much wanted to find out what was happening at Skeabrae, Twatt and Grimsetter, where new airfields were under construction.

Hatston (HMS *Sparrowhawk*) was, of course, started before the war, early in 1939, and was just operational when the crunch finally came on 3 September.[1] It remained operational, flying anti-submarine patrols and shipping strikes off Norway, until December 1940 after which its main function was the training of squadrons disembarked from aircraft carriers visiting the Flow and assisting these carriers with repairs to aircraft, supplying spares and so on.

Early in the war single-engined Skuas were disembarked from the *Ark Royal* and based at Hatston for a time, from where they carried out many long patrols over an unfriendly North Sea in the hope of attacking enemy shipping. The *Ark Royal* squadrons were again land-based at Hatston in March 1940, just in time for the Scapa Flow air-raid season. This time they came under the operational control of RAF Coastal Command giving fighter cover to convoys, among other duties, and during the raids over the Flow they claimed two German planes destroyed and four probables.

It was good training for what was to come when these three Naval squadrons, 800, 801 and 803, flew offensive missions against shipping off the Norwegian coast from April to October, using anything from two to 20 aircraft at a time. The Skuas, however, were operating at their extreme range and many did not make it back to Hatston, often having to 'ditch' short of their base owing to lack of fuel.

One of their most successful exploits was on 10 April 1940, only about 12 hours before the Luftwaffe made its last big, and unsuccessful, attack on Scapa Flow.

Led by Captain R. T. Partridge RM, 16 Skuas — seven from 800 Squadron and nine from 803 — each carying one 500 lb semi-armour-piercing bomb, took off from Hatston just before dawn and climbed north-east into the growing daylight — destination Bergen. Two hours later they made landfall in Norway with precision and accuracy, dead on schedule. Below them alongside the quay in Bergen harbour they saw what they were looking for — the 5,600-ton German cruiser *Königsberg*, flagship of Scouting Forces, Norway. No time was wasted as they pressed home their dive-bomb attack from 8,000 feet in face of intense anti-aircraft fire, with such precision that three direct hits were scored on the cruiser as well as many damaging near-misses. In the grim knowledge that the Skuas had only just enough fuel to reach Bergen, attack and get back to base, they made for home fast, after confirming that they were leaving the *Königsberg* nothing more than a blazing hulk which subsequently turned over and sank.

Four-and-a-half hours after leaving Hatston they were touching down again on its narrow runways watched over by the nearby old Norse Cathedral of St Magnus in Kirkwall, which had seen so many forays to and from Norway in its time but perhaps none more epoch-making than this, for they had, in fact, made naval history. The *Königsberg* was the first major warship ever to be sunk in battle by aircraft alone.[2]

There was a price to be paid, of course. Only 15 Skuas came back — one was missing and four others were damaged by flak; but the German losses were even heavier that day, for not only did they lose a warship but later on that night many of their aircraft were lost in the big Scapa Flow raid.

Later that year on 1 October, Swordfish single-engined biplanes, affectionately known as 'Stringbags', from Hatston made a torpedo attack on the battleship *Scharnhorst* as she steamed down along the Norwegian coast, but the mission was not a success and two of them were shot down.[3]

Even after Hatston turned over to a mainly training role some operational sorties were flown from it, notably one on 22 May 1941 when a Martin Maryland bomber of 771 Squadron (Fleet Requirements Unit) based in Orkney, piloted by the Squadron's CO, took off with Commander Rotherham, Executive Officer of the station, as navigator. The weather was vile with low cloud and poor visibility — it was so bad, in fact, that the RAF had decided to cancel its planned reconnaissance flights.

But it was known that the huge new battleship *Bismarck*, pride of Hitler's navy, was at sea and had last been seen, before the weather closed in, anchored in a fjord near Bergen. There

were grave fears that she was making a break for the open
Atlantic to wreak havoc among the Allied convoys. The Maryland circled Bergen and district in thick cloud and intense flak.
There was no sign of the *Bismarck* where she was known to have
been moored. The very substantial bird had flown — but where?
There was no time to search for her in the murk of cloud and
mist. It was vital to get the news of her having sailed to the C-in-
C Home Fleet in Scapa as soon as humanly possible. It was so
important, in fact, that they decided to break radio silence. They
called up RAF Coastal Command. No response. Commander
Rotherham and his pilot then decided to use their own 771
Squadron frequency. As it happened, one of the squadron's
other aircraft was over Scapa Flow, towing a target for the
Fleet's high-angle gunners. The radio operator on board picked
up the Maryland's signal and passed it at once to the flagship.
The Fleet put to sea without delay and the sinking of the
Bismarck a week later is now naval history.[4] But the first moves
in that triumphant pursuit all over the North Atlantic sprang
from an enterprising and hazardous reconnaissance flight from
HMS *Sparrowhawk* on the shores of Kirkwall Bay.

Hatston had another distinction. It was one of the first, if
not **the** first, British Service station in this country to house and
train members of the United States Navy after America came
into the war in December 1941. The US aircraft carrier *Wasp*
was used to ferry fighters from the United States to the besieged
island of Malta in April 1942. She came into the Flow as part of
a US Task Force which also included the battleship *Washington,*
two heavy cruisers and six destroyers, and she flew off three
squadrons of Vindicators to be temporarily based at Hatston —
the airfield having been cleared of all other aircraft by flying
them to the Twatt airfield (HMS *Tern*) in the West Mainland, 16
miles away. The American squadrons stayed for five weeks
training and flying routine anti-submarine patrols for the Home
Fleet, before being re-embarked on the *Wasp* for their final
destination in the Mediterranean.[5]

The Americans came back to Hatston in the autumn of 1943
when their carrier *Ranger* was attached to the Home Fleet and its
aircraft were flown off to carry out intensive training,
culminating in some very successful operations against enemy
shipping on the Norwegian coast after they re-embarked on their
parent carrier.

So involved with the many aspects of naval air activity did
Hatston become that at the end of the war it was claimed with
some justification that it was unusual for any senior member of
the Fleet Air Arm not to have had some connection with HMS

Sparrowhawk, and it was estimated that no fewer than 200 different naval air squadrons spent some time there during the war.[6]

The last FAA unit at Hatston was 719 Helicopter Flight, equipped with Hoverflies, which was there until September 1945.

After the war Hatston became for a time Kirkwall's civil airport, its hutments being used as temporary housing for the burgh, and it is now the town's industrial estate, having been de-requisitioned only in 1962.

The other three World War II airfields in Orkney all date from 1940. Twatt and Skeabrae were to be naval stations and Grimsetter, just east of Kirkwall, was for the RAF. In fact, it worked out rather differently, for the RAF took over Skeabrae before it was completed in 1940, and Grimsetter changed over from the RAF to the Navy in 1943 when it became HMS *Robin* and then reverted to the RAF again in July 1945. It is now, of course, Kirkwall's civil airport.

Work began on Twatt in June 1940, being carried out largely by Royal Marine Engineers, the first party of naval personnel arriving on 1 March 1941 to a very incomplete air station. By June it was ready for its first aircraft, 812 Squadron followed by 821, 880, 809 and 819 Squadrons FAA up until March 1942, with work on accommodation going on all the time. It was still a 'satellite' of Hatston and, indeed, had to take all the normal Hatston aircraft when the American squadrons from the *Wasp* arrived in April 1942.

Later that year four other FAA squadrons were based there on what was now known as HMS *Tern,* preparing for 'Operation Torch', the North African landings, and in August the station was up-graded from one-and-a-half squadrons to an independent command of three-and-a-half squadrons. The WRNS quarters were opened in March 1944 and the original six Fighter Director Wrens received reinforcements of 150 girls.

An indication of *Tern's* growth is shown by the fact that in 1941 its ground transport consisted of one motor-bike, one three-ton truck, one fire engine and an ambulance, whereas by 1945 it had a fleet of 103 vehicles of all types. On the welfare side it had five football pitches, two hockey pitches, one rugger pitch, one netball pitch and a squash court as well as a cinema-cum-gym.

The Fighter Director School was run from Twatt, the associated radar station at Hesta Geo on the North Shore, Birsay, becoming operational in April 1943, and between May 1943 and June 1945 no fewer than 4,281 students passed through on instruction.

In the twelve months leading up to D-Day, the station's

more or less resident 771 Squadron carried out 4,072 exercises amounting to 10,838 flying hours in weather which had gales on 19% of the days; rain on 74%; snow on 10% and hail on 17% — there appears to be no record of the percentage of fine days but there must have been one or two. Some 20 different types of aircraft used the station which in its early days had been described as 'this clearing in the primeval heather'; these included Seafires, Hurricanes, Rocs, Beauforts, Fulmars and Albacores, not forgetting the 'Stringbags' and the Walruses. It was said that before Twatt was first commissioned as HMS *Tern,* the captain-designate sent a signal to the Admiralty suggesting that the name RNAS Twatt should be changed 'as it might give rise to unseemly mirth'.

One of the last squadrons to use it was 802 with Seafires — the naval version of the Spitfire — which were there until 20 July 1945. The station's own 771 Squadron left five days later, and Twatt became a reserve station under Lossiemouth.[7]

Skeabrae, which is contiguous with Twatt, had been started by the Navy as a satellite for Hatston early in 1940 but was handed over incomplete to the RAF on 2 May that year, in order to meet urgent fighter requirements following the raids on the Flow, and also for the Norwegian campaign which was still in progress. The first RAF personnel arrived on 15 August to find the place still more or less a wilderness, with everything behind schedule due to bad weather and the acute labour shortage in Orkney. There was no water — except the puddles — no power and no sanitation. It was also felt that the planning left a lot to be desired, the administrative block and the technical buildings being crowded together, making them very vulnerable to air attack.

As far as is known, the first aircraft to land at Skeabrae was a Miles Whitney Straight of Station Command Flight on 15 September, and the two RAF fighter squadrons which had been promised turned out to be in actual fact 804 Squadron of the Fleet Air Arm with its Gladiator biplanes and a Martlet which arrived on 25 October. Three RAF Hurricane squadrons did duly arrive early in January 1941. They had frequent skirmishes with prowling enemy aircraft, usually Dorniers or Junkers, but on one occasion they came across one of the huge four-engined Condors which apparently got away. Spitfires were stationed at Skeabrae from time to time and in February 1944 two of them from the renowned 602 (City of Glasgow) Squadron, shot down a Messerschmitt 109G which they encountered at 37,000 feet some 50 miles out to sea, chasing it down almost to sea level in a 400 mph power dive. At the time 602 was 'resting' at Skeabrae and the two aircraft involved in this sortie were Spitfire VIIs, also known as Strato-Spits, having been specially designed for high-altitude work as was the Me 109. The Spitfire pulled out of the dive but then had to crash-land in Stronsay. The pilot was unharmed.

611 Squadron RAF shot down a Ju 88 engaged on photographic reconnaissance over the Flow in October 1944, and a few days later they got another off Norway while on escort duty with a coast strike formation.

A Canadian squadron took over the Scapa defence from January to April 1945, and the last two squadrons to be based on Skeabrae were 603 to July 1945 and 451 until September when the war was, of course, over.[8]

Grimsetter came into operation on 17 October 1940 as the Fighter Sector Station in 14 Group RAF when the operations room staff moved across from Wick. It was a satellite station of Skeabrae for 18 months, until 132 Squadron arrived fully equipped with Spitfires on 11 June 1942 and stayed until September when another Spitfire squadron, the 129, took over until the spring of 1943.

Then, on 7 July that year, the Navy took over, having already had a few FAA Seafires from 800 Squadron based there before the RAF Spitfires moved over to Skeabrae. It was commissioned as HMS *Robin* on 15 August with Avengers, Fireflies, Wildcats, Swordfish, Corsairs, Barracudas, Tarpons and Hellcats using it at various times. The first complete FAA unit to be stationed there was a squadron of 12 Tarpons disembarked from the carrier *Ravager* to carry out a working-up programme.

Altogether from commmissioning day until VE Day, 20 front-line squadrons were flown off carriers in the Flow to Grimsetter for training and working-up, and newly formed units like 1770, 880 and 801 Squadrons carried out programmes lasting several months before embarking on the serious business of operational duties.

And very typically, expansion and reconstruction work put in hand in November 1943 was still in progress on VE Day — shortage of labour, lack of material and changing priorities being the excuses as usual. But at least Kirkwall got a civil airfield out of it all.[9]

CHAPTER 34

At The Peak

THE CHRISTMAS DAY gift of a Ju 88 at the end of 1940 did much to boost the morale of the Orkney defences, and effectively prevented any feeling of anti-climax which might have begun to set in after the big air attacks of the spring had petered out, giving place to sporadic sorties and reconnaissance flights by single, or only small numbers of, enemy aircraft. The threat of bigger attacks being resumed had by no means passed, especially now that the Fleet was constantly on the move in and out of the anchorage, and full scale invasion by land forces still remained at least a possibility. The Scapa defences were geared to meet both eventualities, but always they had to be strengthened and brought into line with the latest weaponry as the technology of war advanced with terrifying acceleration. There could be no relaxation.

Three weeks after the Christmas Day Ju 88 in Orkney, RAF fighters from Sumburgh in Shetland shot down a marauding He 111 on Fair Isle, an indication that the area was still of considerable interest to the Germans. They had a closer look at the Flow itself on 11 February when yet another Ju 88 came from the north, circling Flotta and Burray at 19,000 feet before making off over Copinsay, helped on its way by 133 rounds of HAA fire and the RAF fighters from Wick.

A much more serious intrusion into Orkney air space occured at midday on 8 March in Sanday, where a radar station similar to those at Netherbutton and in South Walls was under construction at Start Point. A Ju 88 came in from the north-east and circled the site before diving on the RAF camp being built nearby, letting go four bombs. Two hit the camp, one did not explode, but the other destroyed four huts, killing one civilian workman and injuring five others. The plane returned and this time dived to 500 feet, machine-gunning the camp as it approached before climbing steeply to seaward the way it had come. There were no guns in Sanday at this time, the station still not being operational, and the fighters failed to make contact.[1]

There was another attack on the Sanday station in June,

when four more bombs were dropped, causing little or no damage. Sanday also had trouble when a floating mine drifted ashore near Kettletoft Pier, where it exploded, damaging houses all round.

Some time earlier, in March, the unlikely target of Auskerry to the east of Orkney, inhabited only by lighthouse-keepers, had been bombed; and in May an enemy aircraft slipped in over the Pentland Firth, shut off its engines and dived to 2,500 feet on Flotta where it let go two flares, it being night time, and two 1000 lb bombs which narrowly missed an LAA gun site. It then for good measure shot down a barrage balloon in flames, before making for home over Holm. No one was injured. There was low cloud at the time and it was thought that the balloon barrage flying above the cloud cover had given away the position of the anchorage.

In June several aircraft carried out a raid, crossing Orkney from west to east to drop bombs on Grimsetter airfield as well as machine-gunning the civilian workers' camp and killing one man. They also machine-gunned Hatston, where one man was injured.[2]

Further out there were two attacks on convoys in the Cape Wrath area during June, one of them by ten Ju 88s, the biggest single formation seen in the area for nearly a year. They had come round the north of Orkney following the Fair Isle channel; then, after the attacks in which several merchant ships were sunk, they made their way back through the Pentland Firth. Peter Stahl in *The Diving Eagle — A Ju 88 Pilot's Diary* describes these raids from the Luftwaffe point of view. On 1 June he made a solo flight to attack shipping reported near Orkney:

> I have to pull up into the clouds . . . to avoid smashing into their high rocky cliffs. In the clouds I keep on climbing in a westerly direction until I come out on top, and then we try to find the area where Scapa Flow should be. Apparently we are just about right because we suddenly draw some hefty fire from heavy AA guns. Here I press haphazardly on the button and let my bombs drop into the clouds.

So much for the Luftwaffe's precision bombing.

Of the attack on the 30-ship convoy off Cape Wrath three days later Stahl claims a hit on a 500-ton ship and adds: 'On the way past, the Orkneys report their presence with a shower of heavy AA shells.'

Even as late as 23 March 1943 one Luftwaffe pilot took off

from Aalborg in Denmark to carry out a photographic reconnaissance of the Flow. The pictures he obtained were flown direct to Hitler on his return because at this time the Germans feared that the Allies were about to open up the Second Front with an invasion of Europe, and the British Fleet would, of course, have been an important part of any such operation. The invasion did not, in fact, take place until the following year but the pilot, interrogated by RAF Intelligence Officers after being taken prisoner when shot down on a later mission, claimed to have identified 36 warships in the Flow on that earlier reconnaissance.

He said he had flown over the Flow at 35,000 feet, above cloud base, but had nevertheless encountered extremely accurate AA fire which, in spite of his evasive action, followed his every movement. He thought that an under-estimate of his speed saved him from being shot down. He was then set upon by three RAF fighters and only escaped them by diving into cloud at 3,500 feet.[3]

And so, with these persistent probings by the enemy planes, there was no feeling among the defenders of Scapa Flow that they were in a backwater of the war. Indeed there was continued reinforcement of both men and matériel until at least mid-1943, during which period the overall defence force was at its peak in both efficiency and numbers. The garrison probably totalled between 25,000 and 30,000 servicemen and women more or less evenly divided between the Army and Navy, with a smaller proportion of RAF personnel. The civilian labour force stood at between 3,000 and 4,000 men.[4] These totals do not, of course, include the crews of the sea-going naval and merchant ships which contributed an additional, fluctuating and quite literally, 'floating population'. Rear Admiral Macnamara, Rear Admiral at Scapa for much of the war, speaking at a fund-raising function in Kirkwall in August 1945, put the total garrison at '40,000 at times'.[5]

One area of defence to be strengthened was the protection of important targets against low-flying attack, and for this the 147 Z Battery with its 64 rocket projectors was brought in to supplement the LAA Bofors and Vickers guns. These projectors were really an early, and rather primitive, system of rocket-propelled explosive missiles, often described as being like dustbins packed with unpleasantness, fired in great numbers to blow up in the path of diving aircraft. When they went off they filled the sky with shell splinters, and it was sometimes suggested that they were more lethal to those on the ground below the bursts than to the aircraft for which they were intended. Be that as it may, they could cover a lot of vulnerable sky round vital targets such as the radar station at Netherbutton or airfields like Hatston where they were also sited. Later they were moved to Flotta, and Netherbutton had to make do with AALMGs manned by 478 LAA Battery.

The Navy did not relax either, continuing to build up the on-shore facilities to massive proportions, as well as maintaining and increasing the off-shore defences. 'R' Plan was coming to fruition.

In 1939 just before the outbreak of war, the newly appointed King's Harbour Master, Commander Oswald Frewin, on inspecting his new charge and the future Base at Lyness had described it contemptuously as — 'a muck heap run by the Boom Defence Depot and about three different contractors. Not the worst Spanish quay was so devastatingly cluttered up,' he wrote.[6]

There was a half-finished quay of about 400 feet in length with quite inadequate flat space behind it, usually inches deep in mud, to serve the needs of the Boom Defence and the growing Base. Work was in progress on the underground oil tanks behind Lyness, and this needed up to a thousand workmen. These, and other contractors' men, as well as naval personnel, needed accommodation urgently in what Frewin drily described as 'an island with Alaskan amenities'. The result was that camps, civil and naval, mushroomed in all directions with a complete lack of central planning. It was said that the huts of these early camps and the camps themselves were so close together that an incendiary raid carried out with a strong wind would have been utterly disastrous. Fortunately it did not happen.

In 1939 there had been 400 men working on the underground tanks inside Wee Fea behind Lyness, but the labour situation became increasingly more difficult as the war progressed. Miners from the English coalfields were imported for the specialised tunnelling work and later on, in October 1941, a party of Norwegian miners from the pits in Spitzbergen, evacuated during a British raid on the islands, were also employed under the Hoy hills. It was September 1942 before the first of these tanks was completed, and the sixth and last was finished and filled in August 1943, bringing the total underground oil storage capacity up to 100,000 tons.

But it was six months later still, in the spring of 1944, before the KHM's pet aversion, the 'muck heap run by the Boom Defence and contractors', was finally replaced, by which time so much money had been spent on it that it was rechristened 'the Golden Wharf'. In 1939 the estimated cost had been put at £35,000 — probably at least £8 million by 1980 standards. Its 600-foot length with depths of water up to 29 feet eased the docking situation considerably, though the need for it had to a great extent passed by the time it was completed. Even in 1943 when it was still incomplete, and again the following year, it handled 97,000 tons of cargo.

Quite apart from the inadequate quay it replaced, piers generally — or rather the lack of them — were a problem round the base. At the outbreak of war there had been only one wooden pier at Lyness — and it was alleged to have been officially condemned as unsafe in 1918. It was, nonetheless, still going strong on VE Day and even after that.

The Navy badly needed something much better, and quickly, so three new piers were commissioned for Ore Bay, two of them, the North Pier and the South Pier at Rinnigal, being of steel construction designed and built by Sir William Arrol and Co. who began work on them in July 1940. The North Pier took only six months to complete and was operational by January 1941, the one at Rinnigal taking longer but still being ready by October 1941. The West Pier was Admiralty-designed of concrete construction, built by Balfour Beatty. It took much longer to construct, not being finished until November 1942.

The North Pier was used mainly for the naval ferries operating on a regular schedule round the Flow, and for the water boats and provision ships, as well as for landing libertymen off the destroyers moored in Gutter Sound so that they could stretch their legs and enjoy what amenities there were ashore. West Pier was used by small craft and tugs, while stores and hydrogen bottles for the balloons were landed at Rinnigal. In the end, none of the three piers was considered to be entirely satisfactory for the very heavy volume of traffic and passengers they subsequently had to carry.

On Flotta, Gibraltar and Sutherland Piers were constructed of stone and concrete respectively, as well as a tubular steel jetty on Roan Head opposite the Calf of Flotta known as the Clubhouse Pier — the Officers' Club and Golf Course, as in the First War, being in this area. It was July 1943 before Gibraltar Pier was ready.[7]

Another Flotta pier had been built of concrete by the military in Pan Bay just before the war, but was of little use as vessels of any size at all could get alongside only at the top of the spring tides. It rejoiced in the name of 'The Folly', sometimes with the addition of the name of the man who was thought to have been mainly responsible for its design and siting.

The Navy, of course, also used the peacetime civilian piers

at Longhope, Scapa, and St Margaret's Hope, while the balloon barrage trawlers docked at Holm Pier. Stromness Harbour and its piers were mainly the province of the Army.

There was yet another, and important, wooden jetty at Houton, one of the Mainland terminals for the two-hourly ferry service operated by the Navy throughout the war and even afterwards for a time, used by service personnel but also available to civilians. There were four main Scapa Flow ferry routes — Lyness to Scapa Pier, usually operated by the *Sir John Hawkins;* Lyness-Longhope; Lyness-Houton-Stromness-Flotta-St Margaret's Hope; and Lyness-Fara-Cava. The South Isles have never had a better ferry service.[8]

In August 1940 while all this expansion and reconstruction was going on, Rear Admiral P. Macnamara replaced Rear Admiral Lyster as Rear Admiral Scapa, in charge of building up the Base and its administration. There was plenty to build up and administer, with the total number of shore-based naval personnel on the pay roll standing then at 12,500.

The 'crew' of HMS *Proserpine,* the Lyness Base, was housed in two camps at Haybrake, but it was March 1942 before the HQ offices nearby were completed and occupied. The CO *Proserpine* by this time was Captain C. B. Amery-Parkes and it was 18 months later still, in September 1943, before the main naval HQ and Communications Centre for the Scapa Base at Wee Fea was ready and manned by ACOS and his staff. ACOS was now Vice-Admiral L. V. Welles, who had taken over from Binney in January 1942.

The Communications Centre was the culminating point in this vital sphere of wartime activity at Scapa. In 1939 there had been only a few telephone and teleprinter circuits round the Base, along with wireless telegraphy (W/T) operating from the submarine depot ship *Greenwich* and the *Iron Duke*. After the *Iron Duke* was bombed and beached, the communications staff were moved ashore to operate from very cramped temporary quarters. What was known as a 'copper ring' had been installed round the Flow by the Post Office just before the war for the Navy which, it was claimed, provided a telephone service equal to that of a small town.

Unfortunately, with the services working in their own watertight compartments, the Army apparently knew nothing of this facility for quite a time, and it was only when war broke out that they were connected up with it.[9] Even as late as March 1940 the Army was complaining bitterly about jammed telephone lines during the first spring air attack. Now with the new Centre at Wee Fea all defence sectors in the Scapa perimeter were in direct communication by phone and by radio telephone (R/T). Not surprisingly the communications staff for this ACOS HQ rose from 80 in November 1939 to 270 in 1944 — 230 of them WRNS — who handled 8,800 phone calls a day in 1943 and 1944.

All the main fleet buoys in the anchorage, such as 'A' buoy for the C-in-C's flagship, were connected by underwater cable to the Centre and thence to the outside world, while the 'copper ring' of earlier days had been supplemented by a submarine cable right round the Flow. Scapa was, incidentally, the first communications centre to operate teleprinters over a radio link instead of by the normal land line. It was first used between Orkney, Shetland and the north of Scotland as early as 1940, long before Wee Fea was built.[10]

The first girls of the WRNS arrived at Lyness in January 1943 but they had been in Orkney long before that. The official Naval account of their arrival in the islands is couched in rather peculiar terms, saying: 'The first WRNS came minus uniforms, very seasick and with an abysmal ignorance of all things naval, in 1939.'

They served at Hatston and HMS *Pyramus* in Kirkwall, their quarters being substantial huts built in Buttquoy Park, which was still known as 'the Wrennery' long after the war when the huts became temporary housing for Kirkwall Town Council. They also served at the Twatt and Grimsetter aerodromes (HMS *Tern* and *Robin*).

The official record of their service in Orkney is again ambiguously worded, stating: 'The WRNS who served in Orkney and Shetland have probably been more directly in contact with the Navy than any others in the British Isles.'[11] A statement of fact, no doubt, but one which might have been more felicitously phrased.

HMS *Proserpine* was, incidentally, in two parts. Lyness was obiously the main one, but there was also a *'Proserpine Thurso'* dealing with the railhead and Scrabster terminals of the communication system between the Base and the south. It also had out-stations, mainly radio and radar, at Cape Wrath, Bower and Wick. One of its main concerns was the handling of the 'Jellicoe Specials', the troop trains which ran daily, or rather nightly, between Euston in London and Thurso, carrying personnel of all three services north to join their ships and units, or south for welcome leave or posting.

Like their predecessors of the First War, after which they were named, these 'Jellicoes' had their problems. Early in 1940, for instance, the north of Scotland was more or less blotted out by blizzards. One 'Jellicoe' left Euston about 8 p.m. on 3

February — it arrived in Thurso on the 8th, having taken four days on the 120-mile section of line between Inverness and Thurso alone. No doubt its weary occupants were glad to enjoy the hospitality of the Royal and Pentland Hotels in Thurso which catered for the travelling troops up until 1942 when the official Transit Camp was opened.[12]

It happened again in February 1941, when all army leave was stopped owing to the line being blocked by snow. Churchill, by this time of course Prime Minister, just managed to get through in his special train going south before the Highland Line became completely impassable. He had been paying his third wartime visit to the Home Fleet in the Flow, having travelled north to wish Lord Halifax God-speed as he left aboard Britain's newest battleship, HMS *King George V,* to take up his appointment as Ambassador to the United States. The Prime Minister was accompanied by Mrs Churchill and by Harry Hopkins, President Roosevelt's confidant and personal emissary. Pearl Harbour and the United States' entry into the war, of course, was still nearly a year away. After seeing Halifax off, the Churchills and Hopkins inspected some of the ships and defences when Mrs Churchill 'excelled all others in nimbleness of skipping and scrambling from one destroyer to another', but — 'Hopkins nearly fell into the sea,' according to Churchill himself, writing in Volume III of his *The Second World War — The Grand Alliance.*

A fortnight later, leave from Orkney was interrupted again when the railway line near Invergordon was blocked by enemy action, presumably bomb damage.

During 1942 and '43 HMS *Proserpine* spawned two other 'ships', HMS *Pomona* and HMS *Pleiades,* thereby along with Northern Patrol's HQ, HMS *Pyramus* (the Kirkwall Hotel), minding the Navy's classical 'Ps' and leaving the more earthy 'Q' Plan to the Army.

HMS *Pleiades* was the Drifter Pool, with its HQ on board the *Dunluce Castle* controlling about a hundred drifters and trawlers at the peak, as well as a fleet of smaller craft and the ferry services round the Flow.

A number of motor fishing vessels (MFVs) were specially designed by the Admiralty for such drifter patrol and communications work in time of war, with the idea that in peacetime they could be used by the fishing industry as true drifters. As it turned out, however, they were like many other dual-purpose ideas — not much good for either. The Drifter Pool found that the traditional steam drifters of the north-east coast fishing ports were far and away the best possible vessels for this arduous naval work, just as they had been in 1914-1918.

After the war the fishing industry did not show any great enthusiasm for the new MFVs either, and two of them ended up as the ferries *Hoy Head* and *Watchful* on the Orkney South Isles run where they did yeoman service though they could hardly be described as the acme of luxury from the passengers' point of view.

HMS *Pomona* was the Boom Defence Command responsible for the 6.51 miles of steel nets and buoys in and around the Flow. The three main booms across Hoxa, Switha and Hoy Sounds had all been laid, if somewhat incompletely, just before the war; now they were finished off and, in fact, had two lines of nets across each channel as well as other booms inside the Flow itself, such as the one between Hunda and the Calf of Flotta which thickened up the Hoxa obstructions.

Scapa Boom Defence, which for a time had the former London County Council (Metropolitan Asylums Board) training ship *Exmouth* as a depot ship, employed 1,100 RN personnel and 130 civilians working on 16 special boom defence vessels with their easily recognisable hauling gear forward, looking like some sort of primeval sea monsters with long blunt snouts, as well as a dozen trawlers. It was hard tedious work, either lying at the booms to open and close the gates for the Fleet or having to turn out in vile weather to repair nets damaged by heavy seas or perhaps by one of the ships making a hash of going through the gate, as the battleship *Prince of Wales* did in October 1941 when she put the Hoxa boom out of action for some time.[13]

Later the *Exmouth* became a depot ship for submarines and it was during this phase of her career that a submarine rating on board claimed 'that he had been told by God to fire a torpedo!' And obeying that Divine injunction he had done so, much to the consternation and annoyance of such slightly lesser deities as Commanders RN and Chief Petty Officers.

Protection of the Fleet in harbour against real attack by torpedo-carrying aircraft exercised the minds of the naval staff at Scapa for quite a long time, and they never really solved the problem. Smoke screens laid by the ships themselves were tried out and later smoke generators were based on Cava, but the efficacy of these naturally depended on wind direction.

Another idea was to put a six-mile-long screen of 30-foot-high anti-torpedo baffles mounted on Tank Landing Craft (LCTs) round the anchored fleet, but this was not a success. They proved a menace in bad weather and the KHM reported that 'so far as is known they never caught any torpedoes but they did catch quite a number of ships which dragged . . . during one or two of the numerous gales'. There was a general sigh of relief in HMS *Proserpine* in 1944 when the imminent D-Day landings in France demanded all available LCTs for their primary purpose of putting tanks ashore in France — and in any case by that time the danger of aerial torpedo attack on Scapa seemed to have receded.[14] Fortunately it never happened anyway.

Moorings for the different classes of ships were pretty widely spread throughout the anchorage, most of them having been laid and allocated before September 1939. By 1943/44 the general scheme had settled down with the capital ships south-west of Fara, the escort carriers and cruisers south of Cava, and the destroyers in Gutter Sound. Oilers anchored north of Cava with ammunition ships west of it, while depot and supply ships moored east of Ore Bay and in West Weddel Sound, with minesweepers in Outer Hope. For a time, while the anti-torpedo baffle scheme was being tried out, the LCTs with their own temporary tubular steel jetty at North Ness were moored in Inner Hope, Longhope itself being a general anchorage. For its own Base vessels HMS *Proserpine* had moorings more or less separate from those of the Fleet proper, with store, depot and hospital ships in Gutter Sound, West Weddel Sound and Longhope, while boom defence ships and some minesweepers were allocated Rysa Sound.[15]

For off-shore defence, the first controlled minefields had been laid as part of 'R' Plan during 1940, and work on these and the associated indicator loops continued, with double-banking of the minefields at the main entrance as well as of the booms themselves. Hoxa, for example, got its second controlled minefield in January 1941, and the doubling up of the Hoy Sound minefields took place between the Clestrain shore and Bring Head in Hoy shortly afterwards. There was also a very sensitive indicator loop in this area, Loop 13, which could record even small wooden craft, and just south of it was a line of depth charges which cynics said was 'intended at least to scare the enemy'.

Indicator loops had been established further out in Hoymouth in 1940, with their shore station near Stromness, but they were never very successful, being frequently damaged by the strong tides in this exposed position. None of them survived any of the five winters without having to be replaced, but a radar station at Breckness in Outertown taken over later by the Army operated successfully right through until it was dismantled in 1945.

Harbour Defence Asdic (HDA) was another system for detecting submerged U-boats to be tried out from Flotta in early

1940. This was the very successful Asdic used on destroyers, corvettes and escort vessels adapted for use from the shore. Two more were used inside Hoxa Sound from July 1942, and later still in 1944 yet another two were tried further out to sea, but the tide swirls provided some very strange and false indications of contacts and so did shoals of fish. By autumn of that year it was decided that HDA was not entirely satisfactory in Orkney conditions, and the Navy reverted to their more traditional and proven methods of detection from land.

The controlled mine loops themselves quite often became defective and dangerous and the only way to get rid of them was to press the button and let them blow themselves up with, it was claimed, 'definite advantage to morale'. Apparently there was nothing quite so good as a nice big harmless bang to cheer up the troops. Then, of course the loops had to be relaid by the base ships, *Helvig* and *Alca,* a more or less annual chore. The Scapa Minelaying Command was also used for experimental work.[16]

In this waiting period after the 1940 raids, the Army was by no means idle either, but continued to build up both the AA and Coast Defences as well as preparing for possible invasion. In addition to the Z Battery of what the traditional gunners regarded as unguided, or even misguided, AA missiles, the Vickers LAA guns were replaced on many sites by the more efficient 120 rounds-a-minute Bofors which fired two-pound, graze-fuse shells.

Training and the prevention of boredom became of paramount importance for all units, and for the gunners practice shoots were carried out on Borwick Hill on the west coast between the Bay of Skaill and Yesnaby where the Navy also had a firing camp for HA guns, mainly their pompoms.[17]

By the end of 1940 four HAA gun sites, two in Hoy and one each in Flotta and on the Mainland, had been equipped with radar GL, and not long afterwards radar control of some searchlights had also been introduced, although sound location remained the standard method of controlling lights until the lights themselves became obsolescent.

It was now ordained that the famous Scapa Barrage would only be fired 'if three or more aircraft attacked', and it would consist of two minutes gunfire at heights of 1,500 feet to 2,000 feet, mainly to deal with a first wave of raiders in conditions of poor visibility and to deter dive-bombing and torpedo attacks.[18]

During 1942/43 both HAA and LAA defence of Twatt and Grimsetter airfields was stepped up, the guns coming from, among other places, Carness, where they were replaced by dummies, while as early as April 1943, with the period of light nights beginning, two searchlight batteries were sent to England and not replaced, the Scapa AA lights being thinned by nearly a half to 48 sites.[19] It was the shape of things to come, but in the meantime particular attention was being paid to the camouflage of the remaining isolated sites which had frequently been selected for unwelcome attention by the Luftwaffe.

Ground defence of Skeabrae airfield was taken over by the RAF Regiment, so relieving the infantry units which had been performing these guard duties. There was already co-operation between the Army and the RAF who, since the beginning of 1941, had been working together in the joint Gun Operations and Sector Control Room just outside Kirkwall for the co-ordination of guns and fighters during air attacks or intrusions by reconnaissance aircraft. There was another and rather unusual example of inter-service co-operation when LAA, searchlight and balloon detachments became responsible for lighting beacons on the foreshore so that the Fleet could pick up moorings when it came into the Flow during the hours of darkness.[20]

Static beach defences against invasion were established by the Army in a number of areas, including the Bay of Meil and Berstane Bay to the east of Kirkwall where there were landmines and barbed wire; Inganess Bay where anti-tank obstacles were constructed and a minefield planned to cover Grimsetter airfield; while Dingieshowe at the head of Deer Sound also had strong defences with concrete anti-tank 'dragons' teeth', steel hurdles and covering infantry positions. The infantry units during 1941 included 9th Gordons at Tormiston, Dounby, Waithe, Orphir and Binscarth; 15th Argyll & Sutherland Highlanders at Ayre Mill, Mayfield, St Mary's (Holm), Towerhill and Sunnybank (both St Ola); B Coy 12th HLI at Skeabrae and B Coy Royal Scots Fusiliers at Lyness.

But the opportunity to follow the advice of the Commander of OSDef, Major General Kemp to his troops early in 1941 to 'live dangerously, take risks and to Hell with Safety First' fortunately never came in its most acute form, although the Commander's exhortation did elicit the query 'Us, too?' from the ATS girls.

CHAPTER 35

Salvage Operations

THERE WAS an important arrival in the Flow on 26 August 1940 when the *Admiralty Floating Dock (AFD) No. 12* picked up its moorings in Gutter Sound. It could take any ship up to the 1,500-ton Tribal class destroyers and it did not have long to wait for its first customer which was, in fact, one of the 'Tribes', the *Bedouin* which went in for repair on 9 September, followed not long afterwards in November by another destroyer, the *Mendip,* the whole of whose stern had been blown off by a depth-charge. In December the dock was joined by a 30-ton floating crane.

By the time *AFD 12* left Scapa for the Far East in June 1945 it had handled 345 ships, including 263 British destroyers and 80 assorted submarines, trawlers, corvettes and frigates as well as some US and USSR destroyers, the last ship docked being HMS *Onslow* — on VE Day.

Closely associated with the floating dock, of course, were the salvage operations of the Base and quite naturally these increased in volume as the stress of war brought ever more hazardous conditions, not only to warships but perhaps even more to merchantmen. Metal Industries Ltd, after the prodigious feats of raising so many of the First War German Fleet from the bottom of Scapa Flow, was probably the most expert and certainly the most experienced salvage organisation in the world — and it was on the spot.

Only a few weeks before the outbreak of war the firm under its renowned Chief Salvage Officer, Thomas McKenzie, had raised the 26,000-ton battlecruiser *Derfflinger* from her 150-foot-deep resting-place between Cava and Hoy. With war imminent she was towed, bottom-up, and moored in shallow water off Rysa, there to await events — and the events lasted six years till peace came again and she could be taken south for breaking. Metal Industries had been about to pull out of Scapa after raising the *Derfflinger* as the Navy wanted to clear Lyness and the Flow generally, pending the arrival of the Fleet should war come.

It came perhaps a bit sooner than expected and Metal

Industries were still there — fortunately for the Navy. Their floating crane was soon in demand and so were the firm's two salvage ships, *Metinda* and *Bertha*. The firm's divers carried out the first survey on the *Royal Oak* just after she had been sunk, and they started salvage operations on the old *Iron Duke* immediately after she had been bombed and beached near Lyness during the first air-raid in 1939. Her quarter-deck was under water and she had a 20-foot hole in her port side open to the sea. It was a unique experience for some of the salvage men who were all familiar enough with battleships, but for quite a few it was the first time they had seen the inside of a submerged warship the right way up, having always worked on the capsized German vessels. Soon the two MI ships were joined by others, *Salvage King, Indefatigable, William H. Hastie* and a couple of the ubiquitous drifters.

On 1 June 1940 Metal Industries took over all Admiralty salvage work in the area, though still retaining civilian status, and McKenzie, who later held the rank of Commodore, became Chief Admiralty Salvage Officer for the North of Scotland, Orkney, Shetland and for a time Faroe, where he established a salvage base in Torshavn during 1942/43. It was a big enough area of ocean, hostile in more senses than one, even for a man of his genius.

He and his teams proved their worth in the first year of their Admiralty work, during which period they carried out successful salvage operations on 19 naval vessels, including two cruisers, five destroyers, and 18 merchant ships totalling 74,000 tons gross. One of the first casualties they attended to was the troopship *Arama* which was refloated after running aground on Cava in June 1940.

During the entire six years of the war Metal Industries carried out no fewer than 2,247 operations including the clearing of 435 propellers and the recovery of 147 anchors, and among the many other objects they brought up from the seabed were the remains of the electrically propelled torpedoes which sank the *Royal Oak,* so establishing beyond doubt that it was enemy U-boat action which caused the disaster and not sabotage. The firm's repair depot at Lyness carried out in all some 8,487 major or minor repairs to auxiliaries and merchant ships.

In spite of the hazards of war, bad weather rather than enemy action caused most trouble to shipping in the area. For instance, nine merchant ships went ashore through stress of weather in one night during November 1941. And during another period of storm in December 1942 two cruisers, one RFA tanker, one collier and a drifter fouled baffles at the booms, and two other merchant ships also ran aground — all in one dark, dirty night. As Mackenzie wrote later, 'these were two occasions on which salvage resources were somewhat stretched.' And that is a masterpiece of understatement.

The most difficult time experienced by Mackenzie and his salvage men came during a period of very foggy weather in August 1944. Describing the incident, or rather incidents, the Navy's dossier on Scapa, probably quoting Mackenzie's own words, says:

> Never before had so many ships been in such difficulties in the Pentland Firth as there were on this occasion when two American convoys met in the thickest fog for years.
>
> Some ships were in collision twice, many ships anchored in impossible places steaming at full speed with both anchors down, alternately ringing their bells and blowing their whistles, while others spent their time steaming in ever-decreasing circles. On such rare occasions as the fog lifted for a few minutes the sight which presented itself was indeed fantastic.

Strangely enough, out of all this maritime mayhem no ships were lost, or perhaps it would be more accurate to say that none were sunk — they were certainly lost. Two were brought into the Flow very badly damaged, one of them with only a foot of freeboard. The *Goldsmith* was refloated from Little Skerry and the *Alexander Ramsay* from Holburn Head just outside Scrabster, but the others, nearly all scarred to some extent from their encounters with one another but still afloat, proceeded on their way, presumably rejoicing. It must have been a nautical nightmare.

Some of the other vessels requiring attention from time to time included the 10,000-ton Danish tanker *Danmark,* torpedoed in Inganess Bay early in 1940 by *U 23* commanded by Lieut. Commander Otto Kretschmer, one of Germany's U-boat aces like Prien; the Greek destroyer *Adrias,* refloated from Stroma in August 1942; the cruiser *Argonaut* which ran aground a few weeks later; the Norwegian tanker *Vardefjell,* torpedoed off Kirkwall in January 1943, her after half being towed in to Inganess Bay; the escort carrier *Chaser,* refloated after running aground inside the Flow itself in July 1943; the hospital ship *Dinard* which managed to run aground twice in Longhope and which was refloated on both occasions; and yet another escort carrier, the *Nabob,* which was patched up in Scapa after being torpedoed at sea in August 1944.

And then, putting them down instead of lifting them, Metal

Industries sank a dozen blockships across the various channels before the Churchill Barriers were complete. They were still operating for the Admiralty after VE Day and, in fact, they refloated yet another American Liberty ship, the *Eugene T. Chamberlain,* from Auskerry where she had run aground, on VJ Day.

CHAPTER 36

The Kirkwall Base

HMS *PYRAMUS*, the requisitioned Kirkwall Hotel, HQ of the Northern Patrol and Contraband Control, was perhaps not, strictly speaking, part of the Scapa defences but it was nevertheless closely associated with them. The cruisers of the Patrol, ranging wide into the North Sea and Atlantic, stopped and searched any ships which aroused suspicion of trading with the enemy. In cases of doubt they were brought in to Kirkwall where the Contraband Control took over to ensure that neither enemy personnel nor material useful to the enemy slipped through the blockade. It was a job that often caused considerable friction among the neutrals whose ships were detained. On occasion there might be anything up to a hundred merchantmen ranging from 1,000 tons to 20,000 tons lying in Kirkwall Roads, waiting for clearance. Tankers, and there were sometimes ten of them, had to wait in Inganess Bay or Shapinsay Sound, being segregated for obvious safety reasons from the harbour installations and other ships.

The Contraband Control arrived in Kirkwall on 16 September 1939 and Vice-Admiral Max Horton, whose exploits in the Baltic as a submarine commander during World War I had brought him great renown, took over command of Northern Patrol in October. He was to earn even greater fame later on in World War II as the victor of the Battle of the Atlantic against the U-boats, when he was C-in-C Western Approaches.

Attempts to protect the Contraband Control anchorage by booms were unsuccessful. Nets were laid from Thieves' Holm off Carness and from Stromberry in Shapinsay to meet in the middle of the String, but this idea failed utterly owing to the tideway and they had to be sunk almost as soon as they were laid. Another boom from Rerwick Head in the East Mainland to the Fit o' Shapinsay was also tried in an attempt to close the String but it did not stand up to the weather for more than a few months, so it too was abandoned and the Navy relied on A/S indicator loops and controlled minefields to cope with any U-boat intrusion from then on. These were laid from Rerwick

Head to Hacksness in Shapinsay to close the String, and from Galtness on the other side of Shapinsay and Gairsay to seal off the northern approach to the harbour.

In Kirkwall itself which the Navy more or less took over at the outbreak of war, accommodation was at a premium in the early days, and not only the Kirkwall Hotel but also the St Ola and Queen's Hotels were requisitioned. Meil's fish store on the Ayre Road and the shipping stores on the pier were taken over by the Navy's supply department; the ground floor of the Masonic Hall in Castle Street was earmarked as a Sick Bay and the top floor of Messrs Flett & Son, Anchor Buildings, just across from the Base HQ, became the Naval Mail Office, and later the Base information centre and library was also housed there. In addition a hutted camp was built at the Willows where the Infant and Primary Schools now stand, and there was another for the WRNS at Buttquoy which up till then had been an open field. Both of these, along with the hutted quarters at Hatston, became temporary housing schemes after the war, helping to solve or at least alleviate Kirkwall Town Council's immediate post-war housing problems.

Kirkwall's normal pre-war water supply system from the catchment on the side of Wideford Hill was quite inadequate for the needs of the increased Services population. In fact, at times it had hardly been adequate for the normal civilian population before the war. And to make matters worse the ships anchored in the Bay also had to be supplied.

The nearest additional water in any quantity was the Kirbister Loch in Orphir, six miles away and the Admiralty put in a pumping station there, laying pipes to the Kirkwall catchment reservoir, at a cost of some £100,000 — about £2½ million by 1980 reckoning. So, the ships and the Navy got their water and the town got a more adequate water supply when peace came — everybody was happy except the Navy, who had put in the new installation, especially when the Admiralty discovered that the Town Council was still charging them the full water rates, or at least trying to. Admiral Macnamara was to write in the story of the Base: 'This is almost the sole occasion in which Orcadians have been known to make a near illegitimate profit out of the war.' There is no indication of how significant that word 'almost' might be in his statement.

The Admiralty also put in hand a scheme for supplying Lyness with extra water by tapping Heldale Water on the other side of Hoy in February 1940. Both sources of supply are still being used.

Admiral Horton and most of his staff left Kirkwall in

January 1941 and the minefields to the eastward were abandoned in July 1943, the last of the Contraband Control staff having left in May 1942; but HMS *Pyramus* continued to 'sail' on until October 1943 when it ceased to be an operational unit, and in 1945 a WRNS officer took over command.

CHAPTER 37

Off-Duty

AS THE ENEMY intrusions grew smaller and less frequent, so the threat from that other insidious foe, boredom, loomed larger among the troops who, though much nearer geographically to their families in the south than their comrades-in-arms overseas, still felt tantalisingly far from home — so near and yet so far, with the stormy Pentland Firth in between. The majority found themselves in uncongenial surroundings which could at times be malevolent and were certainly unfamiliar to people brought up in big cities or in the softer atmosphere of the English countryside where the sun was warmer in summer and the wind neither so violent nor so cold in winter, and where there was little or none of what Orkney's unwilling guests described as its gale-borne 'horizontal rain'. Keeping comparatively warm and dry through the island winters became a major preoccupation, especially when it was alleged that Orkney's climate consisted of 'nine months' winter and three months bad weather'.

Sometimes all this brought on feelings of deep depression which soon earned itself the designation of 'Orkneyitis', an acute form of 'browned-offness'.[1] It was not a new complaint. Orcadians themselves, or at least a few of them, had suffered from something very like it in the past and had even dignified it by the name *melancholia Orcadensis.* The symptoms, and possibly the cure in those otherwise happier times, was for the sufferer to retire to bed with piles of books and other creature comforts at the onset of winter and to remain there until spring was well advanced the following year — a form of hibernation, in fact.

This, of course, was not a practical proposition under wartime Service conditions — unfeeling and unsympathetic sergeants would see to that — but nonetheless everything else possible had to be done to maintain the morale and health, both physical and mental, of the thousands of troops cooped up and isolated in small islands with not too much enemy activity to occupy their minds. Training in their military skills had to be maintained but too much of it could be counter-productive, for staleness can sap efficiency and alertness just as badly as lack of practice.

Entertainment and sparetime activities were extremely important, but perhaps even more so was freedom from worry about health. They must be kept fit with sports and other physical activities, but they also had to be sure that if anything did go wrong there were the medical staff, the hospitals and the equipment to deal with such situations, be it injury or disease. Fortunately there were few serious epidemics apart from an outbreak of meningitis very early in the war which claimed some lives, and as there were few military hospitals at this time, the cases, which were mainly from the Army, were often treated aboard the Navy's hospital ships.[2]

At the outbreak of the war in 1939 the Navy's Sick Bay at Lyness consisted of two small wooden huts where patients had to wait outside in the very open air for attention and treatment. Early in 1940 the hospital ships *Varna* and *Amarapoora* arrived in the Flow and a Military Hospital was also set up in Kirkwall which, like all the medical establishments in Orkney, provided treatment for patients from all three Services and also for civilians from the various firms of contractors on defence works.

Accommodation was still inadequate but the position was eased in October 1940 when Sick Quarters with 66 beds, subsequently increased to 110, were opened at North Ness, three-and-a-half miles from Lyness. It catered for patients from Hoy, Flotta, Cava, Fara and South Ronaldsay although the Army did have a small hospital at Stanger Head and another one in South Ronaldsay, while later there was an Army Camp Reception Station also at Flotta.[3]

The Base Medical Officer, Surgeon Commander I. Cusack, reported that the civilian camps and kitchens were dirty as were the cooks who were also inexperienced, as a result of which there was a large incidence of diarrhoea, scabies and lice among the civilian labour force. This was not so in the Service camps and when, in 1941, all naval personnel in the Base were examined as to general health and cleanliness, the standard was found to be high.[4]

An isolation hospital was opened at Houton in 1941, and Woodwick House in Evie with its wooded policies and sheltered gardens became a convalescent home for navy men including members of the crews of auxiliaries and drifters. It was run by Toc H.

There was also an air ambulance service by two aircraft equipped to carry two 'cot cases' each should specialised emergency treatment further south be required, although most cases were carried by one or other of the hospital ships such as the *Isle of Jersey.* The *Amarapoora* was withdrawn from Scapa in 1943. In addition to the naval Sick Quarters and the main military hospitals in Kirkwall, the Army also had hospitals in Stromness and Dounby and at Kirbister in Orphir, as well as smaller units. The sick Servicemen and women in Orkney during the war were well cared for, and everything possible was done to maintain their health so that they did not often have to use these still very necessary medical facilities. The Navy even went so far as to employ a rat-catcher in Hoy to prevent possible spread of infection, even though rats were seldom seen inside Service camps.

But it was not just physical bodies which had to be looked after; minds needed relaxation and stimulation too. Perhaps the most important item in this context was the introduction and maintaining of regular leave rosters with extra days added to allow for travelling time. In addition, units were changed round every now and again, not only within OSDef itself but within the United Kingdom defences. There was, for instance, a big exchange of AA units during 1941 when some of those brought north under the 'Q' Plan in late 1939 and early 1940 were relieved by equivalent units from the south. Similar changes were also made among the coast defence gunners.

All of this movement kept OSDef's own troopship, mv *Earl of Zetland,* which was normally engaged on the Shetland inter-island service of the 'North' Company in peacetime, very busy on her daily trips between Stromness and Scrabster. During the war years she steamed over 100,000 miles, carrying some 600,000 often very seasick soldiers to and fro across the Pentland Firth. The older ss *St Ninian* from the same Company was, of course, doing similar service for the Navy between Lyness and Scrabster as she had done in the First War, and in World War II she carried half as many men again as the *Earl* at 900,000 or so.[5] And there were quite a few of her passengers too, seamen though they might well be, who were very thankful to see the earth-bound Jellicoe special standing steady and motionless at the platform of Thurso railway station after a dirty crossing.

Leaves, however, were pretty few and far between, even if they were reasonably regular — red-letter days with the intervening grey ones ticked off in eager anticipation on the calendar. But how to fill in the off-duty hours of those grey days? Service people are, as a rule, good at providing their own entertainment and those who were in only for 'the duration' were no different. Indeed, having been drawn from such a wide spectrum of British life, there was an abundance of talent in the Forces and they put it to good use.

OSDef was no exception. With between 30,000 and 40,000 troops, counting the Navy, to draw on, they had their own concert parties, produced their own plays, danced to their own bands and debated the 'shape of things to come' in their own discussion groups; but one big problem was how to give this rather amorphous mass of diverse humanity thrown together by force of circumstances over which they had no control, some sense of unity — of 'belonging', as it were, over and above their military commitment.

Eric Linklater, the Orkney author, at the time a Royal Engineer Major in OSDef, came up with the idea of a garrison weekly newspaper devoted entirely to matters of interest to Service people. There had, of course, been Forces publications like 'The Concentrator' and ships' magazines in the First War, and already by 1940 several small unit journals such as 'The Island Times' of Flotta were springing up; but they catered for just the one unit or group of units and not for the whole garrison. Usually they were duplicated off the battery office typewriter when it was not being used to churn out Part I Orders, and were full of 'in' jokes like a school magazine. They tended to divide rather than unify. The Linklater idea was for a much bigger and properly printed publication produced by professional newspapermen, and there were plenty of them in OSDef. The result was 'The Orkney Blast' which first appeared on 17 January 1941 just a week after its founder and first editor, Eric Linklater, had been posted to the Public Relations department of the War Office in London. There were plenty of aspirants to carry on his work.[6]

One of the team of professional journalists making up the editorial group was Gerald Meyer who had worked in Fleet Street before the war. Along with Alan Richards of 'The Coventry Standard' he subsequently became joint editor for the greater part of 'The Blast's' four-year run. The paper was put together editorially in OSDef HQ in Stromness but printed at The Kirkwall Press each week after the county weekly, 'The Orcadian', had finished its run. After the war, following another spell in Fleet Street, Geremy — which was his usual pen-name — having married an Orkney girl, returned to the islands and for the next 35 years edited that same county weekly.

Finding its way into the most isolated sites and remote units, 'The Blast' was a potent binding force of considerable influence, keeping the garrison in touch with its individual and disparate parts, and with the outside world as well, emphasising and reflecting OSDef's unique 'personality'. It naturally reported and commented on the various social and sporting activities within the garrison, encouraging discussion and criticism among its readership as well as reviewing world affairs and the conduct of the war itself. News of forthcoming attractions in the entertainment world was a regular feature and so were the glamorous pin-up girls, not quite so bereft of clothing as nowadays perhaps, but their 'come-hither' smiles must have gladdened many a lonely heart and made its owner do a re-count on the number of days to his next leave.

Many units took up gardening very seriously as a spare-time activity and as a means of providing the cookhouse with fresh vegetables in season but some of them went even further, straying over into agriculture, with poultry and pig-keeping. Other less sedentary types started up a cycle club with organised outings. 'The Blast' encouraged these activities not only by reporting them but by running competitions like the one for 'best garden', won by a military hospital.

Radio sets for information and entertainment were an important factor in a unit's welfare scheme — no TV in those days of course — and as early as May 1940 OSDef A & Q was reporting a serious shortage of sets. Two hundred were needed.

By that time there were already two mobile cinemas in operation, one in Hoy, the other on the Mainland, and two more were needed at least. Later still more permanent cinemas such as the Naval Cinema in Kirkwall's Temperance Hall and the Strond in Holm were established in main centres, and the Naval Cinema at Lyness went on long after the war until the Base closed down. There were orchestras and dance bands as well as the more formal regimental bands which visited the area from time to time — and dances, dances, dances. As one Kirkwall matron remarked 'forty years on' — 'My, we girls had a marvellous time — dances every night of the week somewhere.'

Drama groups sprang up and organisations catering for even wider artistic interests, like the Kirkwall Arts Club which had sections for art, music and literature as well as drama, provided cultural oases in a wilderness of military life. The Arts Club had its origin among the Fleet Air Arm personnel at Hatston but was open to everyone interested including civilians — and it continued after the war, still going strong nearly half a century later.[7] One of its founder members was the actor Donald Hewlitt who after the war became well known on TV as well as the West End stage, often in military roles.

In addition to all this 'do-it-yourself' entertainment there were the professional shows, with stars of stage, screen and concert hall imported at frequent intervals by ENSA and later by CEMA. In the early days there had been difficulty in getting accommodation for members of professional concert parties coming to Orkney, the '5th Q Plan Progress Report' stating that lodgings in Stromness were costing about £2 2s in 1940, 10 shillings to 15 shillings more than the performers were prepared to pay. An attempt was being made to get more pay for the artistes to cover the discrepancy, and this seems to have been successful.

The 'big names' began to come — and they came in a constant stream, some of the 'biggest names' in show business: names like Leslie Henson who made the King laugh on one of his visits to the Fleet; Tommy Handley of ITMA fame, a household name in those dark days; Vera Lynn, the Forces Sweetheart; Lancashire's and the world's 'lass', Gracie Fields, who sang from the balcony of the Stromness Hotel among other places; George Formby; Flannigan and Allan; Will Hay; Will Fyffe; Evelyn Laye, star of so many glamorous musicals, who shook one small coast defence battery in Hoy by dropping in on them to sing before breakfast; the sophisticated Gertrude Lawrence who starred so brilliantly in Noel Coward roles; and from France, the legendary vivacious Francois Rosay. Earlier there had been Beatrice Lillie, Douglas Byng and Tommy Trinder — it was a scintillating line-up.

On the more serious side there were concerts by Yehudi Menuhin; Pouishnoff, the pianist; Joan Hammond, the soprano; Leon Goossens, the supreme oboeist; the Boyd Neel Orchestra, and many more besides.[8]

They sang, played and performed on makeshift stages in unit canteens and dining-halls away out in the heather, in messes or in more sophisticated surroundings aboard ships — the *Dunluce Castle,* for instance, had a properly equipped 250-seat theatre on board and so did the ss *Autocarrier,* the requisitioned Southern Railway car ferry fitted out as a welfare ship for the Merchant Navy crews of the auxiliaries and DEMS (Defensively Equipped Merchant Ships); but the stars needed real theatres to give of their best. And they got them.[9]

Kirkwall's Garrison Theatre was a massive Nissen hut type of structure near the Ayre Mills, on the site now occupied by the Ortak jewellery workshop. Stromness had one of the first Garrison Theatres at the North End where there is now a swimming pool, and there were others in Flotta and near Lyness, which also had its Globe Theatre built by the Marines. There were, in fact, a number of smaller theatres constructed by the units themselves. They were fully used.

The *Autocarrier* had arrived at Scapa in July 1941 and besides its 230-seat theatre which, like the others, doubled as a cinema when there was no ENSA show and as a church or chapel on Sundays, she also had recreation rooms, an officers' lounge, men's canteen, showers, a NAAFI shop and a licence to sell beer. She was for Merchant Navy men only and was part of the Merchant Navy Welfare Scheme.

Another ship catering for the welfare of seamen was the *Sir William Archibald* of the Royal Mission for Deep Sea Fishermen which was towed to Scapa from Lowestoft in July 1940 and anchored in Ore Bay for the use of the drifter crews. She was there for five years, and until the Mission's hut was built ashore she had up to a thousand men on board at one time or another each week.[10]

All over the world during the Second War, and possibly in the first one as well, Servicemen, especially soldiers, seemed to develop an insatiable thirst for tea, hot, strong and very sweet, which they would swill down in vast draughts whenever opportunity permitted, day or night. Oh yes, they would drink beer as well given the chance but 'top of the drinks' was undoubtedly tea. To satisfy this prodigious thirst canteens sprang up all over the area, for the drinkers preferred whenever possible to quench their thirsts in surroundings other than those of their own unit canteens or dining huts — somewhere where there was at least a hint of the civilian life they had left behind them, some place where there were people other than those from the closed society of their own little unit, girls preferably and the older women volunteers who ran the canteens and had the gift of listening sympathetically to tales of woe and perhaps being able to ease the heartache of homesickness and separation.

There was the Pierhead Canteen in Stromness, and the Church of Scotland canteens in the St Magnus Cathedral Hall in Kirkwall and on the Pier Road in St Margaret's Hope, St Mary's Catholic canteen on New Scapa Road, Kirkwall and Toc H in Great Western Road, Kirkwall, which could also provide the luxury of a bath. And there were many more, large and small, some of them the NAAFI's 'wet' canteens which could provide something a little stronger than tea, though some of the connoisseurs claimed it was not all that much stronger. The bar in the Flotta canteen was claimed to be the biggest in Orkney.''

Toc H was a continuation of the servicemen's organisation started in Flanders during World War I by the Reverend Tubby Clayton, who got to know Orkney through his friendship with the Lord Lieutenant, Mr P. N. Sutherland Graeme of Graemeshall, Holm, and also through his association with the Navy. It provided rest centres like the one in Woodwick House, Evie, recreation rooms and as many of the amenities of home life as were possible in wartime conditions. One of them which included the India Room became Kirkwall's peacetime community centre as part of the 'Welcome Home' scheme for returning Kirkwall ex-Servicemen, and there was another called Halifax House, after Lord Halifax, near Lyness. The India Room was so-called because many of Orkney's servicemen had been posted there during the war.

A unique experiment in another kind of canteen was also successfully carried out in Kirkwall during the spring of 1942, when premises and equipment were provided by the Ministry of Labour and National Service on Pickaquoy Road for civilian workmen who had been drafted to Orkney and were engaged on defence contracts. It was opened by ACOS, Vice-Admiral L. V. Welles, who had recently replaced Binney in this appointment, and it was run with great success for quite a long time by the Salvation Army.[12]

All this officially inspired and organised welfare and entertainment played a tremendous part in boosting and maintaining morale in the garrison as a whole, but there was another and quite informal contribution on the personal and individual level which was no less effective. This was the local hospitality offered spontaneously by Orcadians who invited these strangers within their gates into their homes for meals and friendship. There were so many isolated small units often far out in what the troops thought of as the back-of-beyond, but nearly always there was a farmhouse of friendly folk not far away where they were welcome to get their khaki-clad knees under a civilian table which had not suffered noticeably from food rationing.

To be received into a real home was something every Serviceman appreciated, reminding him, as it did, of what he was in uniform to preserve. It had not happened to the same extent in the First War as the 'occupying force' then had been mainly navy men who were either at sea, at anchor out in the Flow or concentrated ashore in the main bases at Longhope, Lyness or Kirkwall. In the Second World War there were at least as many soldiers as sailors in Orkney and they were more widely dispersed among the local people, and as a result there was a considerable measure of integration. Many lasting friendships were forged between Orcadians and their involuntary neighbours which lasted into the peacetime which followed, and indeed, quite a few of the relationships became even stronger and more permanent with some of the troops finding brides among the island girls.

In complete contrast to these informal social contacts there was the other side of the coin in the visits of the great and famous to the Base and its garrison — not so intimate, of course, and sometimes involving extra 'spit and polish' not to mention the troops' pet abomination, 'bull'. All the same, these visitations added welcome variety to the monotony of garrison duties for those involved, though their numbers were necessarily restricted, at least in the early days, for security reasons.

Churchill, as we have seen, was a fairly frequent visitor to the Flow and especially the Fleet as First Lord of the Admiralty and then as Prime Minister. He made two visits in 1941. As well as seeing Lord Halifax off to Washington in the early part of the year he was back again with his full entourage of 'top brass' on 4 August when he boarded the ill-fated battleship *Prince of Wales* — so soon to be sunk by Japanese bombs in the Far East — for his own trans-Atlantic crossing to meet President Roosevelt in Placenta Bay, Newfoundland, for the conference from which emerged the historic Atlantic Charter. Once again Harry Hopkins was with him in the Flow, having arrived, a desperately sick and tired man, from his deliberations with Stalin in Moscow. The C-in-C Home Fleet sent him straight to bed for two days on board the flagship so that he might recoup his strength for the ocean crossing with Churchill.[13]

After the conference Churchill returned to Scapa in the *Prince of Wales* by way of Iceland where he reviewed both British and American troops, arriving back in the Flow on 18 August before returning to London from Scrabster by his special train.

While he was on the other side of the Atlantic Scapa had another very distinguished visitor in the person of King George VI who landed at Hatston airfield on 9 August, having flown north in a bomber accompanied by the most powerful fighter escort ever seen over Orkney. 'The Orcadian' afterwards reported that there had been 'scores of Spitfires and Hurricanes'.[14] He went straight through Kirkwall to Scapa Pier, where he embarked for his visit to the Fleet, and to the Lyness Base where he inspected the 2nd Battalion (Orkney) Home Guard, nicknamed locally the 'Orkney Foreign Legion' because it was mainly composed of civilians from the south working on the various defence contracts in and around Hoy.

He came north to his fleet in Scapa again in June 1942 and then, less than a year later, in March 1943 he made yet another, and peculiarly well-publicised visit to Orkney.

By this time, of course, the Scapa defences were at the peak of their strength and efficiency while the vortex of war was tending to move away from the north, but even so, security over royal visits was usually very tight indeed; but on this occasion, although naturally no official advance notice of the king's itinerary was publicly released, it was a pretty wide open secret in Orkney among both troops and civilians alike. He came into the Flow on board the 36-knot Lightning Class destroyer *Milne,* with an escort which included the Polish torpedo-boat *Orkan,* and was welcomed aboard the flagship, the *King George V,* by the C-in-C Home Fleet, Admiral Tovey, who was about to relinquish his command. He saw the battleships *Duke of York* and *Howe,* both like the flagship of 35,000 tons, and the 5450-ton escort carrier *Scylla,* where he inspected Seafires and Albacores. Altogether he went aboard ten ships, including the 10,000-ton Kent Class cruiser *Cumberland* and the destroyer depot ship *Tyne.*

In the destroyer *Onslaught,* he crossed the Flow to Scapa Pier where he was greeted by ACOS, Vice-Admiral Welles, the Commander OSDef, Major General Slater, who had taken over from Maj. Gen. Kemp in January, the Lord Lieutenant, Mr Alfred Baikie of Tankerness and Sheriff Brown who was CO of the 1st Bn Orkney Home Guard. After inspecting a guard of honour provided by one of the Highland Regiments which had detachments in Orkney at the time, he went by road through Kirkwall where the streets were lined with school children, it being a Saturday, and they having apparently been told the day before that 'a very important person indeed' would be passing through the town. It was also the first time that the Special Constables had appeared in uniform. The king went on to the Fleet Air Arm aerodrome HMS *Tern* at Twatt, and also visited a hospital in the West Mainland before returning to the flagship.

In the evening he landed on Flotta and enjoyed an ENSA show in the Garrison Theatre with a cast led by the comedian Leslie Henson who made him laugh so much that it produced one of the happiest and most relaxed royal photographs of the war. He left by destroyer again next morning after hoisting the traditional signal — 'Splice the Mainbrace.'[15]

George VI was to pay his fifth and final wartime visit to the Flow just before D-Day when he was with his fleet from 10 to 13 May, going aboard many ships as well as putting to sea in the carrier *Victorious,* with the Royal Standard flying proudly at the fore. He was greatly impressed by the landing of some 40 to 50 Barracudas and Corsairs on her flight deck off Orkney.[16] It was on this occasion that there were three crowned heads of state in Scapa Flow at the same time, George VI himself, Håkon VII of Norway and George II of the Hellenes, all of them, of course, connected by marriage.

Apart from monarchs and prime ministers the Flow had plenty of other important visitors in the later stages of the war. A. V. Alexander, First Lord of the Admiralty, who succeeded Churchill in that appointment, was with the Fleet several times from September 1941, including his last trip north in July 1945 when he officially opened the roadway across the Causeways which bear his predecessor's name.[17]

Generals were, if not exactly two-a-penny, at least seen quite frequently in the OSDef area. Sir Alan Brooke, as he was then, had paid a flying visit to Orkney in the summer of 1939 and he returned for a more comprehensive tour of inspection as C-in-C Home Forces in May 1941, a little time before he became CIGS. Montgomery dropped in on one of his morale-boosting visits to troops before D-Day and the GOC-in-C AA Command, Sir Freddie Pile, had a look round what must have been one of his key AA defensive systems, just after Sir Alan Brooke.

Among the clergy visiting the troops were two Moderators of the General Assembly of the Church of Scotland, the Right Reverend Dr J. Hutchison Cockburn of Dunblane Cathedral at the same time as, but not appearing with, Gracie Fields in July 1941, and the Right Reverend A. J. Campbell, Orkney's own Moderator, whose charge was in Evie, who came during August 1945.

CHAPTER 38

The Tumult and the Shouting Die

BY EARLY 1944 Kipling's 'Recessional' began to apply more and more to Scapa Flow. 'The Tumult and the Shouting' had died to a great extent, and even if 'the Captains and the Kings' had not all departed they were certainly getting thinner on the ground as the focus of the war became ever more concentrated on the south of England rather than the north of Scotland, with preparations building up for 'Operation Overlord', the Allied invasion of Hitler's Fortress Europe.

The war, however, was by no means over and the Fleet using its Scapa Base still had to be protected against attack from an enemy only 300 miles away in Norway. The guard which had been so laboriously built up could not now be dropped, although its potency had of necessity to be reduced as the threat of air attack receded to some extent from Orkney while increasing elsewhere. Some searchlights had been moved out of OSDef area early in 1943 and now, almost exactly a year later, in February 1944, three HAA batteries were withdrawn and sent to England where they took the place of units going overseas. They were not replaced. This move marked the beginning of the run-down of the Scapa Flow defences.[1] Several of the gun positions round the Flow were left unmanned.

In June, shortly after D-Day, there was rather an odd instance of 'put and take' with the Navy sinking a couple of blockships in Burra Sound while the RAF were pulling out all the barrage balloons from Scapa to meet the growing menace of the flying-bombs on London. The RAF Regiment's guard on Skeabrae was also withdrawn at short notice for duties further south.[2]

All this time there were constant air-raid alerts and warnings of enemy aircraft approaching the Flow, but they stayed well out of range of the barrage which could still deal a powerful blow and for which the German air crews had a very healthy respect. By December, however, with the war raging on the very frontiers of Germany itself, both east and west, and with the Fleet using the Flow less and less, the danger of an attack had receded to such an extent that the entire 70th HAA Regiment was moved out and sent to England without being replaced. The defences had to be reshuffled but there were now quite a few unmanned gun sites round the anchorage.

Throughout 1944 searchlight crews had been active in a completely different role from that of illuminating targets for the guns — owing to the reluctance of enemy aircraft to come within range, such targets were pretty scarce in any case. The new searchlight role was to provide homing beacons for our own bombers returning to base after being shot up during raids. The method was to expose the searchlights at a low angle pointing directly on the bearing of the nearest airfield, so that the damaged aircraft could fly along a succession of beams until the pilot was able to locate the flarepath of the base. This system of homing could, of course, never be used when there was a danger of the enemy also making use of it to attack airfields. That danger would appear to have been negligible in the northern area by 1944. The last such call for help to be answered by the Scapa searchlight men came at 3 a.m. on 22 December 1944 when a Lancaster bomber, returning from a mission in dire trouble, radioed for beacons and by their assistance was just able to make Wick aerodrome with only a few gallons of fuel to spare.[3]

Three weeks later and such help would have been impossible for all searchlight units of the Scapa defences ceased to be operational, and a week after that, on 22 January 1945, all the guns were taken out of action too, with one exception. In spite of the general withdrawal it was felt necessary to maintain some defence of the Lyness Base with up to 24 LAA guns, and so the RHQ and two batteries of 144 LAA Regt were brought in from Scotland to 'hold the fort' as it were. At the same time 59 HAA Brigade was moved south to the Bristol area, and 29 Searchlight Regt was converted to garrison duties and then withdrawn from Scapa also and sent south.[4]

The War Office now ordered big cuts in the numbers of AA personnel and this was followed by orders for the withdrawal of all remaining HAA, LAA and rocket batteries in preparation for disbandment and possible conversion to new roles, as had already happened to the coast defence gunners in some instances where they had been transferred to infantry regiments or had become field gunners.

Holm Battery's 12-pounders had, in fact, been unmanned and put on a care and maintenance basis as early as 15 November 1943, the Churchill Barriers by this time having rendered any seaborne entry through the eastern channels impossible. Holm's twin-six-pounder was moved and allocated to

South Walls though it seems never to have been mounted. The Burray twin-six went to Graemsay. The days of coast defence artillery generally were numbered and although the guns on the three main entrances to the Flow — Stanger, Hoxa and Ness — remained operational, a move to instal 9.2s at Hoxa never materialised.

With no troops to administer, 58 AA Brigade HQ at Melsetter was disbanded on 14 February 1945, but although the personnel had already been withdrawn, like those of the Mainland-based 59 AA Brigade, which had already been sent south, the guns and searchlights remained in position — just in case — pending the formulation of a new defence policy for Scapa.

A rear party of two officers with gun fitters, limber gunners, cooks and clerks had already been set up to remain behind after the troops had gone, to look after the now deserted guns and other equipment. It formed an HQ with six maintenance parties, including REME personnel, in February and came directly under OSDef HQ.

The two LAA batteries brought up to cover the withdrawal remained on guard at Lyness against possible suicide attacks until the final 'Cease Fire' on 20 May. There had, after all, been just such a 'Kamikaze' attempt at the end of World War I when the submarine *UB 116* tried to force the underwater defences in one last desperate fling and was destroyed in the controlled minefield off Flotta.[5]

The Navy's run-down was almost as speedy and spectacular as the Army's. In April 1944 there was a change of command, Vice-Admiral Sir Henry Harwood relieving Admiral Welles as ACOS. He was to be the last of the four flag officers to hold the appointment during World War II.

A new hutted camp, Haybrake II, opened to take HMS *Proserpine* personnel in June that year but by October another one, Burn Camp on Mill Bay, which had housed the Base Engineer and the Fleet Repair Engineer's office staff, had been evacuated and what few inhabitants it still retained were moved to the already empty camp of 905 RAF Squadron which had moved with its balloons to London.

There was a further reorganisation of naval command in March 1945 as the war in the west moved inexorably towards its victorious climax for the Allies. The appointment of ACOS was dispensed with and the staff reduced. In their place the appointment of Commander-in-Chief (Ashore) was created and the Admiral Superintendent Orkney became Flag Officer Orkney, assuming administrative control of all naval units remaining in the islands. VE Day brought the preliminary steps for the reduction of the Fleet Base and disposal of the huts which had housed the navymen and women through close on six long years of war.[6]

From nearly nothing at all except eight HAA, five coast defence guns, three incomplete booms and an inadequate number of blockships, the Army, the Navy and the Air Force had built up a massive system of defence for the Fleet at Scapa over the years; it was dismantled in a matter of months. It had served its purpose.

CHAPTER 39

Peace At Last

IT HAD BEEN a fine, if hazy, autumn morning round Scapa Flow on 3 September 1939 when World War II began for Britain; it ended at midnight five-and-a-half weary, often tragic years later on a damp, chilly May morning with fog which later turned to torrential rain in Orkney. It was Tuesday, 8 May 1945, VE Day and a national holiday. The next day was a holiday too — and it was wet as well.

For the troops still in Orkney VE Day was said to have been 'like a Sunday' and the soldiers were described as being 'rather glum' as the civilians celebrated, but even these celebrations seem to have been on rather a low key compared with the almost bacchanalian revels in London and elsewhere. Churchill's radio announcement of peace had been thought 'disappointingly brief' but all the ships in Kirkwall and Stromness harbours sounded their sirens and there was a long and thankful 'All Clear' on the air-raid sirens as well — no more heart-chilling 'warbling notes'. But in Orkney the blackout still continued for several days, or rather nights, until the Allies had occupied the Scandinavian airfields used by the Germans and also until all the U-boats had surrendered — just in case . . .

Kirkwall, Stromness and some of the smaller places made what 'The Orcadian' described as 'a plucky if somewhat pathetic show of flags and bunting' which had, of course, been in store since before the war — they were probably last flown on Coronation Day in 1937.

News of the 'Cease Fire' actually reached Kirkwall on Monday, 7 May and was received quietly, with business as usual, for instance, at the Auction Mart, but then for many Orcadian families the war was not over, especially for their menfolk in the Far East where the Japanese were still holding out and were to do so for nearly four more anxious months. Orkney's own 226 HAA Bty, for instance, was engaged in the fighting in central Burma as part of the 101 HAA Regt, its 3.7 guns now turned against ground targets more frequently than aeroplanes. Back home in the islands their kinsfolk lived in a sort of limbo, and it was not until VJ Day on 15 August that Orcadians as a whole felt that they could really celebrate, even though their sons, boy friends and husbands were still on the other side of the world but at least no longer in mortal danger.

Once again there were two days of public holiday, 15 and 16 August, and again there was the sounding of ships' sirens and this time dancing in the streets to the sound of the pipes. As on VE Day there were Thanksgiving Services, and the one in Kirkwall was in St Magnus Cathedral this time — on VE Day it had been in the Paterson Kirk, the Cathedral organ having developed 'engine failure'.

Between the two 'V' Days much was happening in Orkney. The defences round the Flow were being dismantled even faster than after 1918 although not so destructively, the guns and equipment being stored rather than sold off and blown up for scrap. This time, however, there was no great German Fleet sailing into captivity in the Flow although a dozen U-boats were brought in from their wartime lairs in the Norwegian fjords and one of them, the *U 776,* came into Kirkwall with a British crew to go on show to the public in aid of the King George V Fund for Sailors. Speaking at the 'opening' ceremony of this enemy craft, Rear Admiral Macnamara, now Flag Officer Orkney, underlining the importance of the islands to the Navy, said: 'The Fleet based in Scapa Flow was the pivot of this last war and defeated Hitler.'[1]

The First Lord of the Admiralty, A. V. Alexander, opened the Churchill Causeway roads for all traffic on 12 May at Cara in South Ronaldsay, having come from Lyness where he was on an official visit. He was met by the C-in-C Home Fleet, Admiral Sir Henry R. Moore, the Flag Officer, Orkney, along with Rear Admiral Macnamara and the Commander OSDef, Brigadier T. Carson, who had replaced Major General Slater, the command now having been reduced from divisional to brigade status through the withdrawal of troops. The opening ceremony was a bit of a rush job, being apparently slotted into Alexander's programme at the last minute when it was known that he would be in Orkney anyway. It appears that no representatives of any of the local authorities were invited, although the County Surveyor, Mr John Robertson, who had been concerned in the construction of the roads, was present and the Vice-Convener of the County Council, Mr P. N. Sutherland Graeme, on whose land some of the roads were actually constructed, had heard about the ceremony and was also there.[2] It was believed that the Prime Minister, Winston Churchill, had wanted to perform the opening ceremony himself and this would indeed have been appropriate as they bore, and still bear, his name. Orkney had at least got these causeways out of the war — no Government or local authority would have considered building them in peacetime — not to mention a choice of several airfields, quite a few piers and some temporary housing as well as an augmented water supply system which the County Council eventually acquired.

And, of course there were the memories of those six long years of war, many of them sad, quite a few happy, and some frightening.

During the war itself Orkney had fared reasonably well. True, there were the restrictions petty and otherwise which are a concomitant of war, such as rationing of food, fuel and clothing, censorship, travel permits and, for a time, even a curfew, but they do not seem to have been so repressive nor so much resented as in the First War. Perhaps people had become more tolerant and inured to regimentation between the wars, mild though it was by later standards.

Rationing did not present particularly difficult problems to a county whose basic industry was farming; there were always eggs, butter, milk and a chicken or two. Items like sugar, tea and meat, which was rationed from January 1940 until well after the war ended, were short as they were elsewhere but there did seem to be a two-way traffic with members of the Forces — an unofficial give-and-take system which no doubt was without the approval of the authorities, military or civil, but which did make life just that bit easier for all concerned.

Even as early as October 1942 a columnist in 'The Orcadian' was writing:—

> Sometimes people ask if Orkney really knows there is a war on. This question is prompted by a variety of factors. First of all, there is an abundance of food in Orkney. Secondly, there is the ability of the people to go about their normal activities without continually having it in their minds that we are at war, even though the said activities may be closely associated with the war, militarily or otherwise.[3]

But one big difference compared with the First War was that civilians in Orkney came under actual enemy attack, and indeed they were among the very first in Britain to feel the weight of actual war, though it was light compared with the blitz on cities in the south later on.

In November 1944 the County ARP Officer, Alex Doloughan, later to be Deputy Director of Education and deeply involved in youth and community work, reported to the War Emergency Committee that since the beginning of the war the civilian Air Raid Alert had been sounded 65 times although enemy aircraft had been over the area more often than that and, in fact, on two occasions bombs had been dropped when no warning had been sounded. Most people thought the sirens had sounded more frequently but this was apparently not so, according to official statistics. The figures are also borne out to some extent by a comment in 'The Orcadian' during September 1943 that an air raid siren test was to be carried out, adding that the 'sirens have been silent these many moons'.

A total of 228 bombs and two parachute mines fell on land in 16 attacks, three civilians had been killed, 11 seriously injured and five slightly injured. Bombs fell on Hoy and South Ronaldsay five times each; Flotta and Sanday twice; Shapinsay and Burray once each while Suleskerry and Auskerry with their lighthouses were attacked once each with no serious damage. On the Mainland bombs fell in Deerness, Holm, St Ola, Stenness and Tankerness, while Stromness had been machine-gunned along the entire length of the street. Incendiaries had been frequently dropped, setting fire to heather and one stackyard in Stenness.[4]

One problem for the ARP authorities in the early raids was the casual attitude of Orcadians about taking cover and carrying their gas-masks, indeed the Albert Kinema eventually made it a rule that no one would be admitted unless they did have their respirator with them. It was reported in 'The Orcadian' that on the first Saturday evening raid in March 1940 there had been about a thousand shoppers thronging Kirkwall streets when the sirens sounded. Bombs dropped as close as Craigiefield and Hatston but few people took to the public shelters such as the Strynd, a narrow lane which had been roofed over and sandbagged, although the streets did clear apart from the one or two inquisitive citizens who stayed out to see what was happening.[5] The cinema performance just went on and so did a show in the Temperance Hall, but in Hoy a professional variety programme with Beatrice Lillie and Douglas Byng in the cast was interrupted for a short while. In the later raids when the Scapa Barrage was in full blast with shell splinters coming down like iron rain at times, 'having a look' became a very dangerous occupation indeed and, in fact, two civilians in Hoy were injured for this reason during one of the April attacks.[6]

The Orcadians' attitude to these raids was hardly in accord with the German radio's assertion that 'panic reigned in that part of Scotland nearest Norway' — a comment regarded in Orkney

as being about on a par with Hitler's reported announcement
that he intended to 'liberate Orkney and Shetland from the
British Empire'.[7]

The War Emergency Committee to which these statistics
were reported had been set up in June 1941 as the Advisory
Council for the Deputy Commissioner for Civil Defence, Mr H.
W. Scarth of Breckness, who had been appointed on 6 May
1940. It was, in effect, Orkney's War Cabinet dealing with
problems arising between the civilian population and the Forces.
It was not an elected body but included representatives from the
local authorities, the three Services, Civil Defence organisations,
the farming community and business and commercial interests. It
could also co-opt people with specialised skills and knowledge
when necessary. Mr Scarth, an Orcadian himself and a lawyer,
had been County Clerk of Roxburghshire and later became
Convener of Orkney County Council. Towards the end of the
war he joined the Allied Control Commission in Vienna, and Mr
P. N. Sutherland Graeme took over the chairmanship of the
committee. At its final meeting in January 1945 Mr Graeme
recounted what it had done through the war years and the
problems it had had to face.[8]

With Orkney, as he pointed out, the keystone in the
northern sphere of naval operations, so many Service people had
come to the islands that they outnumbered the civilian
population, causing acute housing and accommodation shortages.
This problem had worsened as more civilians and drafted labour
were brought in to work on defence contracts. Orcadians had
sometimes looked on these and the Army as an 'occupation
force', and the sort of friction which could arise was
demonstrated in 1941 when some of the Manchester Regiment
arrived in Orkney direct from garrison duty in Iceland. They had
complained they had been much more kindly regarded by the
Icelanders than by the Kirkwallians. Mr Graeme stressed that
this had not been the general attitude of the county as a whole
but was an example of what was basically a trivial misunder-
standing which the Committee had had to sort out. Another had
been the co-ordination of opening hours between military
canteens and the local pubs.

Bigger problems arose from the congestion on the piers and
in the harbours which had caused many headaches, civilian,
military and naval. Then there had been trouble when the
Artillery carried out shoots over the hills in the West Mainland,
making peat cutting a risky operation. And when the danger of
invasion threatened, the Deputy Commissioner had issued
instructions and suggestions through the Committee as to how

open fields and lochs should be obstructed to prevent landings by gliders and paratroops, and this of course affected the farming community in particular. These were the kind of potential trouble-areas which the Committee with its local knowledge could deal with as it had been a very flexible organisation, Mr Graeme claimed.

One restriction which had proved irksome before the Committee came into existence was the 11 p.m. to 5 a.m. curfew every night, imposed in July 1940 at the height of the invasion scare.[9] Fines of up to £100 could be levied on any civilian found out-of-doors without a police permit and an identity card between these hours — and quite a few late-nighters were quite literally caught out but the fines were usually not more than a pound, although one of them did feel particularly ill-used, having been picked up at 11.10 p.m. One problem the curfew posed was — how to hold a dance when all the girls had to be home by 11 p.m.? It made Cinderella's time-limit of midnight look very liberal. Someone came up with the bright idea — why not start the dances before 11 p.m. and carry on through the night until 5 a.m.? Even without a curfew quite a lot of dancers did not get home before dawn anyway, it was suggested. The idea was tried out first of all in Westray and then in an unspecified parish on the Mainland. It was not a success, according to 'The Orcadian' report which said: 'There were too many people in a small hall and too much 'refreshment' so that a lot had to be carried out and laid out like dead herring.' The rest broke curfew and were home before 5 a.m. with nothing worse than sore heads and a 'ticking-off' from the police. To everyone's relief the curfew was lifted shortly afterwards on 17 August. It had contributed nothing to the anti-invasion awareness any more than the suggestion that Kirkwall's 'Big Tree' in Albert Street should be cut down in order to confuse any German paratroopers who might happen along.[10]

Use of cameras was banned and so were binoculars and telescopes, and there was at least one prosecution when fines were handed out to two men found on the Holm Road with the forbidden instruments. And in November 1940 the term 'horrors of war' achieved an even deeper significance than ever for home-brew enthusiasts with the announcement that no sugar would be made available for the making of their favourite beverage.[11] And it was no use their trying to get a 'cairry-oot' of spirits or wine from the Kirkwall pubs on a Saturday night either, for that too had been banned.[12] In any case the opening hours had been drastically shortened — drinking time was from 6 p.m. to 8 p.m. in the evenings, if there was anything to drink. Perhaps that is

why a labourer in Lyness was fined £5 or 14 days in jail for
'spreading alarm and despondency'.

Another labourer from the south was jailed for 14 days on a
similar charge when he passed on a rumour that a 'north-east
town had been attacked and 300 had been killed'. The permits to
be in Orkney also caused trouble, as when one worker who had
lost his job stayed on without one. He too went to jail for 14
days. And slackers on defence work were not spared. In December
1943 four men engaged on one of Balfour Beatty's contracts,
possibly the Barriers, were found guilty of 'squandering 500
hours on essential work by absenteeism' and were fined amounts
of up to £5.

It was also reported in 1941 that peats were being stolen off
the hill 'by the lorry-load'. Where the fuel for these illicit lorries
had come from to get to the hills was not stated but one East
Mainland farmer some time earlier had been jailed for
'borrowing' Army petrol. There were doubtless others.

The two Town Councils and the County Council continued
to meet at their usual times throughout the war, and Kirkwall
Council on 20 August 1939 had decided that public air-raid
shelters should be provided in the Strynd, the Gas Wynd, the
narrow lane between what is now the British Airways office and
the Aberdeen Savings Bank, Victoria Lane, the Old Castle ruins
which stood in Main Street, The Burn, the lane across from
Leonard's newsagents leading now to the car park, and the
Moosey To'er of the Bishops' Palace. In addition, the power
station then in Junction Road, the War Memorial on Broad
Street and the east window of St Magnus Cathedral were to be
sand-bagged. All street lights were to be put out during the
blackout, but red and blue oil lamps would be placed at
dangerous corners. And a fire pump was to be requested from
the Home Office. The cinema was ordered to close, but at a
special meeting a week or so later this order was rescinded
provided a fireman was on duty during performances.[13]

Then there was the saga of the Peerie Sea dump. For
generations this land-locked stretch of tidal water, once the
winter harbour of viking longships and a potential asset to the
amenities of Kirkwall, had been used as a rubbish tip. In summer
it became not only an eyesore but an affront to the nostrils, as
well as being a health hazard with its rats and flies. Successive
Town Councils reaching back through its stench into the mists of
time had pursued a relentless policy of dither, dump and do
nothing. It was only long after the war, in the 1970s, that the
present boating pond complex came into being.

While Kirkwallians had become inured to its noisome

presence, newcomers were not so tolerant at the best of times, and when these new incomers of 1939 were the Fleet Air Arm personnel at the nearby Hatston airfield and the soldiers who provided their guard, the fat was in the fire — quite literally, as it happened.

The first shot in this 'civil' war was fired by the Commanding Officer at Hatston as early as 13 January 1940 when he wrote to the Town Council complaining about the bad smell from decaying carcases at the Peerie Sea even in winter and expressing apprehension about the danger to the health of his men from the flies in summer should the dump not have been cleaned up by then.

In May that same year the Army joined in when Lieut. Col. Jones of A & Q OSDef wrote to the Council in similar terms, saying that the troops encamped nearby were being affected by the bad smell. He wanted the dump to be set on fire to render it innocuous. The Council agreed to this but insisted that the fire brigade should be in attendance during the incineration — they were pressing for extra fire pumps at the time and they felt this would be an extra lever to move officialdom at the Scottish Office.

It must have been a good fire. Five months later no less a personage than the Commander of all OSDef, Major General Kemp himself, joined in from a considerable height to 'complain about the bad smell' from the Peerie Sea dump as well as the 'smoke and fumes from the fire there'. He wanted the whole thing re-sited in some place where his troops would not be affected — but at the end of 1940 it would not have been easy to find any place on the Mainland out of smelling range of the soldiery. The Council did not agree in any case, quoting the Medical Officer of Health, Dr Bannerman, as saying that it did not present a health hazard.

It did not end there, however. The Army thought up a new approach. The CO 9th Gordons, whose troops were still in their camp at Hatston, wrote to the Council at the end of November about what he called 'The Peerie Sea Dump and Vesuvius', which he pointed out was still burning after having been set alight by the 7th Gordons in the summer, and this in spite of the efforts of the fire brigade to put it out again. In the summer the blaze had not been so important in the light nights but now in the darkness of winter it provided 'an excellent beacon for hostile aircraft', he claimed, asking the Council to move it. The Council, of course, did what all Councils do with a knotty problem when playing for time — remit it to a small committee or to some official. In this case they chose the latter course and it landed in the lap of the Burgh Surveyor, Mr James Couper.

It would appear however, that the dump and its con-
flagration resisted all attempts to move it, for on 13 January
1941 the Council received a letter from an even greater height,
the Senior Naval Officer himself. He pointed out that there was
'considerable glow and sometimes a blaze' from the dump at
night with what he called 'a consequent danger to the Town of
Kirkwall, Hatston Aerodrome and the Gordons' Camp, as it is
well-known that German night bombers will endeavour to attack
any light'.

After that warning shot across its bows the dump disappears
from the Minutes of the Council, as far as the civil war between
the City and Royal Burgh and the Armed Forces of the Crown
are concerned — perhaps the only instance of gas warfare during
World War II; but the same dump continued to advertise its
malodorous presence at the Peerie Sea until well into the 1970s.
But in April 1941 Kirkwall Town Council **did** ordain that its
employees would wear gas masks — if only for familiarisation —
from 11 to 11.15 a.m. every Monday.[14]

Stromness Town Council did not indulge in such internecine
warfare. Two days before war came they decided to construct
public shelters at the Forty-four Steps, Back Lane, Manse Lane,
Graham Place, Alfred Street and Login's Well.[15] They, too, had
ordered the extinguishing of street lights during the blackout, but
in December 1940 there was a slight relaxation of this restriction
when the lamps were painted blue and re-lit. This meant that the
Burgh Lamplighter, Mr William Donaldson, was voted an extra
five shillings a week for the additional work involved.[16]

In general it seems that apart from comparatively minor
tiffs like the Peerie Sea fracas the local authorities and the
Forces got on quite well together, and as we have seen the
civilian population generally and the troops were on good terms
too, again apart from such friction as developed between the
Manchesters and the Kirkwall people. The Orcadians certainly
did their bit with canteens and local hospitality as well as having
such voluntary efforts as the 'Sock-mending Party' which up
until the end of 1942 had darned no fewer than 1,823 pairs of
soldiers' socks, 42 pullovers and 29 sets of underwear — there
are more ways of winning a war than one.

One important aspect of civilian life in wartime Orkney
involving the Councils, the public and the Services was the
number of 'Weeks' — War Weapons Week, Warship Week,
Salute the Soldier Week and many others. These were drives on
a national scale to provide the vast sums needed to keep the war
effort surging along, and every publicity and public relations

AA

effort was harnessed to persuade the already heavily burdened taxpayer to invest still more money in National Savings or, if he so wished, to make outright donations. With a certain amount of razzmatazz they made a welcome break in the monotony of wartime existence with bands playing, big parades, exhibitions, demonstrations of military skills and, of course, dances and social events. One of the first was in August 1940 at the height of the Battle of Britain when Orkney over-subscribed the fund to buy a Spitfire to such an extent that they threw in a Hurricane as well.

At the opening of War Weapons Week a year later, Vice-Admiral Binney, the current ACOS, told Orcadians: '. . . we are able to keep in your waters in the Orkneys a force which is sufficient to defeat the enemy Fleet and to protect the activities of our merchant ships all over the world. Scapa is really the key to the whole thing. Our whole campaign depends on the force that is here. If it were defeated all else would go.'[17] With that reminder ringing in their ears Orcadians over-subscribed that fund too, as they did with those that followed. Warship Week, in which the county undertook to put up the £120,000 needed to build the corvette HMS *Ness,* actually produced more than double that figure, £234,000. The ship was adopted by the county and had her first U-boat 'kill' just before Christmas 1943 and in the meantime Orkney had collected over £300,000 to buy 15 Catalina flying-boats. Immediately following the D-Day landings came Salute the Soldier Week when Orkney pledged itself to equip three paratroop battalions at a cost of £150,000 but, in fact, £256,000 was gathered in, £5,312 in outright gifts. That 'Week' was opened by the Commander of OSDef, Major General Slater, with the Band of the Royal Scots in attendance, and as always on these occasions the Home Guard marched and paraded with the full-time soldiers.

With its long Volunteer and TA tradition, Orkney was justly proud of its civilian soldiers — or should it be, soldierly civilians — an up-dated continuation of the tradition. As we have seen, there had been an immediate response to this new call to arms in the suspense-laden summer of 1940. Orcadians had been among the first to enlist and the first in the country to have defence positions allocated to them. They went from strength to strength throughout the war, raising two battalions although the 2nd Bn covering Hoy, Flotta and South Ronaldsay was composed mainly of contractors' men from the south with about ten per cent Orcadians — hence the nickname 'Orkney Foreign Legion'. It was disbanded early in 1944.

The 1st Bn seems to have been unique in that at one time in

1943 it had an Artillery Platoon equipped with four 75s — the great field gun of the French Army in the First War and still a formidable weapon. This is believed to have been the only Home Guard unit to have had its own artillery — perhaps a recognition of Orkney's Volunteer gunnery tradition. It later became a more mundane mortar platoon.

Besides its ceremonial functions the 1st Bn's more serious duties were to keep watch and ward over the approaches to Scapa Flow and in the islands generally until the regular parades ended at the beginning of October 1944 when the danger of invasion had passed. The official 'Stand Down' came a month later when the Home Guard throughout the country was placed on the Reserve, and in Orkney the occasion was marked by a whip-round for the Red Cross which raised £4,132. The final 'Stand Down' in December saw a muster of 550 men under Lieut. Col. Robert Scarth of Binscarth at a big parade in the Bignold Park, Kirkwall, where it was inspected by the Commander OSDef, Major General Slater, after which they marched through the town with the Lord Lieutenant, Mr Alfred Baikie, taking the salute in Broad Street on a cold wet dismal day. They were headed by their own Pipe Band, and the Band of the Royal Scots was also in attendance.[18] There had been an even bigger parade on the third anniversary of their formation in 1943; when their Pipe Band after the march-past returned to the Bignold Park by way of Clay Loan, the tail of the column was still in Junction Road. But that was all over now. No more spit-and-polish parades, no more 'bull', but no more crawling along damp dirty ditches either, nor freezing in isolated pillboxes waiting for an enemy who never turned up. Now they could sit back and tell each other the tales that old sweats always tell each other while they waited for VE Day and perhaps even more for VJ Day. And while they waited, their thoughts, like those of all Orcadians, turned naturally to the sort of place Orkney would be after it was all over and of how they could best 'Welcome Home' their returning ex-Servicemen and women.

CHAPTER 40

'Sunset'

ORKNEY WAS already a different sort of 'home' from the one these returning Servicemen and women had left, along with their civilian status, those four, five or six years before, and not all the changes were so immediately obvious as the vacant Nissen huts already beginning to rust or the empty gun pits littering the landscape. The mental outlook and attitude both of themselves and of those who had remained behind had changed in varying degrees. At home, as we have seen, the 'occupying force' had been much more closely integrated with the local people than in the previous war. There had been greater opportunities for the exchange of new ideas and opinions between people of widely contrasted experience and from vastly different environments. At the same time those Orcadians in the Forces had become familiar with the wider horizons of the world in greater numbers than ever before. No one would ever be quite the same again.

This broadened vision engendered an atmosphere of restlessness which became manifest during the immediate post-war period in the growing numbers of young people who became dissatisfied with what 'home' had to offer and who sought better opportunities beyond those wide horizons they had come to know in the Services. The so-called 'drift from the isles' gathered momentum as time went on.

It was not, of course, an entirely new phenomenon. Orcadians had long looked overseas to better themselves, but now, with so many having seen what they believed would be the greener grass on the other side of the fence, the pace of this drift began to accelerate. In the 1930s Orkney's population had stayed fairly steady at around 22,000. By 1951, six years after the war, it had fallen but was still around 21,000. Ten years later in 1961 it had dropped dramatically to 18,650 and it continued this downward trend until it touched bottom at just over 17,000 in the early 1970s. Opportunities were just not available in Orkney for ambitious youngsters, or even for the less thrustful. They had to get out.

And so for many of the Orcadians returning in 1946 the

view of 'home' would soon be a distant one from across the wide oceans of the world — a 'home' from whose lack of opportunities they had re-crossed those oceans to escape. But as time passed the view would become more mellow as memories of the islands' drawbacks became softer in the deepening haze of nostalgia, and 'home' would regain some of its romantic appeal for 'there is magic in the distance where the sea-line meets the sky' — but not enough to bring them back again for more than a few weeks every few years or so. In 1946, however, much of this lay hidden in the future.

Those who stayed on in the islands had different problems to face as the rigours of war gave place to a troubled peace and a stern austerity. One major social problem facing Europe as a whole was shortage of adequate housing and although, unlike vast areas elsewhere, little damage had been done to buildings in the islands by enemy action, Orkney had this problem too. It was to be a dominating theme in local affairs for years to come. There was, however, a temporary solution ready to hand in the hundreds of now deserted and empty hutted camps all round the Flow. Few of them could be called desirable residences as they stood, but Orcadians are good at adapting things to their own use. The huts were soon being sold off and many were acquired by local people who dismantled them and then re-erected them in very different guise all over the islands. Usually built up with concrete blocks, many of them became the substantial single-storey houses still seen today around the countryside which may well conceal an inner wooden skin that started off its career as an orderly room or a barrack-room block.

The County Council of the day encouraged this do-it-yourself housing trend — it saved them the trouble of producing a proper housing programme of their own, but the two Town Councils both acquired complete hutted camps in their areas to give them a breathing space while they planned their own schemes. But this all took time with the prevailing shortage of building materials, and some of those who had to wait in these temporary schemes until their real houses were built were often, to put it mildly, impatient and frustrated.

It was not only Orcadians who used these huts for civilian housing. On 3 September 1945 some 250 Frenchmen arrived at Lyness to dismantle the naval huts there and ship them back to the war-devastated areas of France, the French Government having bought them to provide temporary houses. They stayed in Hoy until the spring of 1946, when the last 31 of the contingent sailed back to Calais with the final cargo of huts on 2 May.[1]

Orkney, in fact, had quite an international air that winter

with units of the Polish Army arriving — the 25th Infantry Battalion was at Tormiston Camp in Stenness and at Hillside Camp in South Ronaldsay, and a company of Polish Lancers was at the Brig of Waithe camp.[2] And, of course, there were still quite a few Italian prisoners-of-war around, though an earlier claim in 'The Orcadian' that they were 'thriving on the Orkney climate and in no hurry to go home' is perhaps open to some doubt. But the overall number of troops in Orkney was decreasing all the time through demobilisation and postings.

Early in January 1946 a much reduced OSDef HQ under Brigadier Lawrie moved from the Stromness Hotel to the vacant hutments of the now vacated Fleet Air Arm aerodrome at Hatston, although Movement Control and 1029 Dock Operating Company RE still stayed in the west, along with the Ordnance Corps depots at Deepdale and Navershaw.[3] Vice-Admiral Harwood had, of course, hauled down his flag as ACOS nearly a year before, and the naval command structure had been considerably reduced. Now, in April 1946, Rear Admiral Macnamara who had been so closely connected with the building up of the Base ever since 1940 was also posted away and left Orkney.

On the civilian side, 'Welcome Home' committees had been set up in the various parishes and islands to make arrangements for greeting the husbands, sons, and sweethearts coming back from the Forces as demobilisation got under way.

In Kirkwall and St Ola the aim was to collect £7,000 to provide the welcoming receptions for the homecomers, with the remainder going towards some more permanent recognition of what they had achieved — a community centre perhaps, or an old folks' home, possibly houses for disabled ex-Servicemen: there were plenty of ideas to mull over and discuss. One of the first purchases was, in fact, the former Toc H complex of huts in Great Western Road with the idea of turning it into a community centre so that it would actually be carrying on its role of providing a relaxing meeting place with various amenities, as it had done throughout its six years of war service. It cost £2,250 and the first Welcome Home party was held in it at Christmas 1945.[4] Other areas floated their own ideas of how to greet their returning Service folk both at the time of their return and more permanently.

There was, however, little enthusiasm for making arrangements to celebrate 'Victory Day' in June 1946, though when the day arrived everyone enjoyed the public holiday, the children's sports and so on; but most people had had just about enough of parades and processions to last them a lifetime.[5]

At the beginning of August that year a long naval association with Scapa Flow was severed when the *Iron Duke,* having been refloated from where she had been beached in Longhope, was towed away to Faslane on the Clyde to be broken up. She had been flagship of the Grand Fleet in Scapa when World War I began and Jellicoe came north to hoist his flag on her as Commander-in-Chief. She had sailed from the Flow with him to do battle at Jutland; she was not far away when *Vanguard* blew up off Flotta in 1917, and between the wars she had returned several times. Just before World War II she had come back into Scapa once again as a flagship but not this time in a sea-going role, although she still had a few 'teeth' in the shape of HA guns. Now she was a Base HQ ship until she was bombed and holed in the first Scapa Flow raid by the Luftwaffe and had to be beached, first at Lyness, and subsequently in Longhope where she was still on duty as Base ship HQ for the Auxiliary Patrol of 71/72 Anti-Submarine Drifter Group, a flotilla of Harbour Defence MTBs and occasional flotillas of 'B' type MLs. These craft patrolled inside and outside the booms, round the anchorage itself, and also the exercise areas. For a time in 1945 she also took the minesweepers under her accommodating wing when their parent ship, *Exmouth,* paid off.

During her time in Longhope she had been the source of victuals, clothing and pay for the crews of over 50 vessels of various kinds totalling some 1,600 men. Among other facilities on board she boasted a bakery which produced 1,000 lbs of bread a day and on occasion twice that amount. Now her days were over and she left the Flow for the last time with a crew of only 14 men, piloted by Bill Dass of Longhope, towed by three tugs and *Metinda II* and flying the Red Ensign — not the White, for she was no longer one of His Majesty's Ships. A sad end to a noble career.[6]

She was followed a fortnight later by a former adversary, the *Derfflinger,* which had been waiting bottom-up off Rysa for six years until peacetime made the tow possible.[7]

The departure of the *Derfflinger* cast an economic shadow across the civilian community of Hoy and Walls. After 27 years' association with Scapa Flow, Metal Industries, which had raised so many of these great German warships, announced that they were pulling out of Orkney and concentrating on their Clyde base at Faslane. The move would be completed by early 1947.

About a hundred families in the South Isles and on the Mainland would be affected, and it was estimated that spending power in Orkney would be reduced by as much as £2,500 a week with this close-down.[8] It was the first straw in an economic wind

that became ever chillier and a forceful indication that Orkney
could no longer take full employment for granted; but with no
more sunken ships which could be profitably raised, the
company had little option but to pull out. And this time there
was no Hochseeflotte to surrender and scuttle itself in Scapa.
Only three German escort vessels had been brought to the Flow,
where they were tied up at Lyness waiting to be sold for
breaking. They were joined later by a German destroyer which
was towed in and moored alongside them in Mill Bay, to await
the same fate.[9]

There was still, however, a Royal Naval Base presence in the
Flow — but for how long? Ships such as the ten minesweepers
engaged on clearing the seas, including the North Atlantic, of
mines, did come into Lyness in July and so did the US cruiser
Little Rock and two destroyers about the same time, but other
indications, like the big sale of plant and furniture at Lyness and
Scapa, pointed to a further run-down and possible closure.

The run-down of Army and RAF stores and equipment was
going on apace, too, with sales of huts at Hillside camp in South
Ronaldsay during September, followed by auctions of more huts
and plant such as generating sets and vehicles at Netherbutton,
Skeabrae, Grimsetter and Stromness. In July OSDef, now only a
Lieutenant Colonel's command, had become OSGar — Orkney
and Shetland Garrison — with its HQ still at Hatston but with
Stromness now almost completely 'demilitarised' as more and
more troops headed south to demobilisation, home and civilian
life. The Poles left too in the *St Ninian,* specially charterd to
take them south, but for most of them the chances of an early
return home were remote.[10]

With the minefields around the coast having been swept
there was no longer any need for naval routeing of merchant
ships, so Kirkwall Naval Base announced its closure in December
1946, allowing the Kirkwall Hotel, no longer HMS *Pyramus,* to
revert to its normal civilian function after considerable restoration
and refurbishing.[11]

In spite of the sweeping, mines still came ashore however,
on parts of the coast as widely separated as Copinsay and the
Bay of Skaill, fortunately without causing casualties.

The year ended with a massive disposal sale at Hatston
Military Camp, Caldale RE Depot and other camps round
Kirkwall when 200 cars and lorries, 70 motor cycles and a mobile
crane came under the hammer as well as much other
miscellaneous plant.[12] The war really did seem to be over as
these sales went on at RAF Grimsetter, RAF Ward Hill in South
Ronaldsay, Craigmillar Camp in Stromness, and the big

Command Supply Depot at Deepdale between the Stromness and Dounby roads near the Stenness Loch which was eventually dismantled and closed in February 1948.

Orcadians now once again outnumbered their naval and military 'guests', and the proportion of one to the other continued to swing in the locals' favour. But it was a strange, rather unreal period in the islands' history, the social atmosphere being an odd 'mix' somewhere between the 'now for the hols' end-of-term feeling at school, a sergeants' mess party, and the disposal sale of a firm about to go out of business.

But at least people no longer listened with apprehension for what was believed to be the characteristic uneven throb of German aero-engines, although these were heard again in Orkney skies during 1947 when the three-engined Ju 52 troop-carriers of the Luftwaffe acquired by the newly-formed British European Airways as temporary passenger planes and renamed Jupiters, roared noisily off the Hatston runways on their scheduled and now peaceful missions.[13]

After this war there was to be no gap in the Volunteer tradition of Orkney, for recruiting to a local gunner unit, the 430 (O & S) Coast Regiment RA TA, started up in April 1947 while the Welcome Home receptions for some of the earlier 'Terriers' were still going on — there was one in South Ronaldsay in May that year. The 430 Regt went to Felixstowe for annual camp the following year and also carried out practice firing from Balfour Battery in South Ronaldsay, one of the last times — if not the last — that coast defence guns were fired in Orkney. Coast Defence Artillery was soon to be declared obsolete and the units everywhere were disbanded, but before that the Orkney gunners had converted first to an LAA role and eventually they became infantry, so ending a long gunner tradition.[14]

Although there was no scuttled German Fleet in the Flow this time, there were plenty of sunken ships of one kind or another to raise if the financial incentive became worthwhile — and it did. Britain was short of steel and the British Iron and Steel Federation started a drive in 1948 to produce 14 million tons. The blockships sunk at the entrances to the Flow before the Causeways were built looked like a fruitful source — perhaps as much as 50,000 to 60,000 tons, it was thought.[15]

By mid-February 1948 Arnot Young & Co, Dalmuir, Glasgow were on the job alongside the Causeways with a self-contained salvage ship, the *Miles K. Burton,* which meant that no shore-based accommodation was needed. Metal Industries (Salvage) Ltd, however, although they had pulled out of their Lyness base, were to carry out the actual raising of the hulks under H. Murray Taylor, who had succeeded his father-in-law Thomas McKenzie as MI's Chief Salvage Officer.

The *Miles K. Burton* did not last long on the job. Shortly after she arrived in Scapa she became the victim of bad weather, grounded on No.2 Barrier, and became a total loss. As a result there was some delay in the salvage work but the first blockship, the *Lake Neuchatel,* having been given a new concrete bottom, was raised by Metal Industries in May and towed to moorings under Hunda.[16] Two more, the *Juanita Thorden* and the *Caroline Thorden* — both from the same Finnish shipping line as the ill-fated *Johanna Thorden,* lost with all but five of her crew in the Pentland Firth in 1937 — were refloated and towed away. Althogher, five blockships were raised in 1948.[17]

In 1952 Metal Industries brought a 60-ton floating crane to the Flow and started lifting the guns and turrets which had been blasted off the *Derfflinger* when she was raised and which were still lying on the seabed. They weighed 350 tons apiece and altogether they provided about a thousand tons of valuable steel for yet another rearmament drive then under way on account of the Cold War. The crane also worked on some of the remaining blockships that year. By 1954 a total of 9,300 tons of scrap, including copper and brass from some of the German First War ships, had been exported from Orkney, and Metal Industries had worked on the old *Thames* and *Numidian* in Kirk Sound as well as other blockships from the Second War. The total export also included scrap metal collected on land from the various abandoned military sites by German prisoners-of-war who were housed at Hatston early in 1948.[18]

But it did not include any from the *Royal Oak*. Early in 1949 the Admiralty had been offered a sum, said to be as low as £50, for the ship as she lay near the Gaitnip Banks, but had refused it. A little later they were said to be thinking of offering her for sale but nothing happened, and in 1952 such a transaction was still said to be only 'under consideration'. Nothing definite happened until December 1957, eighteen years after Prien's torpedoes had struck, when the Admiralty suddenly invited tenders for her. Orkney County Council's Convener of the day, Mr Alex Calder, went on record as saying that there would be 'no opposition' to such a transaction — but he was very, very wrong. There was an immediate outburst of rage and criticism from the Orkney public and survivors of the disaster and also from the Convener's own Council; any attempt to raise or salvage the ship would be 'sacrilege', it was said, and a desecration of the tomb of over 800 men to whose memory a plaque had been unveiled in St Magnus Cathedral in 1948. In the face of such violent opposition from all quarters the Admiralty backed down, and the remains of the *Royal Oak* became designated as an official War Grave.[19]

There had been no similar reaction earlier to news that salvage operations were to begin on that other British battleship whose grave and that of over a thousand of her men was also on the bottom of Scapa Flow, the *Vanguard* which blew up while at anchor in 1917. The director of a Glasgow scrap firm, Mr Nundy, who had also been a diver with Metal Industries in the 1930s, had bought the salvage rights on the ship from the Admiralty and with a converted drifter, *Ocean Raleigh,* as salvage vessel, started work on her, bringing up scrap piecemeal. His operations in the Flow went on for several years on other ships as well as the *Vanguard.*[20]

Apart from these comparatively small salvage enterprises the Flow was a quiet place in the late 1940s and 1950s, with local lobster boats and sheltering trawlers more common than warships, but the Navy still had its Base at Lyness, even if it was a mere shadow of its former self. HM Ships came in from time to time to refuel from the tanks which were now surrounded by what looked like a ghost town of derelict buildings and weed-covered foundations whose wooden structures had disappeared. It was difficult to recall the bustle and purposeful activity of less than a decade earlier.

Warships still used the anchorage, however, if only for short periods; Scapa was so ingrained in naval consciousness that it seemed they could not ignore it, although the advent of the atomic bomb had made it unlikely that there could ever again be large concentrations of fighting ships in confined areas like the Flow. Still, one never knew; experts had been wrong before — and in spite of nominal peace the world was a dangerous place, even though the more obvious flashpoints like Korea seemed far away, but then Poland and Czechoslovakia had seemed a long way away in 1939. And there was the enigma of Soviet Russia. Perhaps it would be just as well to keep the Scapa options open.

The battleships *Howe* and *Anson* with the cruiser *Superb* and four destroyers paid a visit in May 1948 and shortly afterwards there was a rumour that the Royal Navy, the Royal Canadian Navy and the United States Navy were considering the Flow as a possible joint base for their three Fleets along with Plymouth and Gibraltar. NATO, of course, had not yet come into being. The rumour never got any further than a speculative newspaper headline.[21]

Fortunately the same applied to another story three years later that the Flow might be used for testing atomic mines, and no more seems to have been heard about atomic mines either.[22] Nor did anything come of newspaper reports at the end of 1957 that Orkney might be chosen as a missile launching site and that the United States was interested in the former RAF and RNAS airfields at Skeabrae and Twatt. Orkney was going through a rather bad economic patch at the time with the consequent depopulation problems, but even so the idea of a missile site in the islands was received with very mixed feelings — but it did not happen either.[23]

The Navy was back again in the summer of 1950 when the new *Vanguard* anchored close to where the remains of her namesake lay off Flotta. She was accompanied by the cruiser *Superb,* a frigate and five destroyers — eight ships in all but described as the 'biggest concentration of warships in the Flow since the war'. Changed days from the hundred or so of 1914 or the fifty and more of 1939.

Vanguard was back again the next year, 1951, with the aircraft carrier *Indefatigable* and the *Indomitable,* flagship of Admiral Sir Philip Vian, hero of the *Altmark* rescue operation in Norway early in the war. So it went on with HM ships coming in dribs and drabs such as the Battle class destroyer *Trafalgar,* flagship of the Reserve Fleet with the C-in-C Reserve Fleet Vice-Admiral Sir Henry McColl on board in 1953, and the depot ship *Maidstone* with her 14 submarines in Kirkwall Bay later that year.

Then in June 1954 came what was really the grand finale and farewell visit of the Home Fleet with once again, and for the last time, the 42,000-ton *Vanguard,* flagship of the C-in-C, Admiral Sir Michael Benny, along with the fast minelayer *Apollo* and eight destroyers including *Agincourt, Aisne, Corunna* and *Barrosa* — fifteen fighting ships in all — dropping anchor off Flotta as in wartime. They were in the Flow for several days and pre-war cruises were recalled when they held their pulling regatta between the ships in glorious summer weather. The First Lord of the Admiralty, J. L. P. Thomas, flew to Orkney to present the regatta prizes, embarking for *Vanguard* in the C-in-C's barge at the tiny pier which had been built on Lamb Holm for the construction of the Causeways.

Vanguard was, in fact, the last of the great battleships to enter the Flow — the days of the big battlewagons as they were affectionately known were over, as were those of the big fleets. Not very long afterwards she was 'mothballed' and eventually broken up, without ever having been in action. When she left the Flow for the last time she went out through Gutter Sound, the channel normally used by the destroyers but not the big ships — perhaps there was something symbolic about it.[24]

The end of Scapa Flow as a naval base was already in sight, although it was still feared rather than recognised at this time as the occasional ship came in and out and there were still over 150 people employed at Lyness.

Then the blow fell. On 14 June 1956 the Admiralty announced that Scapa Flow Naval Base was indeed to close as part of the national £100 million economy drive. Only the Oil Depot at Lyness would remain. The Boom Defence Depot, once HMS *Pomona,* would go and so would the radio station in South Walls. Worse still in some ways was the decision to stop the naval ferry service between Lyness and Houton which had been running twice a day since the end of the war with a fare of 2s (10p) for the crossing, and used by everyone.

But hardest hit, of course, were the people working at Lyness. Thirty 'established' dockyard workers would be re-posted, but 125 non-established workers would get the sack. The Admiralty stated bluntly: '. . . we can no longer see sufficient use of the installations, either in peace or war, to justify the expense of their retention'.[25]

Towards the end of the year there was an amplification of the news with the Admiralty statement that the number of people still to be employed at Lyness would be only 25, and that by the end of 1957 this figure would be down to only 20. It was also confirmed that the ferry service, which had carried 580 passengers in July, would be discontinued and so would the fire service and the cinema.[26] What remained of the Lyness Base would be administered from Rosyth and it would in future be called merely the Admiralty Oil Fuel Depot, Lyness. The appointment of Resident Naval Officer would, however, be retained meantime until the ferry service was disposed of, but he would be responsible for matters afloat only.

For the people of Hoy and Walls, Christmas 1956 and New Year 1957 could hardly be described as a festive season. Since 1924 at least, something had been going on in the Flow to provide them with employment, but first the salvage base had closed down and now the Navy was pulling out. The future in the South Isles looked bleak indeed.

This was all unhappily confirmed by the Defence White Paper of 1957 which announced the closure of four out of ten RNAS stations as well as the Scapa Base, and among other plans put forward by the Defence Minister, Duncan Sandys, was the reduction of the Naval Reserve from 30,000 to only 5,000 and battleships, including *Vanguard,* were to be scrapped. It was a swingeing blow to the Navy, and the other Services suffered equally.

The formal end came on 29 March 1957, a typical early spring Scapa day when the White Ensign was hauled down for the last time, at what was really little more than an amplification of the normal Royal Navy 'Sunset' Ceremony which takes place on board all HM Ships as the Colours are lowered with the setting of the sun.

It is always a poignant occasion but it was doubly significant on that grey day at Lyness with a gusty wind tugging at the Ensign as it sank to the ground. Fewer than 200 people were there to witness the end not only of a chapter in Scapa Flow's long story but of an era in British naval history. There was not even a flag officer present to pay the nation's last respects to a Base where so many sailors from high-ranking Admirals of the Fleet, and indeed First Lords of the Admiralty down to the humblest Able-Bodied Seaman had served their country. The official party which arrived on the still routine naval ferry, an Admiralty-designed MFV, was headed by Captain A. J. M. Milne-Hume RN, Chief of Staff to the Flag Officer Scotland, who was greeted by the Resident Naval Officer, Commander C. C. S. Mackenzie. Rear Admiral Macnamara, who had been so closely connected with the development and running of the Base from September 1940 until the spring of 1946, was unfortunately unable to be present due to illness, and sadly he died only a fortnight later. He was represented by his wife who, of course, also knew Orkney and Scapa well.

Saddest of all was the complete absence of any man-of-war — no battleship, no cruiser, no destroyer, not even a minesweeper to say a last goodbye to an anchorage which had held them literally by the hundred; only one solitary and rather lowly Boom Defence ship, HMS *Barleycorn,* to stand in for all the rest. On second thoughts, however, perhaps it was not so inappropriate. These tough little ships had spent all their time at the Base, mending the nets, opening the gates for their more noble sisters and closing them again once they were inside to ensure their rest and safety. Six long years of unremitting toil and none of the glory. But — they also serve . . .

Nonetheless it was a sad and low-key ceremony when the Guard of Honour mounted by the Orkney TA unit, the 861 (Independent) LAA Battery, Presented Arms as the White Ensign and the 266-foot-long Paying Off Pennant — one foot for every month the Boom Defence Base had been in commission — came fluttering earthwards marking the end of an anchorage whose name had been so much part of the Royal Navy's history for a century-and-a-half.

Epilogue

THIS WAS NOT the end of the Scapa story: far from it. The striking of the White Ensign at Lyness that grey March day in 1957 marked the end of only one of its many chapters, albeit a most important one; but after all, the 145 years as a naval base is little more than a short paragraph in a history that has stretched across at least five millennia. And warships continued to use the Flow from time to time, now coming not only from the Royal Navy but from many nations — America, Holland, Norway and even the former enemy of two world wars, Germany, or at least West Germany, for by this time the North Atlantic Treaty Organisation (NATO) had been set up in answer to the threat from Soviet Russia and the Eastern Bloc.

There was, in fact, visible evidence of that threat in the number of Soviet and other East European warships with their attendant radio-antennae-festooned trawlers hanging around the Orkney coast from Papay and Sanday to Hoy during the late 1960s and early '70s. It was felt that guided-missile cruisers and destroyers were hardly needed to catch herring, and so they were often shadowed by British frigates such as the *Duncan*. As far as is known, however, they never came into the Flow itself.

But their presence did trigger off several combined operations exercises based on Scapa, such as 'Exercise Athens' in 1970 when 3,500 troops, mainly Royal Marine Commandos along with artillery and transport, were landed in Hoy and elsewhere by helicopter from the carrier *Albion,* supported by the frigates *Ajax* and *Cavalier* and the auxiliaries *Tidepool* and *Retainer*. They also put a detachment of frogmen ashore on Rousay from the submarine *Acheron,* as well as mounting guns on Stroma to cover the eastern entrance to the Pentland Firth.

There was an even bigger assembly of NATO ships with troops and aircraft in the Flow two years later for another war game, 'Exercise Trial Strength'. This time there were two commando carriers including the *Albion* again, with escort vessels and fleet auxiliaries including the *Sir Galahad* which was to come to such a tragic end in the Falklands war. With them were 'dozens of helicopters'. Again they carried out landings in various parts of Orkney.

These visits, however, were of comparatively short duration and eventually even the Admiralty Oil Depot, Lyness was closed down leaving only the voluntary Royal Naval Auxiliary Service (RNXS) with its HQ on Scapa Bay to maintain the naval presence ashore in Orkney. These exercises did nothing material for the local population round the Flow beyond providing interesting topics of conversation for a time — but nothing permanent.

The Royal Yacht *Britannia* was a welcome sight in Scapa on several occasions. The Queen and the Duke of Edinburgh with the Royal children were aboard in 1960 for the first state visit after the war, and the Queen and Prince Edward arrived on board when she anchored off Scapa Pier for the royal visit to the County Show in 1978. The Queen Mother preferred to come by air on quite frequent visits from her Caithness home, the Castle of Mey, her helicopter becoming quite a familiar sight. These visits were usually happy occasions but one at least was sad, when she came to Longhope to unveil the memorial to the crew of the Lifeboat there who lost their lives in the Pentland Firth while going to the assistance of the Liberian cargo ship, *Irene,* drifting out of control off South Ronaldsay during the March gales of 1969.

But as time went on there were fewer and fewer people in the South Isles, to greet visitors, royal or otherwise. Some measure of the effect of the closure of the Lyness Naval Base may be seen in the census figures for North and South Walls, the areas most seriously affected. In 1951 there had been 844 people living there; in 1961, four years after the closure, there were only 455. The population had been just about halved. In Flotta it was, if anything, worse over the same ten years with a drop from 215 to 123, and by 1971 there were only 73 people living on an island which in the 19th century had supported over 400. The situation was extremely serious and there seemed to be no ready-made panacea. There had been quite a boat-building boom in Stromness and Burray during the post-war period, but it declined as the fishing industry itself fell on hard times, and farming needed fewer and fewer workers. As we have seen, there was no scuttled German fleet at the bottom of the Flow this time to provide salvage jobs for the people living, and wanting to continue living, in the area. But something **was** moving in Scapa's favour and it too was under the sea, but not under the Flow. It was over a hundred miles away under the North Sea — oil. A lot of money — millions of pounds — would be needed to provide the advanced technology required to bring it to the surface and to Scapa; much more than had been needed to raise

the battleships. Even in their wildest fantasies, no one had
dreamed of such a possibility — certainly not in Orkney. The
Flow's history might well stretch back over 5000 years but this
next phase in it had been waiting and maturing for well over 100
million years — perhaps even 150 million.

Noting that gas and oil had been found in Holland in 1963,
scientists and oilmen began to wonder if these finds were merely
the fringe of yet untapped reservoirs further out to sea. Six years
later in December 1969 they found this was indeed the case. Oil
was found under the middle of the North Sea — and the rush
was on.

Until then Occidental had been one of the lesser-known oil
companies, but they had been carrying out vigorous reconnaissance
and research in the area and following some more oil strikes in
the British sector — the North Sea by this time having been
divided and parcelled out by international agreement — they
formed the Occidental group or consortium in 1971, consisting
of Occidental Petroleum itself, Getty Oil (Britain) Ltd, Union
Texas Petroleum Ltd and Thomson North Sea Ltd. Backed by
20,000 miles of seismic data they applied for, and in March 1972
were awarded, six blocks of the North Sea covering some
316,000 acres, a hundred miles or so east of Wick. They struck
oil there less than a year later in January 1973 — it was a good
field with an estimated recoverable yield of 708 million barrels —
an oilman's barrel works out at about 34 Imperial gallons, or
about 159 litres.

A little over a year later they found another field a few
miles west of the first, and it too showed a potential worthy of
development. The first field, about 135 miles east-south-east of
Orkney, they named 'Piper', the second they called 'Claymore'.

So far so good, but in the meantime they were considering
how and where to handle this oil once it was tapped. Oxy, as the
consortium came to be known, favoured a shore-based operation
— but where?

All through the early 1970s Orkney had been plagued with a
swarm of oilmen — or at least, would-be oilmen. Entrepreneurs
was the kindest word used to describe them. Wild schemes for
filling in bays, flattening hills to provide infill for runways
stretching into the sea for jumbo-jets, massive concrete oil-
platform construction yards in places like Houton and depots
in various places such as Kirkwall Bay — everything, it seemed,
was possible. The sky was the limit. The only trouble was that
many of these 'entrepreneurs' seemed to be very vague as to
where the money for these fabulous projects was coming from.

Orcadians began to get worried. As a whole they had been

only too keen to bring capital and employment to the islands in order to stem the dreaded 'drift' — but was this the answer? Were they about to let the 'djinn out of the bottle?' Would they be able to recognise their own islands when all this happened? And what would happen when it was all over — when the oil ran out? At first sight and at a distance the possibility of an oil boom had seemed like the answer to the islands' prayers. At closer quarters it began to look as if the price might be too high unless it could be controlled. Orkney really wanted to have its cake and eat it too — always a difficult operation.

Orkney County Council, and after the reorganisation of local government in 1974, its successor, Orkney Islands Council, reflected and shared these fears and doubts while recognising the opportunities being offered. They were deeply concerned, and in 1973 while Oxy was evaluating its Piper Field the Council applied for a Provisional Order in Parliament, giving it authority to control industrial development and land-use in certain areas including Lyness, Rysa, Fara, parts of Flotta and Houton as well as some others in the vicinity of Kirkwall.

While all this was fermenting, Oxy had decided that the place to bring the oil ashore was Scapa Flow where such processing as might be necessary could be carried out before the product was shipped out in big tankers. After all, a stretch of water which had sheltered the Royal Navy in two world wars should be good enough for a few tankers, even supertankers. Flotta was not the first choice, but they did finally settle on it after negotiation with the Council, now armed with its controlling powers.

In July 1973 Oxy applied for planning permission to construct an oil terminal on Flotta, and six months later, in January 1974, outline permission for the first phase was granted. Within weeks, if not days, the earth-movers were on the job. They were followed by pipe-laying barges, the huge Italian floating crane laying the single-point mooring at which the tankers would load about a mile or so offshore from the storage tanks, and all the other oil-exploitation paraphernalia on Flotta itself. A 30-inch diameter pipe had to be laid across the open and stormy North Sea to the Piper Field, 135 miles away, and brought into the Flow under the south end of No. 4 Causeway in South Ronaldsay — then on to Flotta and eventually the single-point moorings. And all this time Flotta, the Flow and the South Isles generally were flooded with contractors' men, and there were plenty of jobs for the local people as well.

In the meantime Claymore field had been discovered. Its oil was to be fed into the same pipeline, so the Flotta terminal would have to be extended. Permission for this was granted.

The oil finally began its 135-mile journey from under the bottom of the North Sea to arrive in Flotta during December 1976. And in January 1977, exactly four years from the time Piper had been discovered, a lavish inauguration ceremony of the terminal was held simultaneously in Flotta and in London, with Dr Armand Hammer, Chairman of Oxy, and Mr Tony Benn, then Energy Minister, present on the island to press the appropriate buttons and flick the symbolic switches.

A new chapter in the Scapa story was well under way, and tankers were now to become as familiar a sight in the Flow as once warships had been. Great care had been taken to landscape the terminal and to disturb the environment generally as little as possible — no hills had been torn asunder, no bays or lochs had been filled in and the whole relationship between Orkney and its new set of 'guests' has been, on the whole, harmonious, with both sides on their best behaviour.

There had been fears about the almost inevitable 'spills' of oil and the effect these would have on the environment, perhaps particularly on the bird life which is such a feature of the Flow. There have, of course, been spills, but between December 1976 and December 1984 they totalled only 22, the total volume of oil being spilt amounting to only 168 barrels — less than 6,000 gallons or .00002% of the total processed, it is stated by Oxy, a pretty good record. In fact, most of the instances of oiled seabirds have been traced to sources outside Orkney, not from inside the Flow.

The total cost of the Flotta development with its associated pipelines up to the end of 1984 was put at $650 million, which does not include the cost of the Piper and Claymore rigs which are put at $793 million and $864 million respectively at 1982 costs. By the end of 1984 the amount of oil processed at Flotta from Piper, Claymore and a third associated smaller field, Tartan, was 833 million barrels, the three fields producing 310 million barrels a day, and all this had been loaded into a total of 1,554 tankers during the same period.

Between 275 and 300 people, two-thirds of them Orcadians, are employed on the 365-acre terminal on Flotta in well-paid jobs — just about the same size of local work-force as was employed by Cox & Danks and Metal Industries in the Flow during their salvage operations, but working, one would imagine, in much more congenial conditions.

One disadvantage from the point of view of the Flotta community is that almost all the workforce at the terminal live outwith the island, and commute daily by boat, so that the hoped-for boost to the island population has not taken place, despite the considerable disturbance experienced by the Flotta people during the construction phase.

In addition to the people actually working on Flotta the community at large has reaped financial benefits, not just because of the increased spending power which has been generated, but also through the Islands Council's slice of the oil cake. First of all there was the large disturbance allowance paid to the Council, and there is a continuing levy on every barrel of oil passing through the terminal to swell the Council coffers. Over and above these payments the tankers using the anchorage pay appropriate fees for pilots, tugs and other services, the Council having constituted itself as the Harbour Authority, controlling shipping movements from its pagoda-like HQ on the shores of Scapa Bay where once stood Orkney's first air station in 1914.

There can be no doubt that oil has brought an air of prosperity to Orkney which could have been in a sad economic state without its advent. Young Orcadians have been able to find lucrative and satisfying employment in their own islands without having to go overseas to find it. The 'drift from the isles' has, at least, been stemmed and even reversed.

How long will it last? That seems to be anyone's guess but Oxy's own official estimate is that Piper Field will not run dry before 1993, and Claymore should go on producing for another three years after that. But no one knows what future exploration may reveal to Scapa's advantage. Nor can anyone foretell what will happen when all the oil fields finally run dry, as must happen one day. One thing, however, seems certain. As long as ships sail the northern seas they will turn for shelter and safe anchorage to this great harbour — Scapa Flow.

Abbreviations

AA	Anti Aircraft.
AALMG	Anti Aircraft Light Machine Gun.
ACOS	Admiral Commanding Orkney and Shetland.
AAQMG	Assistant Adjutant and Quarter Master General (also A&Q).
ARP	Air Raid Precautions.
A/S	Anti Submarine.
ASDIC	Allied (or Anti) Submarine Detection Investigation Committee.
ATS	Auxiliary Territorial Service (later WRAC — Women's Royal Army Corps).
BCS	Battle Cruiser Squadron.
BEF	British Expeditionary Force.
BOP	Battery Observation Post.
BS	Battle Squadron.
CEMA	Council for the Encouragement of Music and the Arts.
CH	Chain Home (Radar chain of stations down the East Coast).
CHL	Chain Home Low (chain of radar stations along the east coast capable of detecting low-flying aircraft and surface vessels not covered by CH).
CIGS	Chief of the Imperial General Staff.
CO	Commanding Officer (usually of a senior formation such as an infantry battalion or an artillery regiment — in the Army normally a Lieut. Col. whose subordinate formations such as infantry companies or artillery batteries would be in charge of Officers Commanding (OC), usually Majors).
COCOS	Commanding Officer Coast of Scotland.
CRE	Commander Royal Engineers.
CS	Cruiser Squadron.
DAQMG	Deputy Assistant Quartermaster General.
DEL	Defence Electric Light (Coast Defence searchlights usually 90 cm).
DEMS	Defensively Equipped Merchant Ship.
Do 17	Dornier 17 (German twin-engined bomber also used for reconnaissance).
DORA	Defence of the Realm Act.
ENSA	Entertainment National Service Association.
FAA	Fleet Air Arm.
GL	Gun Layer (Radar coupled direct to AA guns giving them range, bearing and angle of sight).
GOC	General Officer Commanding.
GOC-in-C	General Officer Commanding in Chief.
GOR	Gun Operations Room.
GSO	General Staff Officer.

HA	High Angle (Naval equivalent of Army's AA).
HAA	Heavy Anti Aircraft (usually guns of 3 in, 3.7 in or 4.5 in).
HDA	Harbour Defence ASDIC (see ASDIC).
HE	High Explosive.
He 111	Heinkel 111 (German twin-engine long-range bomber).
HG	Home Guard.
IG	Instructor Gunnery.
JAG	Judge Advocate General.
Ju 88	Junkers 88 (German twin-engine bomber both high-level and dive).
KHM	King's Harbour Master.
LAA	Light Anti Aircraft (40 mm Bofors, Vickers Mk VIII for defence against low-flying aircraft).
LDV	Local Defence Volunteers (later re-named Home Guard).
LMG	Light Machine Gun.
MFV	Motor Fishing Vessel.
MICE	Member of the Institute of Civil Engineers.
ML	Motor Launch.
MTB	Motor Torpedo Boat.
NAAFI	Navy, Army and Air Forces Institute.
NATO	North Atlantic Treaty Organisation.
OSDef	Orkney and Shetland Defences.
OSGar	Orkney and Shetland Garrison.
OC	Officer Commanding (see CO).
PWSS	Port War Signal Station.
RA	Royal Artillery.
RADAR	Radio Detection And Ranging.
RAF	Royal Air Force.
RAOC	Royal Army Ordnance Corps.
RASC	Royal Army Service Corps.
RDF	Radio Direction Finding.
RE	Royal Engineers.
REME	Royal Electrical and Mechanical Engineers.
RFA	Royal Fleet Auxiliary.
RGA	Royal Garrison Artillery.
RM	Royal Marines.
RMA	Royal Marine Artillery.
RMLI	Royal Marine Light Infantry.
RMNBDO	Royal Marine Naval Base Defence Organisation.
RN	Royal Navy.
RNAS	Royal Naval Air Service or Station.
RNO	Resident Naval Officer.
R/T	Radio Telephone.
SMO	Senior Medical Officer.
SNO	Senior Naval Officer.

TA   Territorial Army.

U-boat   Unterseeboot (German submarine).
USN   United States Navy.
USS   United States Ship.

WAAF   Women's Auxiliary Air Force.
WRAC   Women's Royal Army Corps.
WRNS   Women's Royal Naval Service.
W/T   Wireless Telegraphy.

Appendix I

In 1940 Orkney and Shetland Defences listed the following staffs, units and appointments in what was known as its 'Order of Battle'.

OSDEF HQ / **Stromness Hotel**

Commander	Major General G. C. Kemp, MC
ADC	2/Lieut. P. T. K. Anderson
GSO I	Lieut. Col. G. N. Tuck
GSO II	Major C. M. Addersley — Maj. O. R. Jackson
GSO III	Capt. C. O. Penney
GSO III HG	Capt. W. P. Scott.
AA & QMG	Col. S. O. Jones MC
DAQMG	Maj. J. I. A. McDiarmid DSO
DAAG	Maj. R. J. T. Small
Staff Capt. A	Capt. F. D. Parry
Staff Capt. Q	Capt. R. Garden
Intelligence Officer	2/Lieut. J. H. Taylor
Instructor Gunnery	Capt. D. I. Summers
IFC	Capt. J. R. G. Walker — Capt. G. D. Nussey
PAD Officer	Major A. J. Walsh
Camouflage	Lieut. J. C. W. Heath
Cipher	Lieut. F. A. Cary
SAQC	Capt. David Soutar
JAG	Capt. D. B. Keith
Catering Adviser	Capt. H. A. Barr
Camp Commandant	Capt. J. A. Crichton
Education Officer	Maj. G. W. S. Brown
GOR Kirkwall	Capt. T. White — Capt. J. D. Whyte.

58 AA Bde HQ / **Lynnfield, Kirkwall**

Commander	Col. A. C. Hancocks MC
Bde. Major	Maj. S. H. Pierssenne
Staff Capt.	Capt. A. D. D. Lawson
IO	2/Lieut. W. A. W. Miller

59 AA Bde HQ / **Melsetter, Hoy**

Commander	Brigadier C. H. Peck DSO MC
Bde Major	Maj. D. S. Daniel
Staff Capt.	Capt. J. S. T. Andrews
IO	2/Lieut. W. P. M. Watson

COAST DEFENCE
Fixed Defences HQ / **Ness Bty**

Commander	Lieut. Col. J. G. M. B. Cook MC
191 Heavy Bty. Ness	Maj. E. T. Weigall
198 Hy. Bty. Stanger	Maj. J. M. Moar
199 Hy. Bty. SMH	Maj. F. T. D. Buist
O Fortress RE	Maj. E. Linklater

A.A. GUNS
64 HAA Regt. HQ   **Roeberry House**
Lieut. Col. Keith Anderson MC TD

268 HAA Bty. (3.7) F1, F2
Maj. J. H. Curry TD
179 HAA Bty. (3.7) R1, R2
Maj. & Bt. Col. J. P. Dodds
178 HAA Bty (3.7) B1, R4
Maj. I. A. Morton
180 HAA Bty. (3.7) M5, M10
Maj. R. H. C. Herron

70 HAA Regt. HQ   **Hobbister House**
Lieut. Col. C. J. P. Bateson

216 HAA Bty. (4.5) M1, M2
Maj. B. L. E. Herbert
211 HAA Bty. (3.7) M3, M4
Maj. D. H. Phillips
309 HAA Bty. (3.7 mobile) M11, M6
Maj. A. Scarisbrook
212 HAA Bty. (4.5) M7, M8
Maj. G. H. Vanburgh

95 HAA Regt. HQ   **South Walls**
Lieut. Col. F. H. Lawrence OBE MC TD

293 HAA Bty (4.5) H3, H1
Maj. A. B. Scott
226 HAA Bty (4.5) H5, H6
Maj. W. Baird.
204 HAA Bty. (3.7) H4, H7
Maj. R. B. Price

39 LAA Bty. HQ   **Apostolic Hall, Stromness**
Maj. W. A. H. Rowat

142 LAA Bty. HQ   **Haybrake, Hoy**
Maj. J. W. Perry

SEARCHLIGHTS
61 S/L Regt HQ   **St Margaret's Cottage, St Margaret's Hope**
Lieut. Col. H. T. Valentine MC TD

434 S/L Bty.   S. Walls — 24 sites Hoy
Maj. W. N. Ashburner
432 S/L Bty.   Burray & Flotta — 12 sites
Maj. W. L. Pilkington
433 S/L Bty.   S. Ronaldsay — 18 sites
Maj. W. A. Molyneux

62 S/L Regt.
Lieut. Col. J. H. Whitehead

The Ninth, Orphir

437 S/L Bty.
Maj. F. Baines MC TD
436 S/L Bty
Maj. R. Buckley
435 S/L Bty
Maj. R. R. Rainford TD

Quoybanks — 18 sites E. Mainland

Orphir Hall — 18 sites Centre Mainland

Howe — 18 sites W. Mainland

FIELD GUNS
'A' Bty 152 (Ayrshire Yeomanry)
   Field Regt
152 Field Bty

Wideford Farm
Quoydandy

ROYAL ENGINEERS
CRE HQ
Lieut. Col. A. C. Baillie MC

21 Victoria Street, Stromness

274 Field Coy.
Maj. S. R. Russell
276 Field Coy
Maj. R. W. Johnston
279 Field Coy.
Maj. G. G. M. Webster
701 Gen. Con. Coy.
Maj. S. G. Squires

Stromness

North End Camp, Stromness

Roeberry House, S. Ronaldsay

Stromness

RE Workshop
275 Field Coy.
683 Gen. Cons. Coy.
696 Artisan Works Coy.
19 Coy. 4th Stevedore
26 Bomb Disposal Section

Transit Shed, Stromness
Kirkwall
Holm
Longhope
Stromness
Howe

ROYAL SIGNALS
North Signal Section
Signals office
Capt. J. Lothian

School
Stromness Hotel

INFANTRY
7 Bn. Gordons
Lieut. Col. D. W. Hunter Blair
HQ Coy.
Coys

Drill Hall, Kirkwall

Ayre Mill
Stanger's Dock, Stromness; Netherbutton;
Holm

Bn. Cameronians 'F' Coy.
12 Bn. HLI 'D' Coy.

Kirkwall
Wideford Farm

ROYAL ARMY SERVICE CORPS
CRASC HQ
Lieut. Col. Murray Clarkson
O i/c Supplies
Maj. T. White

Commercial Hotel, Stromness

Shearer's Stores Stromness (Supplies Depot)

ORDNANCE CORPS
DADOS
Major D. Larmour — Masonic Hall, Stromness
Depot
Lieut. A. H. Pycock — Stromness Distillery
Workshop
Maj. W. C. Stewart SOME — Caldale
Workshops — Hoy, and S. Ronaldsay
No. 5 Mobile Laundry — Quanterness

Royal Army Medical Corps
Lieut. Col. E. W. Wade DSO — Stromness Hotel
Military Hospital, Kirkwall; Skin Disease Hospital, Dounby; RN Hospital, N. Ness; No. 1 Field Hospital, Kirbister; No. 2 Field Hospital, Stromness; No. 3 Field Hospital, Longhope

Movement Control — Stromness Hotel
Capt. M. J. Hardy — Stromness Hotel

No. 2 Protected Area HQ — Redroofs, Stromness
Maj. J. B. Simpson MC TD

ATS
'A' Coy. No. 1 (Scottish) Group The Mount, Stromness

Pioneer Corps
No.19 Group Auxiliary Military Pioneer Corps Ness, Stromness
Lieut. Col. A. M. Duncan TD

68 Coy.	Sunnybank, Kirkwall
128 Coy.	North End, Stromness
131 Coy.	Longhope
141 Coy.	St Margaret's Hope
143 Coy.	Brig of Waithe
67 Coy.	Gaitnip

RAF
950 B Sqdn.
Wing Co. R. Risk MC

Appendix II

In 1941 Orkney and Shetland Defences HQ produced one of its Operation Orders outlining plans for repelling any invasion by enemy land forces and listed in it the following formations and their locations.

HQ OSDef Stromness Hotel

58 AA Bde. Lynnfield
110 HAA Regt Hobbister House
31 LAA Regt. Howe Camp
136 Z Bty Netherbutton
71 S/L Regt. The Ninth, Orphir

59 AA Bde. Melsetter
99 HAA Regt. Roeberry, S. Ronaldsay
115 HAA Regt. South Walls
59 S/L Regt. St Margaret's Cottage

Commander Fixed Defences Ness Bty.
533 Coast Regt. Stanger Head, Flotta
534 Coast Regt. Ness
536 Coast Regt. Rerwick

Royal Engineers
No. 12 Coy. 21 Victoria Street, Stromness
678 G.C. Coy. Markstone Camp
671 G.C. Coy Hillside Rd, S. Ronaldsay
114 RC Coy. S. Walls
669 AW Coy. S. Walls
593 AT Coy. Castlegate Camp, Stromness
88 BD Section Weyland Bay Camp
994 DO Coy. The Ness, Stromness
O & S Signal Coy. Springfield Camp, Stromness
HQ 207 Infantry Bde. Weyland Bay (for Finstown)
HQ 517 Field Bty. Quoydandy
11 Bn. Gordons Tormiston
15 Bn. A & S Highlanders Sunnybank, Kirkwall
8 (HD) KOSB Millfield Camp, Stenness
HQ 1 Home Guard Union Bank, Kirkwall
HQ 2 Home Guard Lyness
HQ RASC Commercial Hotel, Stromness
HQ RAOC Apostolic Hall, Stromness
HQ RAMC Stromness Academy
Military Hospitals Kirkwall, Kirbister (Orphir), Stromness and Dounby

HQ Pioneer Camp The Ness, Stromness
168 Pioneer Coy. North End Camp, Stromness
14 Pioneer Coy. Gaitnip
104 Pioneer Coy. Bruna Camp, Stromness
62 Pioneer Coy. Longhope
151 Pioneer Coy. S. Ronaldsay
HQ Balloon Command Lyness

Notes

ADM, CAB and WO are the prefixes for Admiralty, Cabinet and War Office documents in the Public Record Office (PRO) Kew.

O and OH followed by the date are the relevant issues of 'The Orcadian' and 'The Orkney Herald' respectively.

OS/T indicates *Orkneyinga Saga* translated and edited by W. B. Taylor.

Other abreviations are:— *Grand Fleet* — Jellicoe (GF); *Bring Back my Stringbag* — Kilbracken (BBS); *Defence of the United Kingdom* — Collier (DUK); *From Dreadnought to Scapa Flow, Vol. I* — Madder (Dreadnought/SF); *The Grand Scuttle* — van der Vat (Scuttle); *My Naval Career* — Fremantle (MNCF); *Naval Battles of World War I* — Bennett (N Battles WWI); *Scapa and a Camera* — Burrows (S&C); *The War at Sea* — Roskill (WaS); *World Crisis 1911-1918* — Churchill (WC).

Chapter 1 — In the Beginning

1. Personal communication from Dr Per Sveaas Andersen, Oslo University; *Orkney Farm Names* — Hugh Marwick.
2. *Orcades or a Geographic and Hydrographic Survey of the Orkney and Lewis Islands in Eight Maps* — 1750 — Murdo MacKenzie.
3. Walter Scott Diary 1814, *Northern Lights*. Byway, Hawick edition p. 64.
4. *Orkney Miscellany*, Vol. IV.
5. *The Orkney Parishes* edited by J. Storer Clouston who extracted the various parish accounts from Sir James Sinclair's Old Statistical Account.
6. *Scapa and a Camera* — C. W. Burrows.
7. *Scapa Flow* — Brown and Meehan.
8. *Orkney Parishes.*
9. *ibid.*
10. *ibid.*
11. *The Highlands and Islands of Scotland* — O'Dell.

Chapter 2 — A Viking Lair

1. *The Northern Isles* edited by F. T. Wainwright — Chapter on Brochs and Broch Builders by J. R. C. Hamilton.
2. *Orkneyinga Saga* edited by A. B. Taylor (OS/T) p. 259.
3. OS/T p. 259.
4. OS/T p. 258
5. OS/T p. 307.
6. OS/T p. 317.
7. OS/T p. 331.
8. *Håkon Saga.*
9. *Håkon Saga.*

Chapter 3 — The Scots Take Over

1. *A Rutter of the Scottish Seas* — Alexander Lindsay, edited by A. B. Taylor.
2. *ibid.*
3. *ibid.*
4. *The Three Voyages of Martin Frobisher, Vol. II p. 2* — Argonaut Press, London 1938.
   This account of Frobisher's second voyage to the Nor' Wast was written by Dionyse Settle, a 'gentleman supercargo'.
5. *History of the Church in Orkney, 1663 to 1688*, J. B. Craven p. 67.
6. *Orkney Feuds and the '45* — R. P. Fereday.
7. *ibid.*
8. The Orcadian (O) 22/5/1909 reprinted from the Edinburgh Magazine 1782.
9. Orkney Parishes.
10. *ibid.*

Chapter 4 — Shape of Things to Come

1. *The Longhope Battery and Towers* — R. P. Fereday.
2. All references from this point are contained in 'Scapa Flow in 1812 — A Memorial to the Lords Commissioners of Admiralty by Graeme Spence late Maritime Surveyor to Their Lordships' edited by P. N. Sutherland Graeme and published in The Orkney Miscellany Vol. IV of the Orkney Record and Antiquarian Society pp 57-64.

Chapter 5 — Lull before the Storm

1. The Orcadian (O) 23/7/1898.
2. *ibid.*
3. *Prince Louis of Battenburg* — Admiral Mark Kerr pp. 116 & 119.
4. PRO WO/55/830 quoted by Fereday in *Longhope Battery and Towers.*
5. Orkney Herald 10/7/1912.
6. O 9/6/1907.
7. O 11/1/1908.
8. O 14/3/08 & 4/4/08.
9. O 18/7/08.
10. O 3/7/09.
11. O 11/5/07 — reprinted from 'Naval Review.'
12. O 25/5/07.
13. O 8/6 & 28/9/07.
14. O 26/10/07.
15. O 13/6/08.
16. O 25/7/08.
17. O 1/8/08 & 15/8/08.
18. O 8/2 & 7/3/08.
19. O 3/4 & 24/4/09.
20. O 1/5, 8/5 & 15/5/09.
21. O 22/5 & 25/9/09.
22. O 19/6/09.
23. O 10/7/09.
24. O 28/8/09.

Chapter 6 — The Pace Quickens

1. Orcadian 29/1/1910.
2. Aberdeen Free Press reprinted in O 19/2/10.
3. *World Crisis* — Winston Churchill, abridged edition pp 92/3.
4. O 30/4/10.
5. O 6/8/10.
6. O 20/8/10.
7. O 5/11/10.
8. O 30/4/10.
9. O 10/12/10.
10. O 30/8/13.
11. O 1 & 8/3/13.
12. O 26/4/13.
13. O 26/4/13.
14. O 8 & 15/5/11.
15. O 6/5/11.
16. *World Crisis* — WSC pp 92/3.
17. O 10/6/11.
18. O 15/7/11.
19. O 12/8/11.
20. O 16 & 30/9/11.
21. O 30/9 & 7/10/11.
22. O 14/10/11.

Chapter 7 — Time Runs Out

1. O 6/4/12.
2. OH 10/7/12.
3. OH 24/7/12.
4. PRO ADM/116/1293 — Report on Flotta landing manoeuvres by RM Expeditionary Force; also O 6/9/23; O 20-27/7 & 3/8/12; OH 17/7/12.
5. O 20/7/12.
6. PRO ADM 1293 Case 11193 Defence Arrangements Scapa Flow 1912-14.
7. ADM 1293.
8. *ibid.*
9. *ibid.*
10. *ibid.*
11. *ibid.*
12. *ibid.*
13. *ibid.*
14. O 14/9/12.
15. O 5/10/12.
16. O 1/3/13.
17. O 22/3/13.
18. O 3-10/5/13.
19. O 7/6/13.
20. ADM 1293.
21. *ibid.*
22. O 13/12/13.
23. O 13/12/13.

Chapter 8 — Zero Hour

1. *The Grand Fleet* — Jellicoe (GF) p. 88.
2. GF p. 90.
3. *World Crisis* — Churchill (WC).
4. *ibid.*
5. *King George VI* — Wheeler-Bennett (KG VI).
6. WC.
7. O 6/9/23 — How Scapa was made Safe.
8. *ibid.*
9. *Dreadnought to Scapa Flow Vol. I* —Arthur Marder p.4 (Dreadnought/SF).
10. O 6/9/23.
11. O 13/8/31.
12. O 6/9/23.
13. O 8/8/14.
14. GF p. 4
15. *ibid.* p. 90.
16. *ibid.* p. 90.
17. *ibid.* p. 26.
18. *ibid.* p. 26
19. *ibid.* p. 26.
20. *ibid.* p. 26.
21. *ibid.* p. 88.
22. *ibid.* p. 93.

Chapter 9 — Settling In

1. GF p. 137.
2. *ibid.* p. 137.
3. *Scapa and a Camera* — C. W. Burrows (S&C) p. 10 and GF p. 80.
4. S&C p. 10.
5. GF p. 80.
6. *ibid.* p. 88.
7. *ibid.* p. 116.
8. *ibid.* p. 116.
9. Dreadnought/SF 1 p. 64.
10. *ibid.* p. 67.
11. GF pp. 142/143; Dreadnought/SF 1 p. 67 and WC.
12. Ministry of Defence, Naval History Branch; GF p. 116; Naval Battles of World War I Geoffrey Bennett (N Battles WWI) p. 134 Pan Books edition.
13. O 17/4 — 1/5 & 15/5/19.
14. GF p. 168.
15. *ibid.* p. 144.
16. WC.
17. S&C p. 10.
18. S&C pp. 83 & 88.
19. GF p. 160.
20. *ibid.* p. 170.
21. *ibid.* p. 176.
22. *Ibid.* p. 184.
23. *ibid.* p. 206.
24. S&C p. 143.

Chapter 10 — Welcome Visitors

1. GF pp. 85, 201; S&C p. 18.
2. S&C pp. 22 and 91.
3. GF p. 229.
4. O 9/10/15.
5. GF pp. 234 and 235.
6. All extracts from personal diary of King George V in Royal Archives Windsor Castle.
7. GF p. 244.
8. KG VI pp. 100 — 102.
9. GF p. 245.
10. O 18 — 25/12/15.
11. O 3/7/15.
12. O 12/6/15.
13. O 10/7/15; 20/6 & 21/12/18.
14. GF p. 264.
15. *ibid.* p. 265.
16. *ibid.* p. 233.
17. *ibid.* p. 254.

Chapter 11 — Out to Battle

1. GF p. 248.
2. *ibid.* p. 255.
3. *ibid.* p. 226.
4. O 13/2/30.
5. GF p. 263.
6. *ibid.* p. 267.
7. *ibid.* p. 269.
8. *ibid.* pp. 297 — 301.
9. *ibid.* pp. 301 & 415; N Battles WWI p. 155.
10. N Battles WWI pp. 178/9.
11. GF p. 389.
12. *ibid.* pp. 400 & 415.

Chapter 12 — Loss of the Hampshire

Unless otherwise indicated by footnotes all references to the sinking of the Hampshire are from Jellicoe's *Grand Fleet* (GF) pp. 422 to 427. and *The Mystery of Lord Kitchener's Death* by Donald McCormick.

1. N Battles WWI p. 155.
2. GF p. 429.
3. *ibid.* p. 434.
4. N Battles WWI p. 254.
5. GF p. 436.
6. *ibid.* p. 434.

Chapter 13 — The Fleet Grows Wings

1. GF p.453.
2. *Bring Back My Stringbag* — Lord Kilbracken (BBS) p. 9.
3. *ibid.* p. 218.
4. *ibid.* p. 22.
5. *ibid.* p. 23.
6. GF p. 107.
7. O 4/5/22.
8. O 6/9/23.
9. GF p. 222.
10. *ibid.* p. 229.
11. *ibid.* p. 269.
12. O 17/6/26.
13. O 11/8/27 — reprinted from Blackwood's Magazine.
14. BBS p. 24.
15. OH 12/2/19.
16. O 12/12/18.

Chapter 14 — The Long Wait

1. O 12/12/18.
2. Victory at Sea — Admiral W. S. Sims USN.
3. O 27/2/19 — reprinted from 'The Chicago Herald.'
4. Extracts from the personal diary of King George V in the Royal Archives.
5. *They Called it Accident* — A. C. Hampshire (TCA) p. 123.
6. *ibid.* pp. 126 — 127.
7. O 26/12/18.
8. As recounted in an interview with Mr A. Flett, Holm, one of the gunners.
9. TCA p. 127.
10. O 21/7/17 & TCA p. 132.
11. *Earl Beatty — The Last Naval Hero* — Stephen Roskill p. 244.

Chapter 15 — The End in Sight

1. O 29/1/20.
2. N Battles WWI pp. 282 & 283.
3. *The Royal Oak Disaster* — Gerald S. Snyder (RODS) p. 35.
4. O 26/4/23 — reprinted from 'The Montreal Star.'
5. O 12/12/18.
6. 'Reminiscences of a Naval Surgeon' — Surgeon Rear Admiral T. T. Jeans — reprinted in O 13/10/27.
7. O 9/12/18.
8. O 29/12/83 and *Early Flying in Orkney* by Dr T. Crouther Gordon DFC.
9. O 16/1/19.
10. O 19/12/18 — reprinted from the 'Daily Mail.'
11. O 16/1/19.
12. *My Naval Career* — Admiral Sir Sydney Fremantle (MNCF) p. 247.

Chapter 16 — 'The Suicide Navee.'

1. MNCF p. 275.
2. *ibid.* p. 275.
3. *ibid.* p. 275.
4. *ibid.* p. 275.
5. *Scapa Flow 1919* — Admiral Friedrich Ruge (RUGE) p. 101 & *Scapa Flow* — Admiral Ludwig von Reuter.
6. RUGE p. 111; *The Grand Scuttle* — Dan van der Vat (Scuttle) Chap. 9 and Reuter.
7. O 26/6/19.
8. O 26/4/23 — reprinted from the 'Montreal Star.'
9. Orkney Sound Archive — from interviews broadcast by BBC Radio Orkney.
10. *ibid.* from the earlier local programme of the BBC, 'Town and Country'.
11. Scuttle p. 176.
12. O 3/7/19.
13. MNCF p. 275.
14. *ibid.*
15. O 12/2/20.
16. MNCF p. 277.
17. *ibid.* p. 280.
18. Scuttle pp. 177, 178.
19. MNCF p. 275.
20. RUGE p. 123; Scuttle pp. 180, 181 and 'The Times' 23/6/19.
21. MNCF p. 279.
22. O 17/7/19.
23. OH 1/10/19.

Chapter 17 — Prosperity and Frustration

1. O 1/7/26.
2. O 5/8/16.
3. O 8/7/26.
4. OH 4/6/19.
5. O 22/5/15.
6. O 12/12/14.
7. O 22/5/15.
8. O 29/1/20.
9. O 24/7/15.
10. O 4/9/15.
11. O 13/2/15.
12. O 30/10/15.
13. O 28/11/18.
14. O 19/12/18.
15. O 29/5/19.
16. O 19/6/19.
17. O 5/8/20.

Chapter 18 — U.S. Navy Re-opens the 'Gate'

Except where otherwise stated all references are to the official account of the minesweeping operation — *Sweeping the North Sea Mine Barrage* published by the United States Navy Department.

Chapter 19 — The Uneasy Peace

1. O 29/4/20.
2. O 25/11/20.
3. O 16/12/20.
4. O 9/11/20.
5. O 5/1/22.
6. O 20/4/22.
7. O 27/4/22.
8. O 3/8/22.
9. O 4/5/22.
10. O 19/4/23.
11. O 28/8/24.
12. O 21/3/29.
13. O 6/5/30.
14. O 22/4/37.
15. O 15/7/37.
16. O 29/4/37.
17. O 20/1/38.
18. O 17 — 31/3/38.
19. O 12/5/38.
20. O 13/10/38.
21. O 29/9/38.
22. O 29/9/38.
23. O 27/10/38.
24. O 2/3/39.
25. O 4/5/39.
26. O 1/6/39.
27. O 31/8/39.

Chapter 20 — Blocked Channels

All references are from 'The Orcadian'
and 'The Orkney Herald' reports
of the relevant dates and Orkney
County Council Minutes.

1. O 24/4/24.
2. O 21/7/21.
3. O 24/4/24.
4. O 3/11/24.

Chapter 21 — Raising the German Fleet

All references to the actual raising of
the ships are from 'The Orcadian'
and 'Orkney Herald' reports of
the relevant dates.

1. O 14 — 21/12/22.
2. O 14/6/23.
3. O 14/2/24.
4. O 7/8/24.
5. O 14/2/29.
6. O 17/12/31.
7. O 7/1/32.

Chapter 22 — New Aerial Horizons

All references are from 'The Orcadian'
and 'The Orkney Herald' reports
of the relevant dates.

Chapter 23 — Count-Down to War

1. O 9/11/20.
2. O 22 — 29/7/20.
3. O 1/10/25.
4. O 11/6/31.
5. O 2/6/32.
6. O 26/4/34.
7. *Defence of the United Kingdom* — Collier (DUK) p.22.
8. *ibid.* p. 62 footnote.
9. *ibid.* p. 69.
10. *War at Sea, Vol. I* Roskill (WaS) pp. 17 & 41; Public Record Office (PRO) ADM 116/4208 — LD 0601/39.
11. PRO ADM/116/4112 and ADM 116/4208.
12. DUK p. 70.
13. DUK p. 77
14. PRO ADM 116/4112 22/7/39.
15. O 24/9/36.
16. PRO ADM 116/5790 (Chronology) and PRO ADM 116/3831 on the blocking of the Scapa Flow entrances.
    ADM 116/5790 is a large dossier apparently compiled by the Historical Section of the Tactical and Staff Duties Division of the Admiralty shortly after the end of World War II. It contains chapters on every aspect of the build-up of the Scapa Flow Base from 1937 onwards and it also contains recommendations as to how such an expansion should be carried out should the need arise again. The chronological section is rather like a War Diary and is the connecting narrative for other chapters.
17. PRO ADM 116/3831 4/10/38.
18. *ibid.* 15/3/38.
19. *ibid.* 1/3/38.
20. *ibid.* 22/9/38.
21. *ibid.* 24/3/39.
22. *ibid.* 25/5/39.
23. ADM 116/5790 27/5/39.
24. ADM 116/3851 26/6/39.
25. *ibid.* 4/7/39.
26. ADM 116/5790.
27. *ibid.*
28. *ibid.*
29. ADM 53/109896 Log of HMS *Nelson* August 1939.
30. PRO WO 166//2507 — 2049 and 3551 War Diaries of 226 HAA Bty, Orkney Fixed Defences and Orkney (Fortress) Company RE (T).
31. ADM 116/5790 and ADM 53/109896.
32. WaS Vol. I p. 47.

Chapter 24 — At War Again

1. PRO ADM 53/109896 (Nelson Log) 3, 4, 5, 6 & 7/9/39.
2. WaS pp. 65 & 69.
3. ADM 116/5790 (Chronology).
4. *ibid.* Chap. XIII. Compiled by OSDef, this chapter deals with the Army's part in the build-up of the Scapa defences.
5. PRO CAB 66/1 (Cabinet Papers).
6. *The Gathering Storm,* Vol. I of *The Second World War* by Winston Churchill, pp. 338 & 339.
7. ADM 116/5790 Chap. XIII.
8. PRO WO 199/952.
9. ADM 116/4208 20/9/39.
10. *ibid.* 23/9/39.
11. ADM 116/4060 Manning of Scapa Flow Defences by Royal Marines — Special Secret Branch Acquaint.
12. *ibid.*
13. ADM 116/4208.
14. ADM 116/4112.
15. ADM 116/4111 Scapa Flow Defences 1917-1940.
16. ADM 116/4060.
17. ADM 116/4112 2 — 3/1/40.

Chapter 25 — OSDef Is Born

1. PRO WO 166/2054 OSDef War Diary.
2. ADM 116/5790 Chap. XIII.
3. OSDef War Diary Appendix I.
4. ADM 116/5790 (Chronology).
5. *King George VI, his Life and Reign* — John W. Wheeler Bennett p. 427.
6. ADM 116/5790 Base ships and extended defences.
7. Scottish Command War Diary.
8. ADM 116/5790 Chap. XIII.
9. *ibid.*

Chapter 26 — Baptism of Fire

1. *The War at Sea* — Roskill p. 71.
2. Führer Conferences on Naval Affairs, Admiralty transcript p. 29 and *Phantom of Scapa Flow* — Kirganoff (Kirganoff).
3. Kirganoff.
4. *ibid.* p. 184.
5. *ibid.* p. 184.
6. PRO ADM 187/2-4 Pink Lists, locations of HM Ships at 1600 hours each day and *Nightmare at Scapa Flow* — Weaver.
7. Führer Conferences and Log of U 47 in same publication.
8. Personal communication from Mr A. Flett.
9. Führer Conferences — log of U 47.
10. ADM 116/5790 and ADM 199/158 (Royal Oak Inquiry).
11. ADM 199/158.
12. OSDef War Diary 15/11/39.
13. *War at Sea* I p. 75.
14. PRO WO 166/2507 (226 HAA Bty. War Diary) and WO 166/2054 (OSDef War Diary and Intelligence Report).
15. WO 166/2049 (Orkney Fixed Defences War Diary).
16. ADM 116/5790.
17. OSDef and 226 HAA Bty. War Diaries with Intelligence Report.

Chapter 27 — Empty Harbour

1. ADM 116/5790 (Chronology) and War at Sea, I p. 77.
2. War at Sea p. 78.
3. *ibid.* p. 80.
4. PRO CAB 65/2 51 (39) 2.
5. CAB 65/3.
6. CAB 65/3.
7. CAB 63 (39) 3.
8. CAB 65 (3) 23/10/39.
9. CAB 65 (3) 30/10/39.
10. CAB 63/4.
11. *The Second World War — The Gathering Storm* — Churchill. Appendix J p. 556.
12. *Mountbatten* — Ziegler p. 126.
13. *War at Sea* I p. 82.
14. CAB 63/4 75th Conclusion 8/11/39.
15. *War at Sea* p. 79.

Chapter 28 — Closing the Gaps

1. ADM 116/5790 (Chronology and Base Ships).
2. *ibid.* (Extended Defences).
3. *ibid.* (Security).
4. ADM 116/4111 Defences 1917-1940.
5. ADM 116/5790 (Base Ships).
6. ADM 116/4111.
7. ADM 116/5790 (Chronology).
8. *ibid.* (Extended Defences).

Chapter 29 — The Army Digs In

1. WO 199/952.
2. WO 166/2049 (Orkney Fixed Defences War Diary).
3. WO 192/109 (Holm Fort Record Book); WO 166/2049, Fixed Defences War Diary.
4. WO 199/952.
5. WO 166/2049 Fixed Defences War Diary.
6. *ibid.*
7. *ibid.*
8. ADM 116/5790 (Extended Defences).
9. *ibid.* (Chap. XIII).
10. *ibid.* (Chronology).
11. *ibid.* (Chronology).
12. WO 166/2055 OSDef AA & QMG War Diary.
13. War Diaries of the individual formations.
14. OSDef War Diary.
15. ADM 116/5790 (Balloon Barrage).
16. ADM 116/5790 (Fighter Cover) and *Action Stations Vol. 7, Military Airfields of Scotland, the North East and Northern Ireland* — David J. Smith (1982).
17. ADM 116/5790 (Fighter Cover).
18. *ibid.* (Chronology).
19. ADM 116/4111.
20. *ibid.*

Chapter 30 — The Bombers come at Dusk

1. Letter from A. Hague, Bromley, Kent, who was Navigating Officer on Fleet Tender B, to Mr Pat Scott, Kierfiold House, Sandwick, Orkney dated 15/1/74, and OSDef War Diary 1/3/40.
2. OSDef War Diary 8/3/40.
3. ADM 116/5790 (Chronology).
4. *ibid.*
5. *Gathering Storm* p. 449.
6. CAB 65/6.
7. *Gathering Storm* pp. 450-452.
8. CAB 65-40.
9. Intelligence Report in OSDef War Diary and Appendix 5B to same Report also in the War Diary.
10. CAB 65-40.
11. CAB 65-40.
12. *War at Sea* p. 155.
13. Intelligence Report and Appendix 5B in OSDef War Diary.
14. CAB 65-40.
15. OSDef War Diary; ADM 116/5790 (Chronology & Chap. XIII).
16. OSDef War Diary.
17. *ibid.*
18. *Orkney Fixed Defences War Diary.*
19. *War at Sea I* p. 157.
20. *ibid.* p. 158.
21. Intelligence Report in OSDef War Diary.
22. *ibid.*
23. ADM 116/5790 (Chap. XIII & OSDef War Diary).
24. Intelligence Report in OSDef War Diary.
25. ADM 116/5790 Chap. XIII.
26. ADM 199/110 79/HD/1161 dated 14/4/40 (Lessons from German Raids on Scapa Flow).
27. OSDef War Diary.
28. ADM 116/5790 (Preface to Chap. XIII).

Chapter 31 — Building the Barriers

Except where otherwise indicated all references are to the papers 'Causeway closing the eastern entrances to Scapa Flow' by J. A. Beath and 'Laboratory Experiments in Connection with closing the eastern entrances to Scapa Flow' by Jack Allen read to the Institution of Civil Engineers, Maritime and Waterways Engineering Division on 26 March 1946 and subsequently published by the Institution.

1. WO 166/2049 Fixed Defences War Diary.
2. *ibid.*
3. ADM 116/5790 (Extended Defences).
4. Fixed Defences War Diary.
5. *ibid.*
6. ADM 116/1293 Defence Arrangements 1912-1914 Case 11193.
7. ADM 116/5790 (Extended Defences).
8. *ibid.*
9. *ibid.*

Chapter 32 — Pinprick Attacks

1. O 16/5/40.
2. O 23/5/40 and WO 109/622.
3. ADM 116/5790 Chap. XIII.
4. OSDef War Diary.
5. *ibid.*
6. Intelligence Report in OSDef War Diary.
7. OSDef War Diary.
8. *ibid.*
9. O 2/1/41.

Chapter 33 — In The Air

1. ADM 116/5790 (Chronology).
2. *Action Stations* Vol. 7.
3. *ibid.*
4. *ibid.* and ADM 116/5790 Chap. V The Naval Air Stations.
5. ADM 116/5790 Chap. V.
6. *ibid.* and Action Stations Vol. 7.
7. Information regarding HMS *Tern* from ADM 116/5790 Chap. V and *Action Stations* Vol. 7.
8. All information regarding Skeabrae from *Action Stations* Vol. 7.
9. All information regarding Grimsetter (HMS *Robin*) from ADM 116/5790 Chap. V and *Action Stations* Vol. 7.

Chapter 34 — At the Peak

1. OSDef War Diary.
2. *ibid.*
3. Air Ministry PoW Report of 12/6/43 quoted in ADM 116/5790 Chap. XIII.
4. OSDef AA & QMG War Diary and ADM 116/5790.
5. O 25/8/45.
6. ADM 116/5790 (King's Harbour Master's Department).
7. *ibid.*
8. *ibid.* (Base Ships).
9. *ibid.* (KHM Dept).
10. *ibid.* KHM Dept. and Base Ships.
11. *ibid.* (WRNS).
12. *ibid.* (Base Ships).
13. *ibid.*
14. *ibid.* (KHM Dept).
15. *ibid.*
16. ADM 116/5790 (Extended Defences).
17. *ibid.* (Chap. XIII and OSDef War Diary).
18. OSDef War Diary.
19. ADM 116/5790 (Chap. XIII).
20. OSDef War Diary.

Chapter 35— Salvage Operations

All details taken from ADM 116/5790
(Salvage).

Chapter 36 — The Kirkwall Base

All references from ADM 116/5790.

Chapter 37 — Off Duty

1. There are frequent references to this malaise in 'The Orkney Blast.'
2. 70 HAA Regt. War Diary 3/3/40.
3. ADM 116/5790 (Chap. VII, Medical Services).
4. *ibid.*
5. *A Northern Saga — A Chronicle of the North of Scotland & Orkney & Shetland Steam Navigation Co. Ltd., during the Second World War* published by the Company.
6. O 23/1/41 and Orkney Blast 17/1/41.
7. O 10/2/44.
8. ADM 116/5790.
9. *ibid.*
10. *ibid.*
11. *ibid.* and OSDef War Diary.
12. O 30/4/42.
13. *The Second World War — The Grand Alliance —* Churchill p. 381.
14. O 14/8/41.
15. O 25/3/43.
16. King George VI — Wheeler Bennett p. 598.
17. O 5/7/45.

Chapter 38 — The Tumult and the Shouting Die

1. ADM 116/5790 (Chronology and Chap. XIII).
2. *ibid.* (Chronology).
3. *ibid.* (Chap. XIII).
4. *ibid.*
5. *ibid.*
6. *ibid.* (Base Ships).

Chapter 39 — Peace at Last

1. O 16/8/45.
2. O 5/7/45.
3. O 20/8/42.
4. O 2/11/44.
5. O 21/3/40.
6. O 11/4/40.
7. O 9/5/40.
8. O 11/1/45.
9. O 4/7/40.
10. O 10/8/40.
11. O 25/11/40.
12. O 21/11/40.
13. Kirkwall Town Council Minutes, August 1939.
14. *ibid.* 13/1/40 to April 1941.
15. Stromness Town Council Minutes September 1939.
16. *ibid.* December 1940.
17. O 21/8/41.
18. O 2/11/44.

Chapter 40 — 'Sunset'

1. O 2/5/45.
2. O 17/1/46.
3. O 10/1/46.
4. O 5/1/46.
5. O 24/4 & 13/6/46.
6. O 8 — 22/8/46.
7. O 29/8 & 12/9/46.
8. O 19/1/46.
9. O 11/7 & 7/11/46.
10. O 11/7/46.
11. O 7/11/46.
12. O 13/12/46.
13. O 22/5/47.
14. O 24/4/47.
15. O 25/12/47.
16. O 13 & 27/5/48.
17. O 30/6/48.
18. O 7/8/52.
19. O 5 — 19/12/57.
20. O 9/5/57.
21. O 11/11/48.
22. O 28/9/50.
23. O 26/12/57.
24. O 17 & 24/6/54.
25. O 14/6/56.
26. O 8/11/56.

Bibliography

Admiralty transcript *Fuehrer Conferences on Naval Affairs 1939.*

Allen, Jack *Laboratory Experiments in Connection with closing the eastern entrances to Scapa Flow.*

Althem, Edward *Jellicoe.*

Bacon, Admiral Sir R. H. *Life of John Rushforth, Earl Jellicoe* and *Life of Lord Fisher of Kilverstone.*

Beasley, Patrick *Room 40: British Naval Intelligence 1914/18.*

Bekka, Cajus *Luftwaffe War Diaries.*

Bennett, Geoffrey *Naval Battles of World War I* and *The Battle of Jutland.*

Bennett, John W. Wheeler *King George VI, His Life and Reign.*

Brown, M. & Meehan, P. *Scapa Flow.*

Burrows, C. W. *Scapa and a Camera.*

Bush, Capt. Eric *Bless this Ship.*

Churchill, Winston *World Crisis 1911-1918* and *The Second World War, Vols. I, II, III.*

Clouston, J. Storer *The Orkney Parishes (Old Statistical Account)* and *History of Orkney.*

Cosgrave, Patrick *Churchill at War: Alone 1939-40.*

Cormack, Alastair and Anne *Days of Orkney Steam.*

Davis, Lieut. Noel (USN) ed. *Sweeping the North Sea Mine Barrage.*

Fereday, R. P. *Longhope Battery and Towers* and *Orkney Feuds and the '45.*

Ferguson, David M. *The Wrecks of Scapa Flow.*

Freivald, Ludwig *The Last Days of the German Fleet.*

Fremantle, Adm. Sir Sydney *My Naval Career 1880-1928.*

George, S. C. *Jutland to Junkyard.*

Hamilton, Brig. J. R. E. *Coast Defence of Orkney in Two World Wars.*

Hampshire, A. Cecil *They called it Accident.*

Haynes, Grace P. *World War I, Compact History.*

Haywood, Victor *HMS Tiger at Bay.*

Jellicoe, Adm. Sir John *The Grand Fleet 1914-1916.*

Johnston, Brian *Fly Navy.*

Kemp, Cmdr. P. K. *Victory at Sea.*

Kerr, Admiral Mark *Prince Louis of Battenburg — Admiral of the Fleet.*

Kilbracken, Lord *Bring Back my Stringbag.*

Korganoff, Alexander *The Phantom of Scapa Flow.*

Linklater, Eric *The Man On My Back* and *The Art of Adventure.*

Low, George *A Tour through Orkney and Shetland.*

Maurice-Jones, Col. K. W. *History of Coast Artillery in the British Army.*

McCormick, Donald *The Mystery of Lord Kitchener's Death.*

McKee, Alexander *Black Saturday.*

McRoberts, Douglas *Lions Rampant.*

Miller, Prof. R. *Orkney*

Morder, A. J. *From Dreadnought to Scapa Flow.*

Munro, Capt. D. J. *Scapa Flow — A Naval Retrospect.*

Prien, Günther *U-boat Commander.*

Roskill, C. S. *Admiral of the Fleet Lord Beatty* and *The War at Sea Vol. I (Official History).*

von Reuter, Adm. Ludwig *Scapa Flow; the Account of the Greatest Scuttle of All Time.*

Robertson, Terence *Night Raider of the Atlantic.*

Rollo, D. *History of the Orkney and Shetland Volunteers.*

Royle, Trevor *The Kitchener Enigma.*
Ruge, Adm. Friedrich *Scapa Flow 1919; the End of the German Fleet.*
Scott, Sir Walter *Northern Lights (Diary).*
Seath, J. A. *Causeways closing the eastern entrances to Scapa Flow.*
Sim, Adm. W. S. (USN) *Victory at Sea.*
Snyder, Gerald S. *The Royal Oak Disaster.*
Stahl, Peter *The Diving Eagle; a Ju 88 Pilot's Diary.*
Taylor, A. B. (ed) *Orkneyinga Saga.*
Wainwright, F. T. (ed) *The Northern Isles.*
Weaver, H. J. *Nightmare at Scapa Flow.*
Woodward, David *The Collapse of Power.*
Ziegler, Philip *Mountbatten.*

North of Scotland Orkney & Shetland Steam Navigation Coy *A Northern Saga.*

Files of *The Orcadian, The Orkney Herald* and *The Orkney Blast.*

Index of Ships

(Royal Navy vessels in italics)

General Index

Aberdeen 13, 14, 87
'A' Buoy 239, 252-3, 335
Aircraft carriers 112, 114, 229, 231
Airlock 210, 214, 217, 221
Air raids 261, 292-304, 318-20
Air Raid Precautions 188-9, 194, 369
Air Raid Warnings (Alerts) 244, 254, 284, 366
Airships 44 (Sanday and Stronsay) 108,111-2, 117-8
Albert, Prince 61, 84, 86, 87, 107, 121-3, 160
Alexander, A. V. (First Lord) 311, 358, 364
Anderson, James 235
Anderson, Sir John (Home Secretary) 293
Archbishop of York 85
Armistice 128, 131, (Terms) 167
Asleifsson, Sweyn 9, 10, 11
Asquith, Herbert (Prime Minister) 56 (in Orkney)
Atlantic 3, 15, 256
   do. Fleet 35, 41, 229
Aurora Borealis 258
Auskerry 43

Baffles, anti torpedo 337
Baikie, Alfred (Lord Lieutenant) 189, 357, 373
Baikie, Provost (Kirkwall) 175, 179
Baikie & Son (contractors) 57
Balfour Beatty Ltd (contractors) 234, 308
Balloonists, German 43 (First Arrival)
Balloon, Kite 114, 116
Balloon, Barrage 246, 272, 285, 288, 359
Balloon Centre No 18 286
Balloon Centre No 20 286
Balloon Squadron No 950 287
Battenberg, Admiral Prince Louis (First Sea Lord) 30, 31, 35, 41, 56, 57, 60, 64, 77
Batteries, Coast 313 (Reorganisation)
   ''   Balfour 278
   ''   Buchanan 277-9, 299, 300, 305
   ''   Burray 277-9, 305-6, 361
   ''   Cara 277, 293, 305
   ''   Carness 277
   ''   Galtness 278, 305

Batteries, Gate 277-8
   ''   Holm 74, 76, 184, 277-9, 305, 360
   ''   Houton 278
   ''   Hoxa 74, 184, 278, 305, 361
   ''   Links 279, 305
   ''   Neb 74, 184, 239, 251, 278, 280, 301, 305, 361
   ''   Ness 74, 185, 190, 239, 251, 278, 280, 301, 305, 361
   ''   Rerwick Head 278
   ''   Scad 277-8
   ''   Stanger Head 74, 86, 190, 239, 251, 278, 293, 301, 361
   ''   Skerry 279 (Hoy)
   ''   Wasswick 278
Battery 226 HAA 189-190, 240, 251, 262-3, 363
Battles, Carbisdale 17
   ''   Clontarf 9
   ''   Dogger Bank 81, 99
   ''   Heligoland Bight 87, 99
   ''   Jutland 12, 68, 99-101, 108
   ''   Knarston 11
   ''   Largs 11
   ''   Summerdale 16, 17
Barrage, North Sea Mine 128, 173
   ''   Scapa Flow AA 295-6, 339
Barrel of Butter 2, 4, 18, 147
Beatty, Admiral Sir David (C-in-C Grand Fleet) 59, 77, 99, 110, 119, 123, 127, 132-3, 173
Beaton, Cardinal 14, 16
Bergen 11, 12, 324
Bignold, Sir Arthur, MP 38
Bignold Park 225, 373
Binney, Vice Admiral T. H. (ACOS) 249, 272, 296, 372
Birsay 42 (Bty), 105, 162-3
Birsay, Brough of 9
Blackout 165, 190, 363
Blenheim (fighter/bomber) 288
'Blimp' (airships) 112, 114
Blockade 122, 128
   ''   Close 39
   ''   Distant 40
Blockships 197, 237, 258, 274-5, 293, 344, 359, 379
Bofors LAA guns 251, 282
Booms 78, 236, 288-9, 301
   ''   Hoxa 4, 234, 236, 241, 337
   ''   Houton 234, 238, 337
   ''   Switha 234, 238, 241, 337

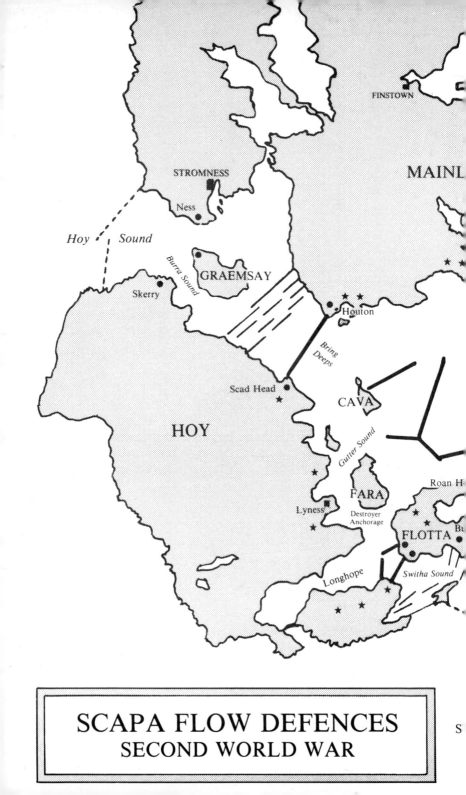

FINSTOWN

STROMNESS

MAINL

Ness

Hoy *Sound*

Burra Sound

GRAEMSAY

Skerry

Houton

Bring Deeps

Scad Head

CAVA

HOY

Gutter Sound

FARA

Roan H

Lyness

Destroyer Anchorage

FLOTTA

Bu

Longhope

Switha Sound

SCAPA FLOW DEFENCES
SECOND WORLD WAR

S